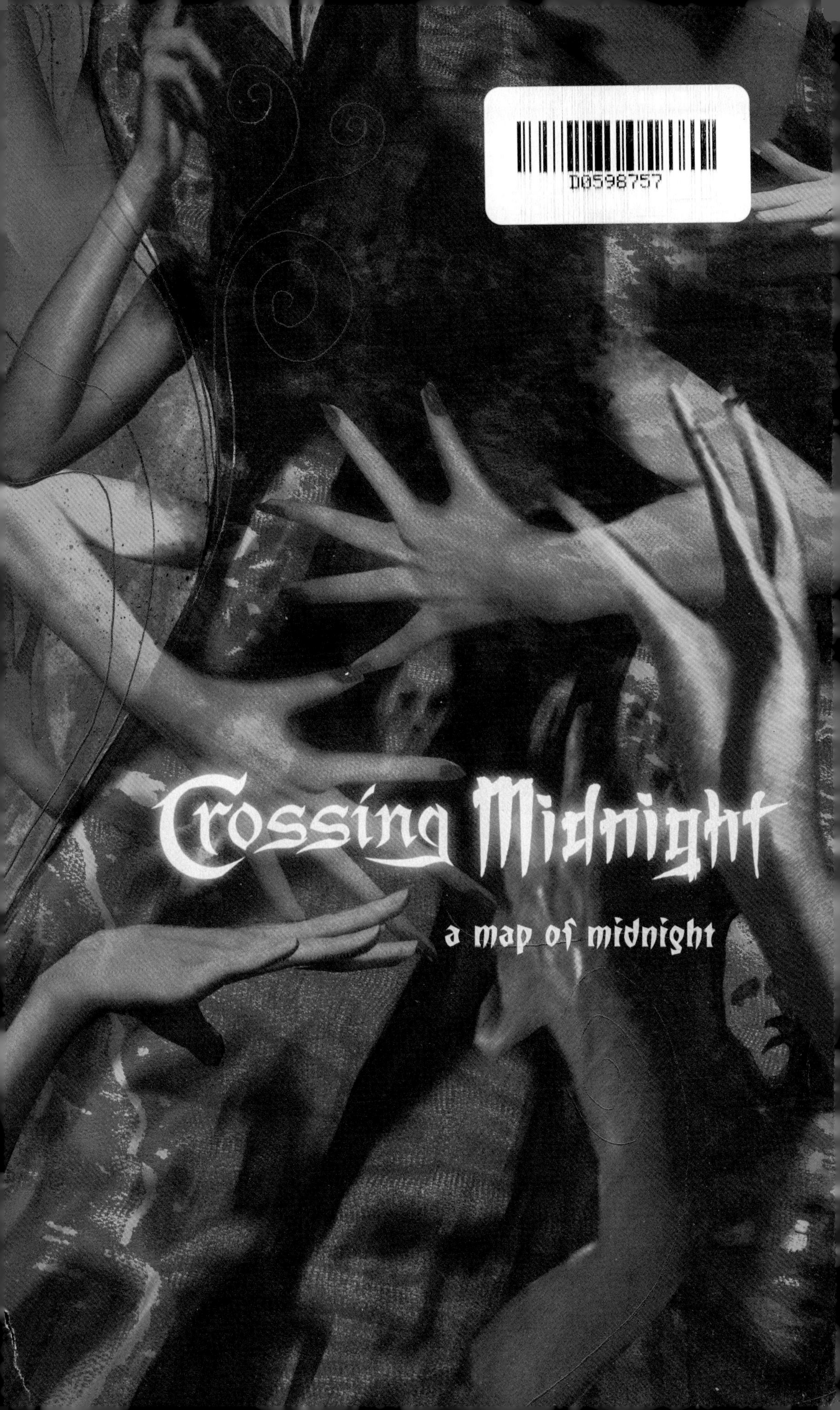
Crossing Midnight
a map of midnight

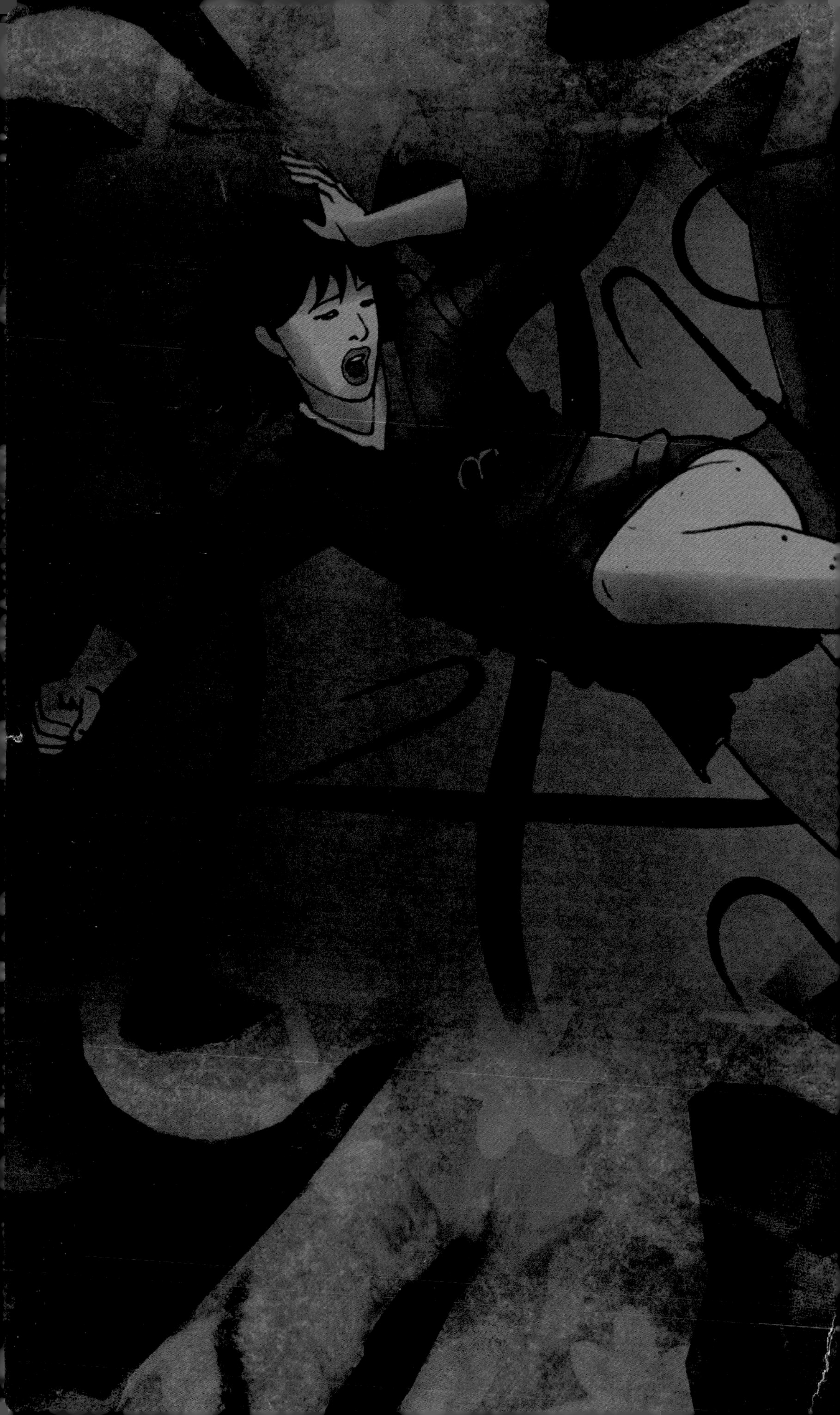

Crossing Midnight

a map of midnight

Mike Carey
WRITER

Jim Fern
Eric Nguyen
PENCILLERS

Mark Pennington
Eric Nguyen
INKERS

José Villarrubia
COLORIST

Todd Klein
LETTERER

J.H. Williams III
ORIGINAL SERIES
COVERS

CROSSING MIDNIGHT created by
Mike Carey and **Jim Fern**

Cover illustration by J. H. Williams III
Logo design by Glenn Parsons of Astrolux Design
Publication design by Amelia Grohman

CROSSING MIDNIGHT:
A MAP OF MIDNIGHT
Published by DC Comics. Cover, afterword and
compilation copyright © 2008 DC Comics.
All Rights Reserved.
Originally published in single magazine form
as CROSSING MIDNIGHT 6-12.
Copyright © 2007 Mike Carey and Jim Fern.
All Rights Reserved.
VERTIGO and all characters, their distinctive
likenesses and related elements featured in this
publication are trademarks of DC Comics.
The stories, characters and incidents featured
in this publication are entirely fictional.
DC Comics does not read or accept unsolicited
submissions of ideas, stories or artwork.

DC Comics, 1700 Broadway, New York, NY 10019
A Warner Bros. Entertainment Company.
Printed in Canada. First Printing.
ISBN: 978-1-4012-1645-0

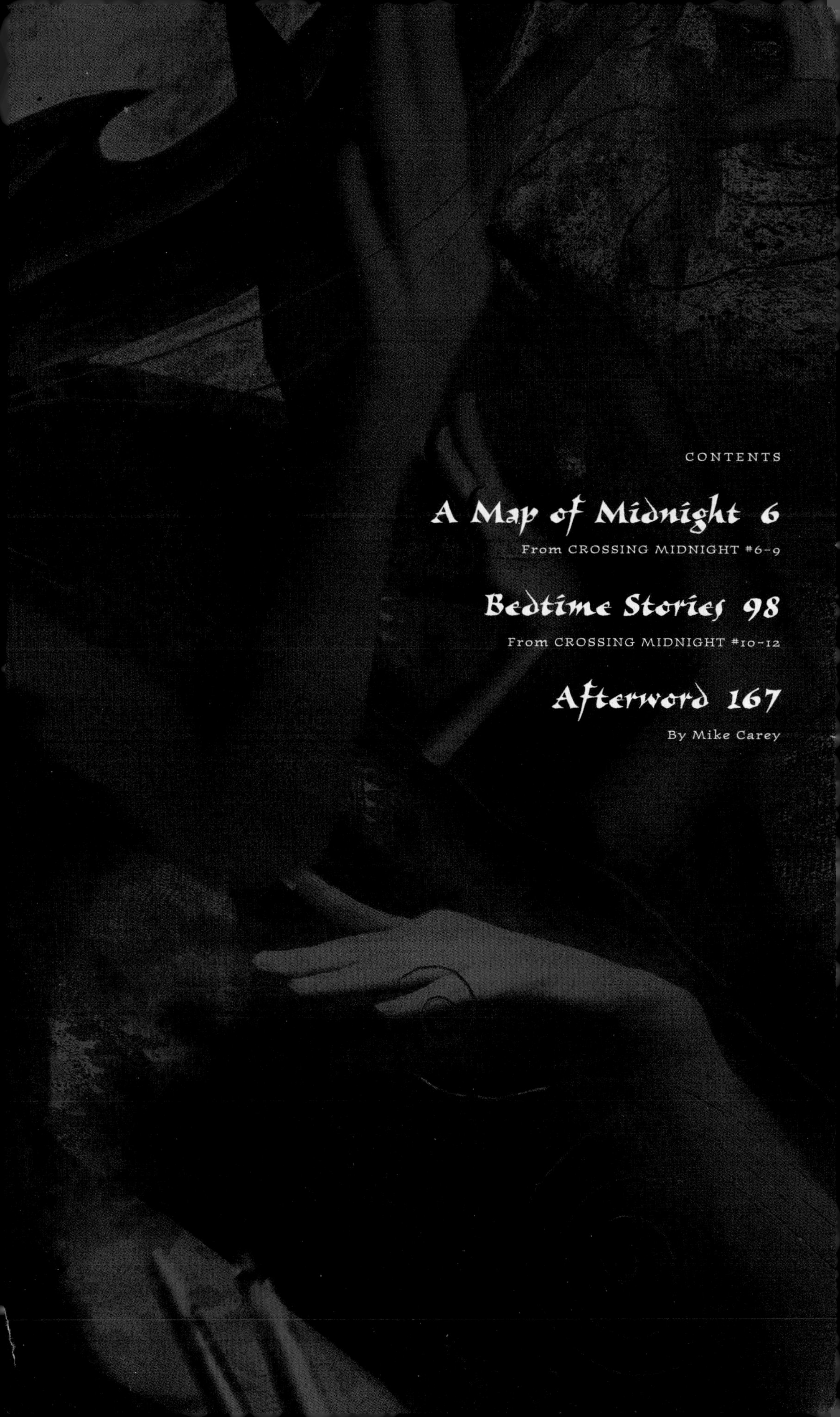

CONTENTS

A Map of Midnight

Written by Mike Carey   Pencils by Jim Fern   Inks by Mark Pennington

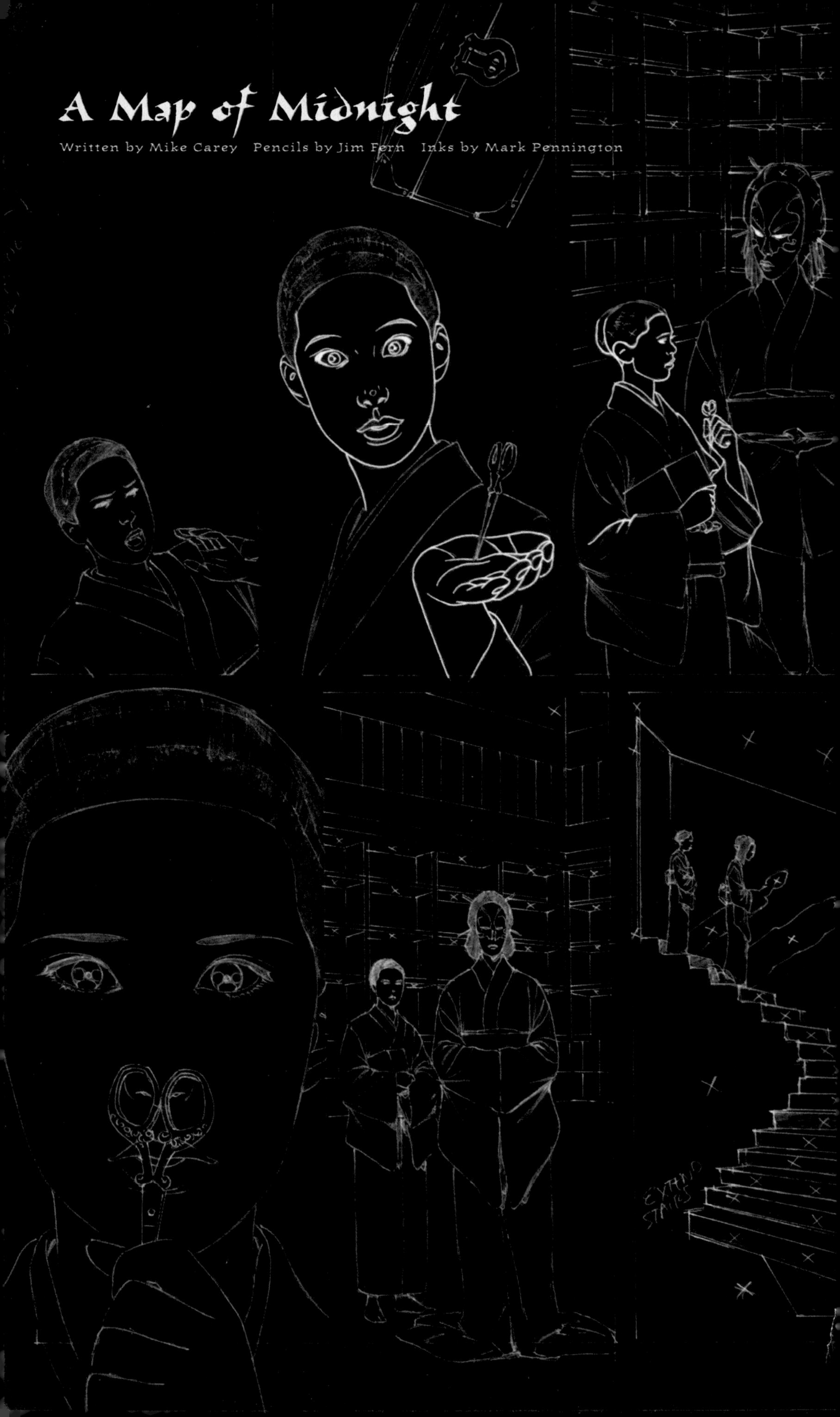

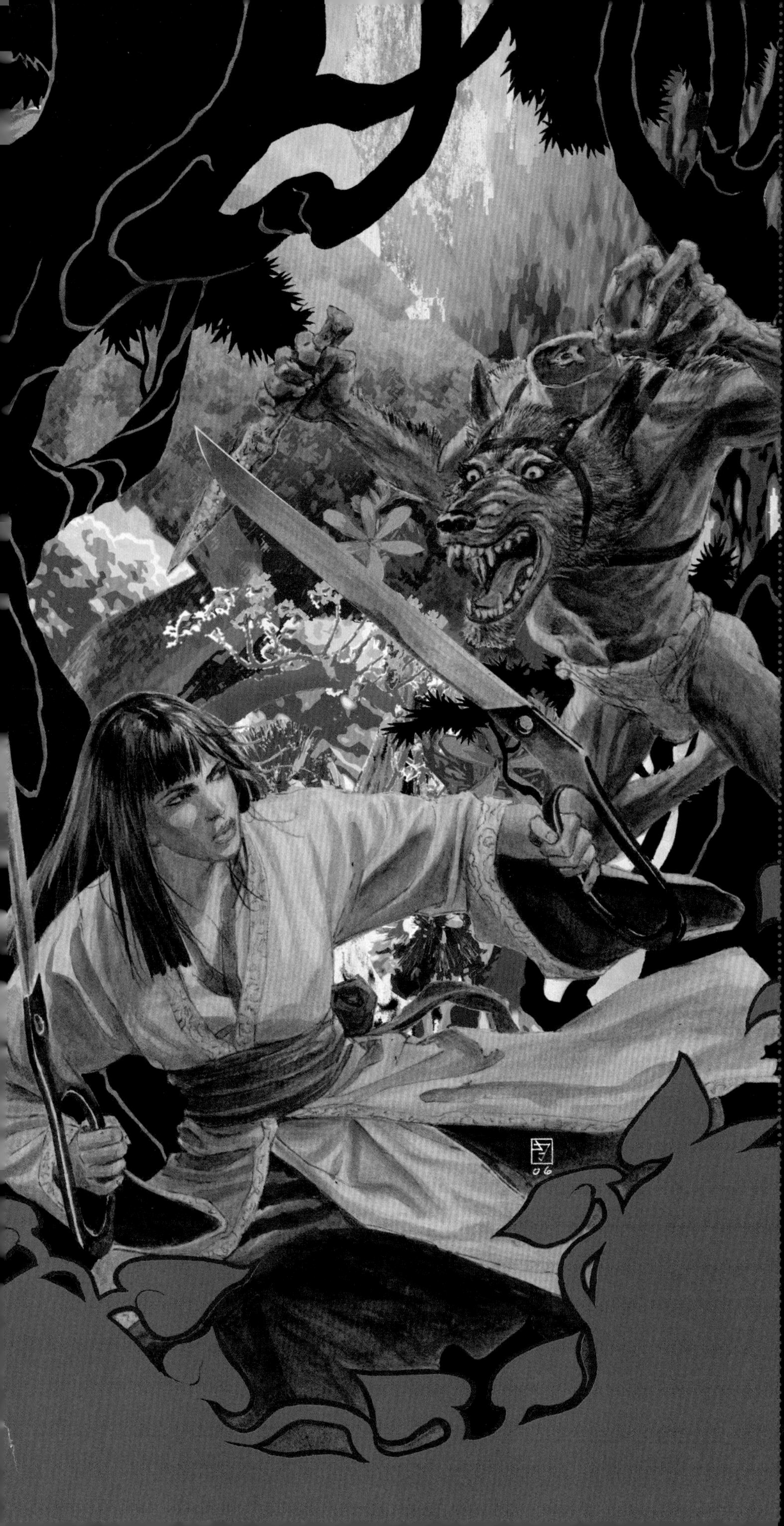

chapter one

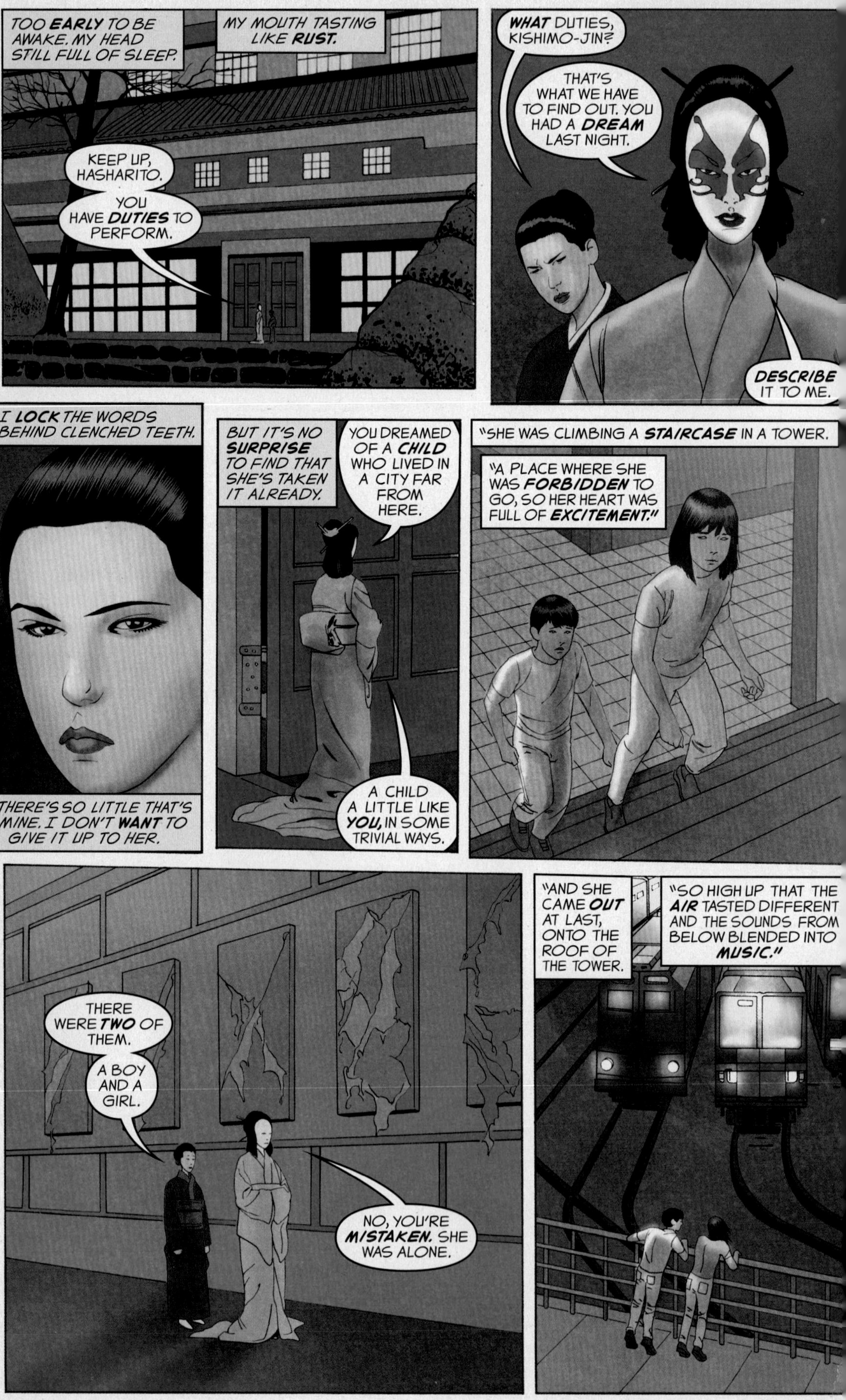
TOO EARLY TO BE AWAKE. MY HEAD STILL FULL OF SLEEP.
MY MOUTH TASTING LIKE RUST.
KEEP UP, HASHARITO.
YOU HAVE DUTIES TO PERFORM.
WHAT DUTIES, KISHIMO-JIN?
THAT'S WHAT WE HAVE TO FIND OUT. YOU HAD A DREAM LAST NIGHT.
DESCRIBE IT TO ME.
I LOCK THE WORDS BEHIND CLENCHED TEETH.
THERE'S SO LITTLE THAT'S MINE. I DON'T WANT TO GIVE IT UP TO HER.
BUT IT'S NO SURPRISE TO FIND THAT SHE'S TAKEN IT ALREADY.
YOU DREAMED OF A CHILD WHO LIVED IN A CITY FAR FROM HERE.
A CHILD A LITTLE LIKE YOU, IN SOME TRIVIAL WAYS.
"SHE WAS CLIMBING A STAIRCASE IN A TOWER.
"A PLACE WHERE SHE WAS FORBIDDEN TO GO, SO HER HEART WAS FULL OF EXCITEMENT."
THERE WERE TWO OF THEM.
A BOY AND A GIRL.
NO, YOU'RE MISTAKEN. SHE WAS ALONE.
"AND SHE CAME OUT AT LAST, ONTO THE ROOF OF THE TOWER.
"SO HIGH UP THAT THE AIR TASTED DIFFERENT AND THE SOUNDS FROM BELOW BLENDED INTO MUSIC."

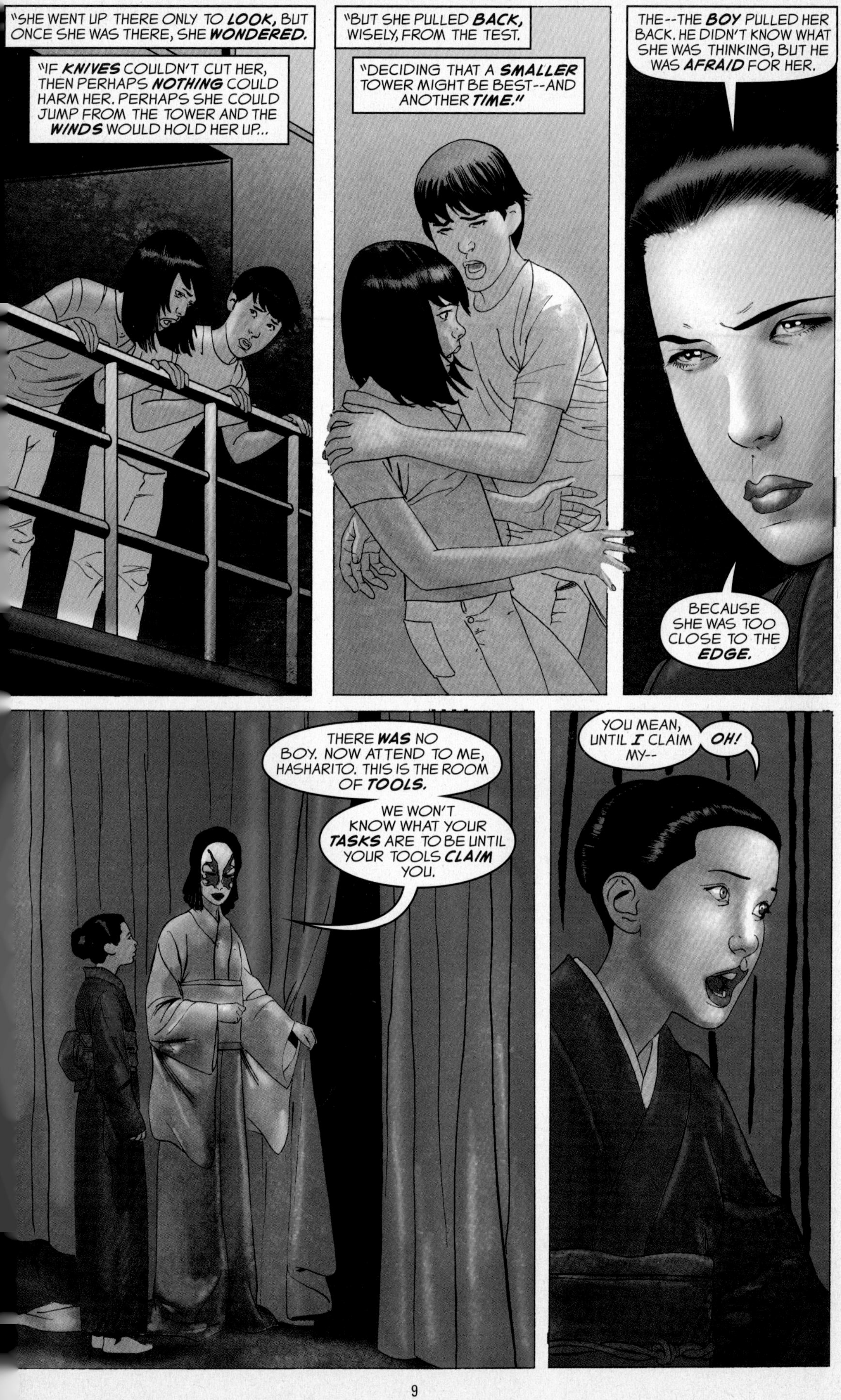
"SHE WENT UP THERE ONLY TO LOOK, BUT ONCE SHE WAS THERE, SHE WONDERED.
"IF KNIVES COULDN'T CUT HER, THEN PERHAPS NOTHING COULD HARM HER. PERHAPS SHE COULD JUMP FROM THE TOWER AND THE WINDS WOULD HOLD HER UP...
"BUT SHE PULLED BACK, WISELY, FROM THE TEST.
"DECIDING THAT A SMALLER TOWER MIGHT BE BEST--AND ANOTHER TIME."
THE--THE BOY PULLED HER BACK. HE DIDN'T KNOW WHAT SHE WAS THINKING, BUT HE WAS AFRAID FOR HER.
BECAUSE SHE WAS TOO CLOSE TO THE EDGE.
THERE WAS NO BOY. NOW ATTEND TO ME, HASHARITO. THIS IS THE ROOM OF TOOLS.
WE WON'T KNOW WHAT YOUR TASKS ARE TO BE UNTIL YOUR TOOLS CLAIM YOU.
YOU MEAN, UNTIL I CLAIM MY--
OH!

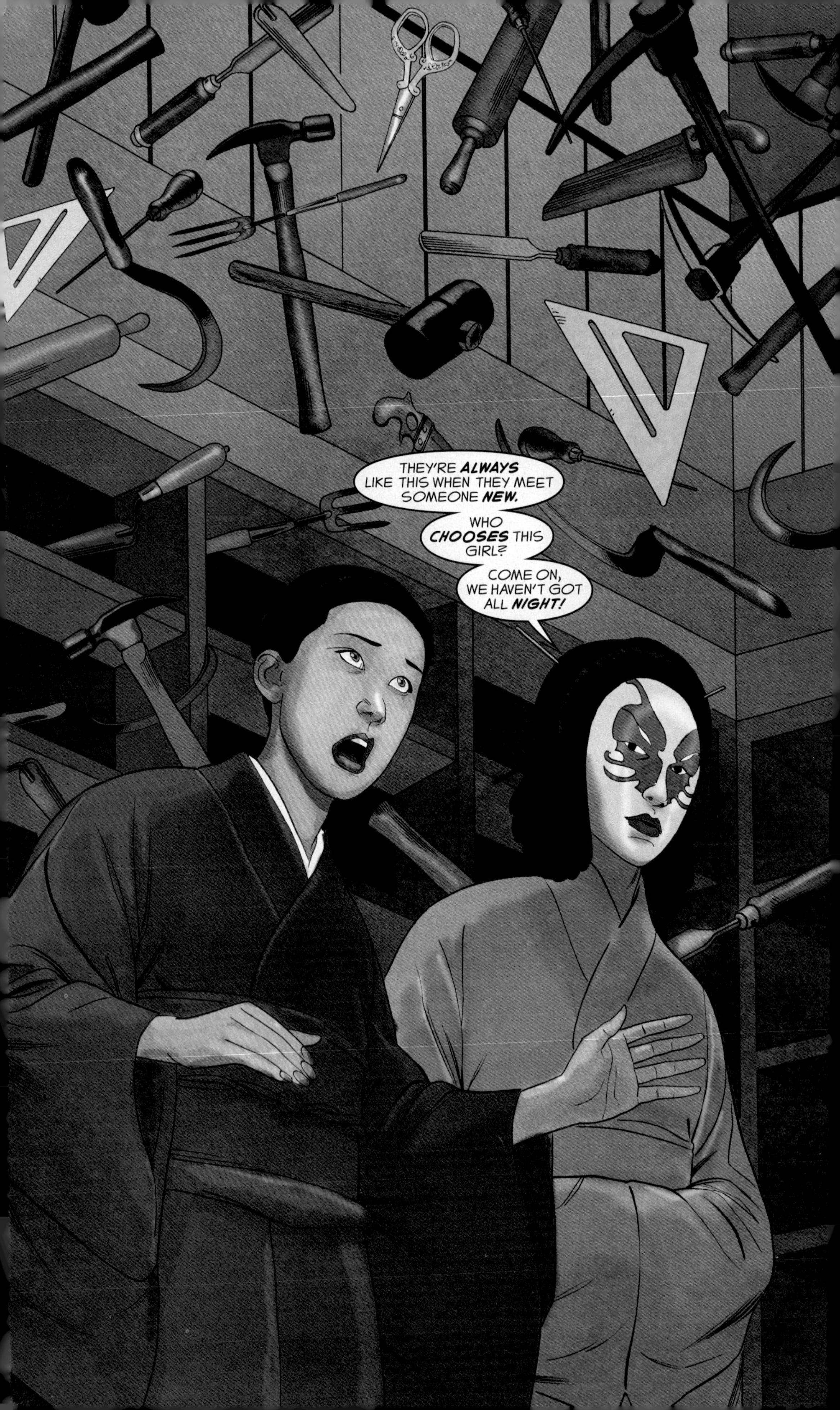
THEY'RE ALWAYS LIKE THIS WHEN THEY MEET SOMEONE NEW.
WHO CHOOSES THIS GIRL?
COME ON, WE HAVEN'T GOT ALL NIGHT!

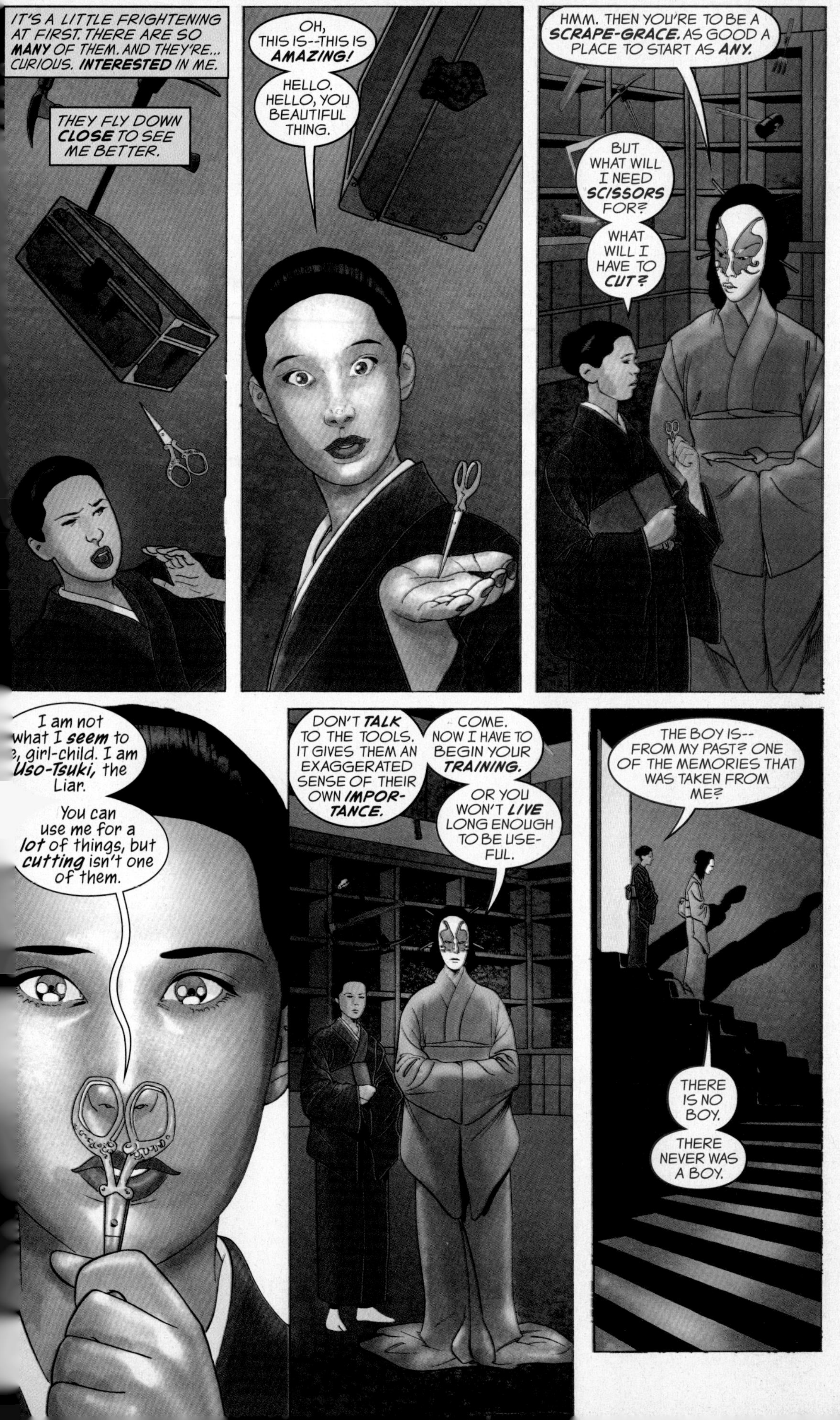

IT'S A LITTLE FRIGHTENING AT FIRST. THERE ARE SO MANY OF THEM. AND THEY'RE... CURIOUS. INTERESTED IN ME.
THEY FLY DOWN CLOSE TO SEE ME BETTER.
OH, THIS IS--THIS IS AMAZING!
HELLO. HELLO, YOU BEAUTIFUL THING.
HMM. THEN YOU'RE TO BE A SCRAPE-GRACE. AS GOOD A PLACE TO START AS ANY.
BUT WHAT WILL I NEED SCISSORS FOR?
WHAT WILL I HAVE TO CUT?
I am not what I seem to be, girl-child. I am Uso-Tsuki, the Liar.
You can use me for a lot of things, but cutting isn't one of them.
DON'T TALK TO THE TOOLS. IT GIVES THEM AN EXAGGERATED SENSE OF THEIR OWN IMPORTANCE.
COME. NOW I HAVE TO BEGIN YOUR TRAINING.
OR YOU WON'T LIVE LONG ENOUGH TO BE USEFUL.
THE BOY IS-- FROM MY PAST? ONE OF THE MEMORIES THAT WAS TAKEN FROM ME?
THERE IS NO BOY.
THERE NEVER WAS A BOY.

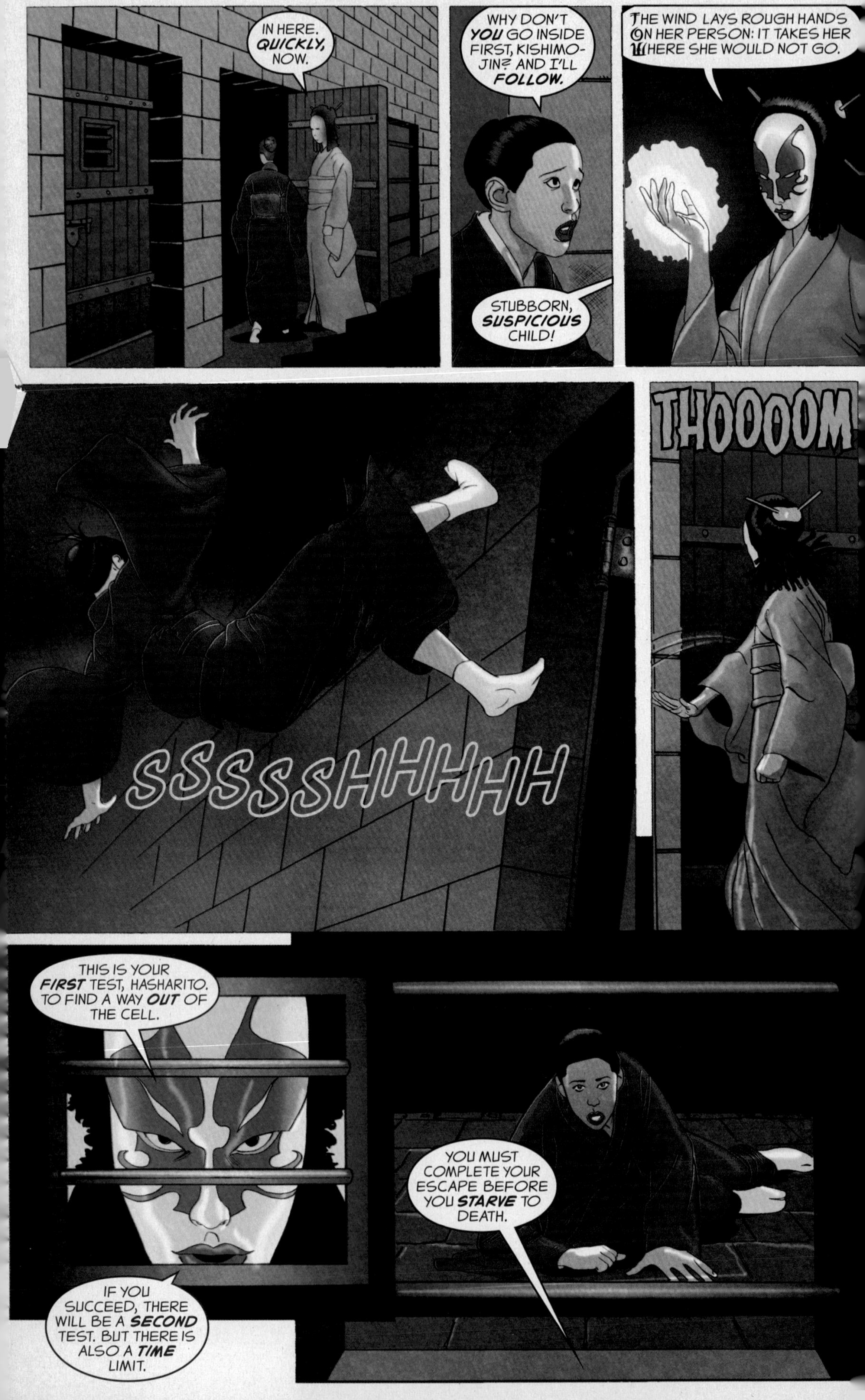
IN HERE. QUICKLY, NOW.
WHY DON'T YOU GO INSIDE FIRST, KISHIMO-JIN? AND I'LL FOLLOW.
STUBBORN, SUSPICIOUS CHILD!
THE WIND LAYS ROUGH HANDS ON HER PERSON: IT TAKES HER WHERE SHE WOULD NOT GO.
SSSSSHHHHH
THOOOOM
THIS IS YOUR FIRST TEST, HASHARITO. TO FIND A WAY OUT OF THE CELL.
IF YOU SUCCEED, THERE WILL BE A SECOND TEST. BUT THERE IS ALSO A TIME LIMIT.
YOU MUST COMPLETE YOUR ESCAPE BEFORE YOU STARVE TO DEATH.

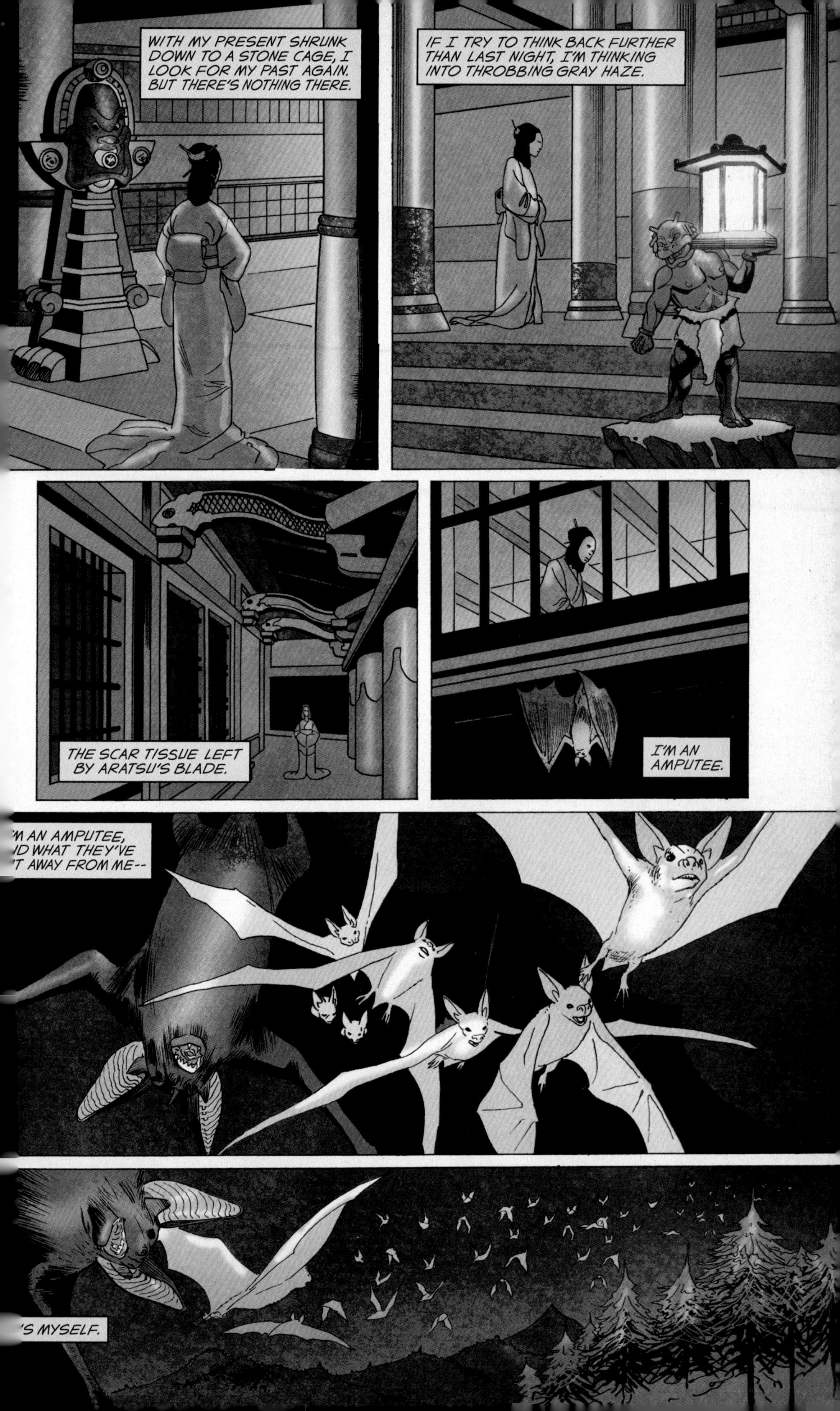
WITH MY PRESENT SHRUNK DOWN TO A STONE CAGE, I LOOK FOR MY PAST AGAIN. BUT THERE'S NOTHING THERE.
IF I TRY TO THINK BACK FURTHER THAN LAST NIGHT, I'M THINKING INTO THROBBING GRAY HAZE.
THE SCAR TISSUE LEFT BY ARATSU'S BLADE.
I'M AN AMPUTEE.
'M AN AMPUTEE, ID WHAT THEY'VE T AWAY FROM ME--
'S MYSELF.

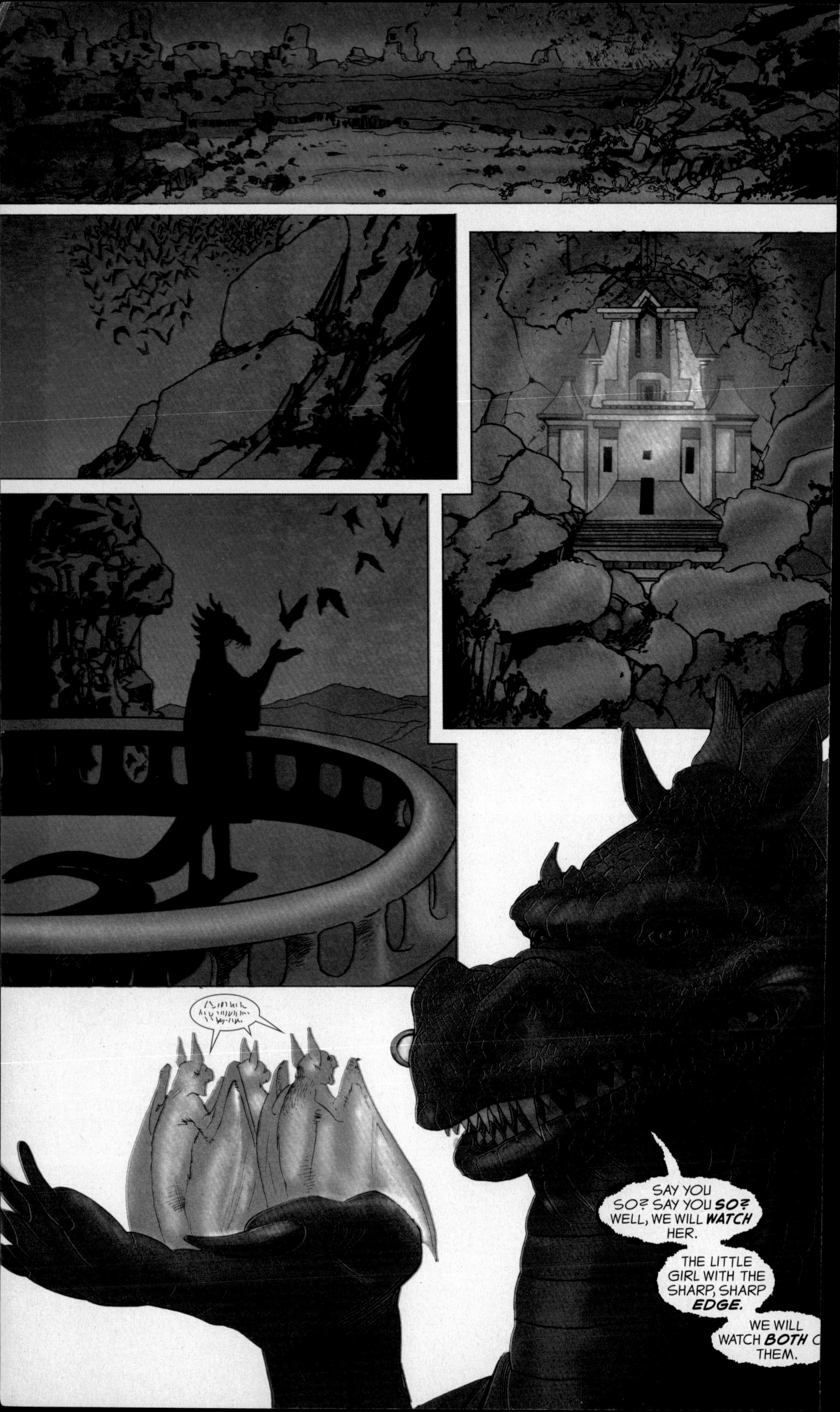
SAY YOU SO? SAY YOU SO? WELL, WE WILL WATCH HER.
THE LITTLE GIRL WITH THE SHARP, SHARP EDGE.
WE WILL WATCH BOTH THEM.

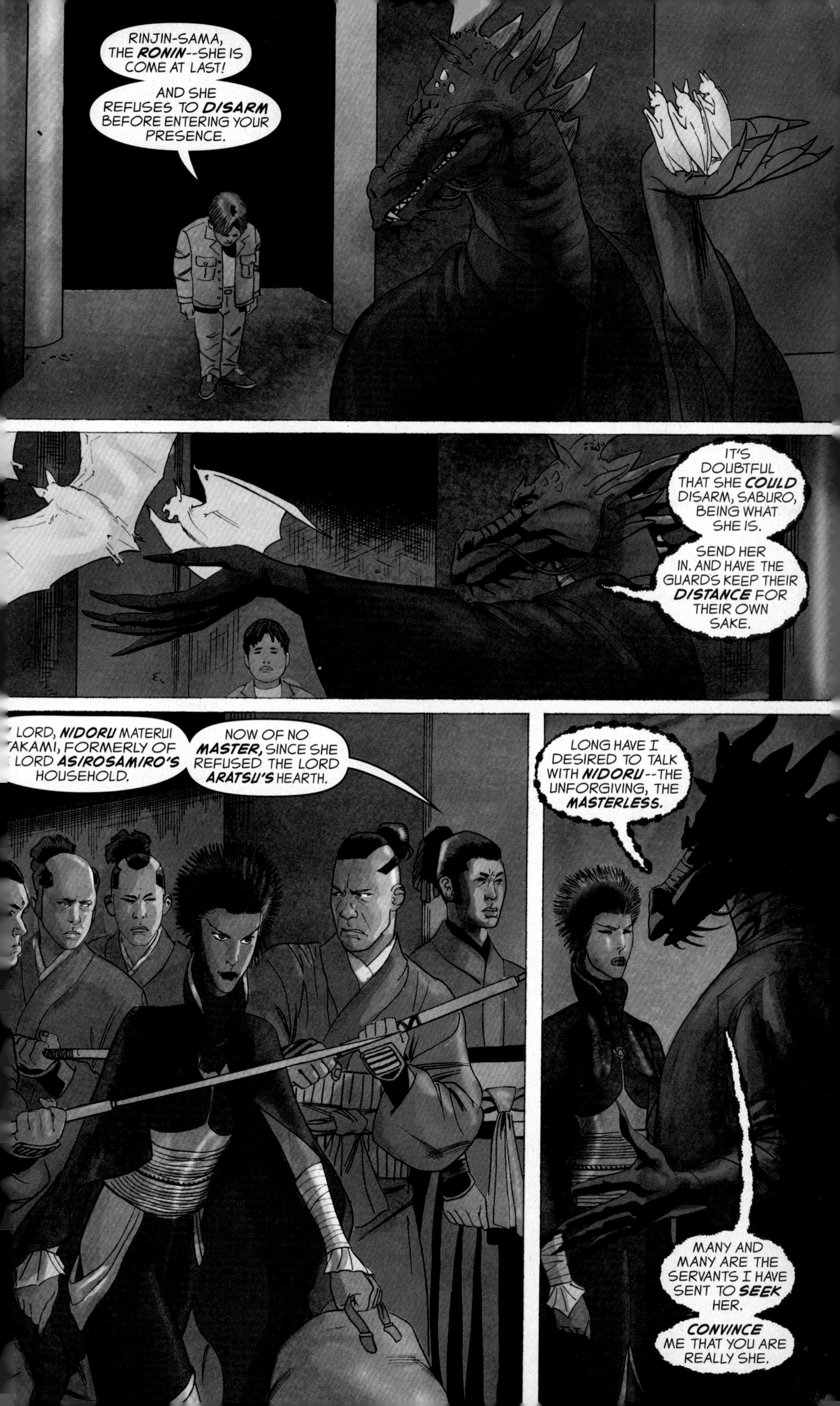

RINJIN-SAMA, THE RONIN--SHE IS COME AT LAST!
AND SHE REFUSES TO DISARM BEFORE ENTERING YOUR PRESENCE.
IT'S DOUBTFUL THAT SHE COULD DISARM, SABURO, BEING WHAT SHE IS.
SEND HER IN. AND HAVE THE GUARDS KEEP THEIR DISTANCE FOR THEIR OWN SAKE.
LORD, NIDORU MATERUI TAKAMI, FORMERLY OF LORD ASIROSAMIRO'S HOUSEHOLD.
NOW OF NO MASTER, SINCE SHE REFUSED THE LORD ARATSU'S HEARTH.
LONG HAVE I DESIRED TO TALK WITH NIDORU--THE UNFORGIVING, THE MASTERLESS.
MANY AND MANY ARE THE SERVANTS I HAVE SENT TO SEEK HER.
CONVINCE ME THAT YOU ARE REALLY SHE.

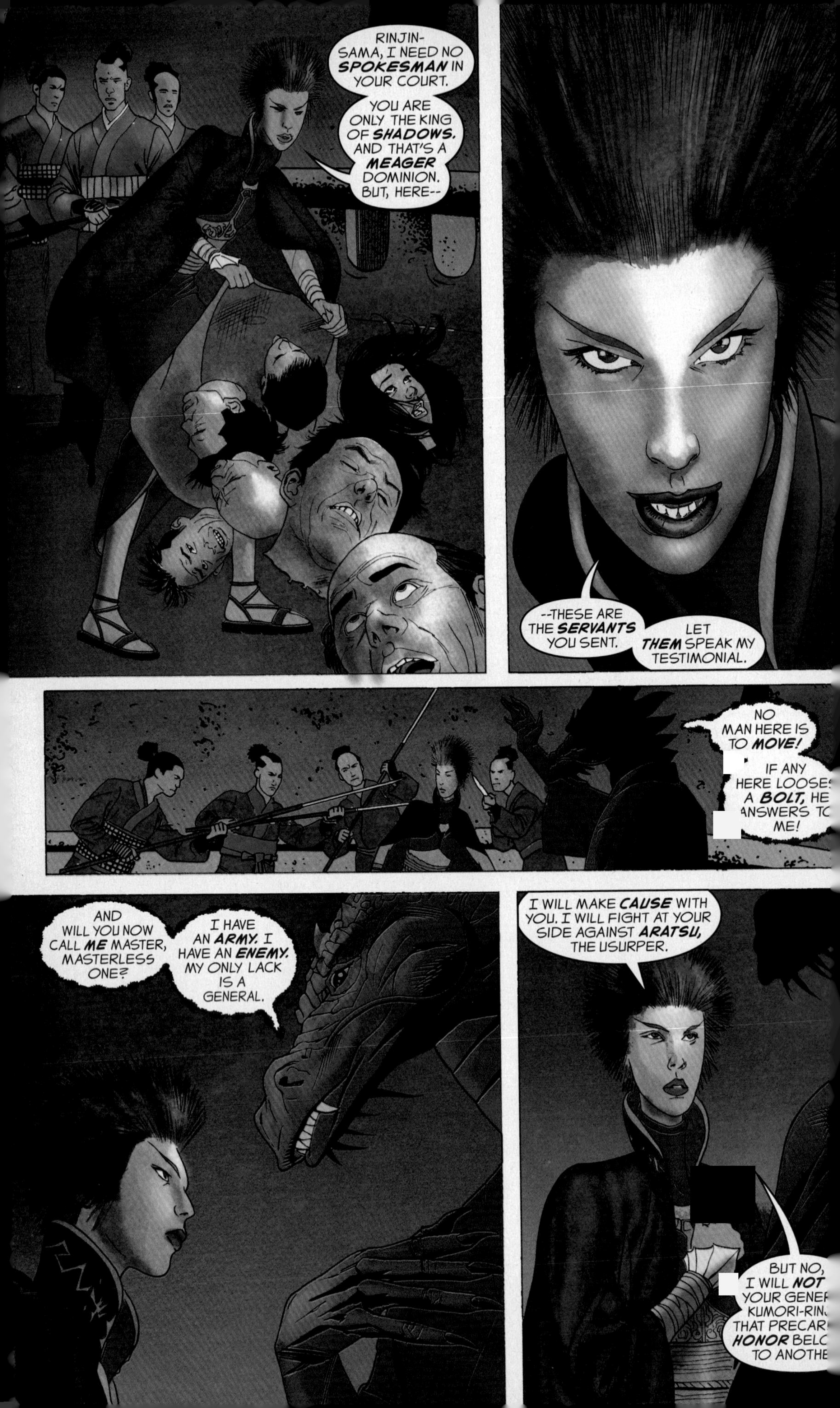

RINJIN-SAMA, I NEED NO SPOKESMAN IN YOUR COURT.
YOU ARE ONLY THE KING OF SHADOWS. AND THAT'S A MEAGER DOMINION. BUT, HERE--
--THESE ARE THE SERVANTS YOU SENT.
LET THEM SPEAK MY TESTIMONIAL.
NO MAN HERE IS TO MOVE!
IF ANY HERE LOOSE A BOLT, HE ANSWERS TO ME!
AND WILL YOU NOW CALL ME MASTER, MASTERLESS ONE?
I HAVE AN ARMY. I HAVE AN ENEMY. MY ONLY LACK IS A GENERAL.
I WILL MAKE CAUSE WITH YOU. I WILL FIGHT AT YOUR SIDE AGAINST ARATSU, THE USURPER.
BUT NO, I WILL NOT YOUR GENE KUMORI-RIN THAT PRECAR HONOR BEL TO ANOTHE

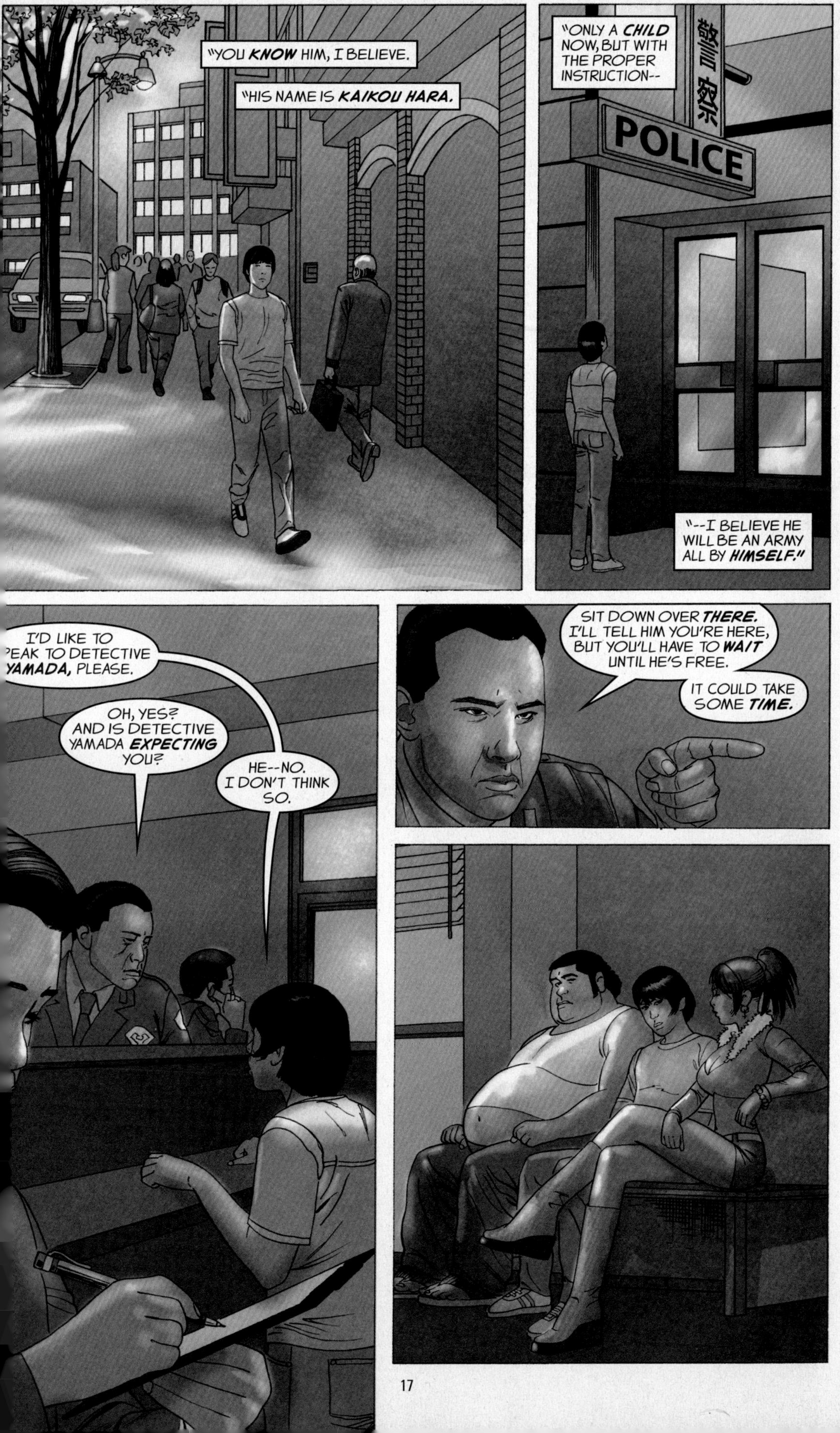

"YOU KNOW HIM, I BELIEVE.
"HIS NAME IS KAIKOU HARA.
"ONLY A CHILD NOW, BUT WITH THE PROPER INSTRUCTION--
警察
POLICE
"--I BELIEVE HE WILL BE AN ARMY ALL BY HIMSELF."
I'D LIKE TO SPEAK TO DETECTIVE YAMADA, PLEASE.
OH, YES? AND IS DETECTIVE YAMADA EXPECTING YOU?
HE--NO. I DON'T THINK SO.
SIT DOWN OVER THERE. I'LL TELL HIM YOU'RE HERE, BUT YOU'LL HAVE TO WAIT UNTIL HE'S FREE.
IT COULD TAKE SOME TIME.

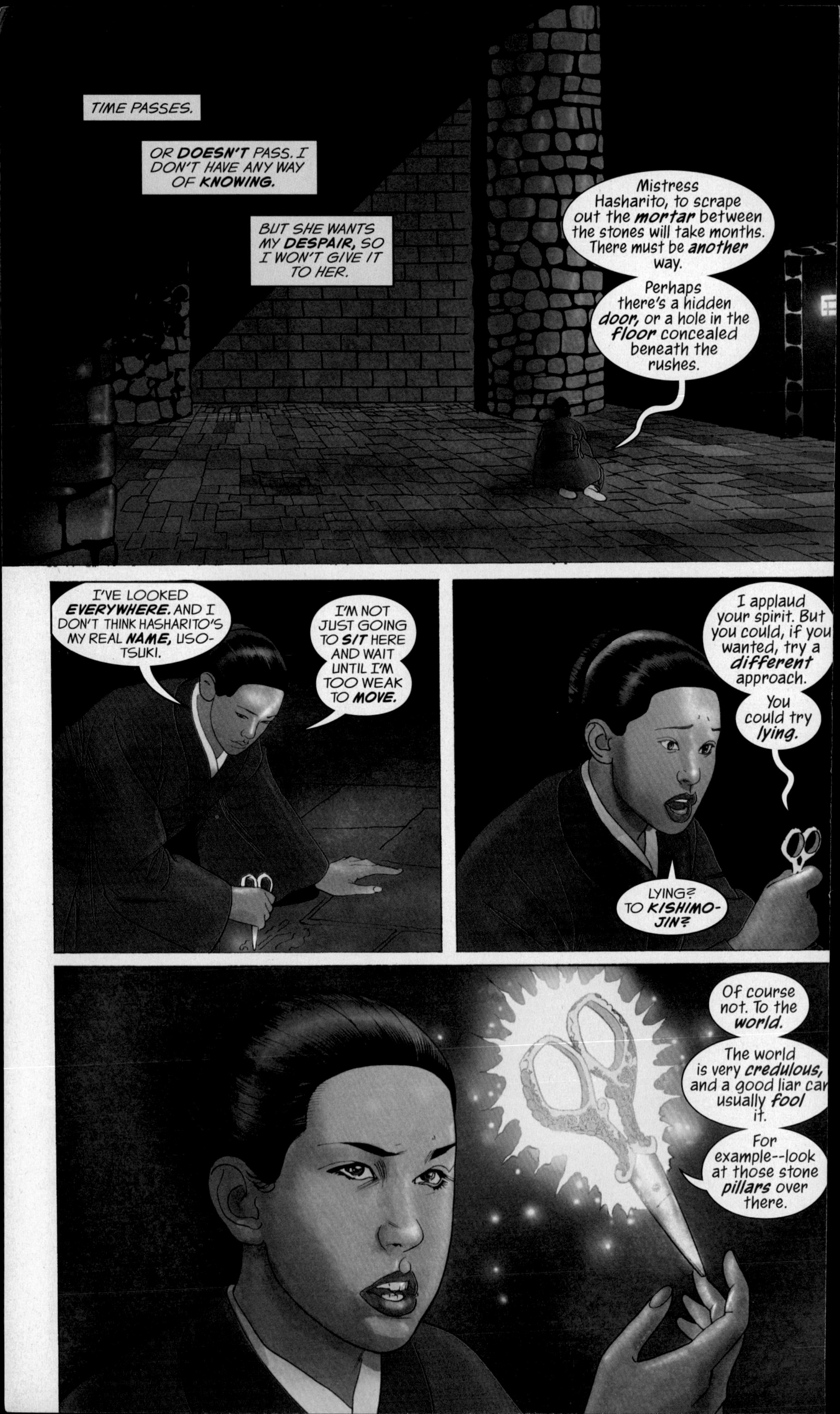
TIME PASSES.
OR DOESN'T PASS. I DON'T HAVE ANY WAY OF KNOWING.
BUT SHE WANTS MY DESPAIR, SO I WON'T GIVE IT TO HER.
Mistress Hasharito, to scrape out the mortar between the stones will take months. There must be another way.
Perhaps there's a hidden door, or a hole in the floor concealed beneath the rushes.
I'VE LOOKED EVERYWHERE. AND I DON'T THINK HASHARITO'S MY REAL NAME, USO-TSUKI.
I'M NOT JUST GOING TO SIT HERE AND WAIT UNTIL I'M TOO WEAK TO MOVE.
I applaud your spirit. But you could, if you wanted, try a different approach.
You could try lying.
LYING? TO KISHIMO-JIN?
Of course not. To the world.
The world is very credulous, and a good liar can usually fool it.
For example--look at those stone pillars over there.

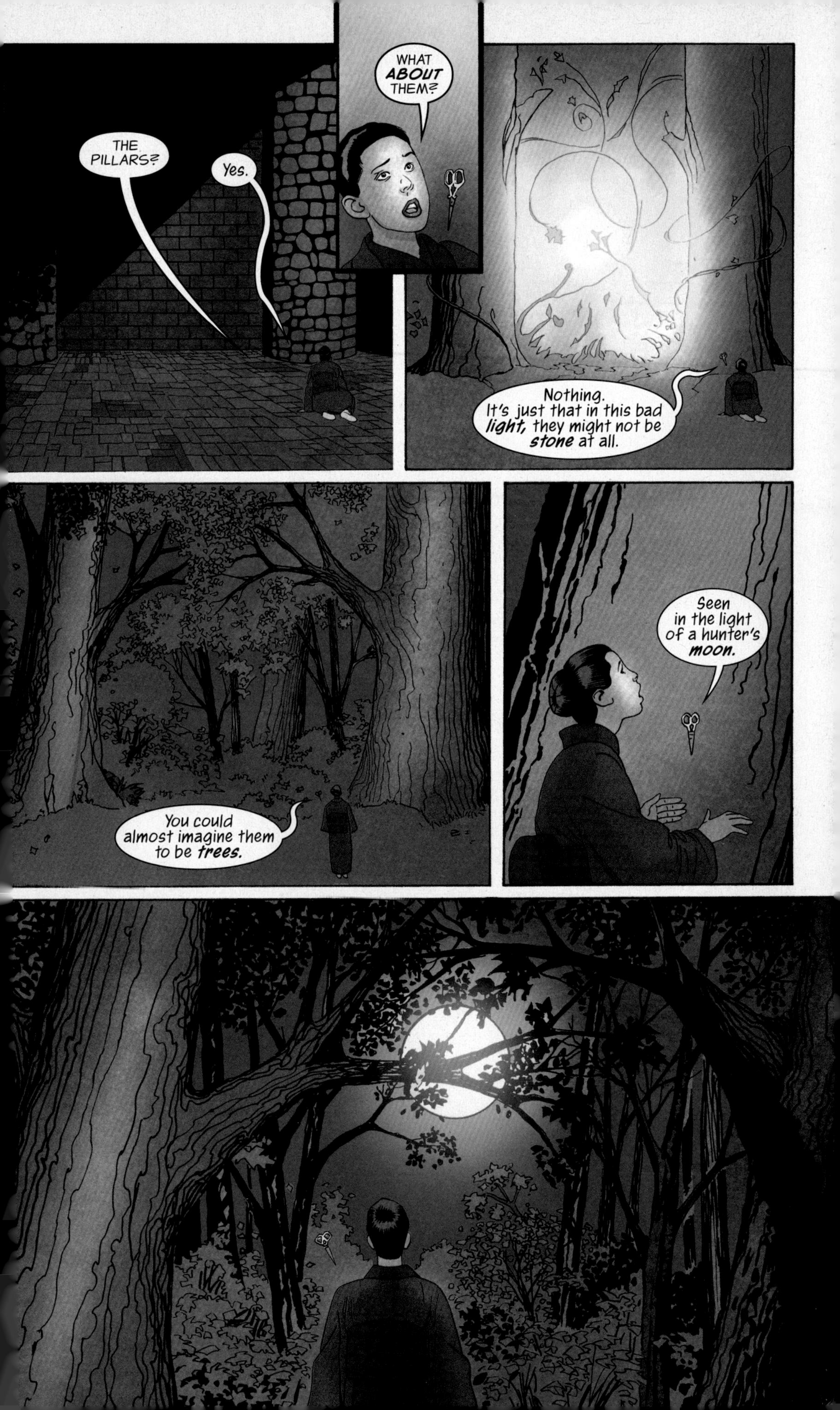
THE PILLARS?
Yes.
WHAT ABOUT THEM?
Nothing. It's just that in this bad light, they might not be stone at all.
You could almost imagine them to be trees.
Seen in the light of a hunter's moon.

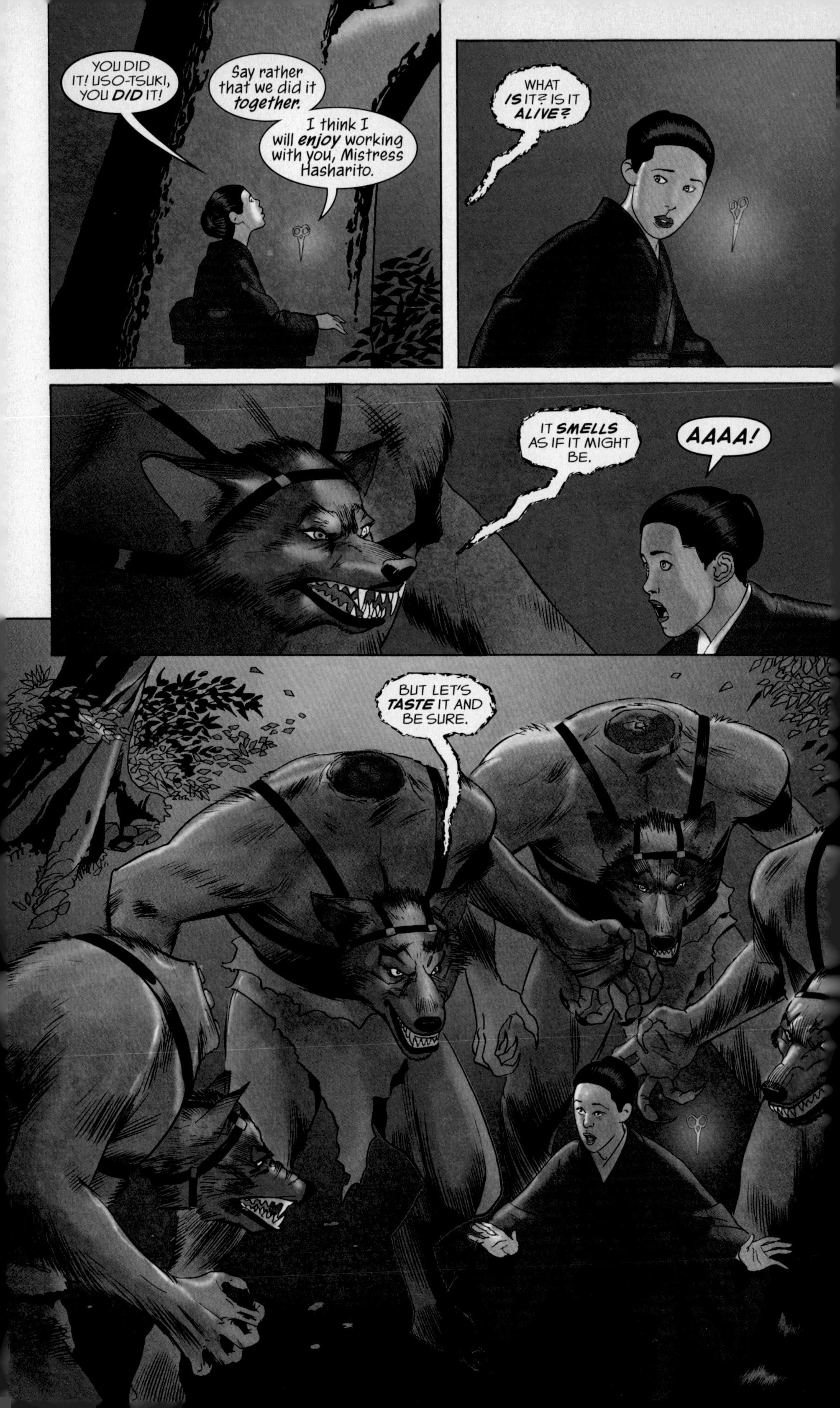
YOU DID IT! USO-TSUKI, YOU DID IT!
Say rather that we did it together.
I think I will enjoy working with you, Mistress Hasharito.
WHAT IS IT? IS IT ALIVE?
IT SMELLS AS IF IT MIGHT BE.
AAAA!
BUT LET'S TASTE IT AND BE SURE.

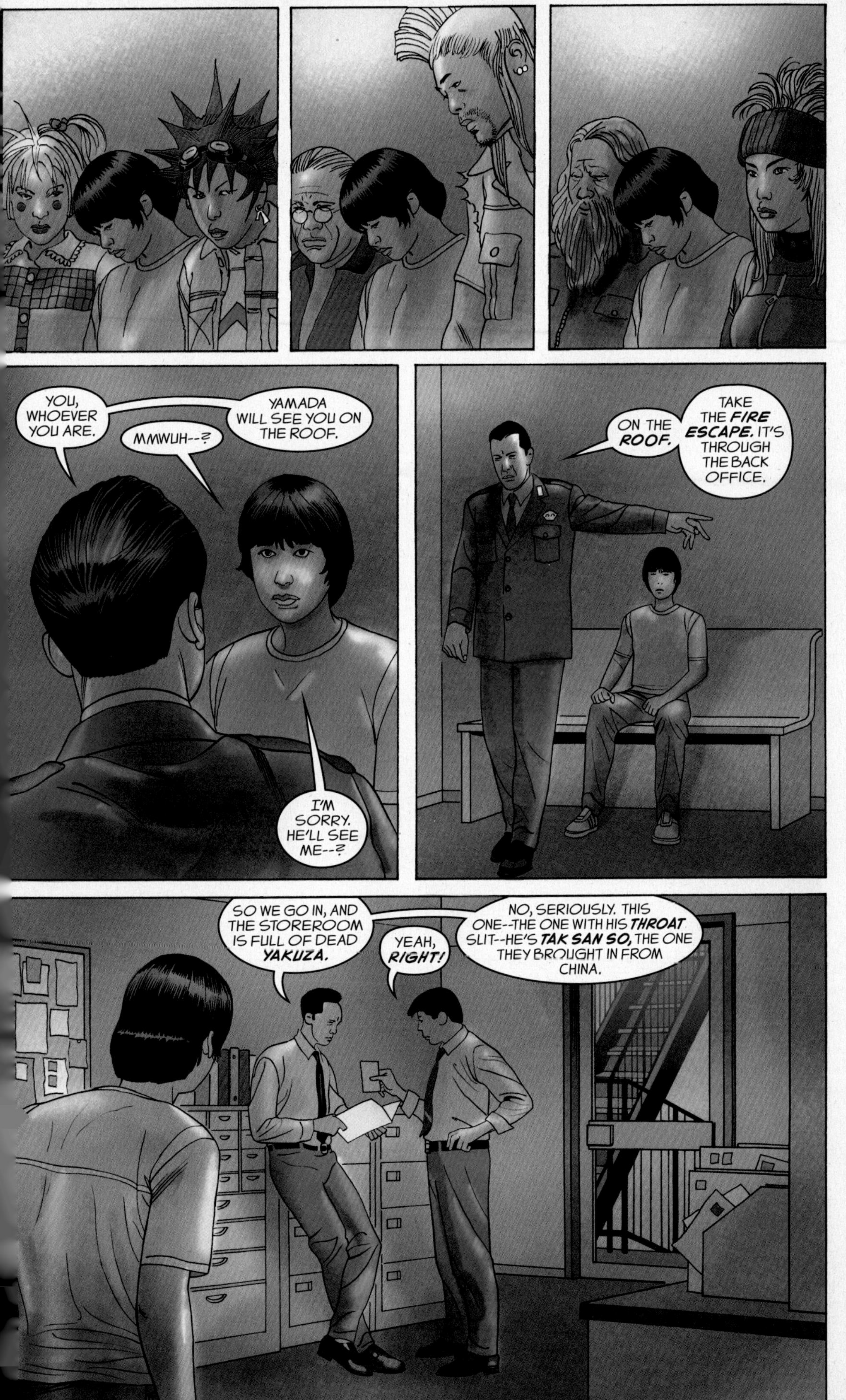
YOU, WHOEVER YOU ARE.
YAMADA WILL SEE YOU ON THE ROOF.
MMWUH--?
I'M SORRY. HE'LL SEE ME--?
ON THE **ROOF.**
TAKE THE ***FIRE ESCAPE.*** IT'S THROUGH THE BACK OFFICE.
SO WE GO IN, AND THE STOREROOM IS FULL OF DEAD ***YAKUZA.***
YEAH, ***RIGHT!***
NO, SERIOUSLY. THIS ONE--THE ONE WITH HIS ***THROAT*** SLIT--HE'S ***TAK SAN SO,*** THE ONE THEY BROUGHT IN FROM CHINA.

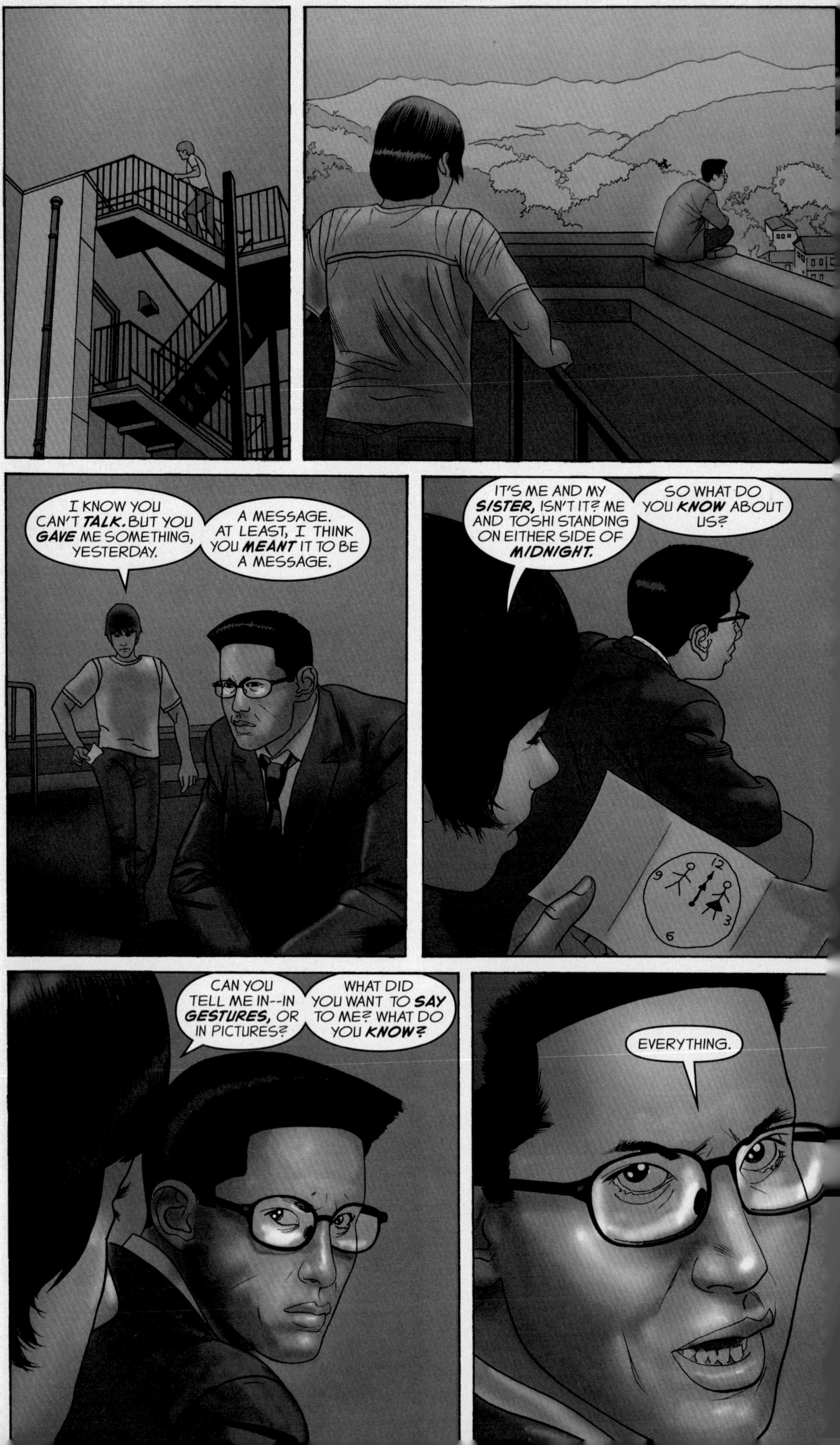

I KNOW YOU CAN'T **TALK.** BUT YOU **GAVE** ME SOMETHING, YESTERDAY.
A MESSAGE. AT LEAST, I THINK YOU **MEANT** IT TO BE A MESSAGE.
IT'S ME AND MY **SISTER,** ISN'T IT? ME AND TOSHI STANDING ON EITHER SIDE OF **MIDNIGHT.**
SO WHAT DO YOU **KNOW** ABOUT US?
12
9
3
6
CAN YOU TELL ME IN--IN **GESTURES,** OR IN PICTURES?
WHAT DID YOU WANT TO **SAY** TO ME? WHAT DO YOU **KNOW?**
EVERYTHING.

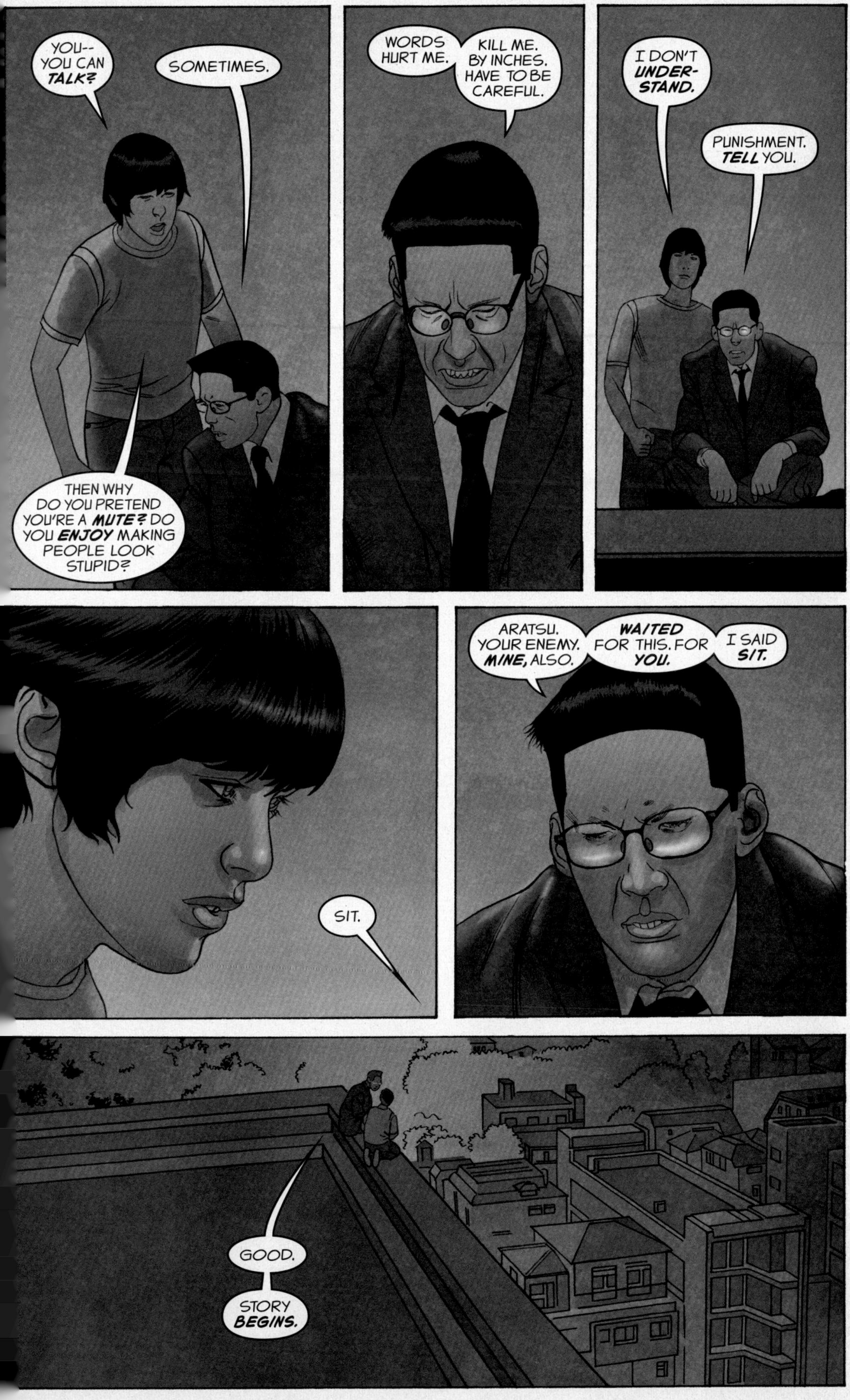

YOU-- YOU CAN TALK?
SOMETIMES.
THEN WHY DO YOU PRETEND YOU'RE A MUTE? DO YOU ENJOY MAKING PEOPLE LOOK STUPID?
WORDS HURT ME.
KILL ME. BY INCHES. HAVE TO BE CAREFUL.
I DON'T UNDERSTAND.
PUNISHMENT. TELL YOU.
SIT.
ARATSU. YOUR ENEMY. MINE, ALSO.
WAITED FOR THIS. FOR YOU.
I SAID SIT.
GOOD.
STORY BEGINS.

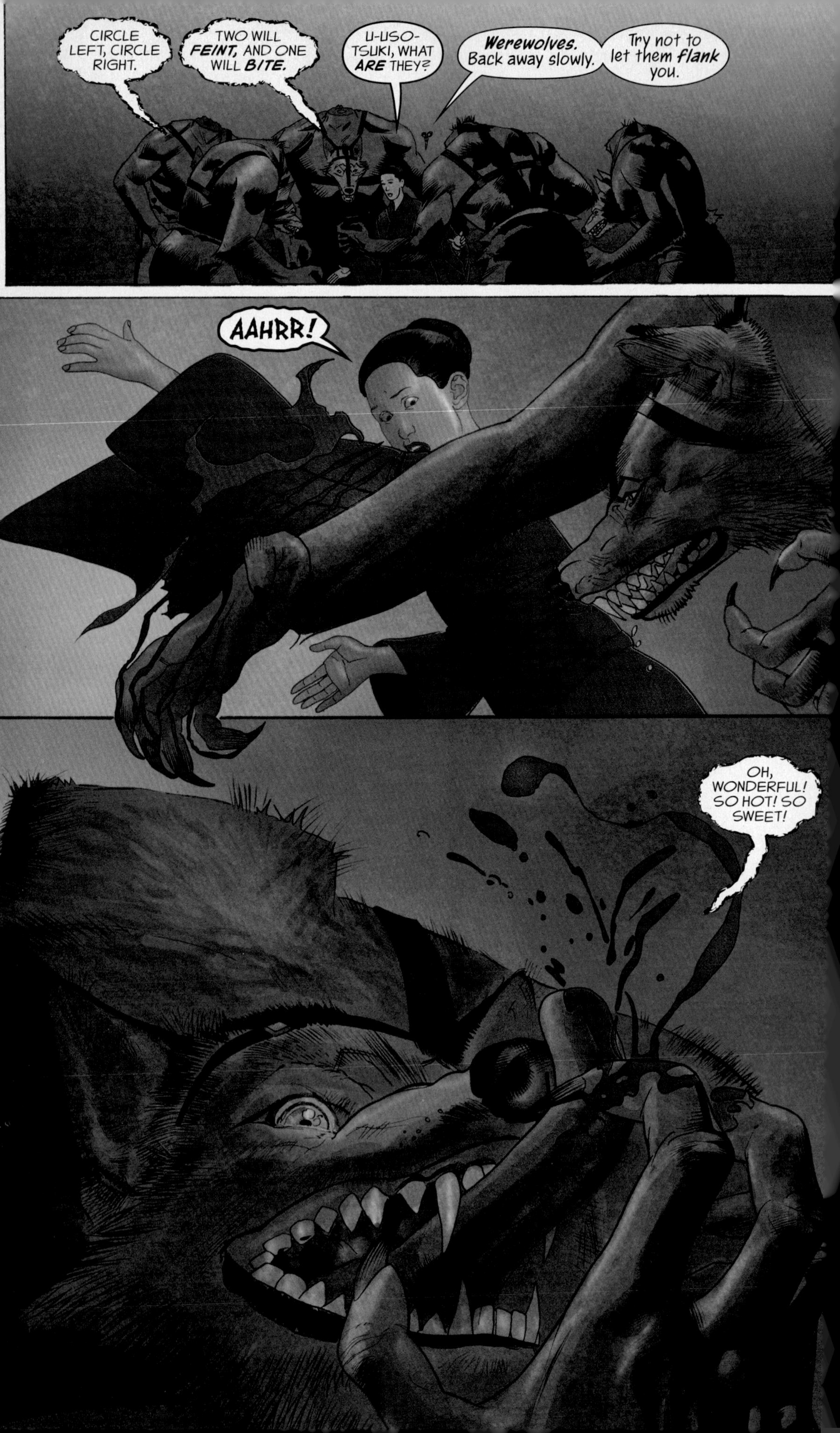

CIRCLE LEFT, CIRCLE RIGHT.
TWO WILL FEINT, AND ONE WILL BITE.
U-USO-TSUKI, WHAT ARE THEY?
Werewolves. Back away slowly.
Try not to let them flank you.
AAHRR!
OH, WONDERFUL! SO HOT! SO SWEET!

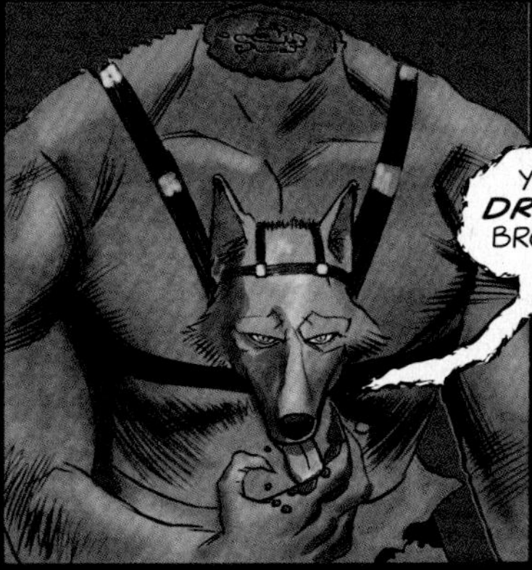
YESSS! **DRINK** HER, BROTHERS!

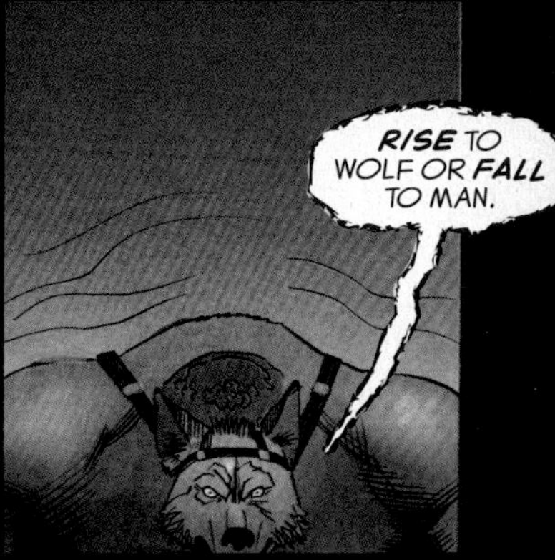
RISE TO WOLF OR **FALL** TO MAN.

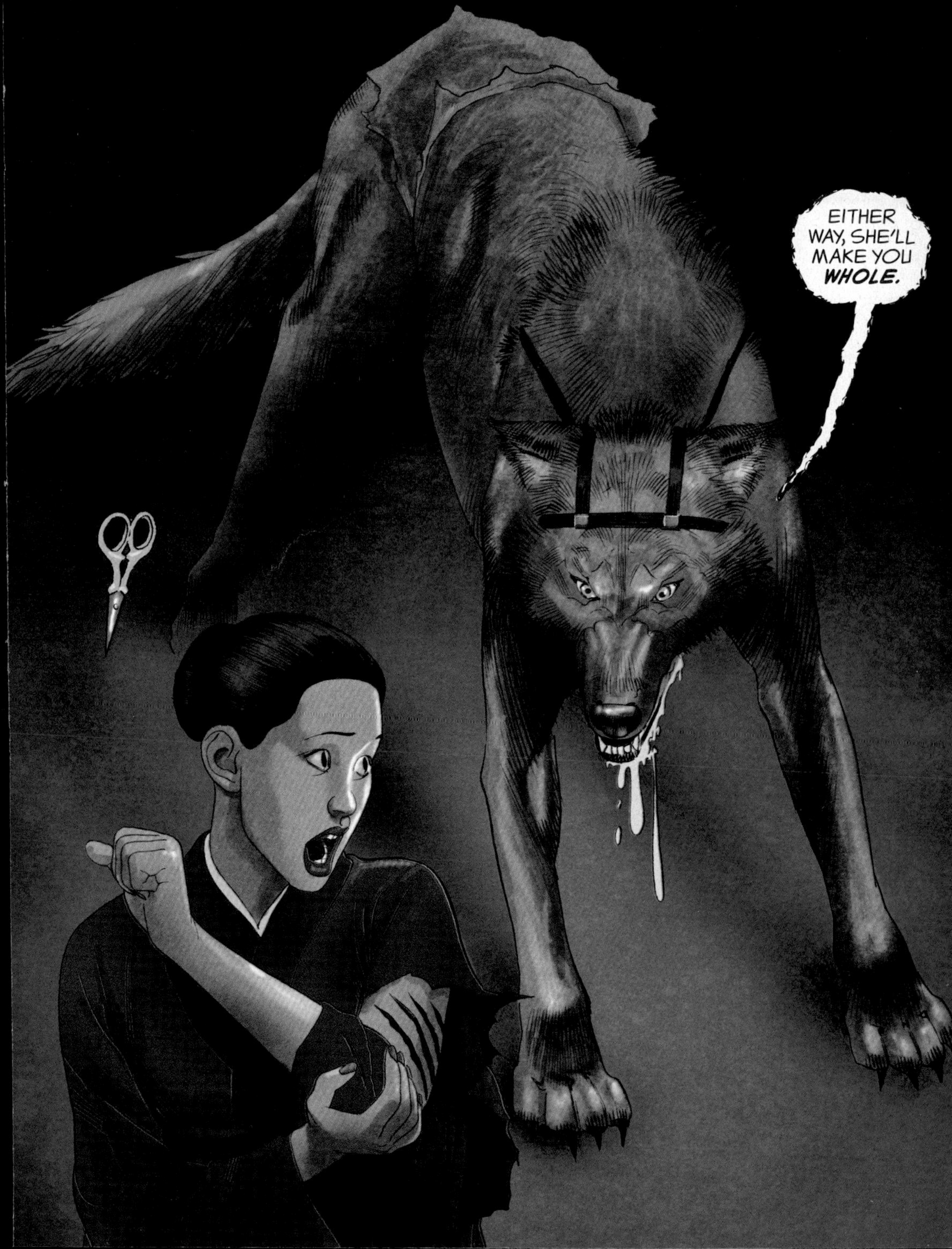
EITHER WAY, SHE'LL MAKE YOU **WHOLE.**

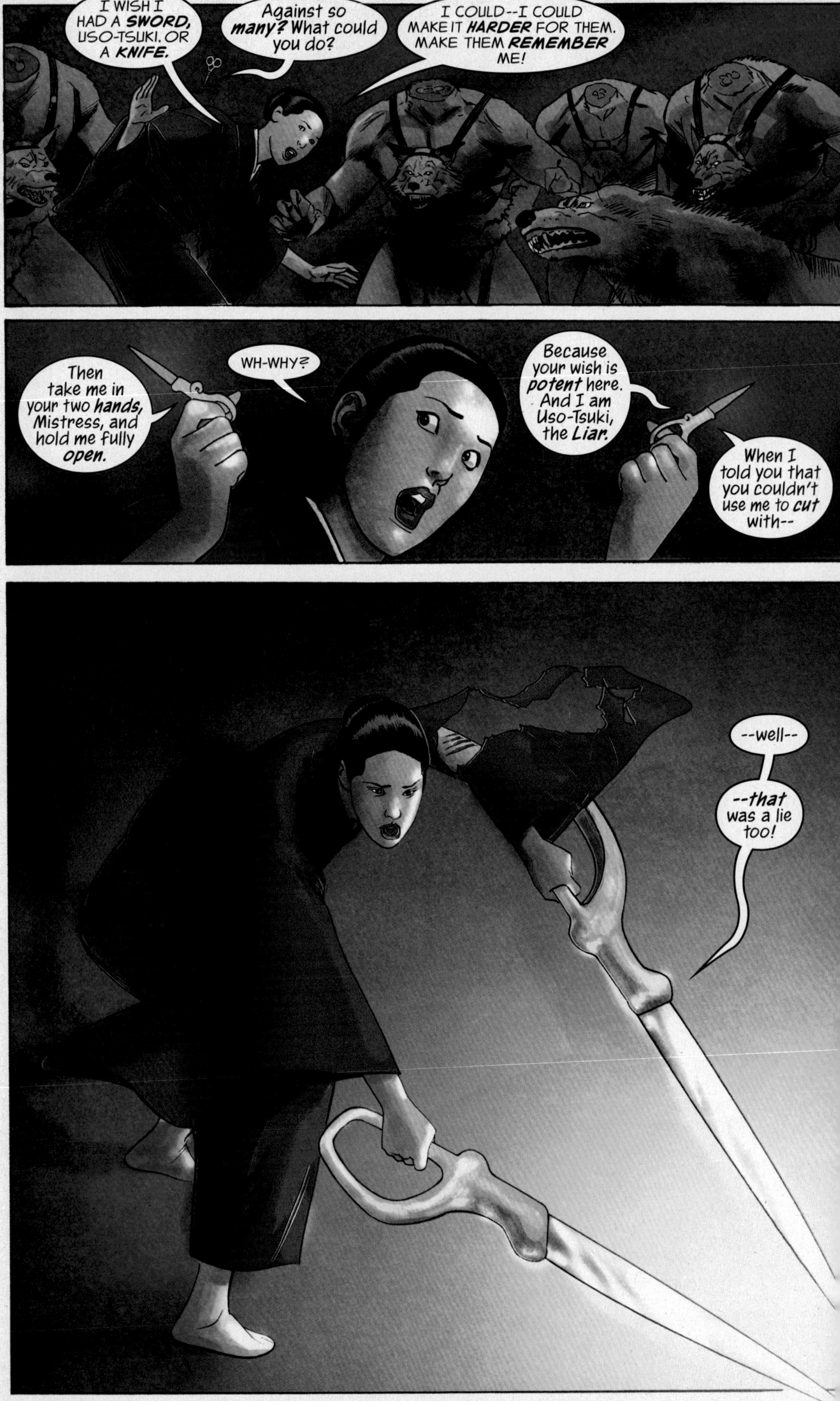

I WISH I HAD A SWORD, USO-TSUKI. OR A KNIFE.
Against so many? What could you do?
I COULD--I COULD MAKE IT HARDER FOR THEM. MAKE THEM REMEMBER ME!
Then take me in your two hands, Mistress, and hold me fully open.
WH-WHY?
Because your wish is potent here. And I am Uso-Tsuki, the Liar.
When I told you that you couldn't use me to cut with--
--well--
--that was a lie too!

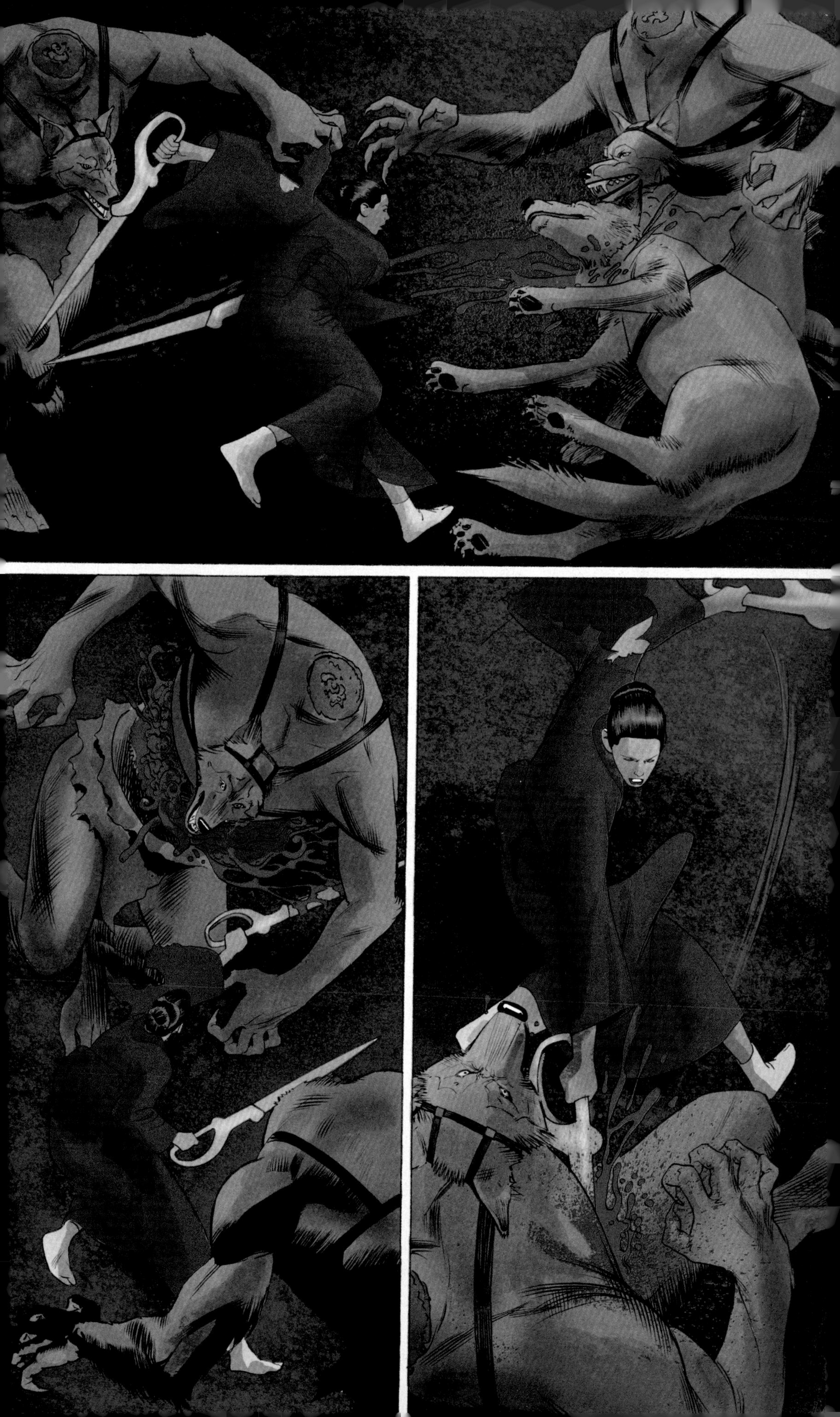

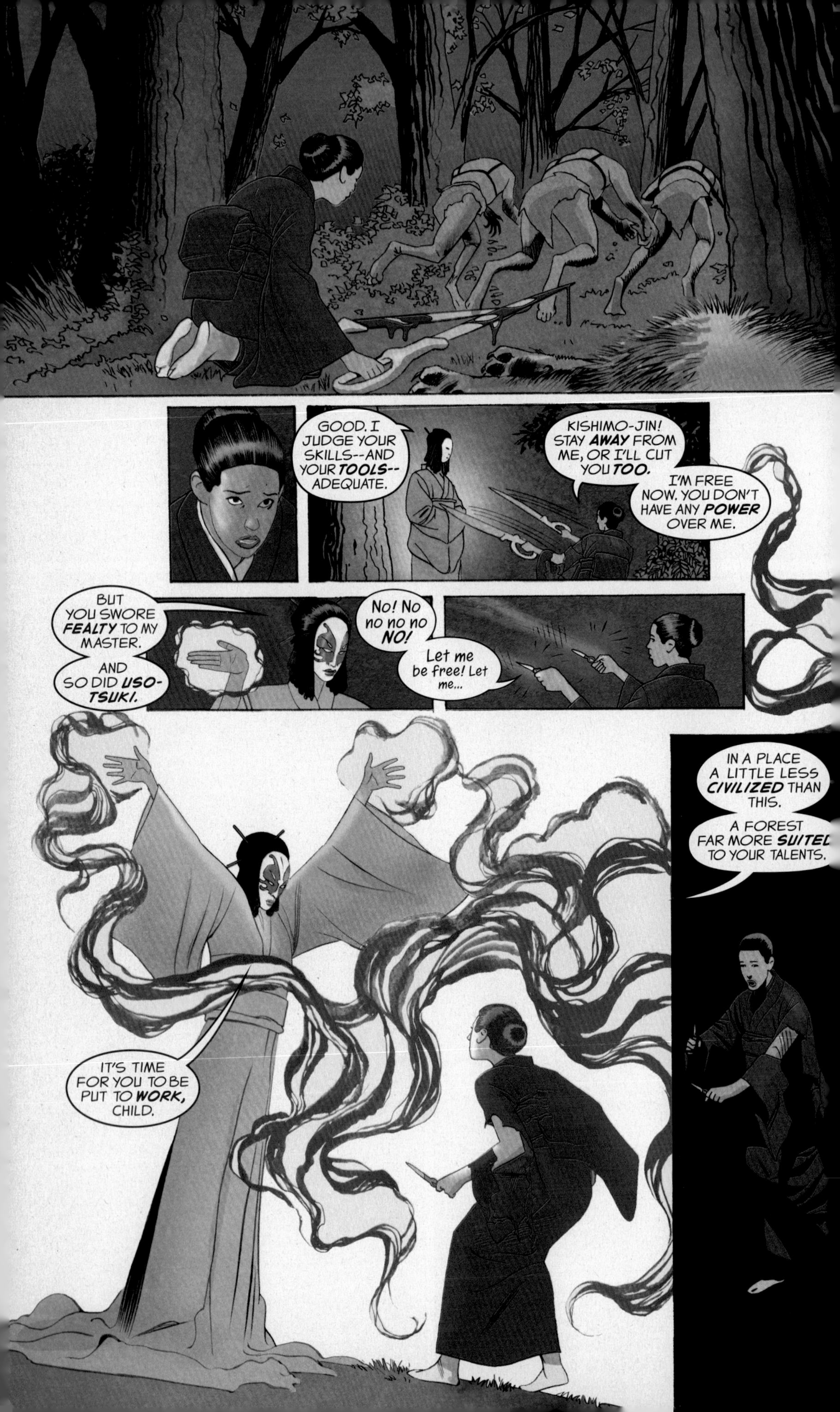
GOOD. I JUDGE YOUR SKILLS--AND YOUR TOOLS-- ADEQUATE.
KISHIMO-JIN! STAY AWAY FROM ME, OR I'LL CUT YOU TOO.
I'M FREE NOW. YOU DON'T HAVE ANY POWER OVER ME.
BUT YOU SWORE FEALTY TO MY MASTER.
AND SO DID USO-TSUKI.
No! No no no no NO!
Let me be free! Let me...
IN A PLACE A LITTLE LESS CIVILIZED THAN THIS.
A FOREST FAR MORE SUITEL TO YOUR TALENTS.
IT'S TIME FOR YOU TO BE PUT TO WORK, CHILD.

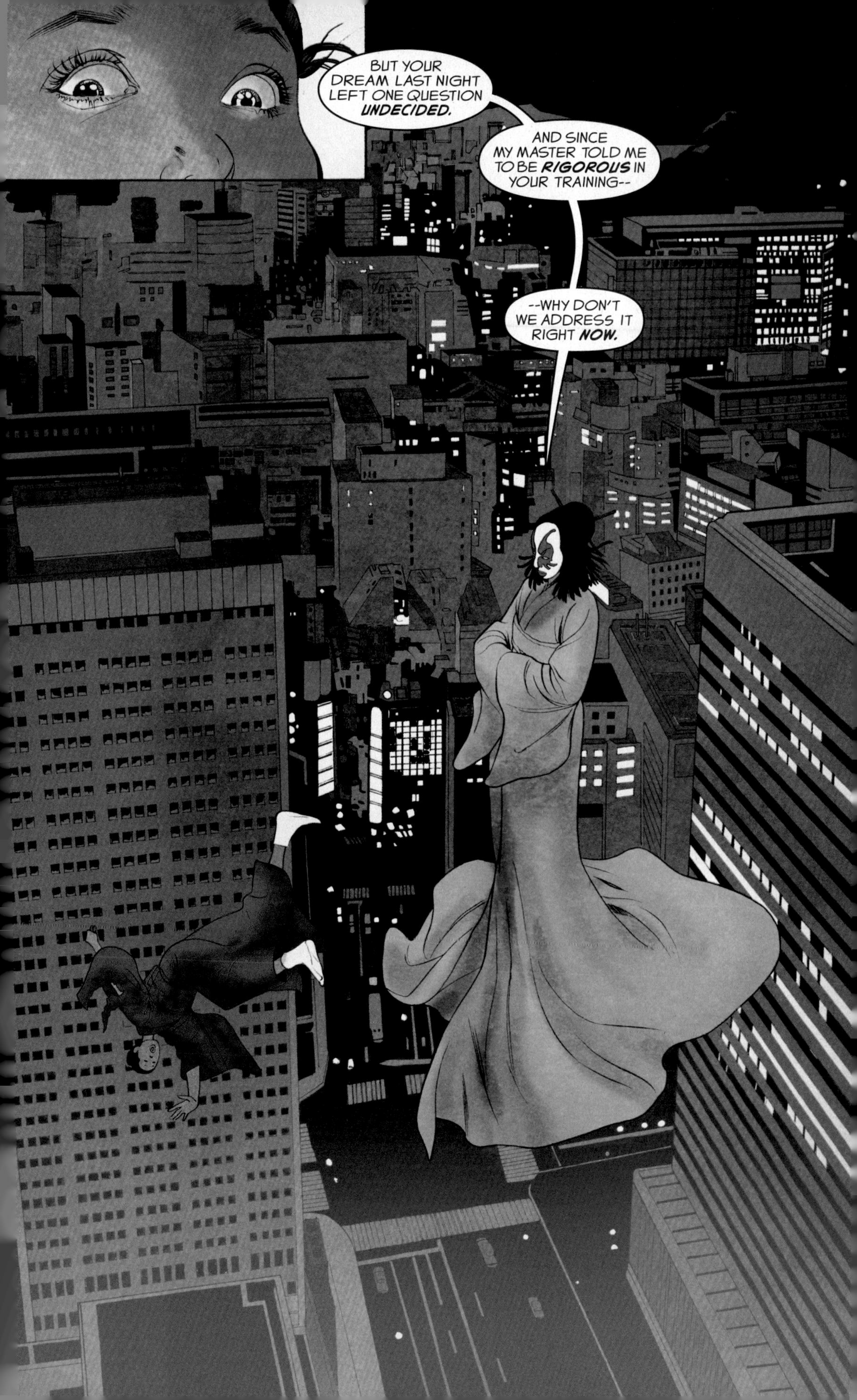
BUT YOUR DREAM LAST NIGHT LEFT ONE QUESTION UNDECIDED.
AND SINCE MY MASTER TOLD ME TO BE RIGOROUS IN YOUR TRAINING--
--WHY DON'T WE ADDRESS IT RIGHT NOW.

chapter two

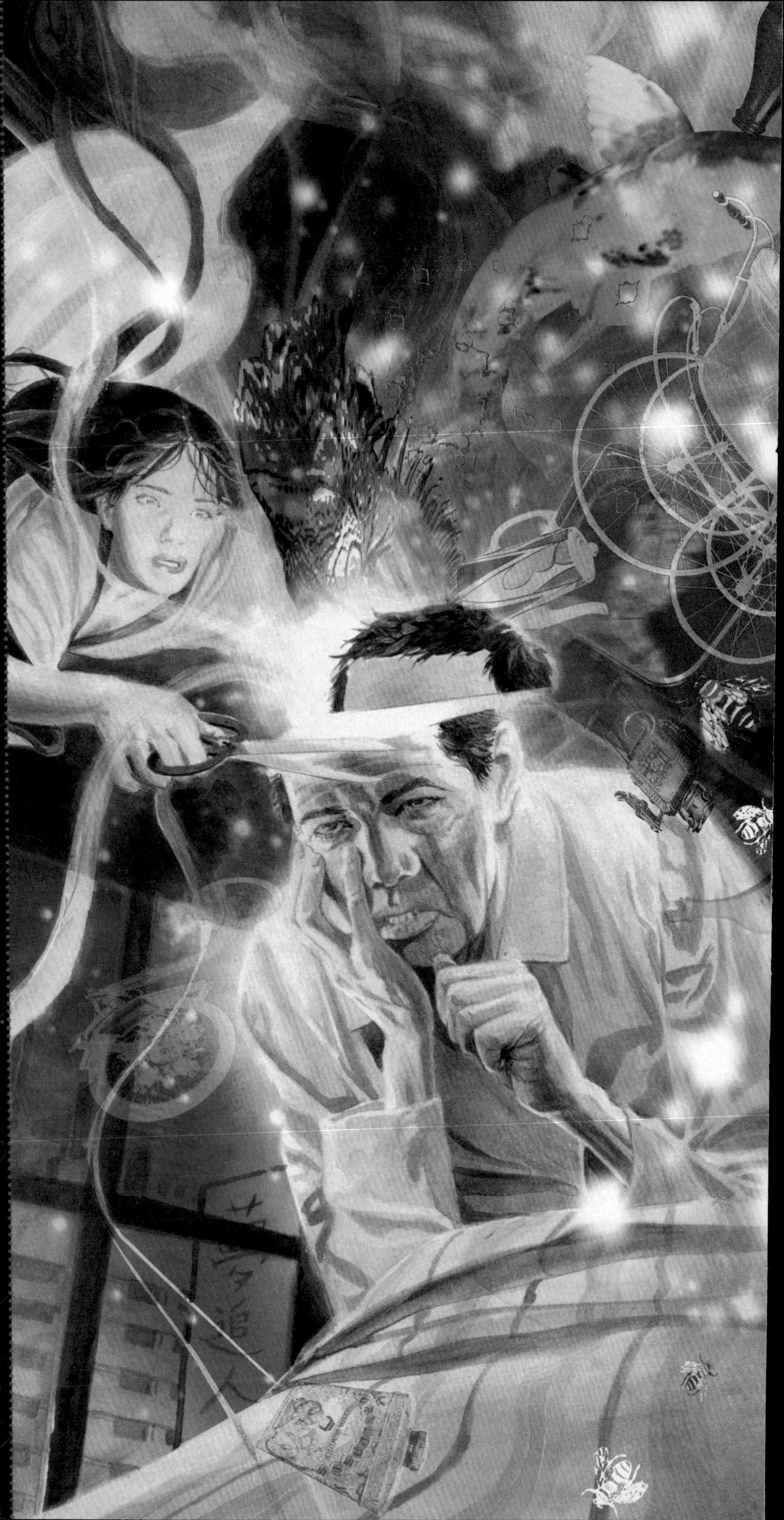

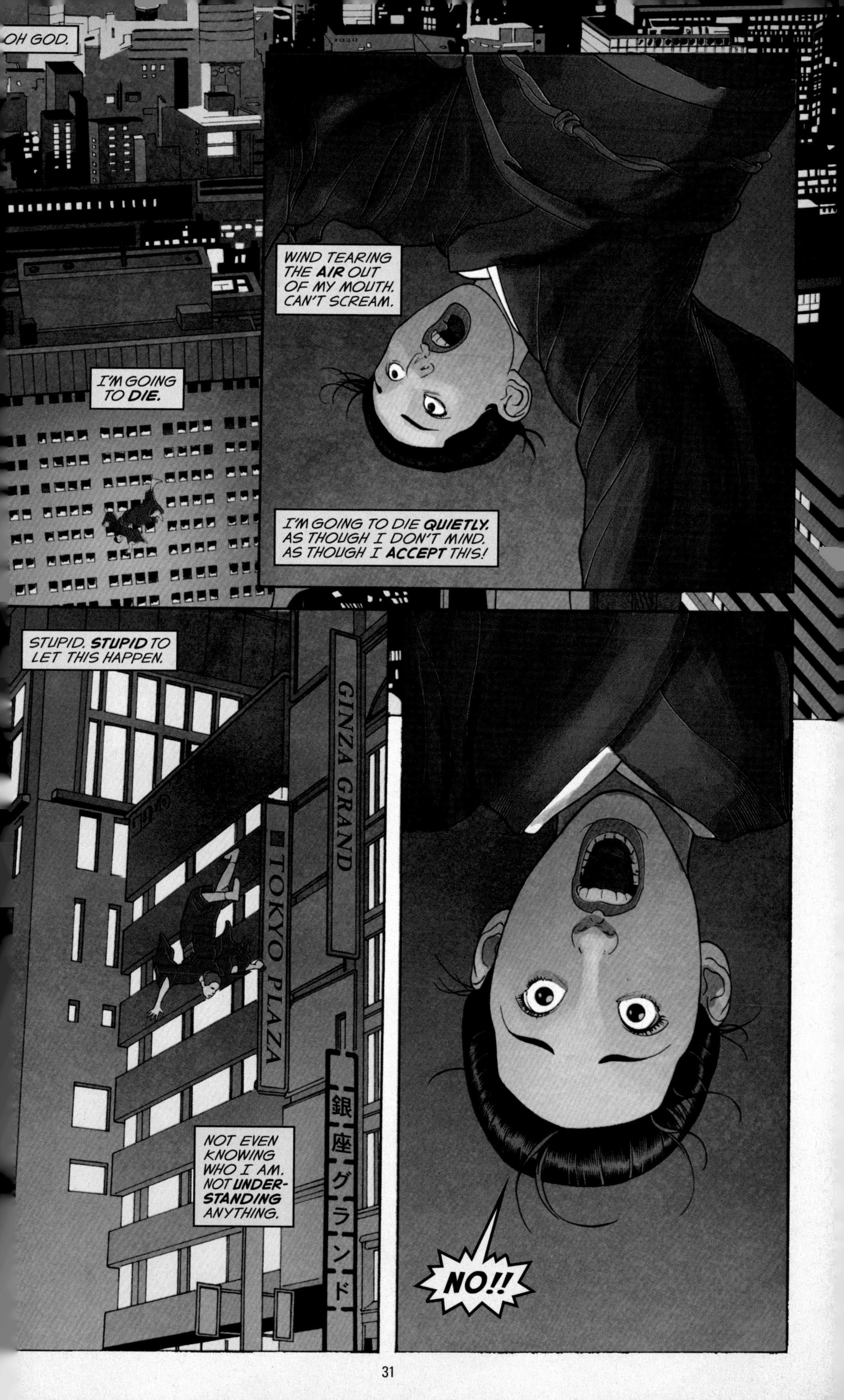
OH GOD.
WIND TEARING THE AIR OUT OF MY MOUTH. CAN'T SCREAM.
I'M GOING TO DIE.
I'M GOING TO DIE QUIETLY. AS THOUGH I DON'T MIND. AS THOUGH I ACCEPT THIS!
STUPID. STUPID TO LET THIS HAPPEN.
GINZA GRAND
TOKYO PLAZA
銀座グランド
NOT EVEN KNOWING WHO I AM. NOT UNDERSTANDING ANYTHING.
NO!!

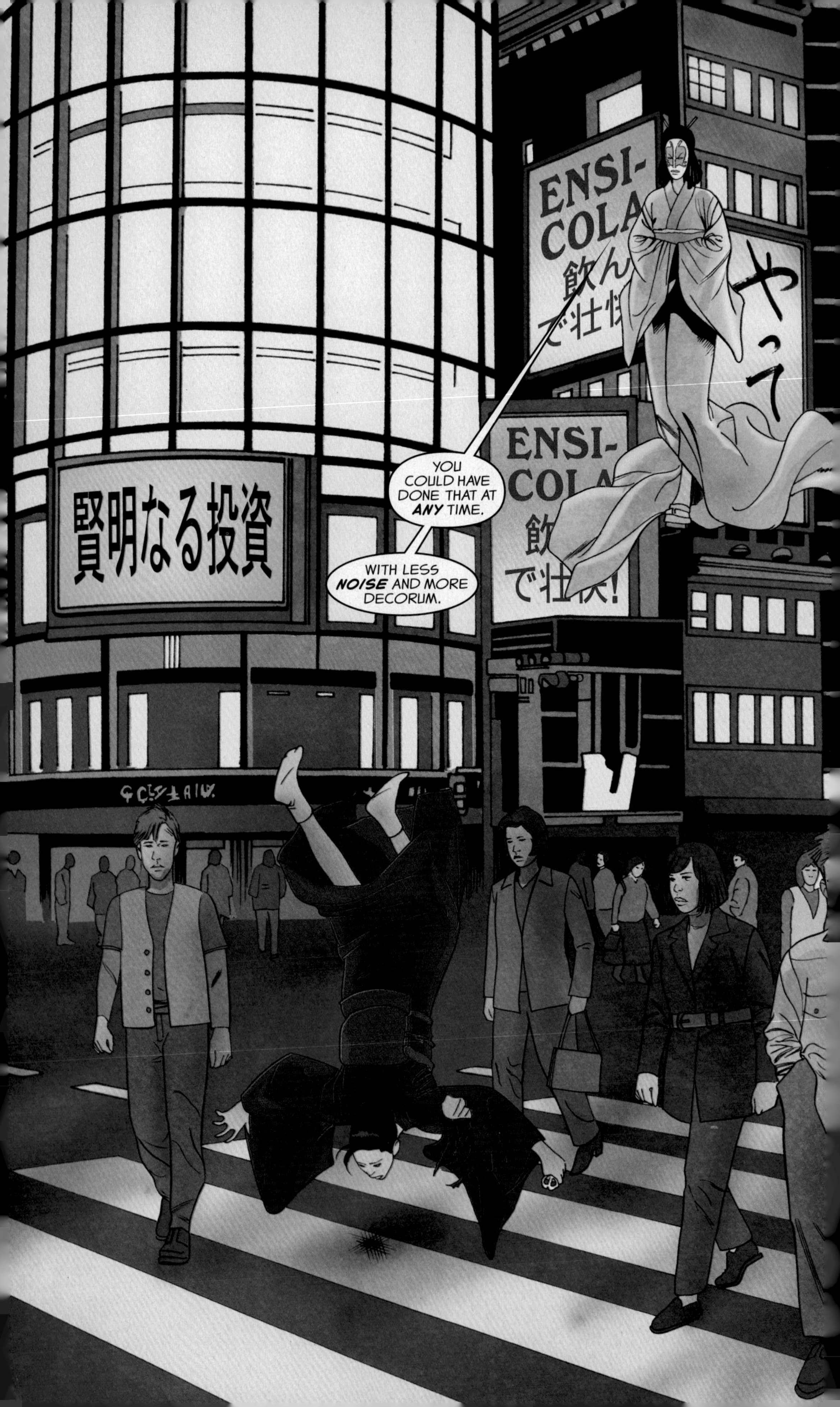

ENSI-COLA
やって
賢明なる投資
YOU COULD HAVE DONE THAT AT *ANY* TIME.
WITH LESS *NOISE* AND MORE DECORUM.

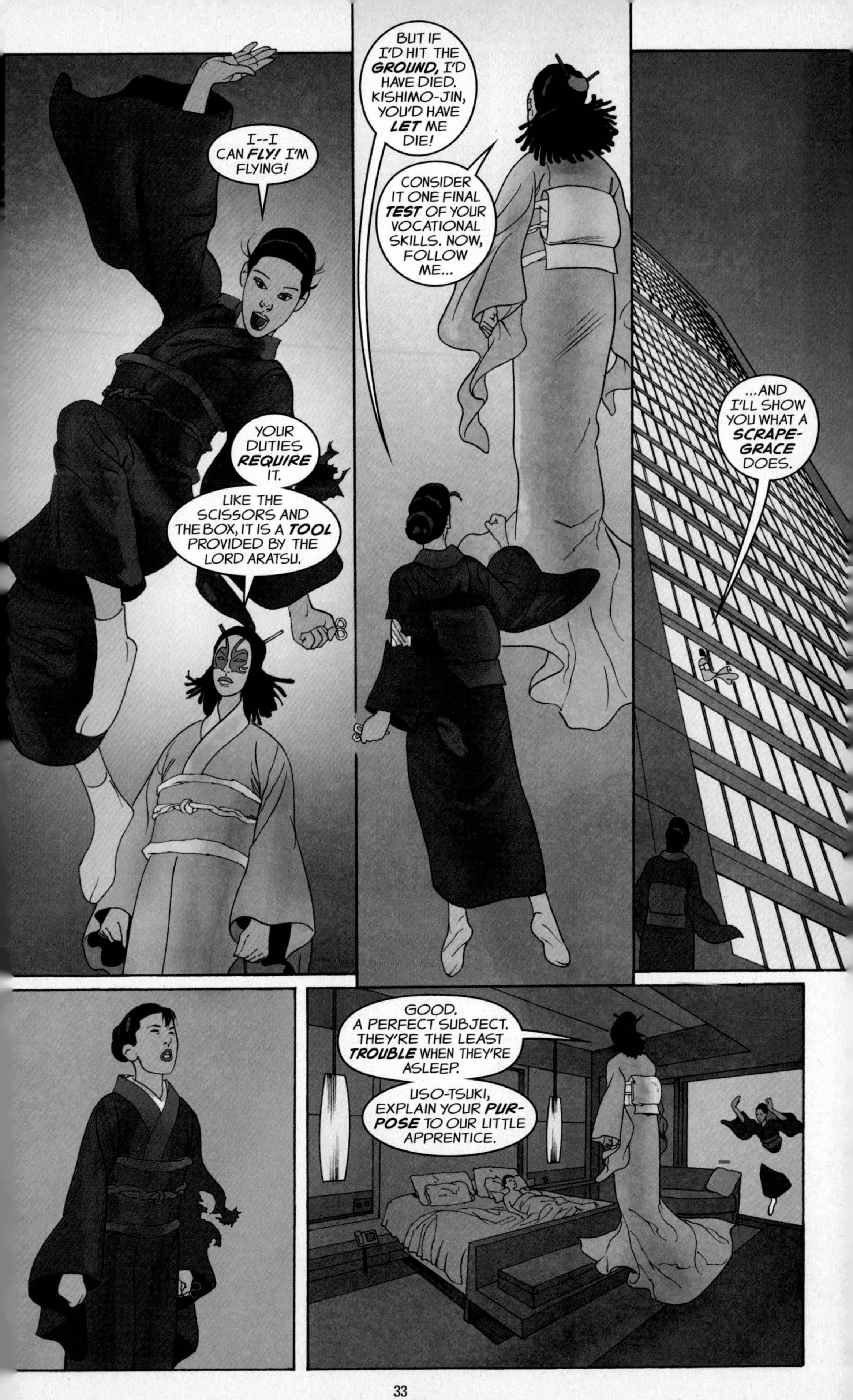
I--I CAN FLY! I'M FLYING!
YOUR DUTIES REQUIRE IT.
LIKE THE SCISSORS AND THE BOX, IT IS A TOOL PROVIDED BY THE LORD ARATSU.
BUT IF I'D HIT THE GROUND, I'D HAVE DIED. KISHIMO-JIN, YOU'D HAVE LET ME DIE!
CONSIDER IT ONE FINAL TEST OF YOUR VOCATIONAL SKILLS. NOW, FOLLOW ME...
...AND I'LL SHOW YOU WHAT A SCRAPE-GRACE DOES.
GOOD. A PERFECT SUBJECT. THEY'RE THE LEAST TROUBLE WHEN THEY'RE ASLEEP.
USO-TSUKI, EXPLAIN YOUR PURPOSE TO OUR LITTLE APPRENTICE.

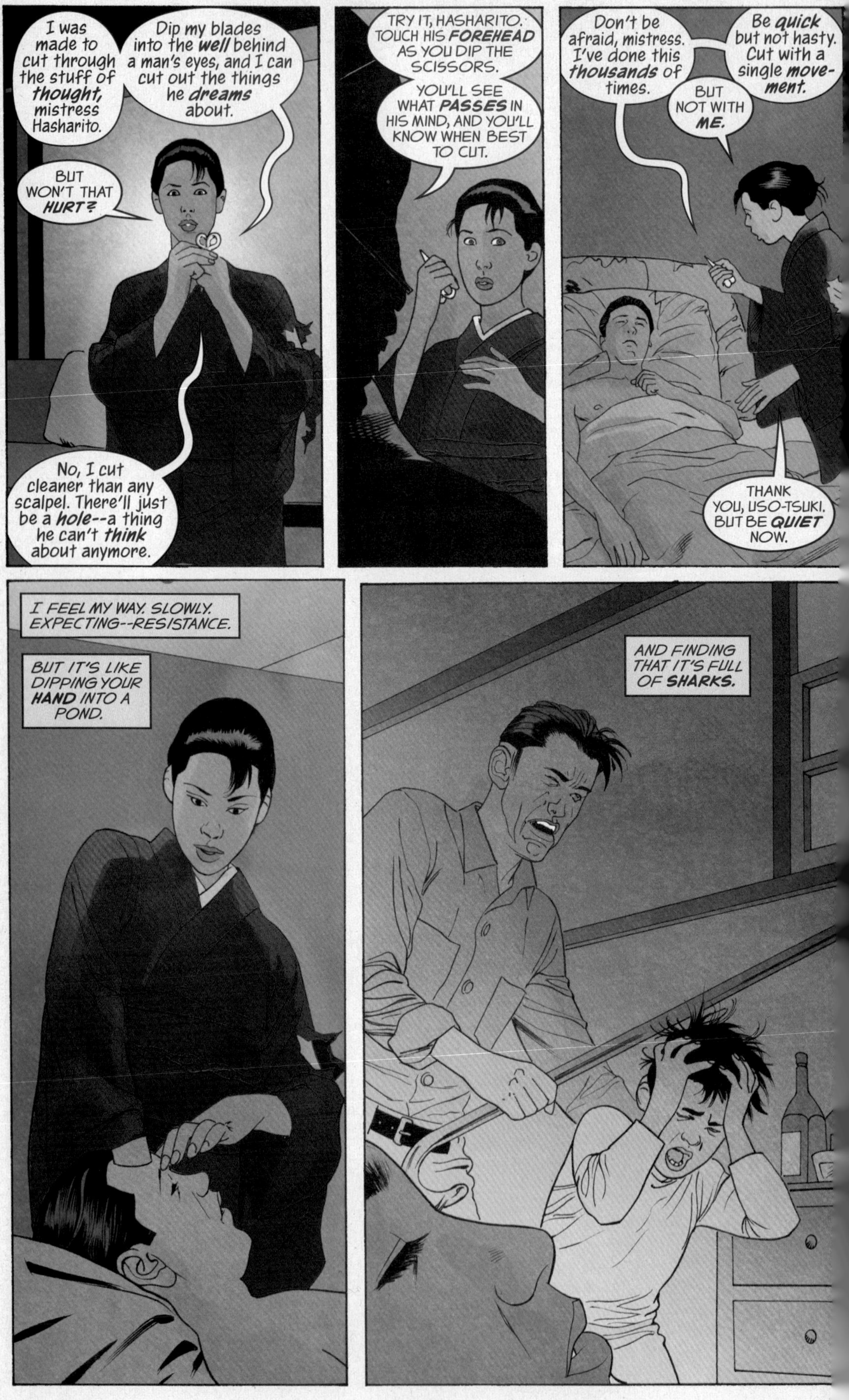
I was made to cut through the stuff of thought, mistress Hasharito.
Dip my blades into the well behind a man's eyes, and I can cut out the things he dreams about.
BUT WON'T THAT HURT?
No, I cut cleaner than any scalpel. There'll just be a hole--a thing he can't think about anymore.
TRY IT, HASHARITO. TOUCH HIS FOREHEAD AS YOU DIP THE SCISSORS.
YOU'LL SEE WHAT PASSES IN HIS MIND, AND YOU'LL KNOW WHEN BEST TO CUT.
Don't be afraid, mistress. I've done this thousands of times.
Be quick but not hasty. Cut with a single movement.
BUT NOT WITH ME.
THANK YOU, USO-TSUKI. BUT BE QUIET NOW.
I FEEL MY WAY. SLOWLY. EXPECTING--RESISTANCE.
BUT IT'S LIKE DIPPING YOUR HAND INTO A POND.
AND FINDING THAT IT'S FULL OF SHARKS.

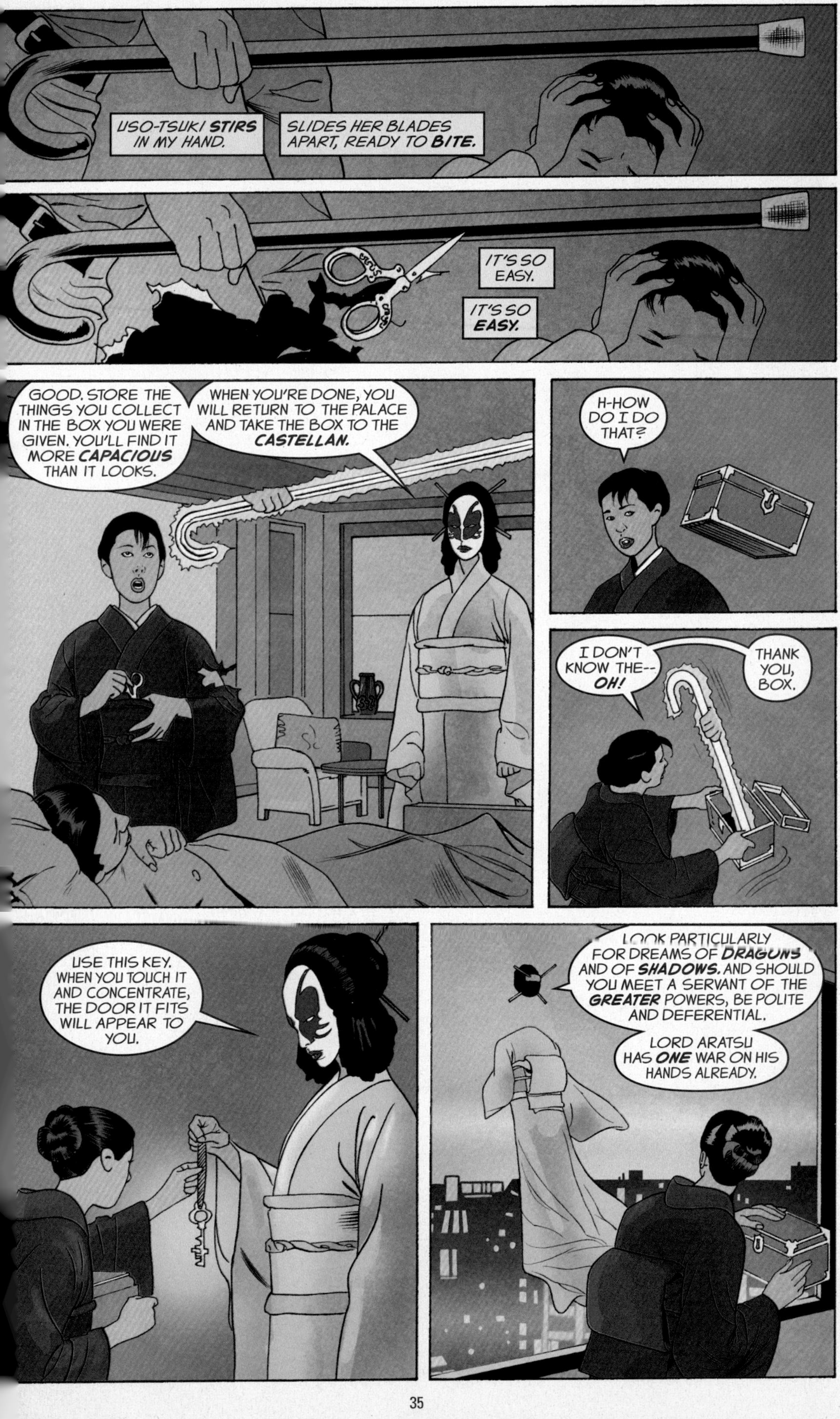
USO-TSUKI STIRS IN MY HAND.
SLIDES HER BLADES APART, READY TO BITE.
IT'S SO EASY.
IT'S SO EASY.
GOOD. STORE THE THINGS YOU COLLECT IN THE BOX YOU WERE GIVEN. YOU'LL FIND IT MORE CAPACIOUS THAN IT LOOKS.
WHEN YOU'RE DONE, YOU WILL RETURN TO THE PALACE AND TAKE THE BOX TO THE CASTELLAN.
H-HOW DO I DO THAT?
I DON'T KNOW THE-- OH!
THANK YOU, BOX.
USE THIS KEY. WHEN YOU TOUCH IT AND CONCENTRATE, THE DOOR IT FITS WILL APPEAR TO YOU.
LOOK PARTICULARLY FOR DREAMS OF DRAGONS AND OF SHADOWS. AND SHOULD YOU MEET A SERVANT OF THE GREATER POWERS, BE POLITE AND DEFERENTIAL.
LORD ARATSU HAS ONE WAR ON HIS HANDS ALREADY.

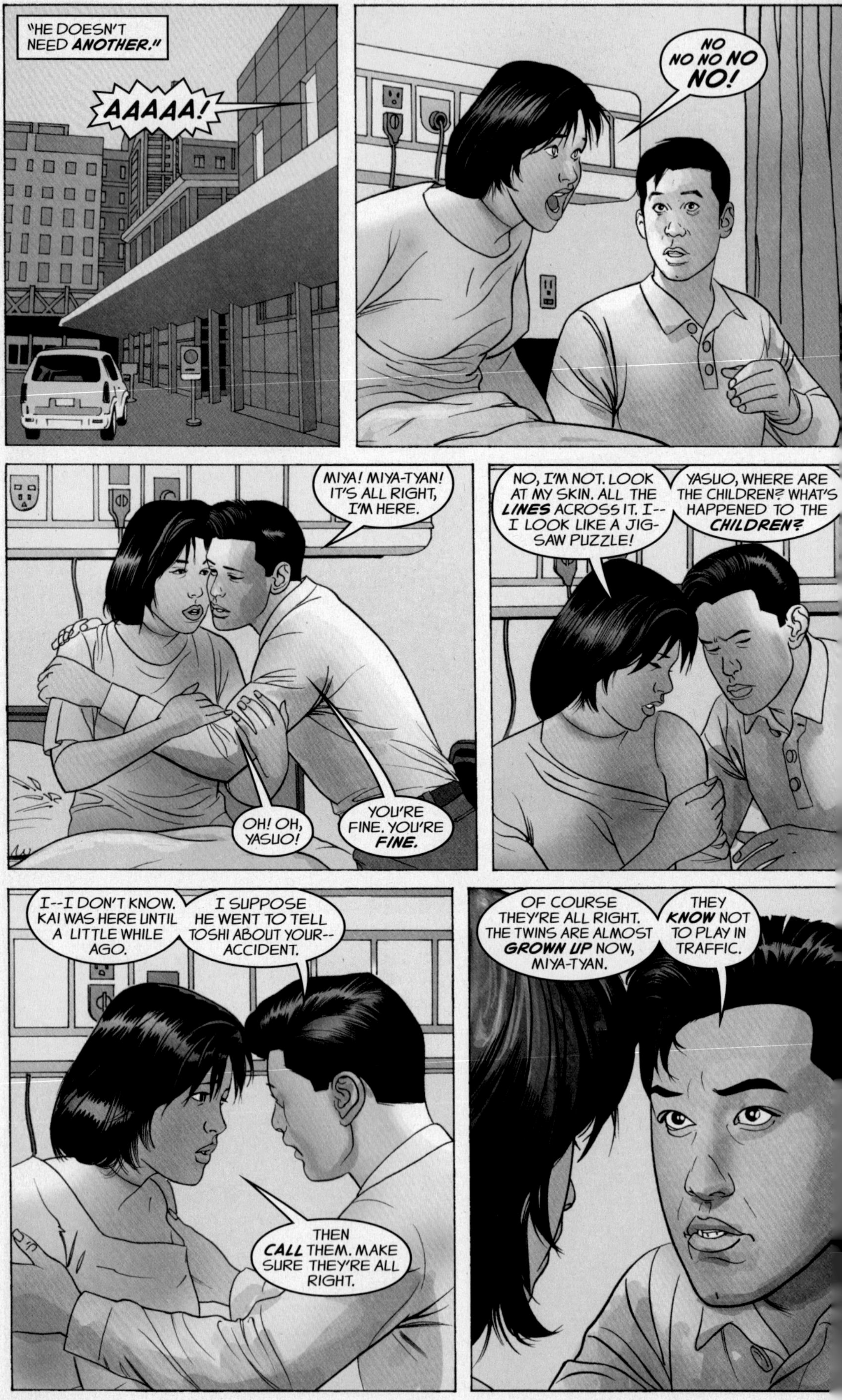
"HE DOESN'T NEED ANOTHER."
AAAAA!
NO NO NO NO NO!
MIYA! MIYA-TYAN! IT'S ALL RIGHT, I'M HERE.
OH! OH, YASUO!
YOU'RE FINE. YOU'RE FINE.
NO, I'M NOT. LOOK AT MY SKIN. ALL THE LINES ACROSS IT. I-- I LOOK LIKE A JIG-SAW PUZZLE!
YASUO, WHERE ARE THE CHILDREN? WHAT'S HAPPENED TO THE CHILDREN?
I--I DON'T KNOW. KAI WAS HERE UNTIL A LITTLE WHILE AGO.
I SUPPOSE HE WENT TO TELL TOSHI ABOUT YOUR-- ACCIDENT.
THEN CALL THEM. MAKE SURE THEY'RE ALL RIGHT.
OF COURSE THEY'RE ALL RIGHT. THE TWINS ARE ALMOST GROWN UP NOW, MIYA-TYAN.
THEY KNOW NOT TO PLAY IN TRAFFIC.

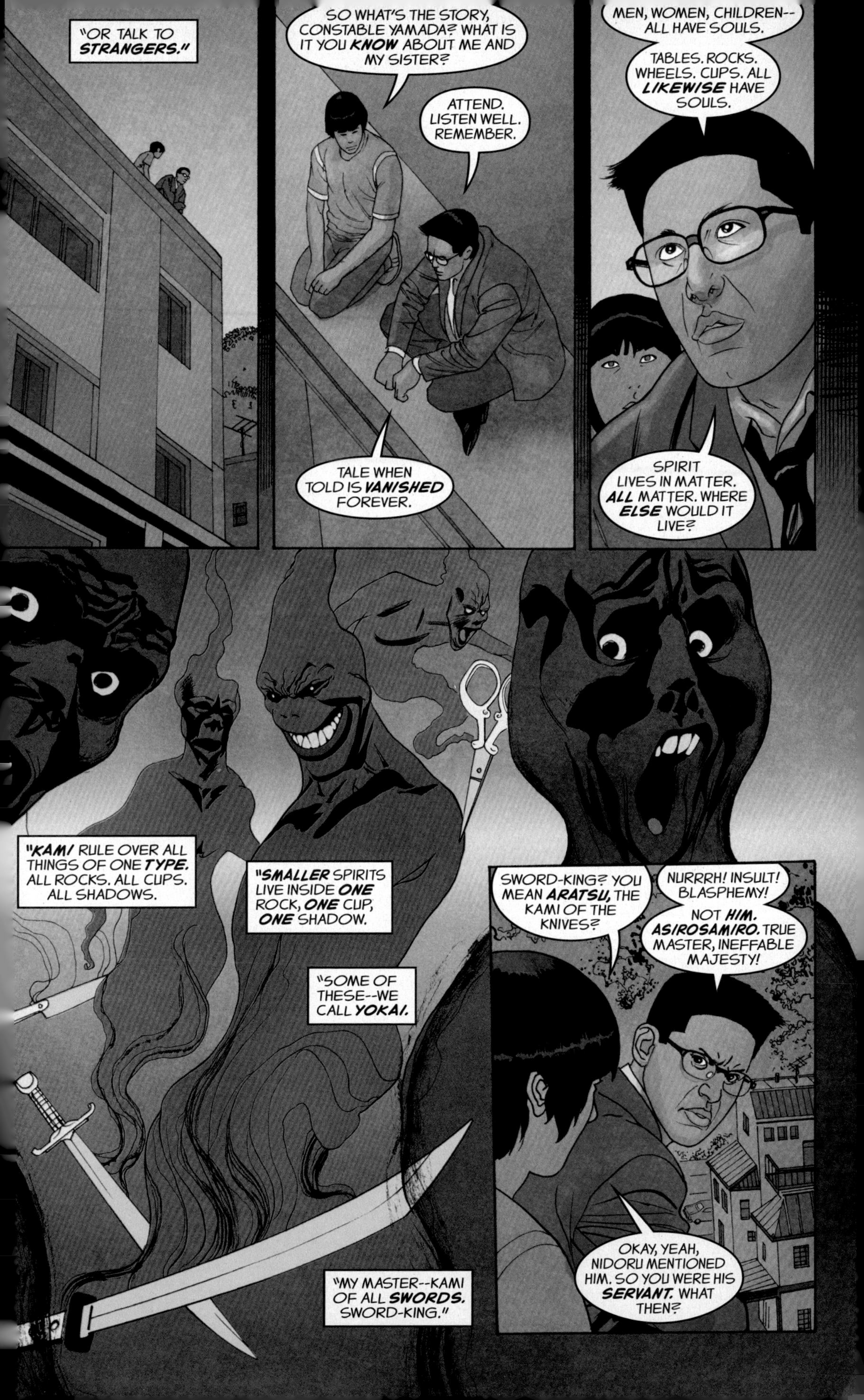
"OR TALK TO STRANGERS."
SO WHAT'S THE STORY, CONSTABLE YAMADA? WHAT IS IT YOU KNOW ABOUT ME AND MY SISTER?
ATTEND. LISTEN WELL. REMEMBER.
TALE WHEN TOLD IS VANISHED FOREVER.
MEN, WOMEN, CHILDREN-- ALL HAVE SOULS.
TABLES. ROCKS. WHEELS. CUPS. ALL LIKEWISE HAVE SOULS.
SPIRIT LIVES IN MATTER. ALL MATTER. WHERE ELSE WOULD IT LIVE?
"KAMI RULE OVER ALL THINGS OF ONE TYPE. ALL ROCKS. ALL CUPS. ALL SHADOWS.
"SMALLER SPIRITS LIVE INSIDE ONE ROCK, ONE CUP, ONE SHADOW.
"SOME OF THESE--WE CALL YOKAI.
"MY MASTER--KAMI OF ALL SWORDS. SWORD-KING."
SWORD-KING? YOU MEAN ARATSU, THE KAMI OF THE KNIVES?
NURRRH! INSULT! BLASPHEMY!
NOT HIM. ASIROSAMIRO. TRUE MASTER, INEFFABLE MAJESTY!
OKAY, YEAH, NIDORU MENTIONED HIM. SO YOU WERE HIS SERVANT. WHAT THEN?

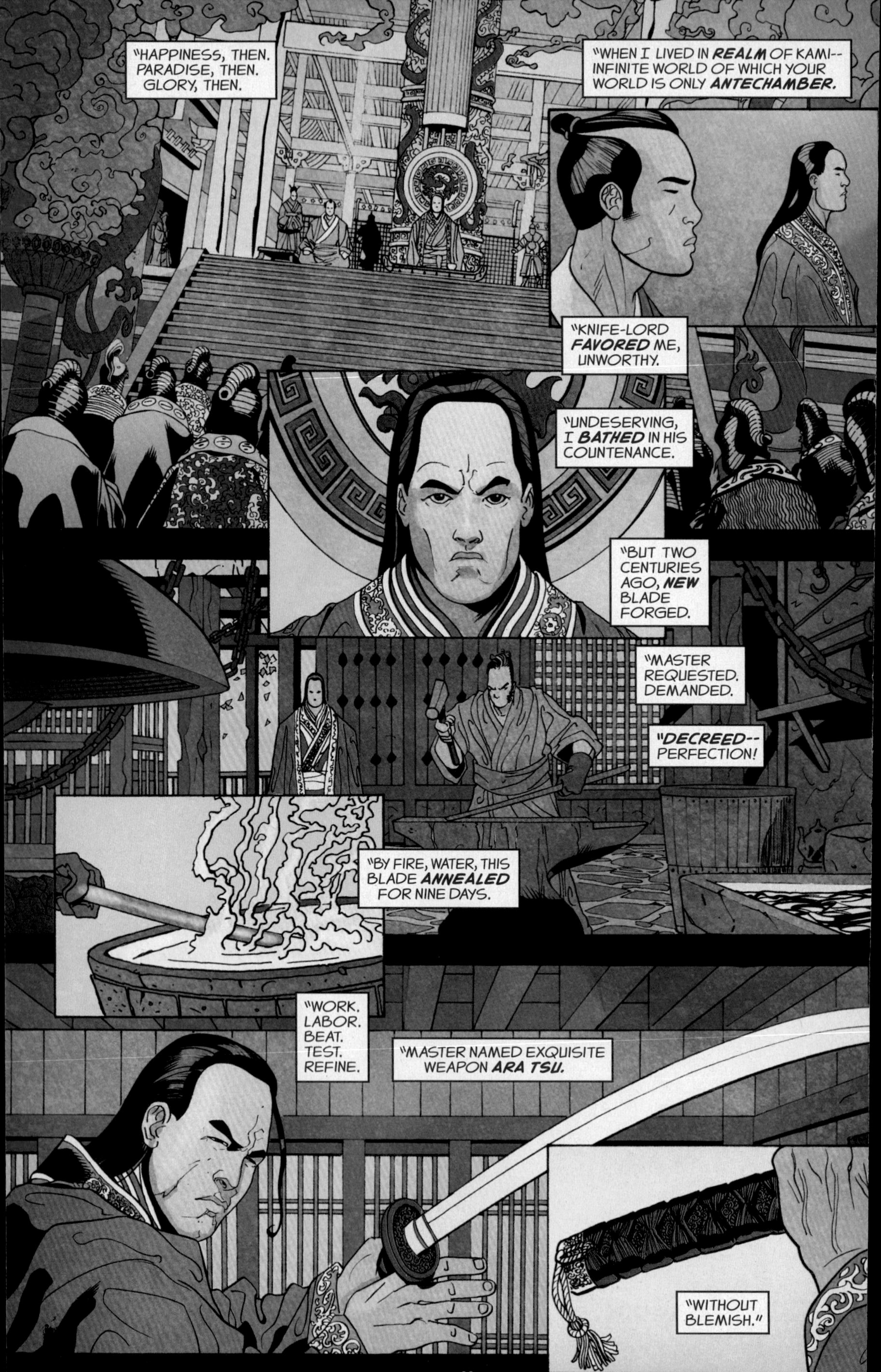
"HAPPINESS, THEN. PARADISE, THEN. GLORY, THEN.
"WHEN I LIVED IN REALM OF KAMI-- INFINITE WORLD OF WHICH YOUR WORLD IS ONLY ANTECHAMBER.
"KNIFE-LORD FAVORED ME, UNWORTHY.
"UNDESERVING, I BATHED IN HIS COUNTENANCE.
"BUT TWO CENTURIES AGO, NEW BLADE FORGED.
"MASTER REQUESTED. DEMANDED.
"DECREED-- PERFECTION!
"BY FIRE, WATER, THIS BLADE ANNEALED FOR NINE DAYS.
"WORK. LABOR. BEAT. TEST. REFINE.
"MASTER NAMED EXQUISITE WEAPON ARA TSU.
"WITHOUT BLEMISH."

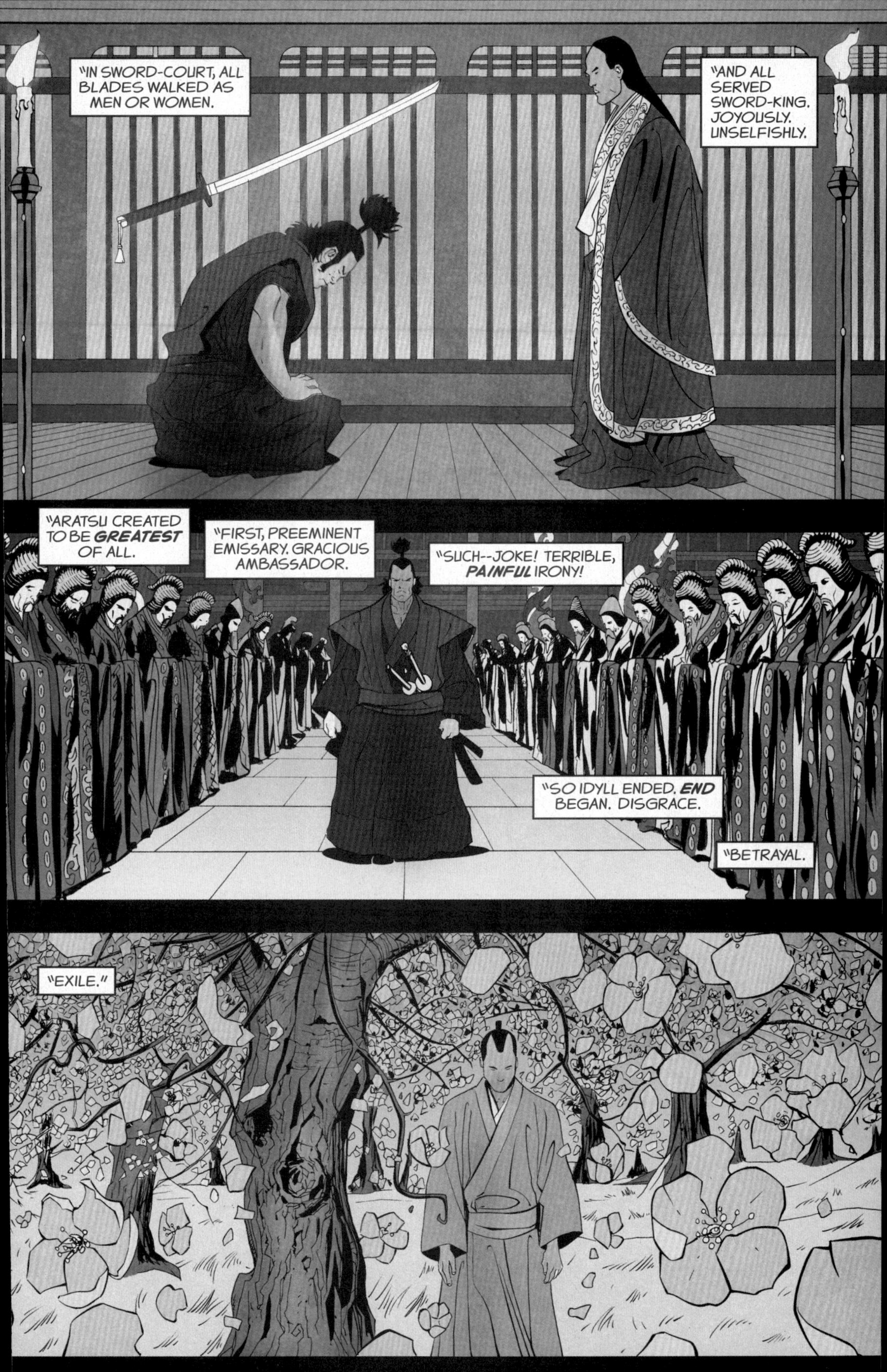
"IN SWORD-COURT, ALL BLADES WALKED AS MEN OR WOMEN.
"AND ALL SERVED SWORD-KING. JOYOUSLY. UNSELFISHLY.
"ARATSU CREATED TO BE GREATEST OF ALL.
"FIRST, PREEMINENT EMISSARY. GRACIOUS AMBASSADOR.
"SUCH--JOKE! TERRIBLE, PAINFUL IRONY!
"SO IDYLL ENDED. END BEGAN. DISGRACE.
"BETRAYAL.
"EXILE."

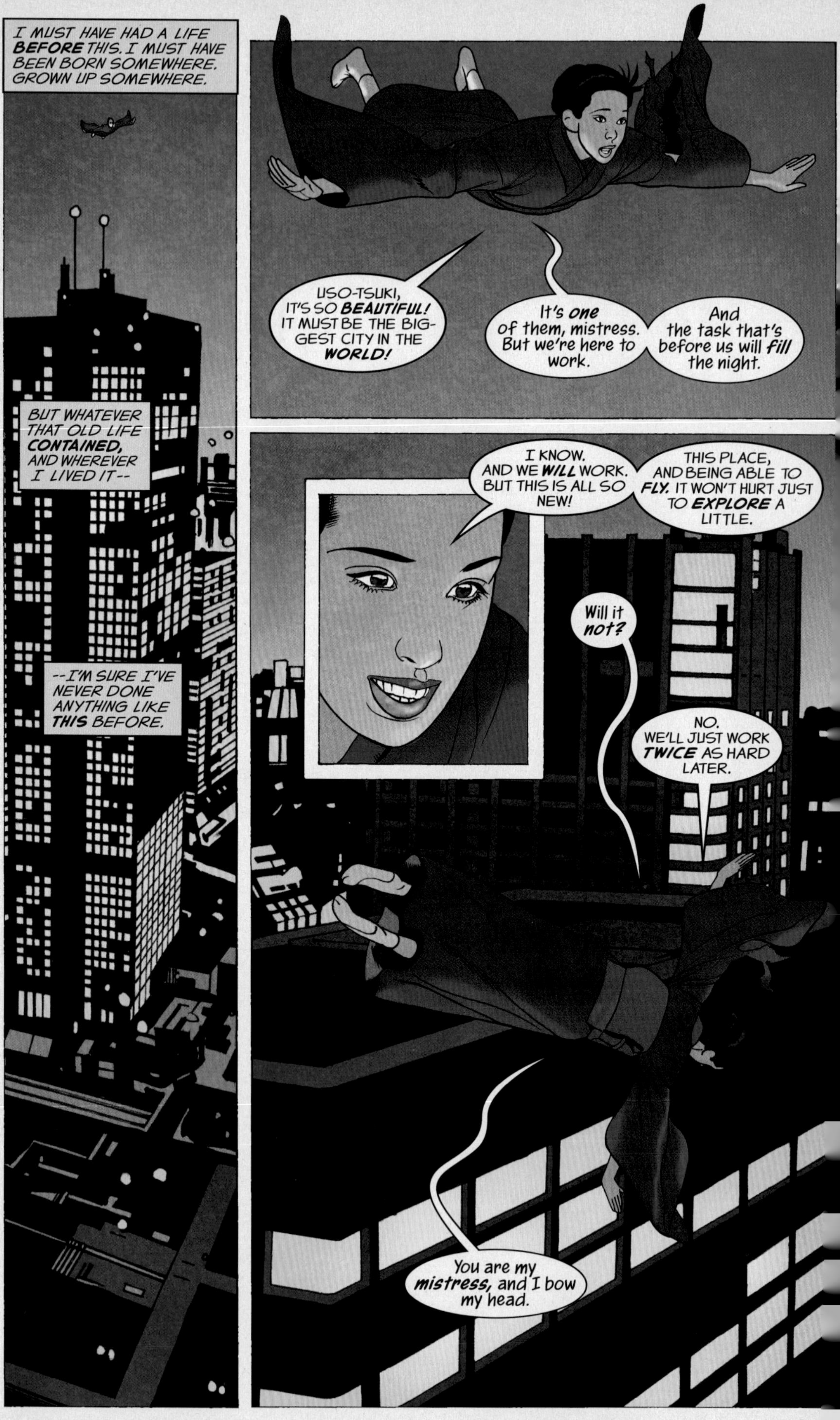
I MUST HAVE HAD A LIFE BEFORE THIS. I MUST HAVE BEEN BORN SOMEWHERE. GROWN UP SOMEWHERE.
BUT WHATEVER THAT OLD LIFE CONTAINED, AND WHEREVER I LIVED IT--
--I'M SURE I'VE NEVER DONE ANYTHING LIKE THIS BEFORE.
USO-TSUKI, IT'S SO BEAUTIFUL! IT MUST BE THE BIGGEST CITY IN THE WORLD!
It's one of them, mistress. But we're here to work.
And the task that's before us will fill the night.
I KNOW. AND WE WILL WORK. BUT THIS IS ALL SO NEW!
THIS PLACE, AND BEING ABLE TO FLY. IT WON'T HURT JUST TO EXPLORE A LITTLE.
Will it not?
NO. WE'LL JUST WORK TWICE AS HARD LATER.
You are my mistress, and I bow my head.

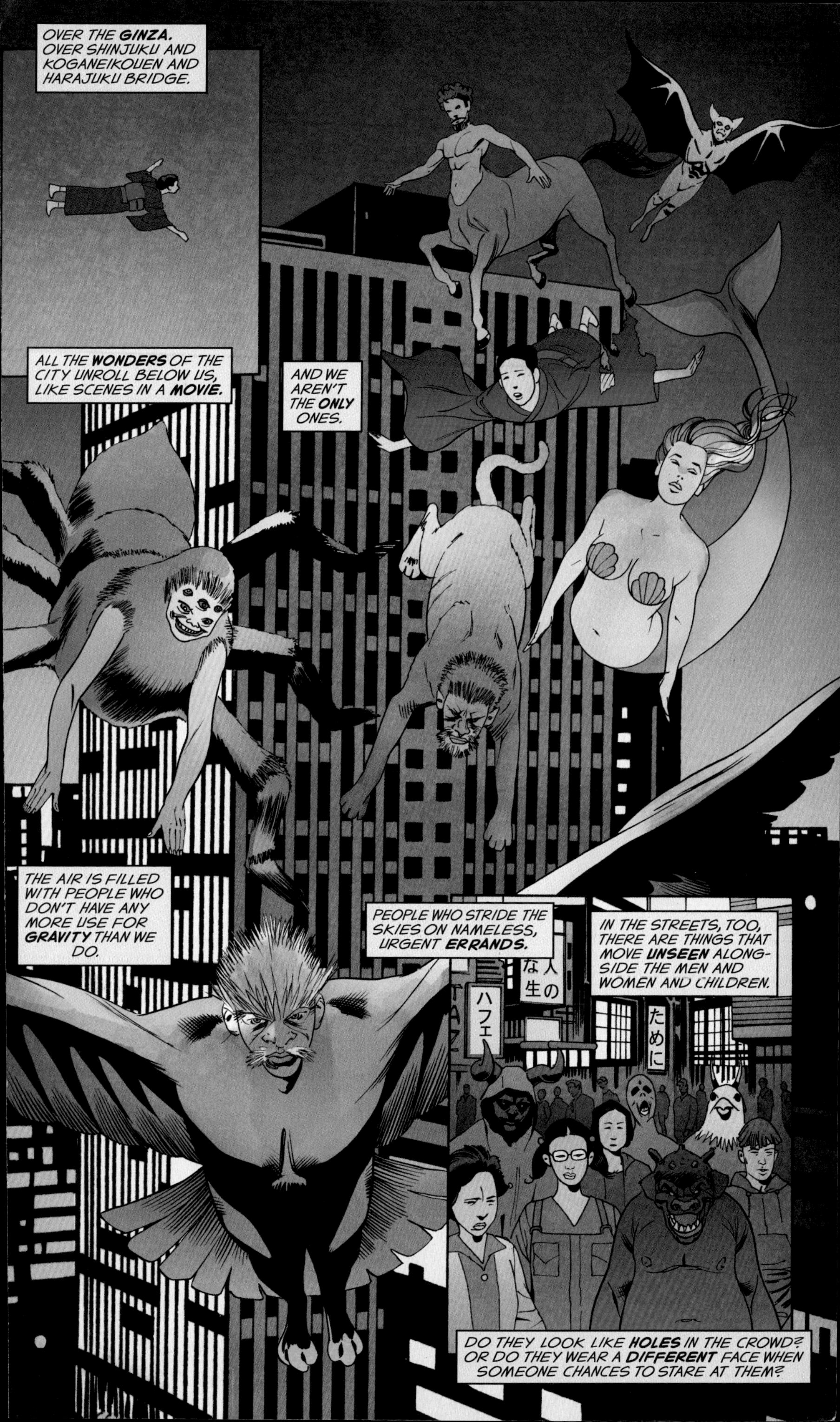
OVER THE GINZA. OVER SHINJUKU AND KOGANEIKOUEN AND HARAJUKU BRIDGE.
ALL THE WONDERS OF THE CITY UNROLL BELOW US, LIKE SCENES IN A MOVIE.
AND WE AREN'T THE ONLY ONES.
THE AIR IS FILLED WITH PEOPLE WHO DON'T HAVE ANY MORE USE FOR GRAVITY THAN WE DO.
PEOPLE WHO STRIDE THE SKIES ON NAMELESS, URGENT ERRANDS.
IN THE STREETS, TOO, THERE ARE THINGS THAT MOVE UNSEEN ALONGSIDE THE MEN AND WOMEN AND CHILDREN.
人の生な
ハフェ
ために
DO THEY LOOK LIKE HOLES IN THE CROWD? OR DO THEY WEAR A DIFFERENT FACE WHEN SOMEONE CHANCES TO STARE AT THEM?

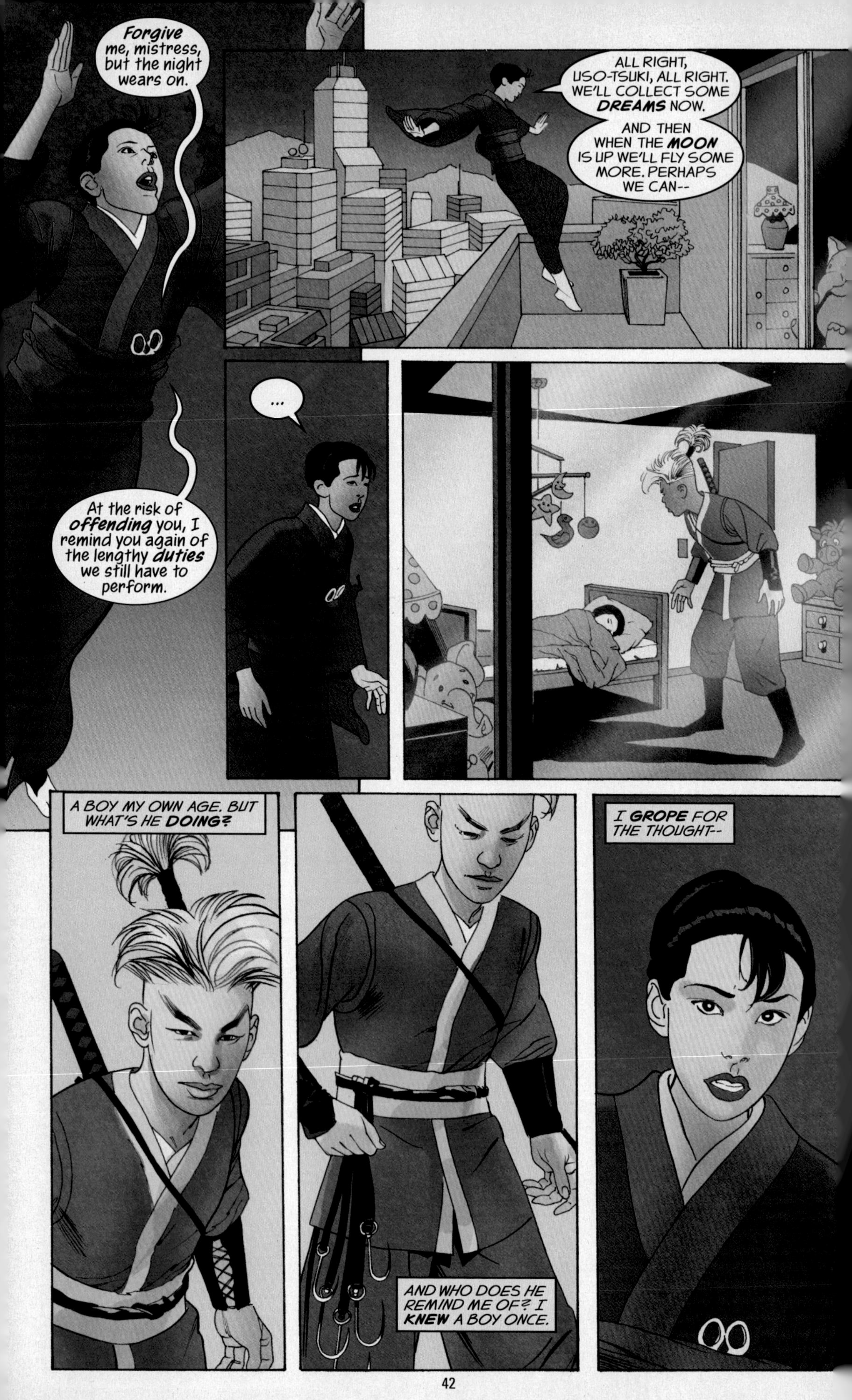
Forgive me, mistress, but the night wears on.
ALL RIGHT, USO-TSUKI, ALL RIGHT. WE'LL COLLECT SOME DREAMS NOW.
AND THEN WHEN THE MOON IS UP WE'LL FLY SOME MORE. PERHAPS WE CAN--
At the risk of offending you, I remind you again of the lengthy duties we still have to perform.
...
A BOY MY OWN AGE. BUT WHAT'S HE DOING?
AND WHO DOES HE REMIND ME OF? I KNEW A BOY ONCE.
I GROPE FOR THE THOUGHT--

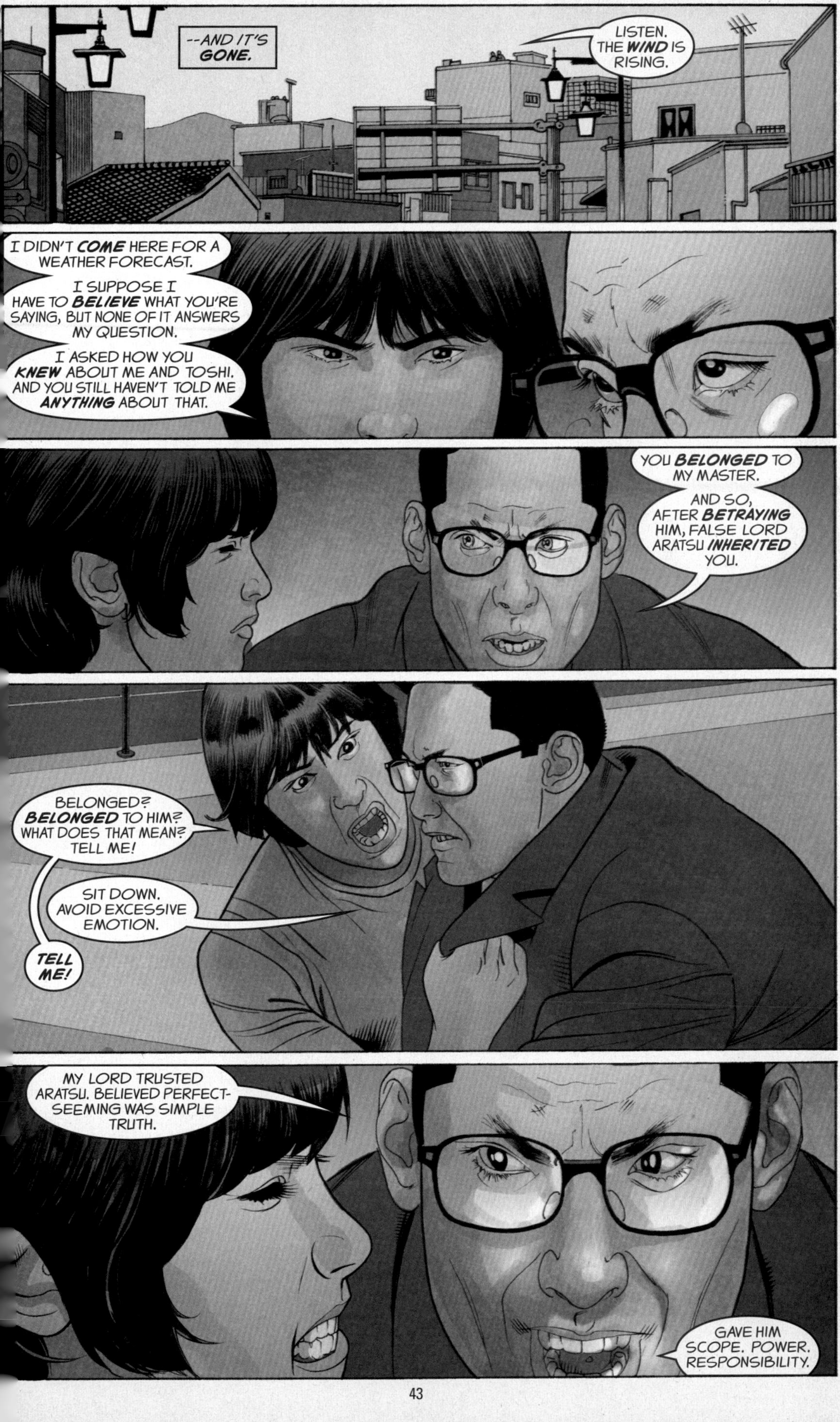
--AND IT'S GONE.
LISTEN. THE WIND IS RISING.
I DIDN'T COME HERE FOR A WEATHER FORECAST.
I SUPPOSE I HAVE TO BELIEVE WHAT YOU'RE SAYING, BUT NONE OF IT ANSWERS MY QUESTION.
I ASKED HOW YOU KNEW ABOUT ME AND TOSHI. AND YOU STILL HAVEN'T TOLD ME ANYTHING ABOUT THAT.
YOU BELONGED TO MY MASTER.
AND SO, AFTER BETRAYING HIM, FALSE LORD ARATSU INHERITED YOU.
BELONGED? BELONGED TO HIM? WHAT DOES THAT MEAN? TELL ME!
SIT DOWN. AVOID EXCESSIVE EMOTION.
TELL ME!
MY LORD TRUSTED ARATSU. BELIEVED PERFECT-SEEMING WAS SIMPLE TRUTH.
GAVE HIM SCOPE. POWER. RESPONSIBILITY.

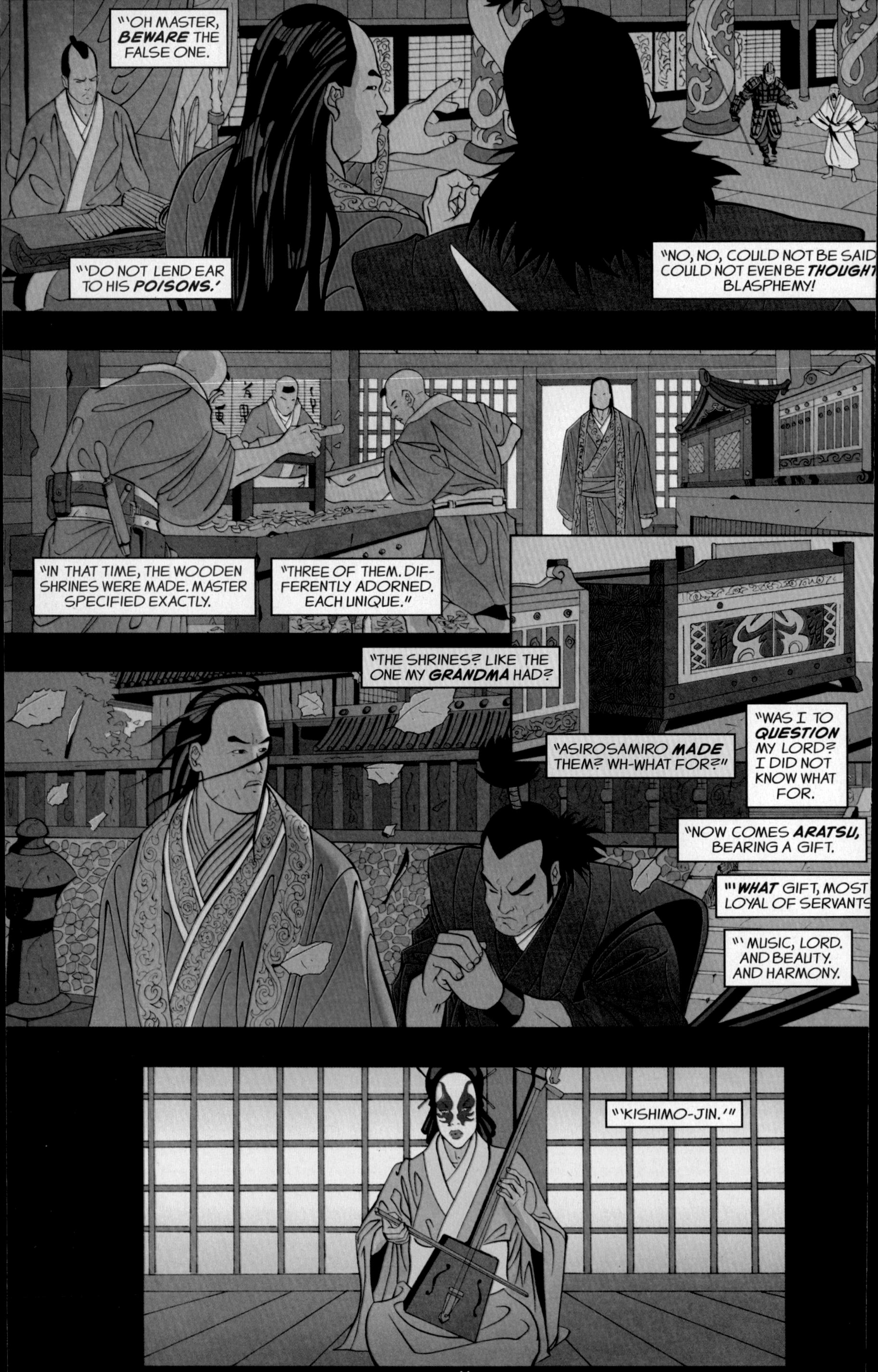
"'OH MASTER, BEWARE THE FALSE ONE.
"'DO NOT LEND EAR TO HIS POISONS.'
"NO, NO, COULD NOT BE SAID COULD NOT EVEN BE THOUGHT BLASPHEMY!
"IN THAT TIME, THE WOODEN SHRINES WERE MADE. MASTER SPECIFIED EXACTLY.
"THREE OF THEM. DIFFERENTLY ADORNED. EACH UNIQUE."
"THE SHRINES? LIKE THE ONE MY GRANDMA HAD?
"ASIROSAMIRO MADE THEM? WH-WHAT FOR?"
"WAS I TO QUESTION MY LORD? I DID NOT KNOW WHAT FOR.
"NOW COMES ARATSU, BEARING A GIFT.
"'WHAT GIFT, MOST LOYAL OF SERVANTS
"' MUSIC, LORD. AND BEAUTY. AND HARMONY.
"'KISHIMO-JIN.'"

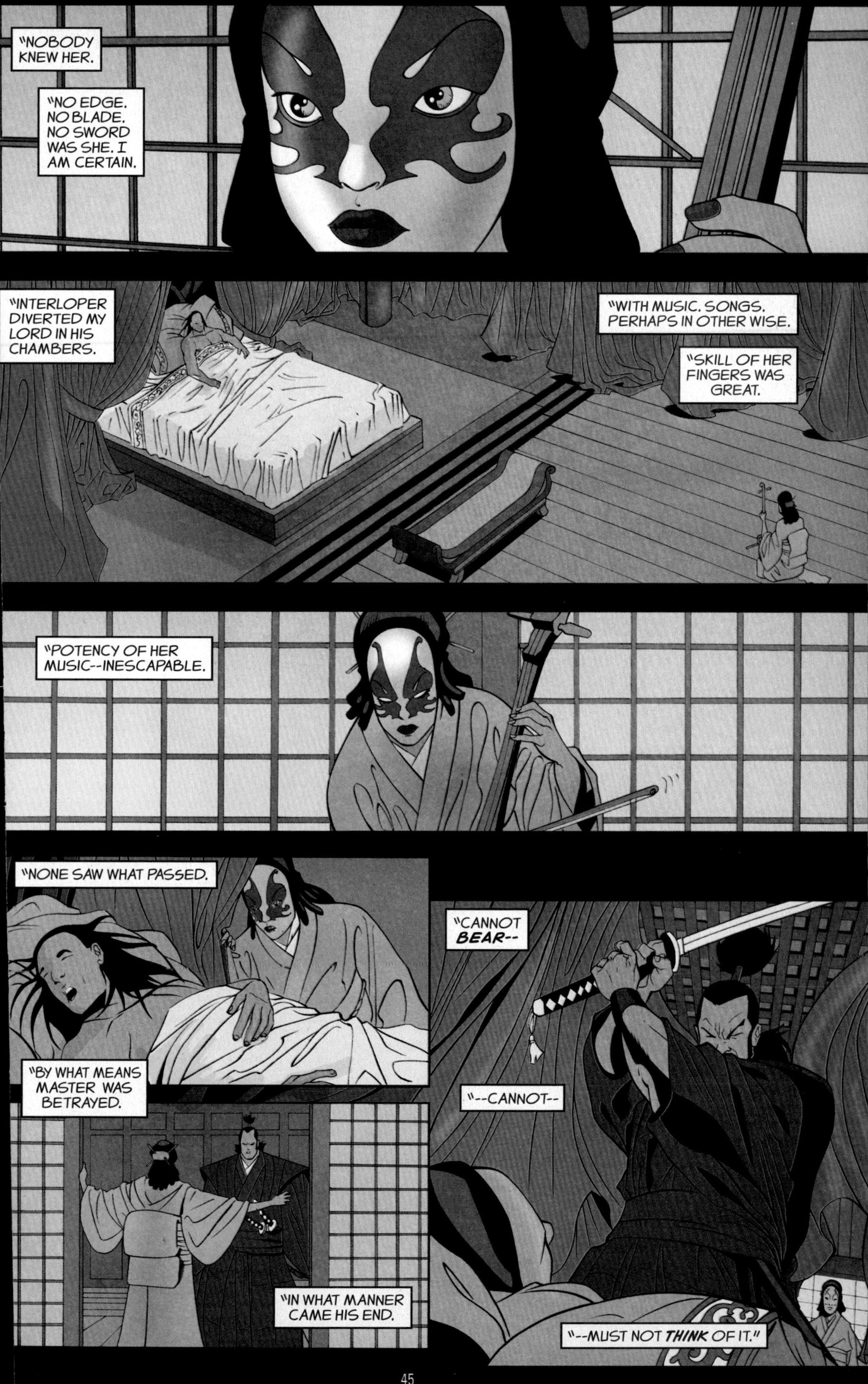
"NOBODY KNEW HER.
"NO EDGE. NO BLADE. NO SWORD WAS SHE. I AM CERTAIN.
"INTERLOPER DIVERTED MY LORD IN HIS CHAMBERS.
"WITH MUSIC. SONGS. PERHAPS IN OTHER WISE.
"SKILL OF HER FINGERS WAS GREAT.
"POTENCY OF HER MUSIC--INESCAPABLE.
"NONE SAW WHAT PASSED.
"BY WHAT MEANS MASTER WAS BETRAYED.
"IN WHAT MANNER CAME HIS END.
"CANNOT BEAR--
"--CANNOT--
"--MUST NOT THINK OF IT."

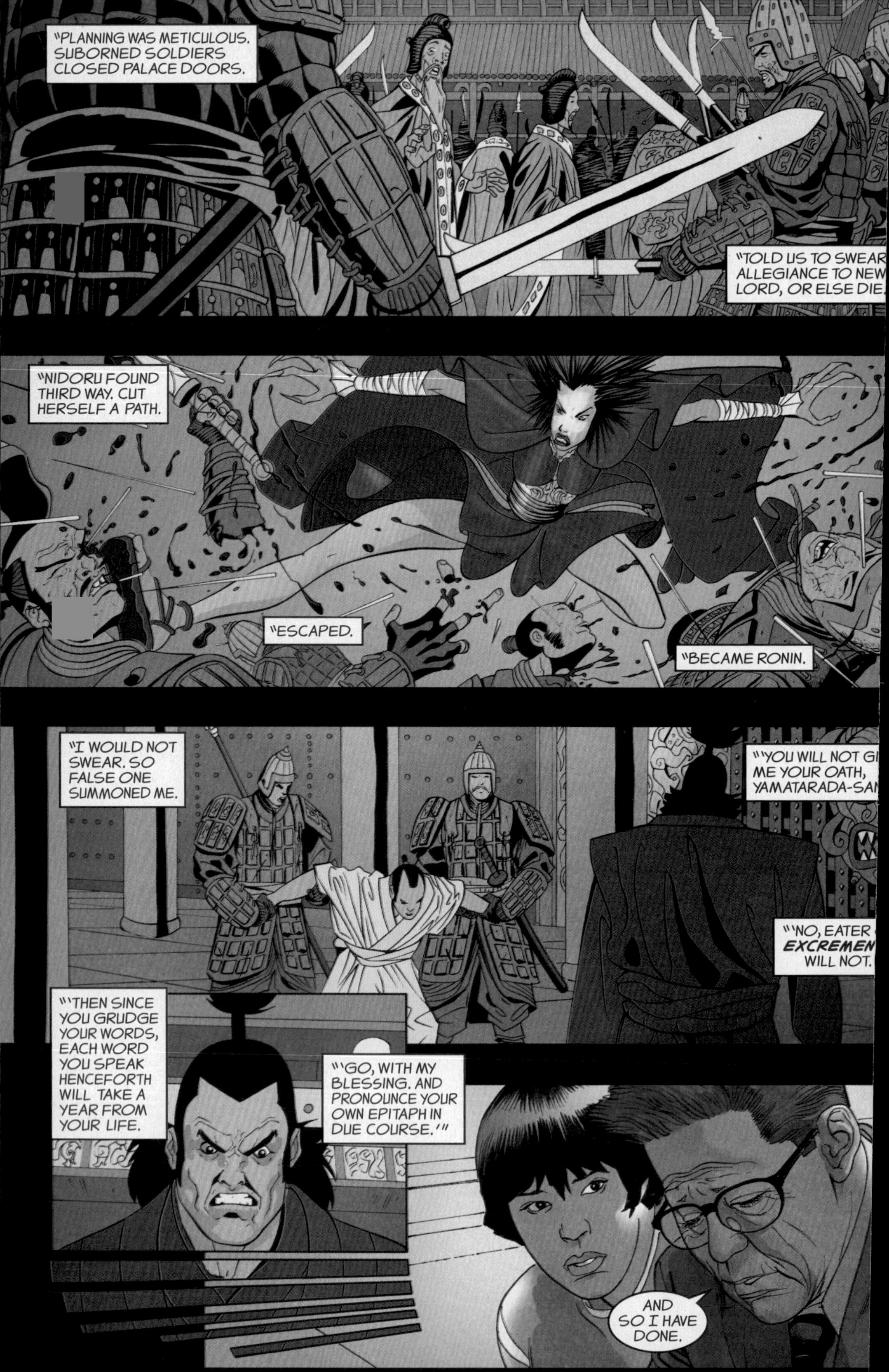
"PLANNING WAS METICULOUS. SUBORNED SOLDIERS CLOSED PALACE DOORS.
"TOLD US TO SWEAR ALLEGIANCE TO NEW LORD, OR ELSE DIE.
"NIDORU FOUND THIRD WAY. CUT HERSELF A PATH.
"ESCAPED.
"BECAME RONIN.
"I WOULD NOT SWEAR. SO FALSE ONE SUMMONED ME.
"'YOU WILL NOT GI ME YOUR OATH, YAMATARADA-SAN
"'NO, EATER EXCREMEN WILL NOT.
"'THEN SINCE YOU GRUDGE YOUR WORDS, EACH WORD YOU SPEAK HENCEFORTH WILL TAKE A YEAR FROM YOUR LIFE.
"'GO, WITH MY BLESSING. AND PRONOUNCE YOUR OWN EPITAPH IN DUE COURSE.'"
AND SO I HAVE DONE.

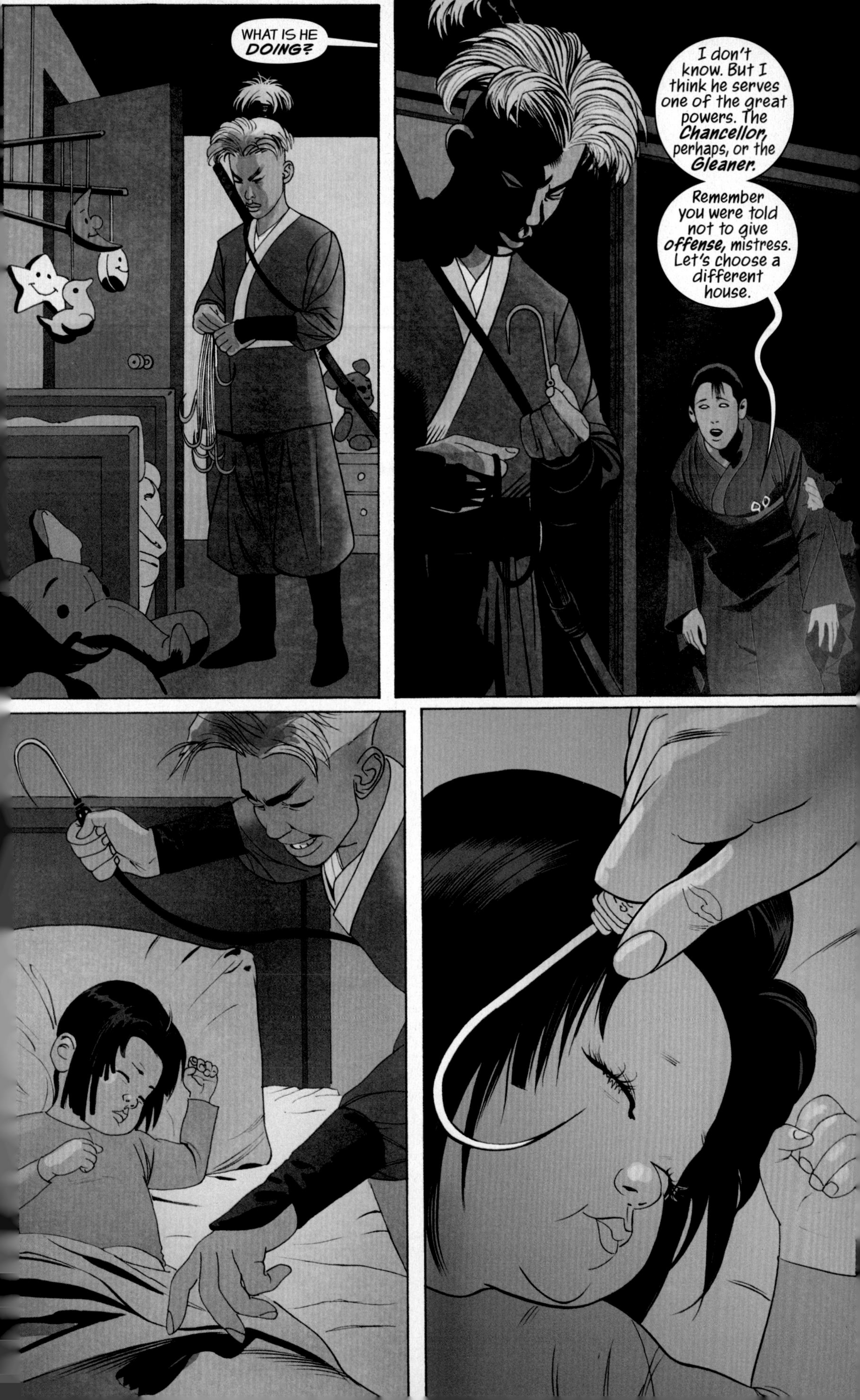

WHAT IS HE DOING?
I don't know. But I think he serves one of the great powers. The Chancellor, perhaps, or the Gleaner.
Remember you were told not to give offense, mistress. Let's choose a different house.

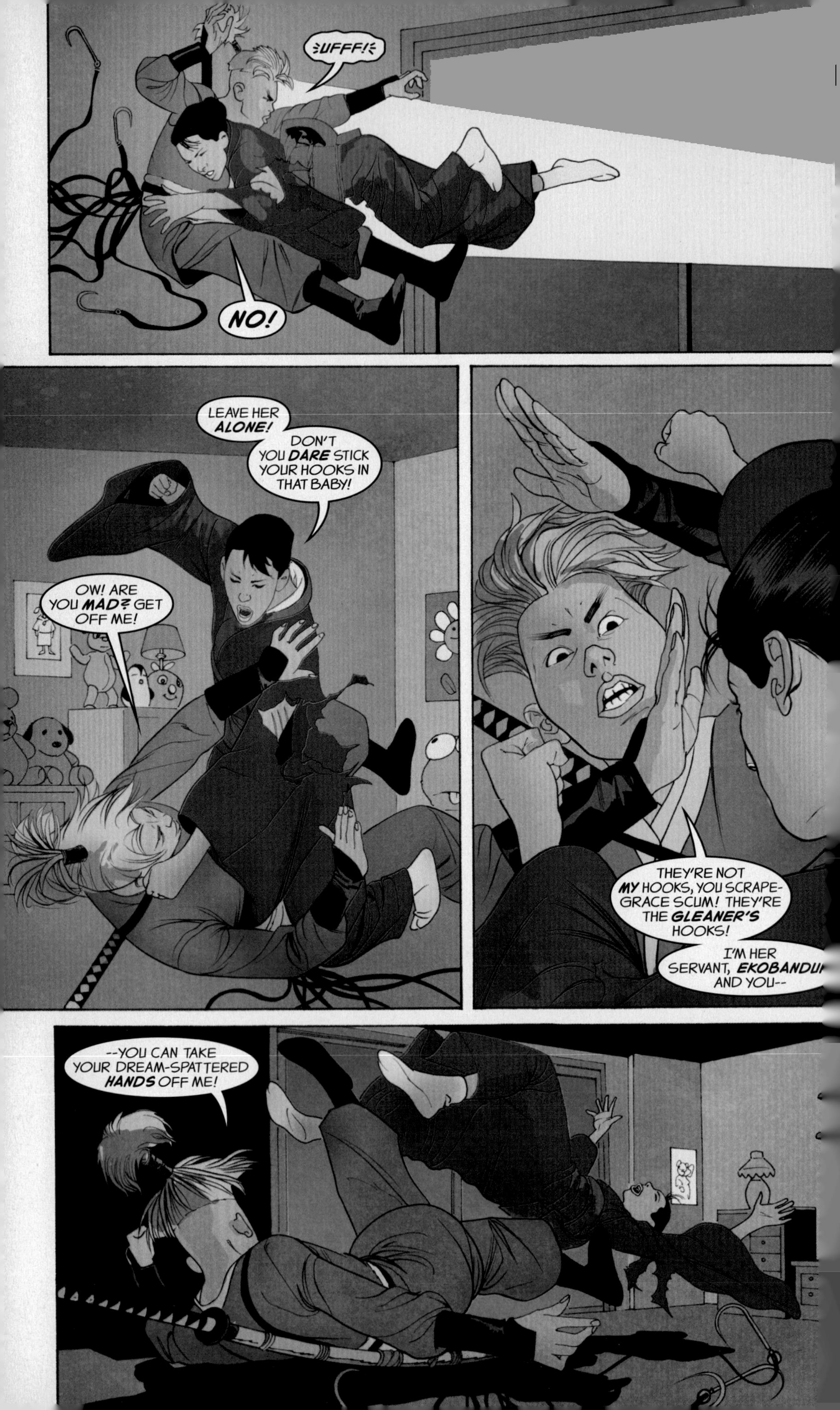
UFFF!
NO!
LEAVE HER ALONE!
DON'T YOU DARE STICK YOUR HOOKS IN THAT BABY!
OW! ARE YOU MAD? GET OFF ME!
THEY'RE NOT MY HOOKS, YOU SCRAPE-GRACE SCUM! THEY'RE THE GLEANER'S HOOKS!
I'M HER SERVANT, EKOBANDU AND YOU--
--YOU CAN TAKE YOUR DREAM-SPATTERED HANDS OFF ME!

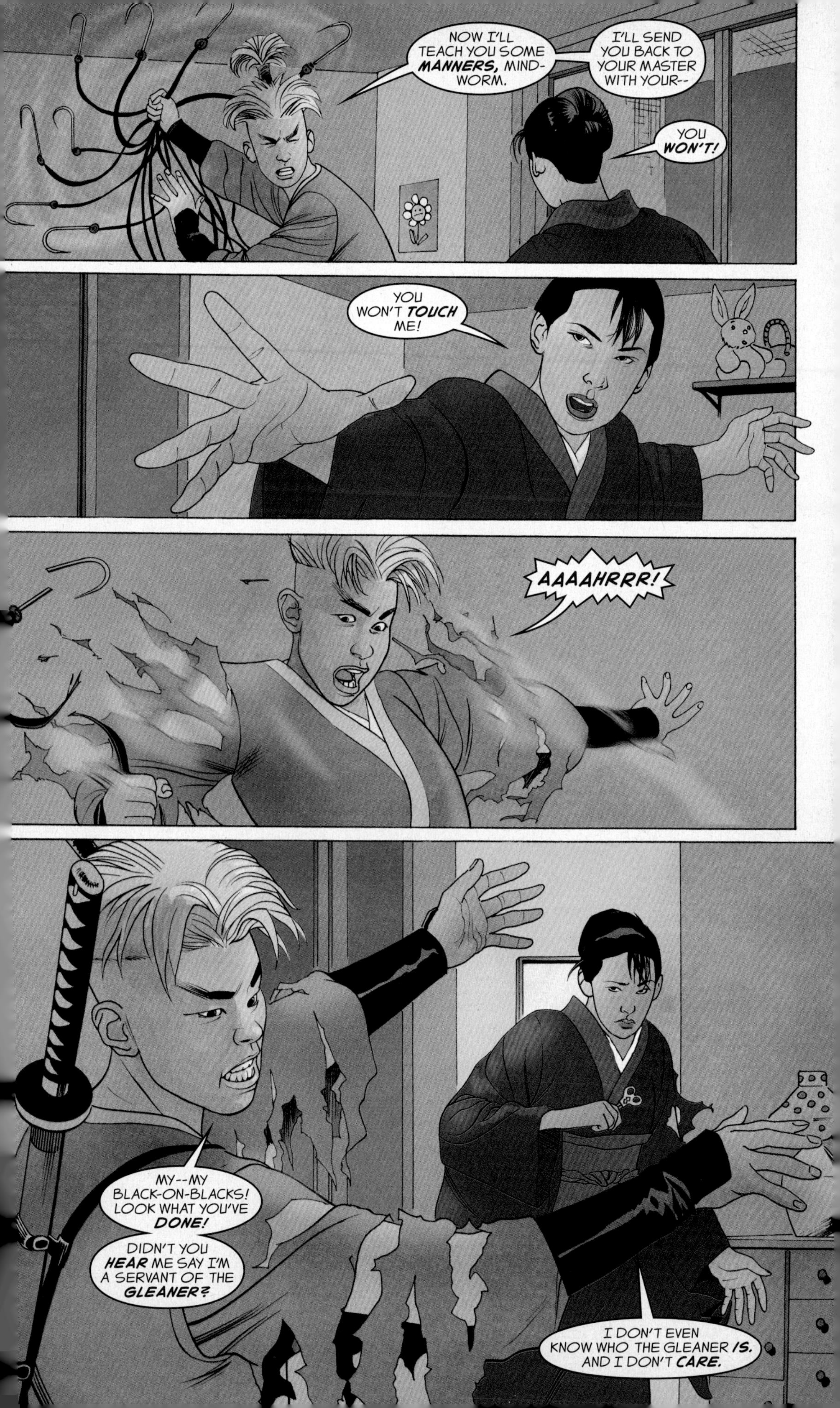

NOW I'LL TEACH YOU SOME MANNERS, MIND-WORM.
I'LL SEND YOU BACK TO YOUR MASTER WITH YOUR--
YOU WON'T!
YOU WON'T TOUCH ME!
AAAAHRRR!
MY--MY BLACK-ON-BLACKS! LOOK WHAT YOU'VE DONE!
DIDN'T YOU HEAR ME SAY I'M A SERVANT OF THE GLEANER?
I DON'T EVEN KNOW WHO THE GLEANER IS. AND I DON'T CARE.

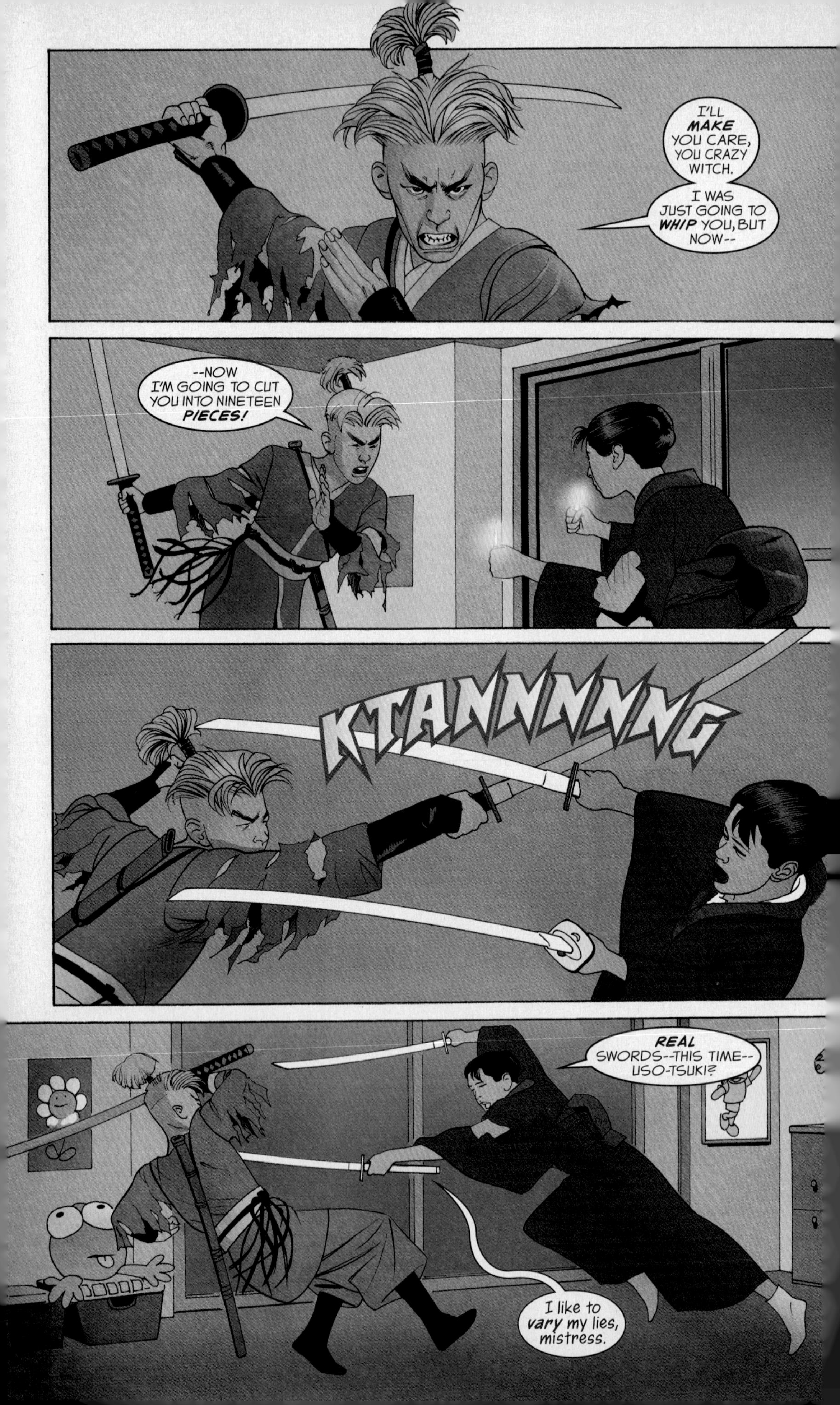
I'LL MAKE YOU CARE, YOU CRAZY WITCH.
I WAS JUST GOING TO WHIP YOU, BUT NOW--
--NOW I'M GOING TO CUT YOU INTO NINETEEN PIECES!
KTANNNNNG
REAL SWORDS--THIS TIME-- USO-TSUKI?
I like to vary my lies, mistress.

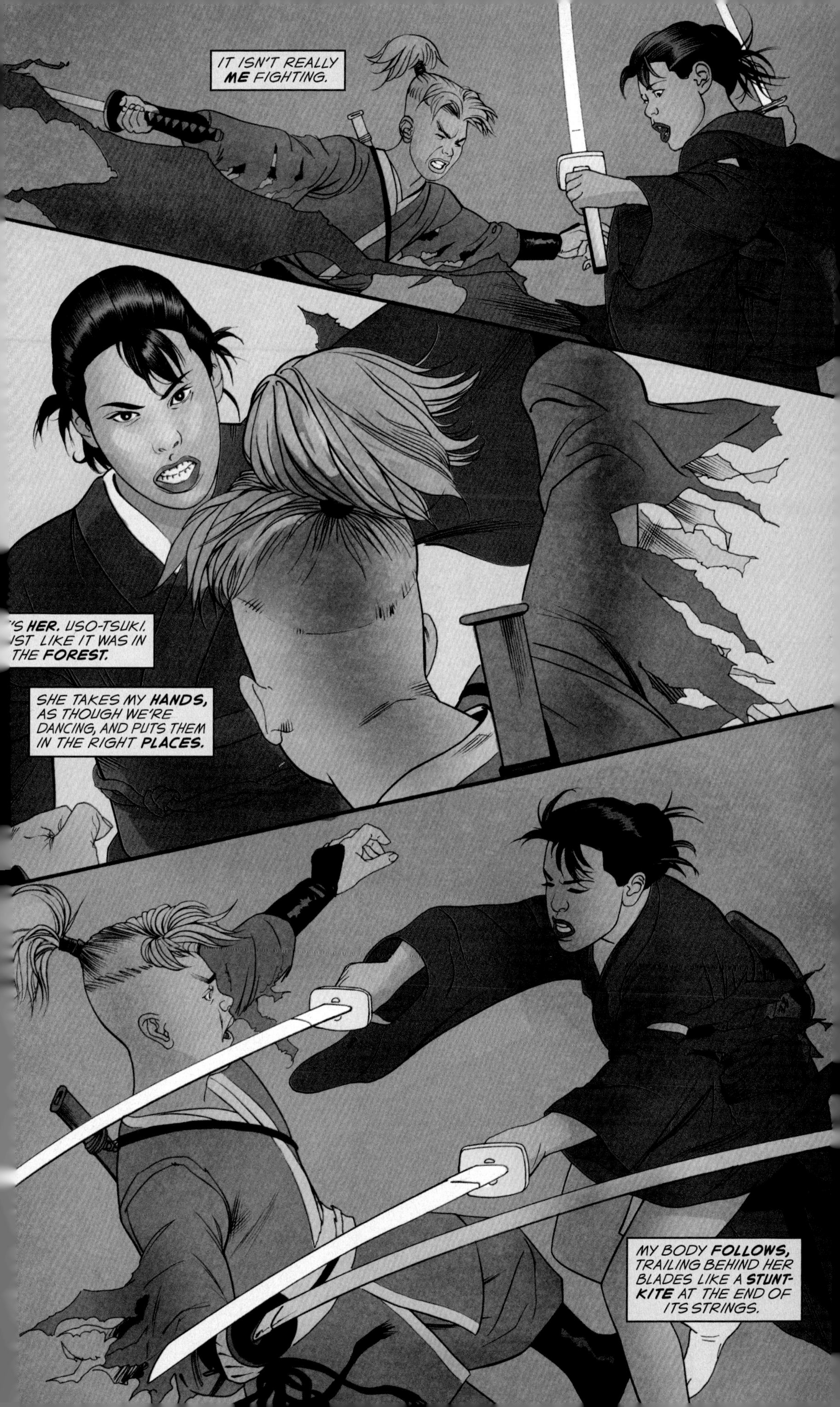
IT ISN'T REALLY ME FIGHTING.
'S HER. USO-TSUKI. ST LIKE IT WAS IN THE FOREST.
SHE TAKES MY HANDS, AS THOUGH WE'RE DANCING, AND PUTS THEM IN THE RIGHT PLACES.
MY BODY FOLLOWS, TRAILING BEHIND HER BLADES LIKE A STUNT-KITE AT THE END OF ITS STRINGS.

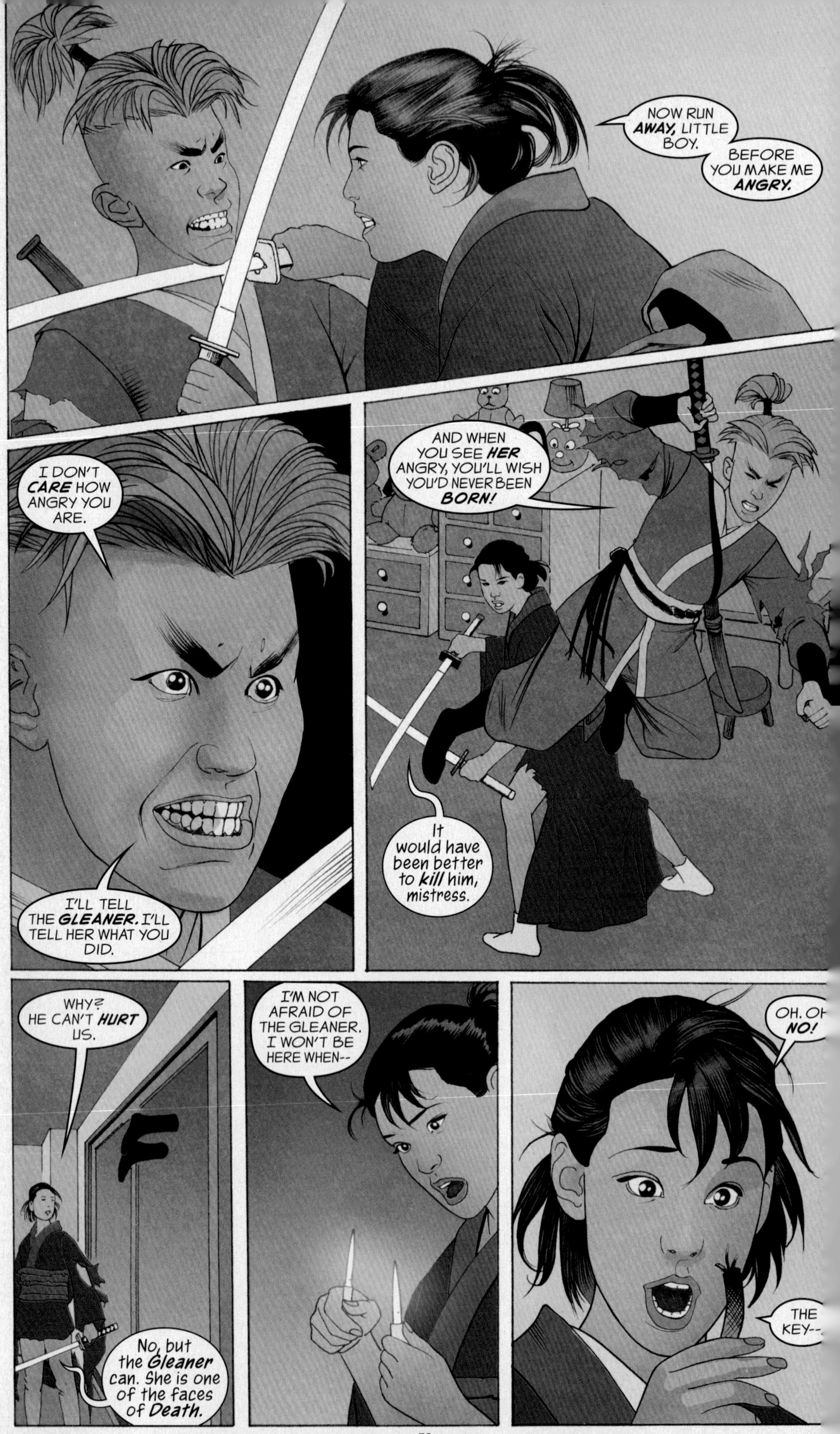
NOW RUN AWAY, LITTLE BOY.
BEFORE YOU MAKE ME ANGRY.
I DON'T CARE HOW ANGRY YOU ARE.
I'LL TELL THE GLEANER. I'LL TELL HER WHAT YOU DID.
AND WHEN YOU SEE HER ANGRY, YOU'LL WISH YOU'D NEVER BEEN BORN!
It would have been better to kill him, mistress.
WHY? HE CAN'T HURT US.
No, but the Gleaner can. She is one of the faces of Death.
I'M NOT AFRAID OF THE GLEANER. I WON'T BE HERE WHEN--
OH. OH NO!
THE KEY--.

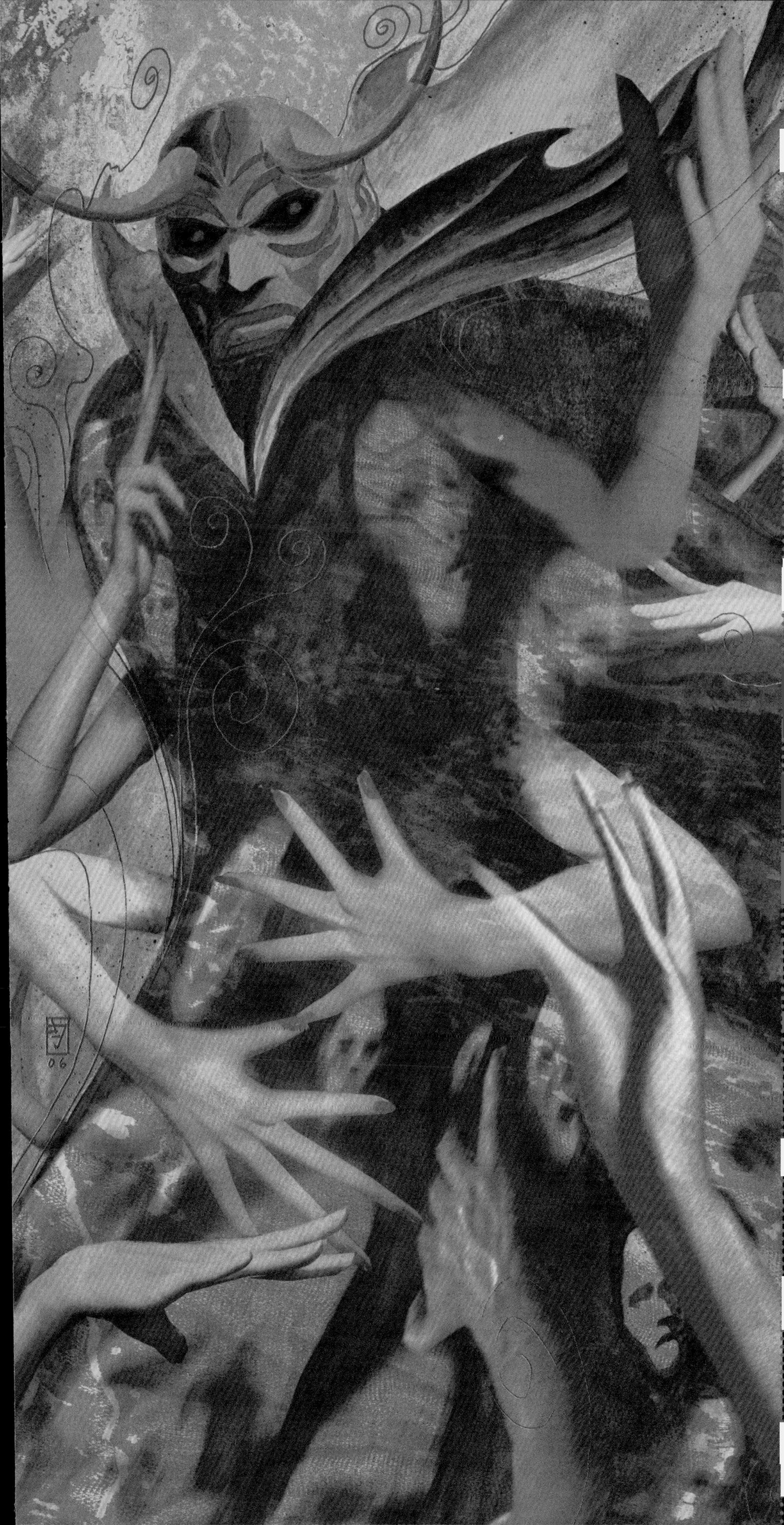

chapter three

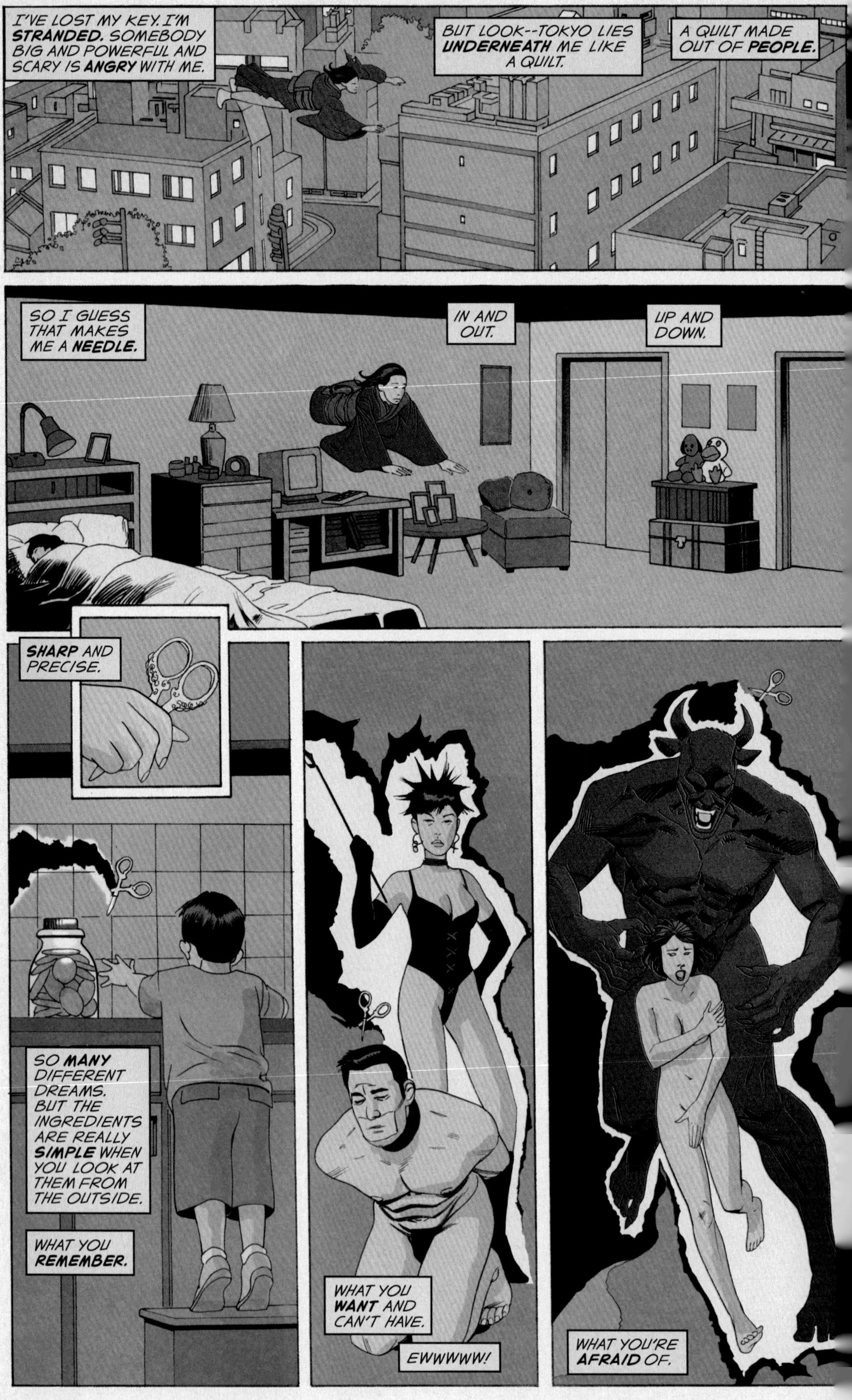

I'VE LOST MY KEY. I'M STRANDED. SOMEBODY BIG AND POWERFUL AND SCARY IS ANGRY WITH ME.
BUT LOOK--TOKYO LIES UNDERNEATH ME LIKE A QUILT.
A QUILT MADE OUT OF PEOPLE.
SO I GUESS THAT MAKES ME A NEEDLE.
IN AND OUT.
UP AND DOWN.
SHARP AND PRECISE.
SO MANY DIFFERENT DREAMS. BUT THE INGREDIENTS ARE REALLY SIMPLE WHEN YOU LOOK AT THEM FROM THE OUTSIDE.
WHAT YOU REMEMBER.
WHAT YOU WANT AND CAN'T HAVE.
EWWWWW!
WHAT YOU'RE AFRAID OF.

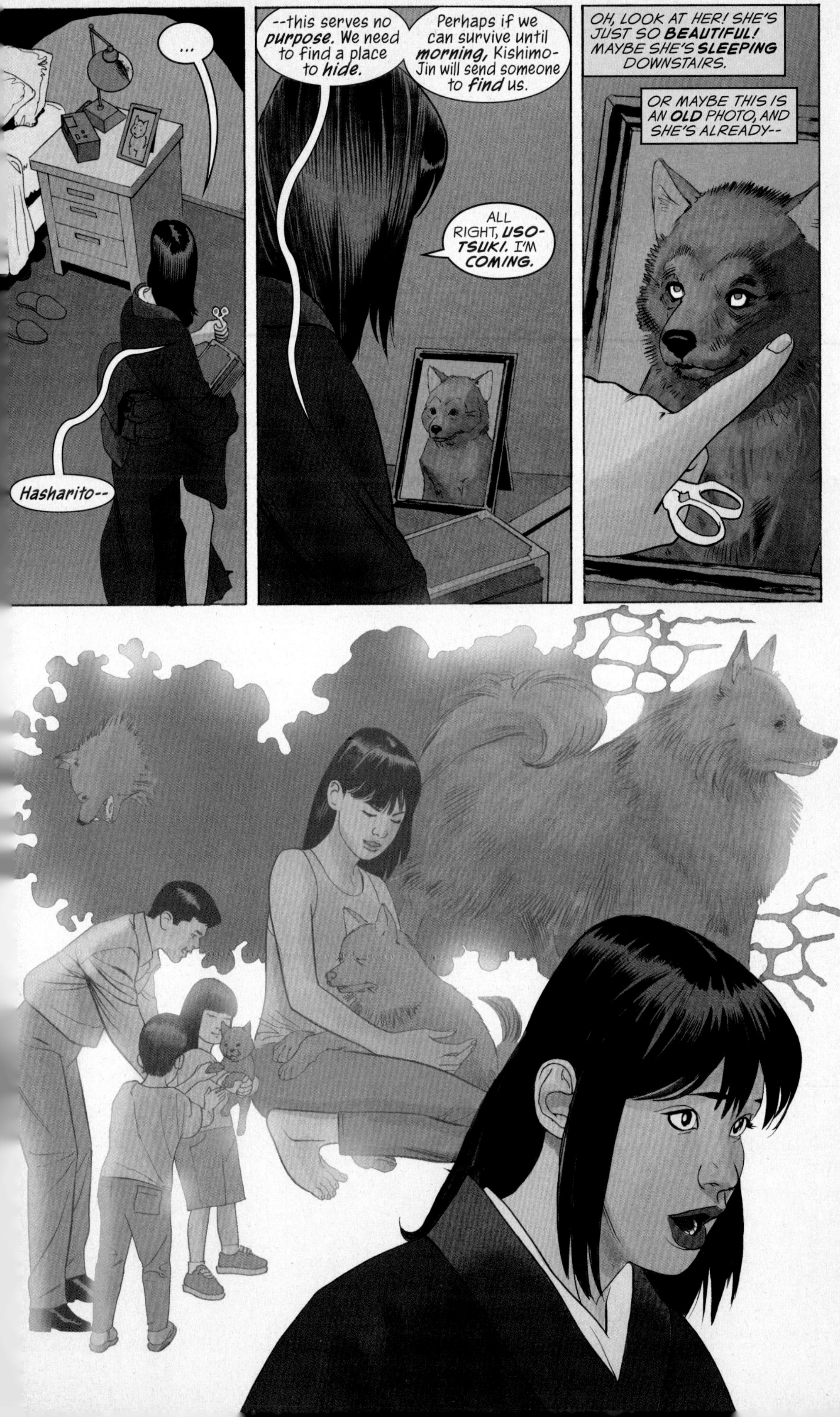
...
Hasharito--
--this serves no **purpose.** We need to find a place to **hide.**
Perhaps if we can survive until **morning,** Kishimo-Jin will send someone to **find** us.
ALL RIGHT, **USO-TSUKI.** I'M **COMING.**
OH, LOOK AT HER! SHE'S JUST SO **BEAUTIFUL!** MAYBE SHE'S **SLEEPING** DOWNSTAIRS.
OR MAYBE THIS IS AN **OLD** PHOTO, AND SHE'S ALREADY--

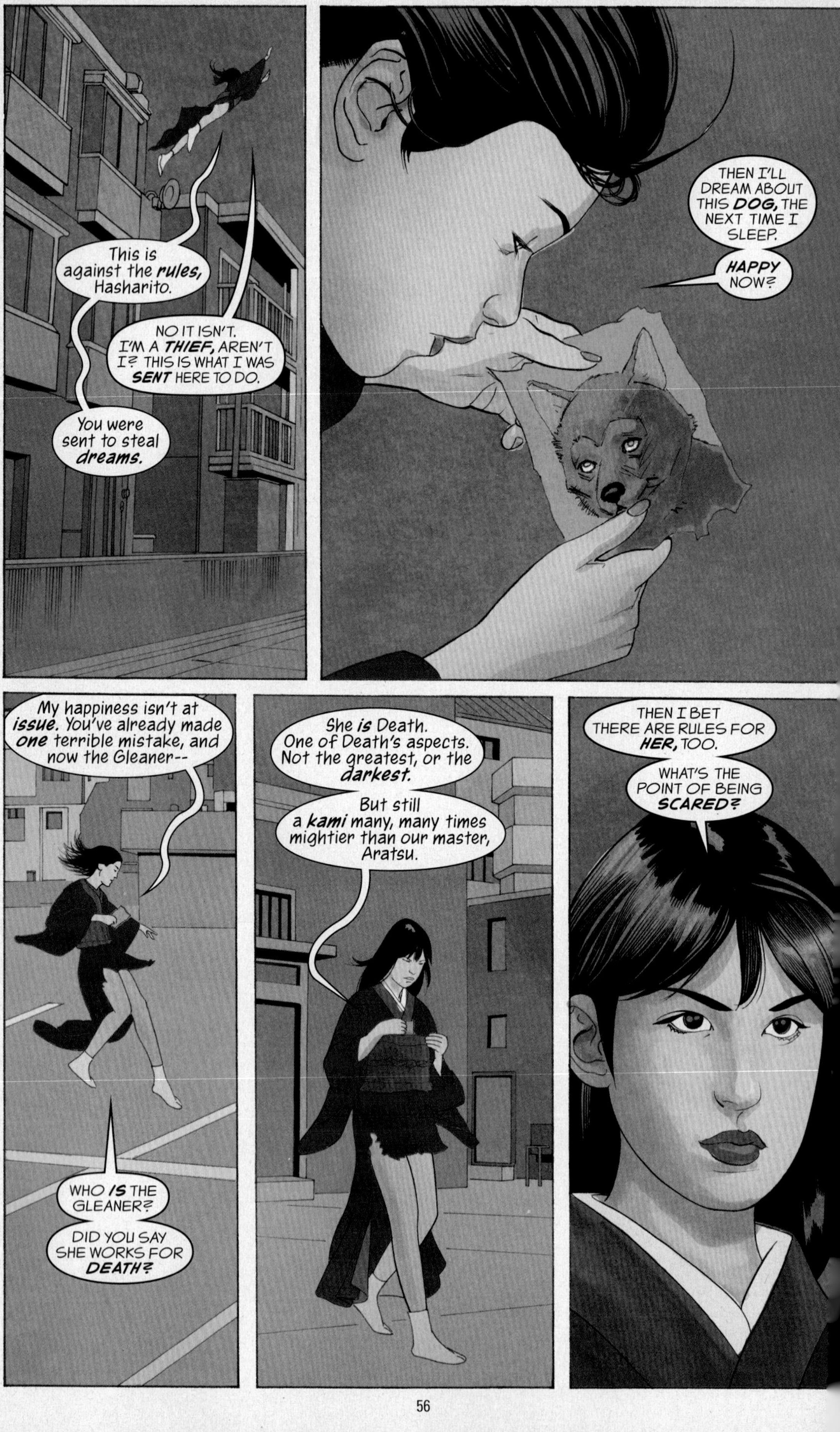
This is against the rules, Hasharito.
NO IT ISN'T. I'M A THIEF, AREN'T I? THIS IS WHAT I WAS SENT HERE TO DO.
You were sent to steal dreams.
THEN I'LL DREAM ABOUT THIS DOG, THE NEXT TIME I SLEEP.
HAPPY NOW?
My happiness isn't at issue. You've already made one terrible mistake, and now the Gleaner--
WHO IS THE GLEANER?
DID YOU SAY SHE WORKS FOR DEATH?
She is Death. One of Death's aspects. Not the greatest, or the darkest.
But still a kami many, many times mightier than our master, Aratsu.
THEN I BET THERE ARE RULES FOR HER, TOO.
WHAT'S THE POINT OF BEING SCARED?

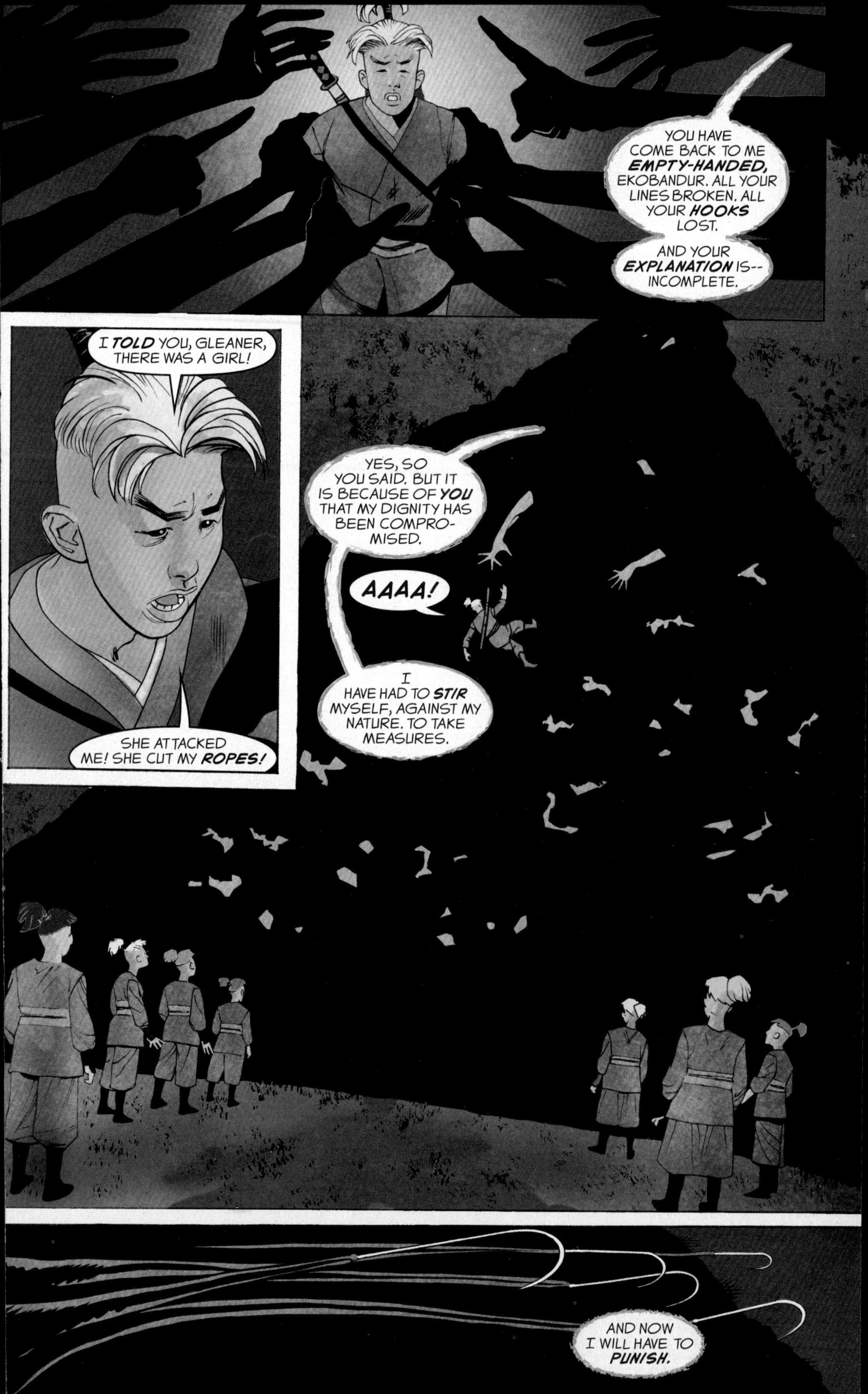
YOU HAVE COME BACK TO ME EMPTY-HANDED, EKOBANDUR. ALL YOUR LINES BROKEN. ALL YOUR HOOKS LOST.
AND YOUR EXPLANATION IS-- INCOMPLETE.
I TOLD YOU, GLEANER, THERE WAS A GIRL!
SHE ATTACKED ME! SHE CUT MY ROPES!
YES, SO YOU SAID. BUT IT IS BECAUSE OF YOU THAT MY DIGNITY HAS BEEN COMPRO-MISED.
AAAA!
I HAVE HAD TO STIR MYSELF, AGAINST MY NATURE. TO TAKE MEASURES.
AND NOW I WILL HAVE TO PUNISH.

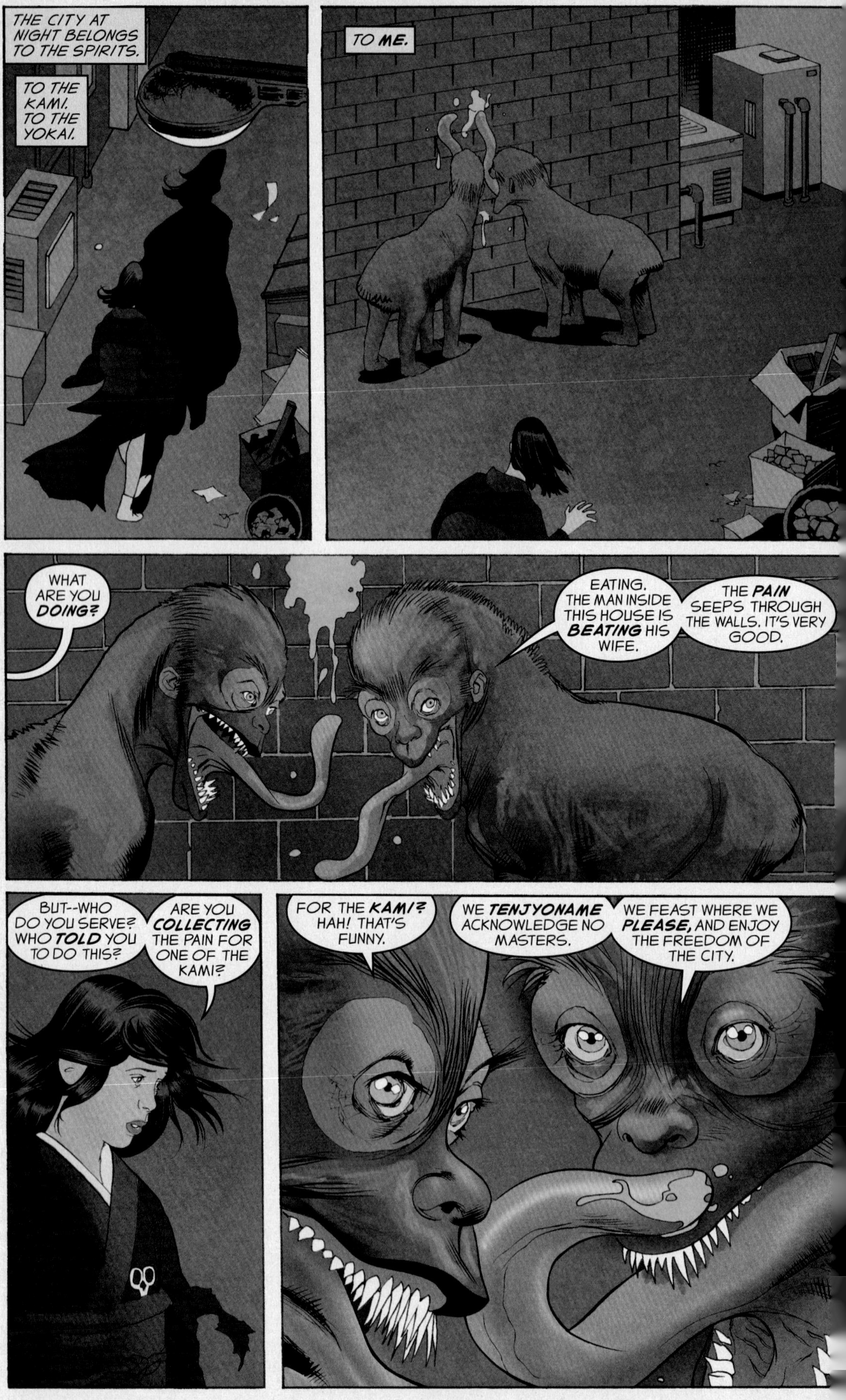
THE CITY AT NIGHT BELONGS TO THE SPIRITS.
TO THE KAMI. TO THE YOKAI.
TO ME.
WHAT ARE YOU DOING?
EATING. THE MAN INSIDE THIS HOUSE IS BEATING HIS WIFE.
THE PAIN SEEPS THROUGH THE WALLS. IT'S VERY GOOD.
BUT--WHO DO YOU SERVE? WHO TOLD YOU TO DO THIS?
ARE YOU COLLECTING THE PAIN FOR ONE OF THE KAMI?
FOR THE KAMI? HAH! THAT'S FUNNY.
WE TENJYONAME ACKNOWLEDGE NO MASTERS.
WE FEAST WHERE WE PLEASE, AND ENJOY THE FREEDOM OF THE CITY.

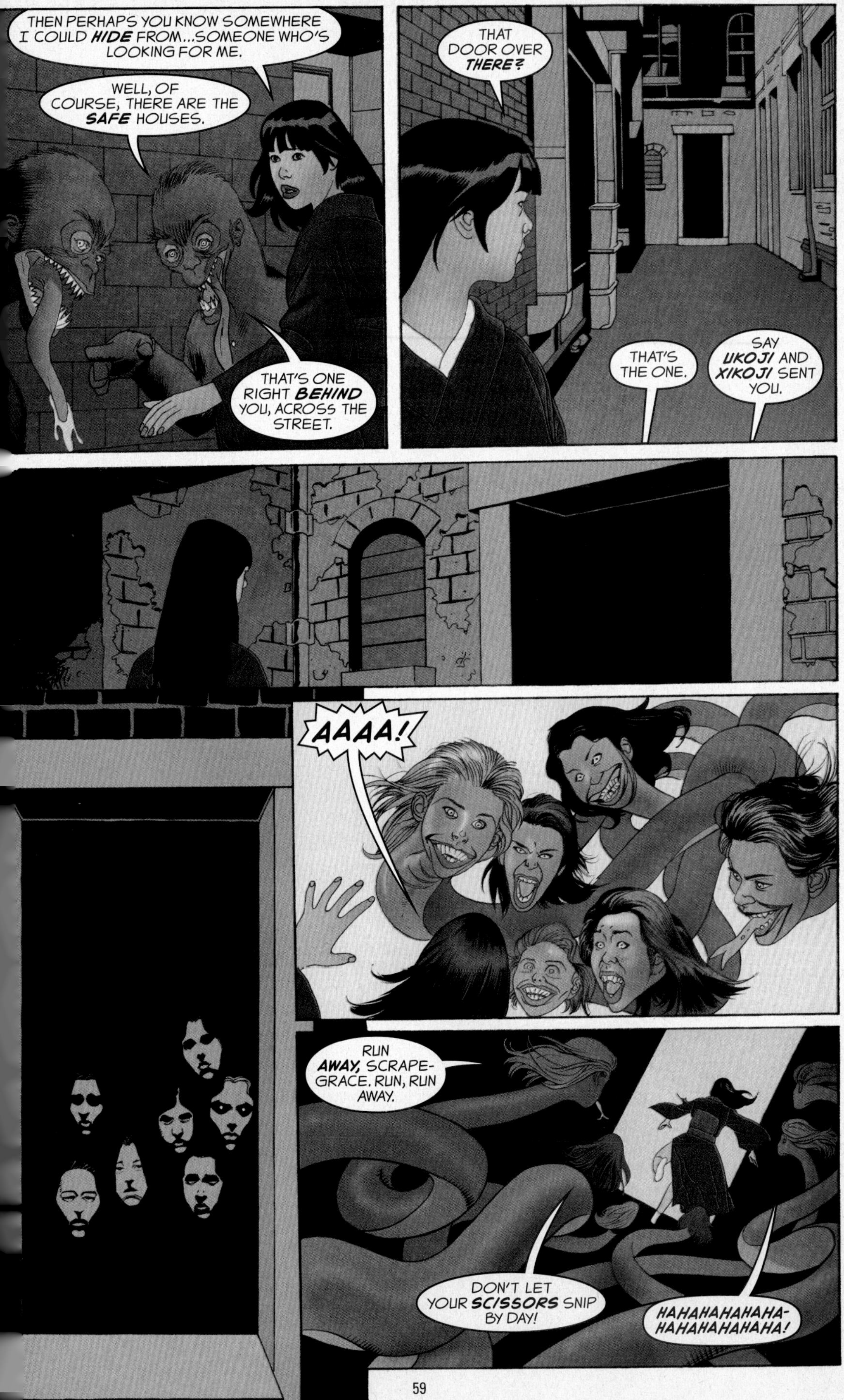
THEN PERHAPS YOU KNOW SOMEWHERE I COULD HIDE FROM...SOMEONE WHO'S LOOKING FOR ME.
WELL, OF COURSE, THERE ARE THE SAFE HOUSES.
THAT'S ONE RIGHT BEHIND YOU, ACROSS THE STREET.
THAT DOOR OVER THERE?
THAT'S THE ONE.
SAY UKOJI AND XIKOJI SENT YOU.
AAAA!
RUN AWAY, SCRAPE-GRACE. RUN, RUN AWAY.
DON'T LET YOUR SCISSORS SNIP BY DAY!
HAHAHAHAHAHA-HAHAHAHAHAHA!

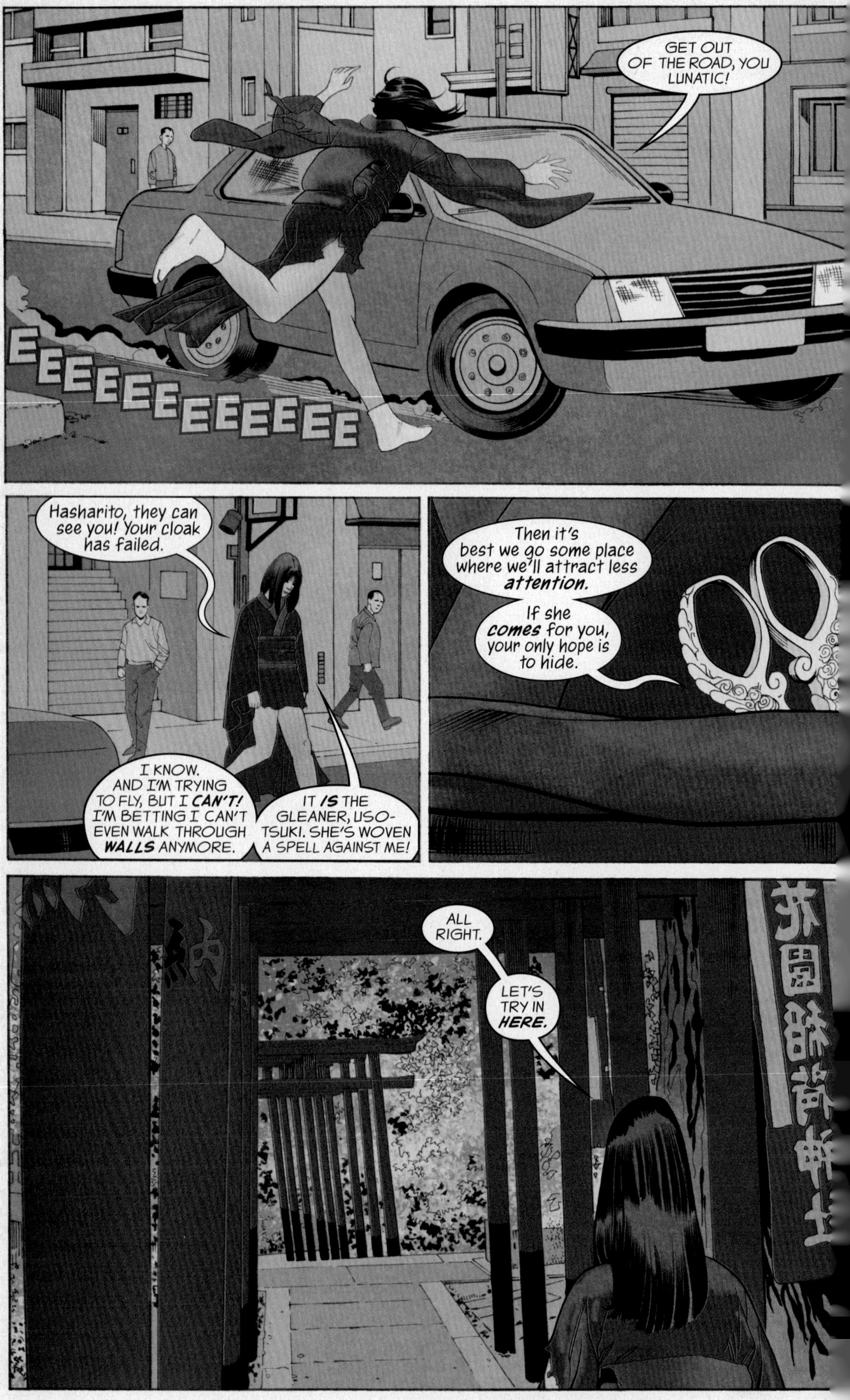
GET OUT OF THE ROAD, YOU LUNATIC!
EEEEEEEEEEEEE
Hasharito, they can see you! Your cloak has failed.
I KNOW. AND I'M TRYING TO FLY, BUT I CAN'T! I'M BETTING I CAN'T EVEN WALK THROUGH WALLS ANYMORE.
IT IS THE GLEANER, USO-TSUKI. SHE'S WOVEN A SPELL AGAINST ME!
Then it's best we go some place where we'll attract less attention.
If she comes for you, your only hope is to hide.
ALL RIGHT.
LET'S TRY IN HERE.

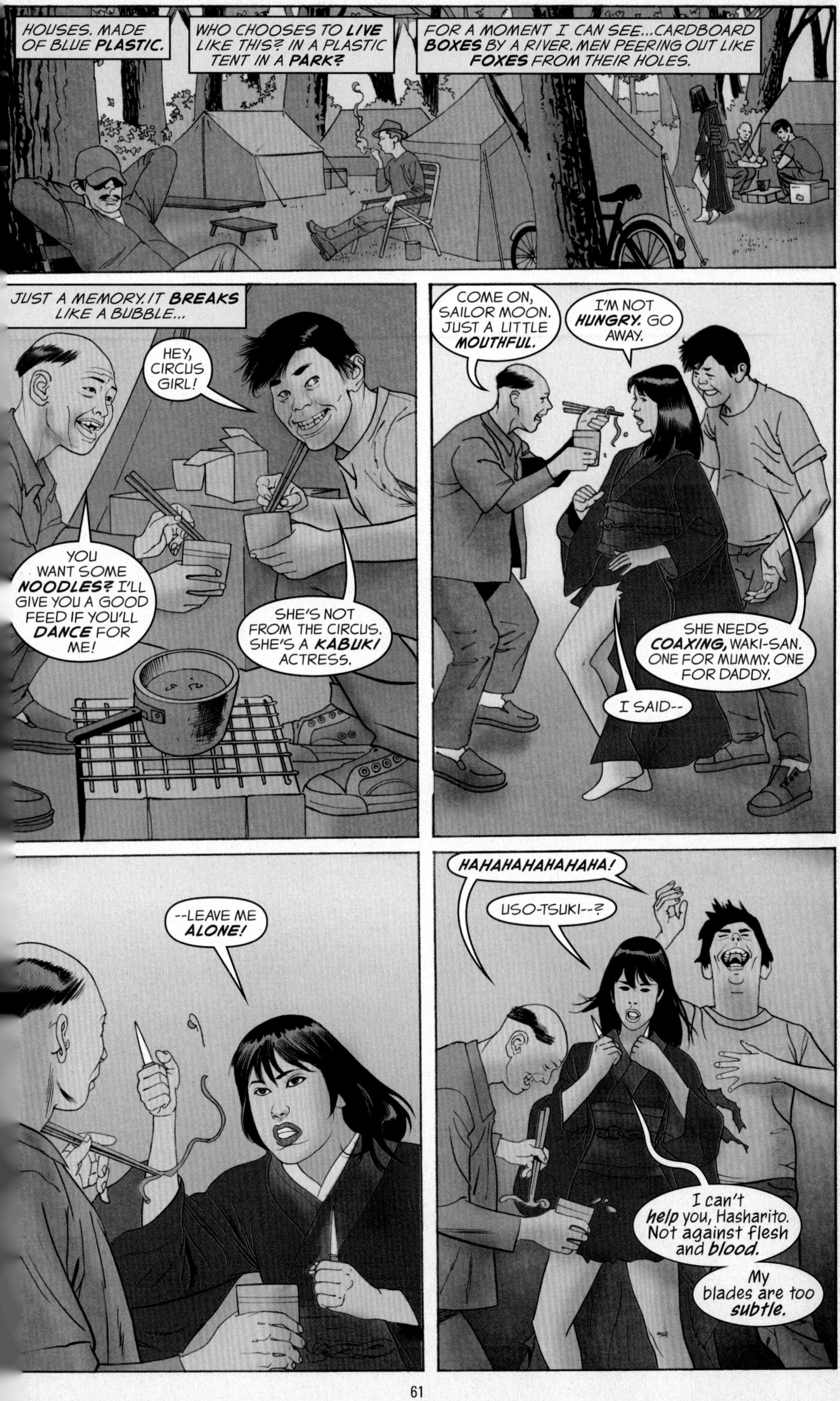
HOUSES. MADE OF BLUE PLASTIC.
WHO CHOOSES TO LIVE LIKE THIS? IN A PLASTIC TENT IN A PARK?
FOR A MOMENT I CAN SEE...CARDBOARD BOXES BY A RIVER. MEN PEERING OUT LIKE FOXES FROM THEIR HOLES.
JUST A MEMORY. IT BREAKS LIKE A BUBBLE...
HEY, CIRCUS GIRL!
YOU WANT SOME NOODLES? I'LL GIVE YOU A GOOD FEED IF YOU'LL DANCE FOR ME!
SHE'S NOT FROM THE CIRCUS. SHE'S A KABUKI ACTRESS.
COME ON, SAILOR MOON. JUST A LITTLE MOUTHFUL.
I'M NOT HUNGRY. GO AWAY.
SHE NEEDS COAXING, WAKI-SAN. ONE FOR MUMMY. ONE FOR DADDY.
I SAID--
--LEAVE ME ALONE!
HAHAHAHAHAHAHA!
USO-TSUKI--?
I can't help you, Hasharito. Not against flesh and blood.
My blades are too subtle.

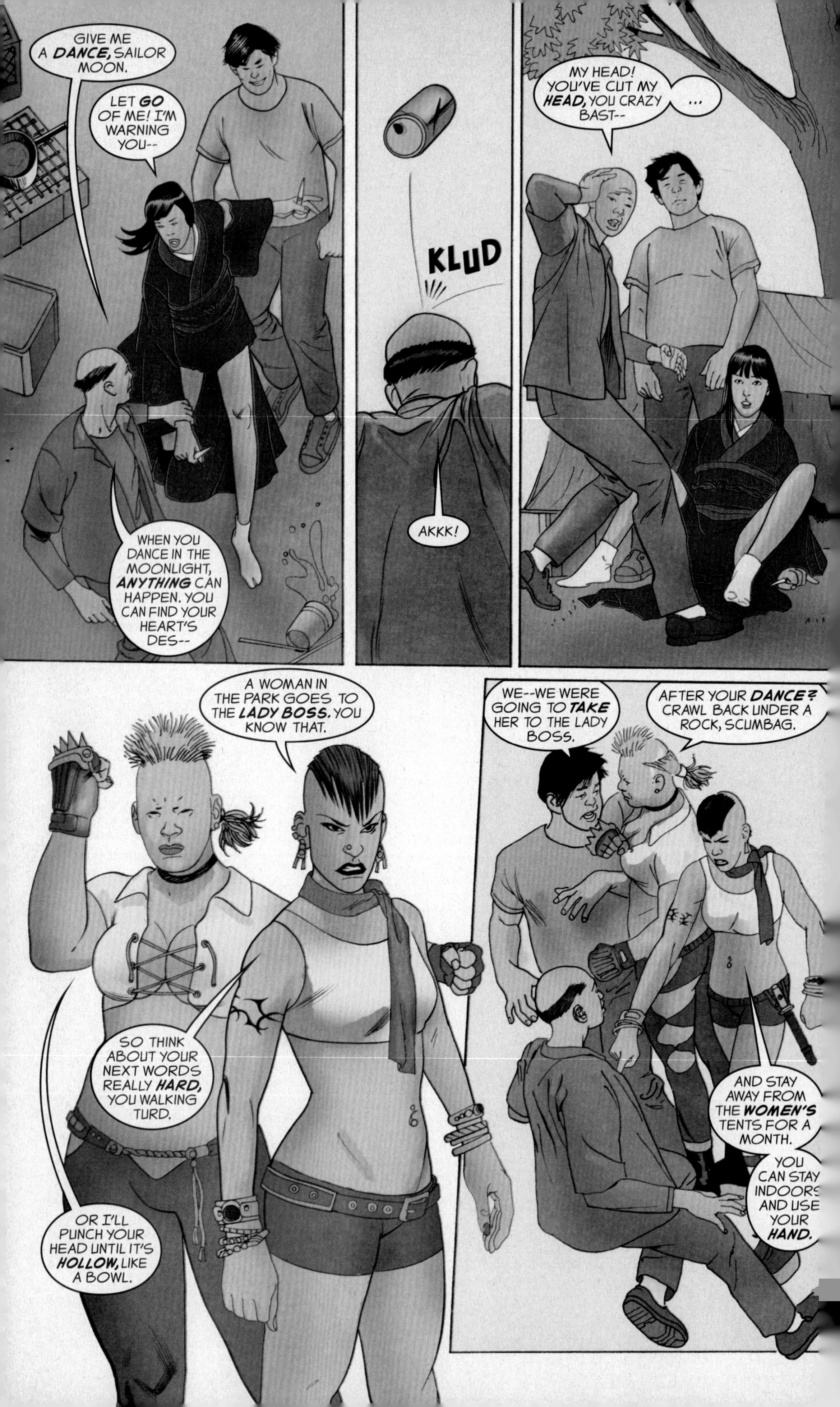

GIVE ME A **DANCE**, SAILOR MOON.
LET **GO** OF ME! I'M WARNING YOU--
WHEN YOU DANCE IN THE MOONLIGHT, **ANYTHING** CAN HAPPEN. YOU CAN FIND YOUR HEART'S DES--
KLUD
AKKK!
MY HEAD! YOU'VE CUT MY **HEAD**, YOU CRAZY BAST--
...
A WOMAN IN THE PARK GOES TO THE **LADY BOSS**. YOU KNOW THAT.
SO THINK ABOUT YOUR NEXT WORDS REALLY **HARD**, YOU WALKING TURD.
OR I'LL PUNCH YOUR HEAD UNTIL IT'S **HOLLOW**, LIKE A BOWL.
WE--WE WERE GOING TO **TAKE** HER TO THE LADY BOSS.
AFTER YOUR **DANCE?** CRAWL BACK UNDER A ROCK, SCUMBAG.
AND STAY AWAY FROM THE **WOMEN'S** TENTS FOR A MONTH.
YOU CAN STAY INDOORS AND USE YOUR **HAND.**

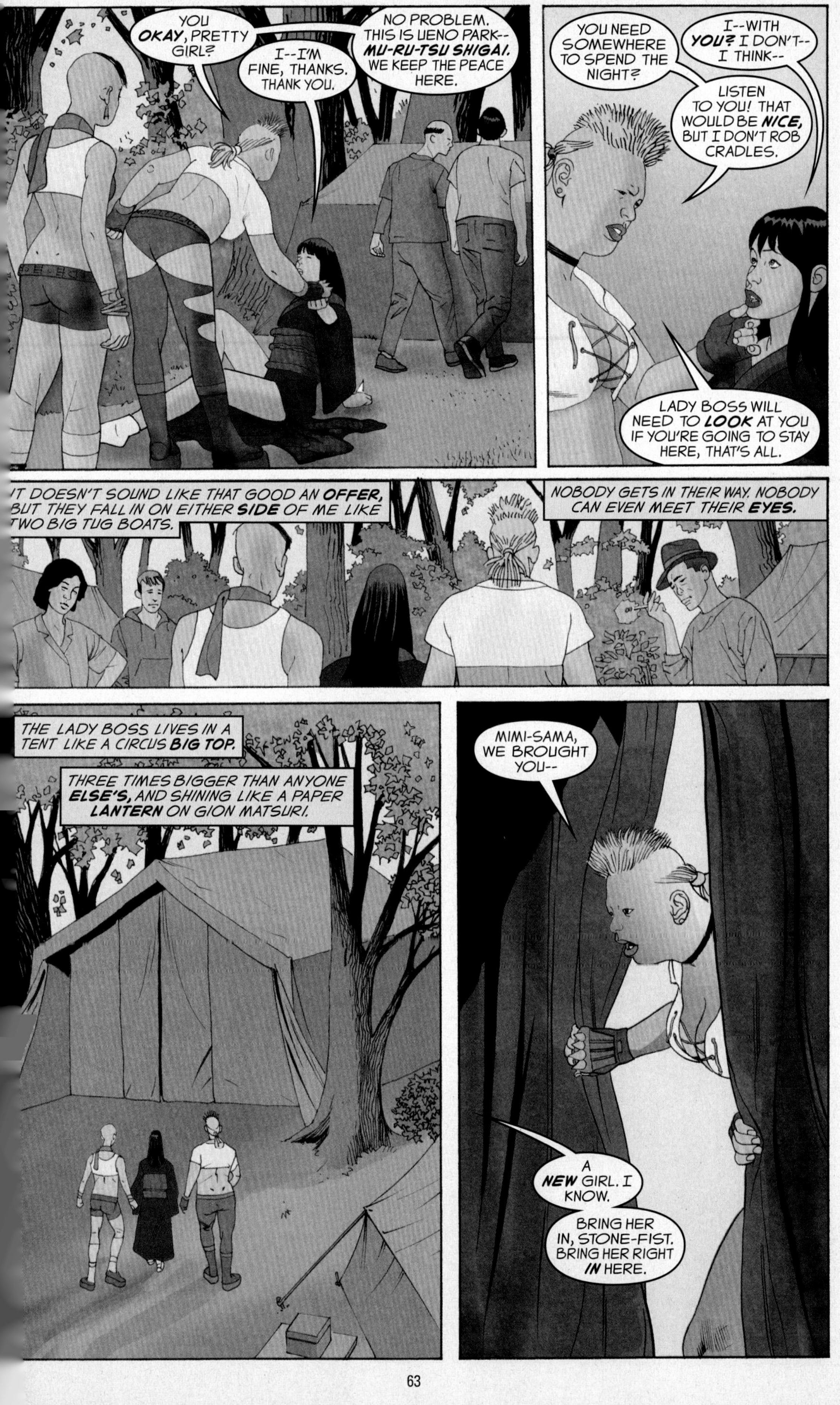
YOU OKAY, PRETTY GIRL?
I--I'M FINE, THANKS. THANK YOU.
NO PROBLEM. THIS IS UENO PARK-- MU-RU-TSU SHIGAI. WE KEEP THE PEACE HERE.
YOU NEED SOMEWHERE TO SPEND THE NIGHT?
I--WITH YOU? I DON'T-- I THINK--
LISTEN TO YOU! THAT WOULD BE NICE, BUT I DON'T ROB CRADLES.
LADY BOSS WILL NEED TO LOOK AT YOU IF YOU'RE GOING TO STAY HERE, THAT'S ALL.
IT DOESN'T SOUND LIKE THAT GOOD AN OFFER, BUT THEY FALL IN ON EITHER SIDE OF ME LIKE TWO BIG TUG BOATS.
NOBODY GETS IN THEIR WAY. NOBODY CAN EVEN MEET THEIR EYES.
THE LADY BOSS LIVES IN A TENT LIKE A CIRCUS BIG TOP.
THREE TIMES BIGGER THAN ANYONE ELSE'S, AND SHINING LIKE A PAPER LANTERN ON GION MATSURI.
MIMI-SAMA, WE BROUGHT YOU--
A NEW GIRL. I KNOW.
BRING HER IN, STONE-FIST. BRING HER RIGHT IN HERE.

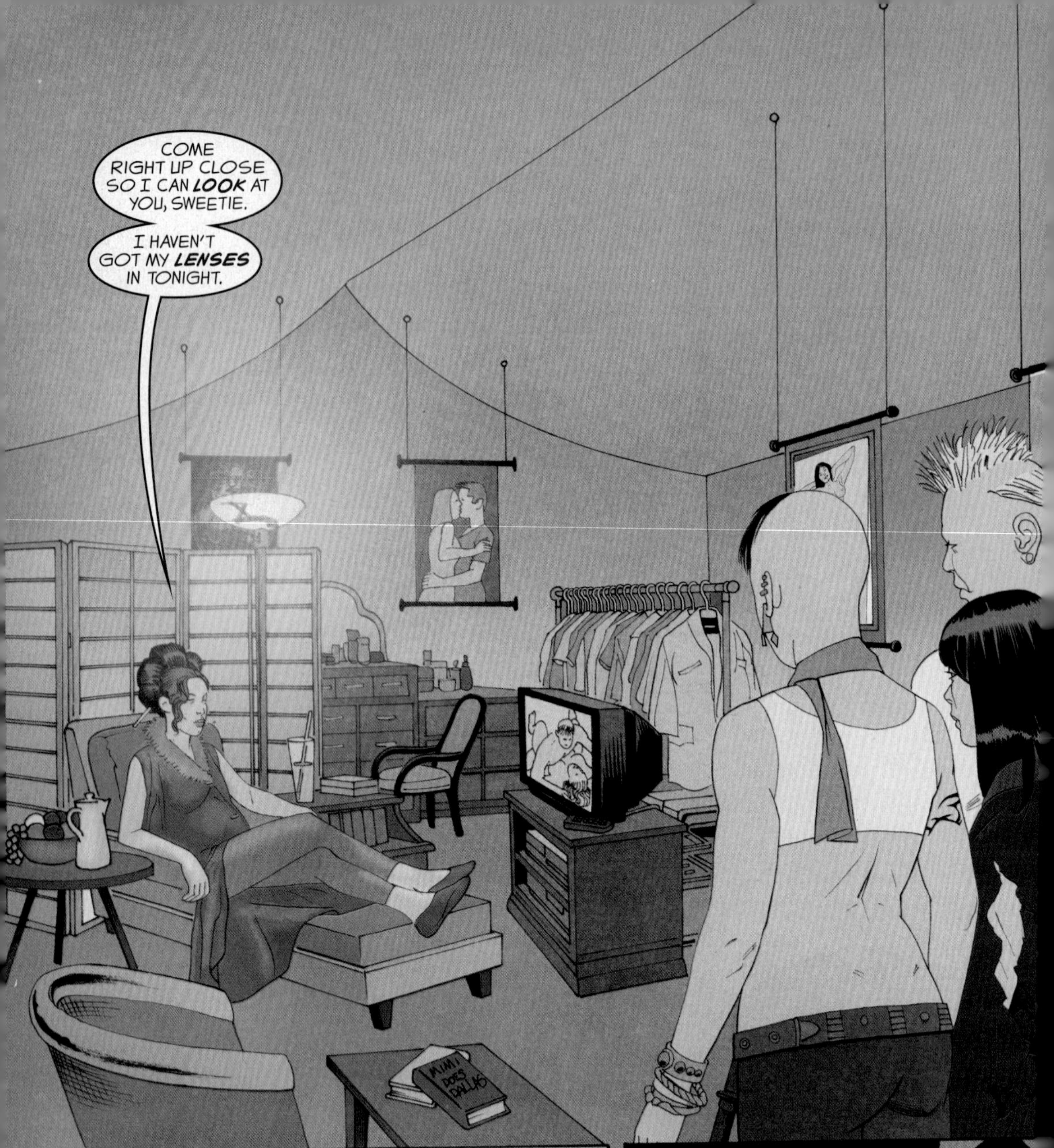
COME RIGHT UP CLOSE SO I CAN **LOOK** AT YOU, SWEETIE.
I HAVEN'T GOT MY **LENSES** IN TONIGHT.
MIMI DOES DALLAS

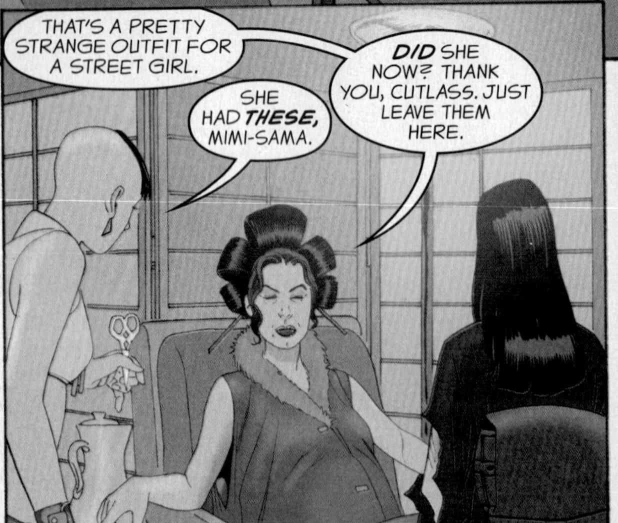
THAT'S A PRETTY STRANGE OUTFIT FOR A STREET GIRL.
SHE HAD **THESE,** MIMI-SAMA.
DID SHE NOW? THANK YOU, CUTLASS. JUST LEAVE THEM HERE.

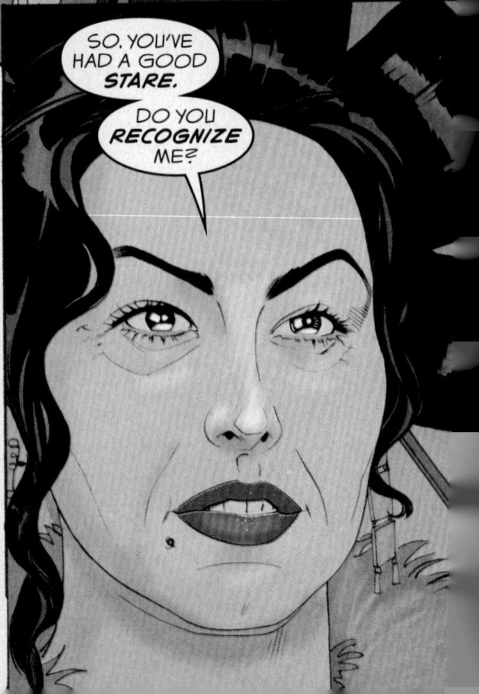
SO. YOU'VE HAD A GOOD **STARE.**
DO YOU **RECOGNIZE** ME?

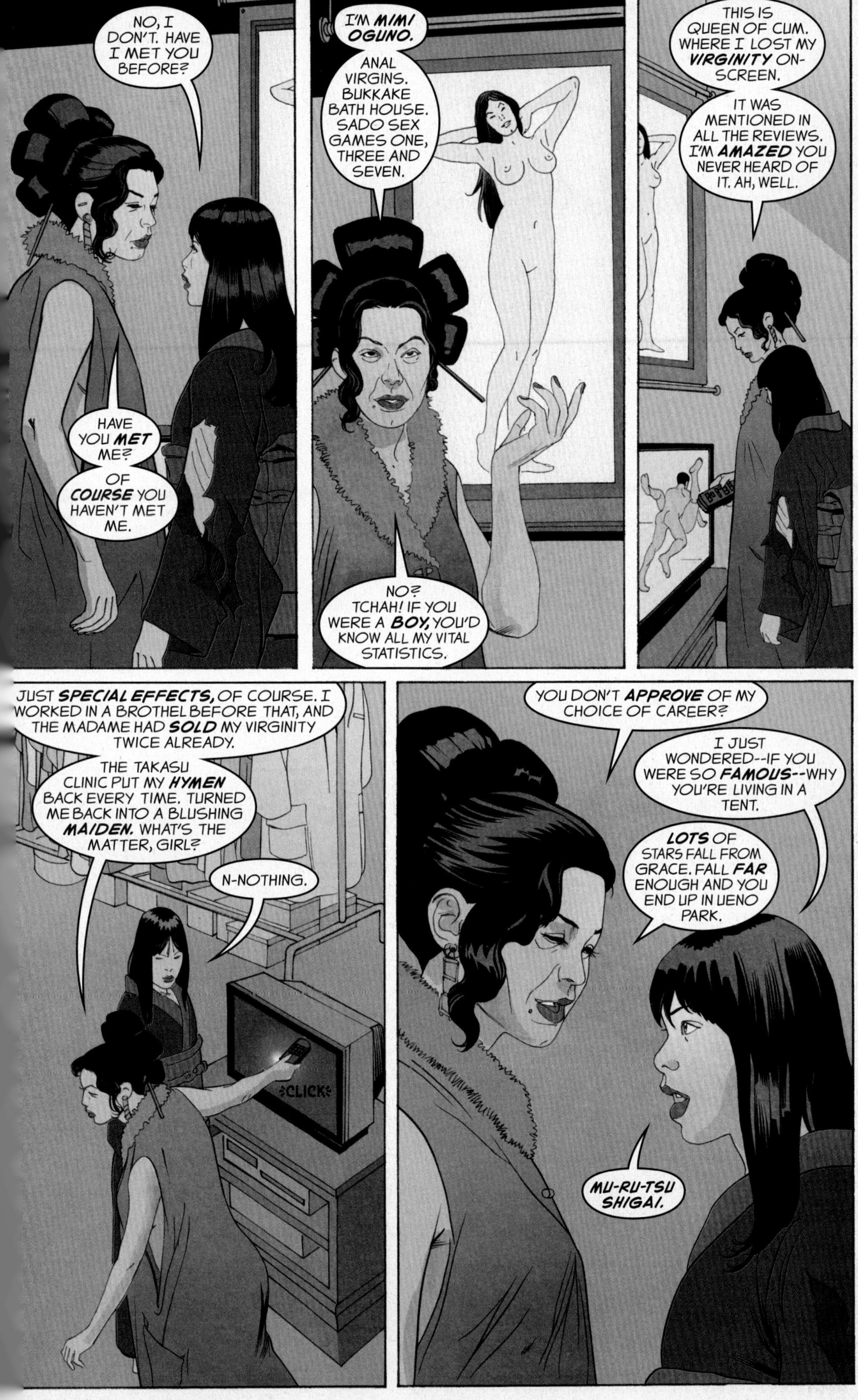
NO, I DON'T. HAVE I MET YOU BEFORE?
HAVE YOU MET ME?
OF COURSE YOU HAVEN'T MET ME.
I'M MIMI OGUNO.
ANAL VIRGINS. BUKKAKE BATH HOUSE. SADO SEX GAMES ONE, THREE AND SEVEN.
NO? TCHAH! IF YOU WERE A BOY, YOU'D KNOW ALL MY VITAL STATISTICS.
THIS IS QUEEN OF CUM. WHERE I LOST MY VIRGINITY ON-SCREEN.
IT WAS MENTIONED IN ALL THE REVIEWS. I'M AMAZED YOU NEVER HEARD OF IT. AH, WELL.
JUST SPECIAL EFFECTS, OF COURSE. I WORKED IN A BROTHEL BEFORE THAT, AND THE MADAME HAD SOLD MY VIRGINITY TWICE ALREADY.
THE TAKASU CLINIC PUT MY HYMEN BACK EVERY TIME. TURNED ME BACK INTO A BLUSHING MAIDEN. WHAT'S THE MATTER, GIRL?
N-NOTHING.
CLICK
YOU DON'T APPROVE OF MY CHOICE OF CAREER?
I JUST WONDERED--IF YOU WERE SO FAMOUS--WHY YOU'RE LIVING IN A TENT.
LOTS OF STARS FALL FROM GRACE. FALL FAR ENOUGH AND YOU END UP IN UENO PARK.
MU-RU-TSU SHIGAI.

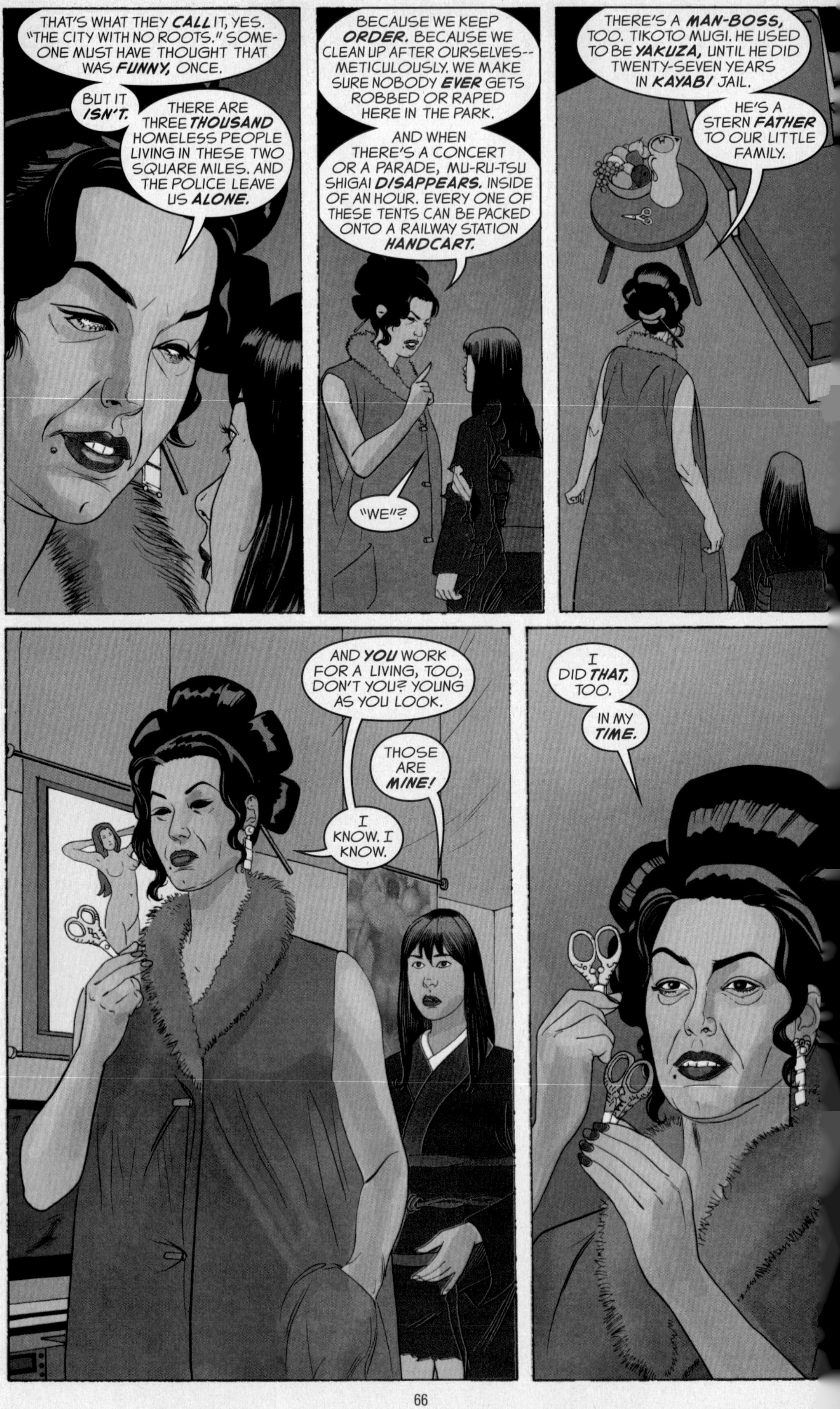

THAT'S WHAT THEY **CALL** IT, YES. "THE CITY WITH NO ROOTS." SOMEONE MUST HAVE THOUGHT THAT WAS **FUNNY,** ONCE.
BUT IT **ISN'T.**
THERE ARE THREE **THOUSAND** HOMELESS PEOPLE LIVING IN THESE TWO SQUARE MILES. AND THE POLICE LEAVE US **ALONE.**
BECAUSE WE KEEP **ORDER.** BECAUSE WE CLEAN UP AFTER OURSELVES-- METICULOUSLY. WE MAKE SURE NOBODY **EVER** GETS ROBBED OR RAPED HERE IN THE PARK.
AND WHEN THERE'S A CONCERT OR A PARADE, MU-RU-TSU SHIGAI **DISAPPEARS.** INSIDE OF AN HOUR. EVERY ONE OF THESE TENTS CAN BE PACKED ONTO A RAILWAY STATION **HANDCART.**
"WE"?
THERE'S A **MAN-BOSS,** TOO. TIKOTO MUGI. HE USED TO BE **YAKUZA,** UNTIL HE DID TWENTY-SEVEN YEARS IN **KAYABI** JAIL.
HE'S A STERN **FATHER** TO OUR LITTLE FAMILY.
AND **YOU** WORK FOR A LIVING, TOO, DON'T YOU? YOUNG AS YOU LOOK.
THOSE ARE **MINE!**
I KNOW. I KNOW.
I DID **THAT,** TOO.
IN MY **TIME.**

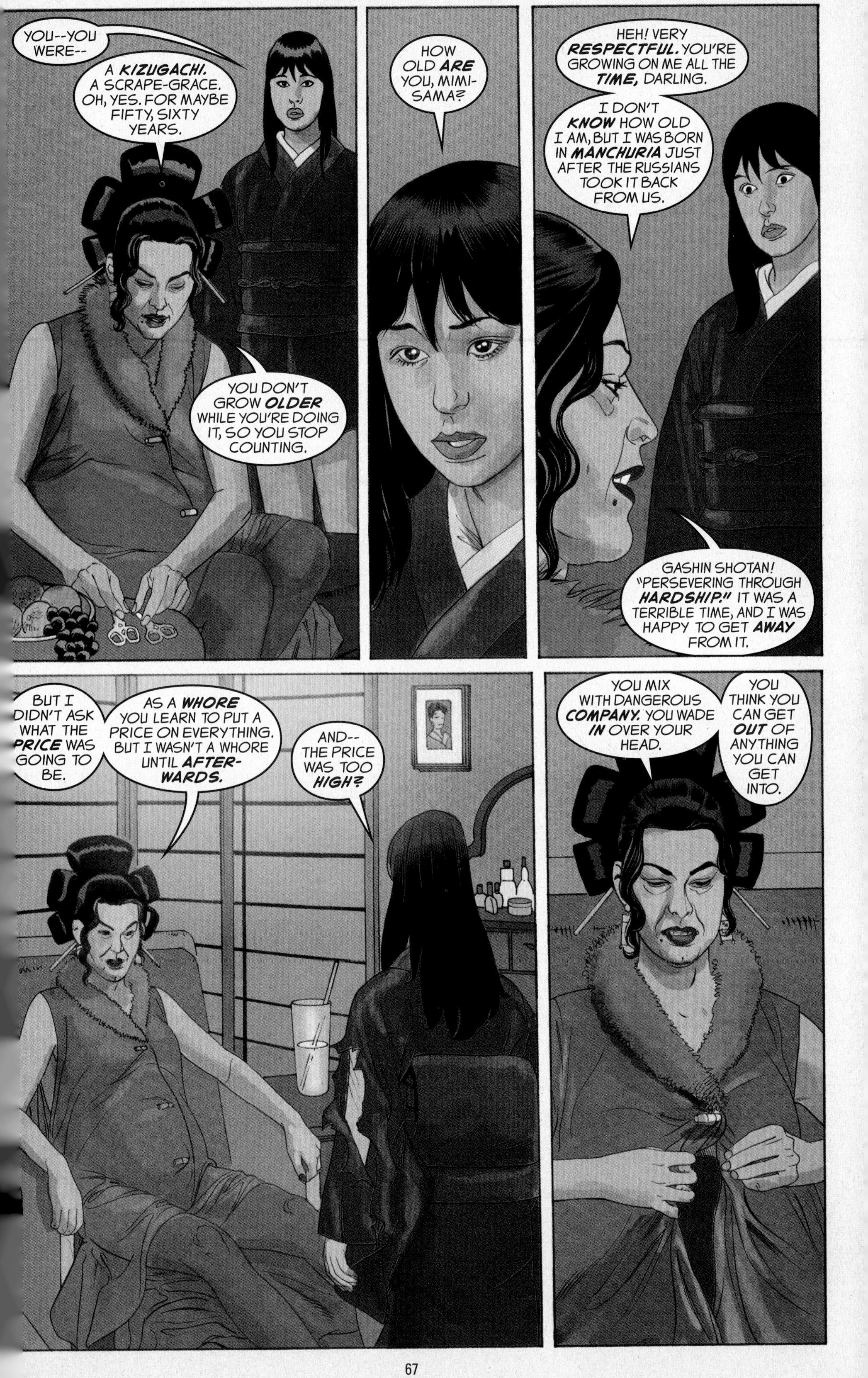
YOU--YOU WERE--
A KIZUGACHI. A SCRAPE-GRACE. OH, YES. FOR MAYBE FIFTY, SIXTY YEARS.
YOU DON'T GROW OLDER WHILE YOU'RE DOING IT, SO YOU STOP COUNTING.
HOW OLD ARE YOU, MIMI-SAMA?
HEH! VERY RESPECTFUL. YOU'RE GROWING ON ME ALL THE TIME, DARLING.
I DON'T KNOW HOW OLD I AM, BUT I WAS BORN IN MANCHURIA JUST AFTER THE RUSSIANS TOOK IT BACK FROM US.
GASHIN SHOTAN! "PERSEVERING THROUGH HARDSHIP." IT WAS A TERRIBLE TIME, AND I WAS HAPPY TO GET AWAY FROM IT.
BUT I DIDN'T ASK WHAT THE PRICE WAS GOING TO BE.
AS A WHORE YOU LEARN TO PUT A PRICE ON EVERYTHING. BUT I WASN'T A WHORE UNTIL AFTER-WARDS.
AND-- THE PRICE WAS TOO HIGH?
YOU MIX WITH DANGEROUS COMPANY. YOU WADE IN OVER YOUR HEAD.
YOU THINK YOU CAN GET OUT OF ANYTHING YOU CAN GET INTO.

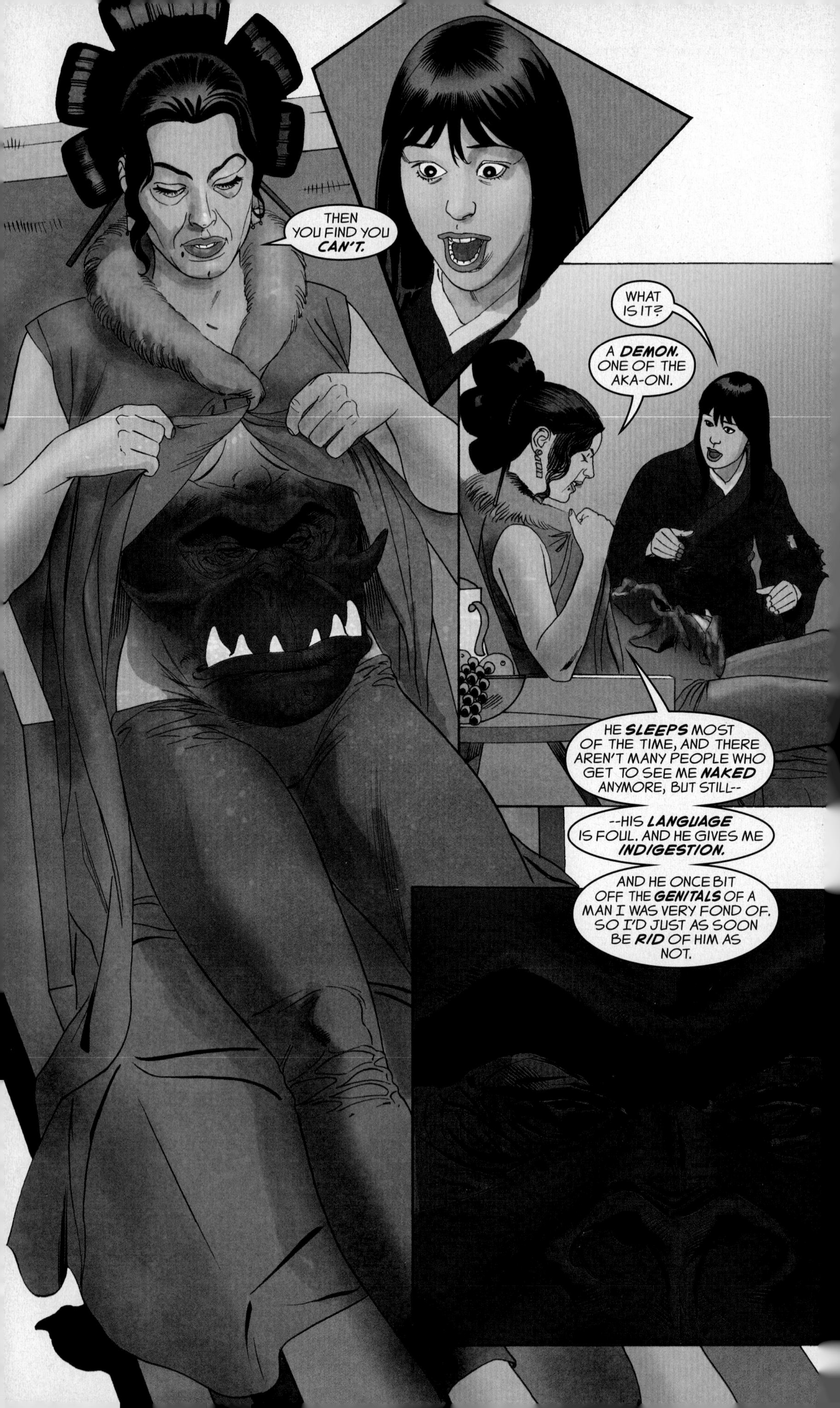
THEN YOU FIND YOU CAN'T.
WHAT IS IT?
A DEMON. ONE OF THE AKA-ONI.
HE SLEEPS MOST OF THE TIME, AND THERE AREN'T MANY PEOPLE WHO GET TO SEE ME NAKED ANYMORE, BUT STILL--
--HIS LANGUAGE IS FOUL. AND HE GIVES ME INDIGESTION.
AND HE ONCE BIT OFF THE GENITALS OF A MAN I WAS VERY FOND OF. SO I'D JUST AS SOON BE RID OF HIM AS NOT.

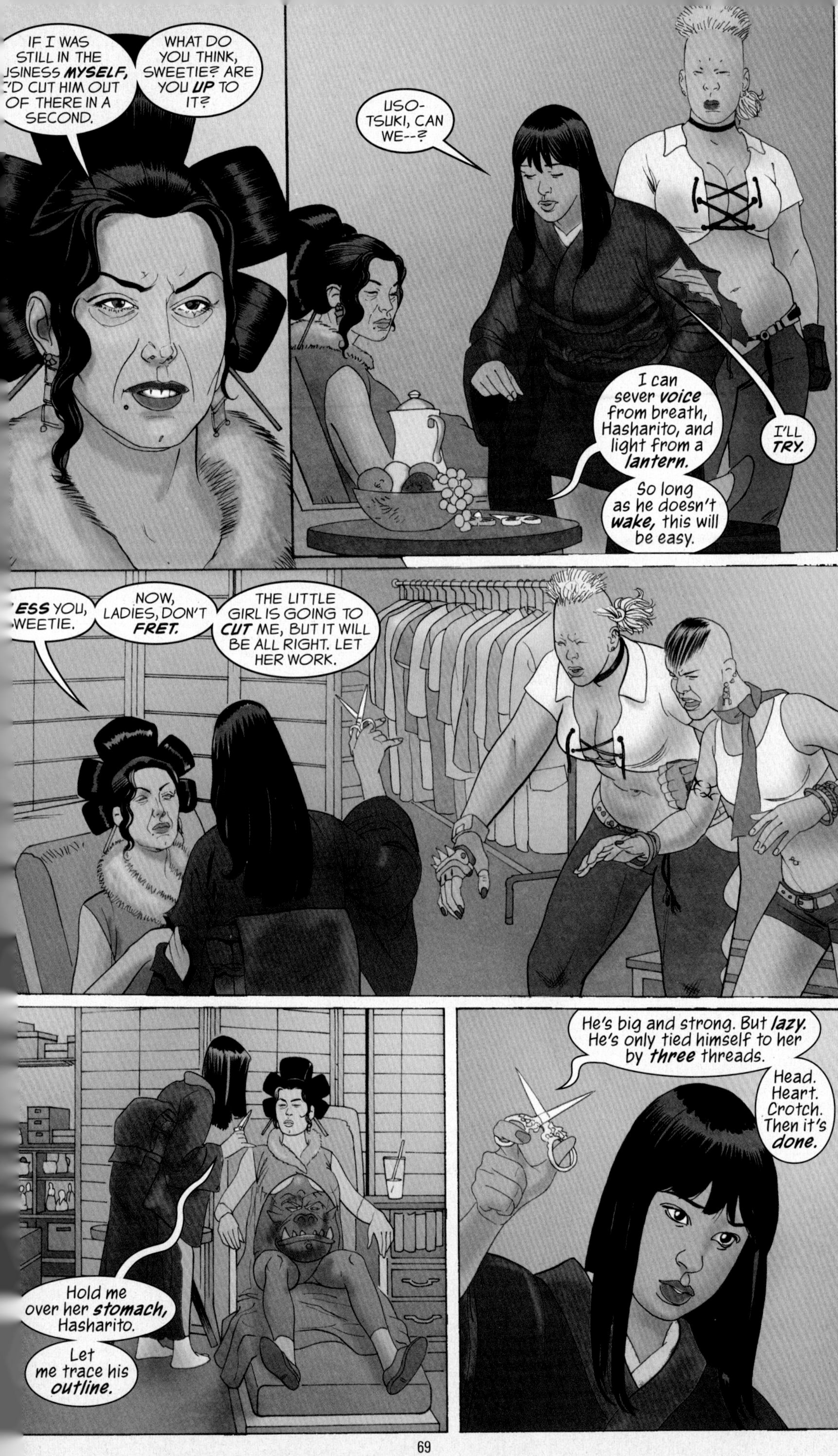

IF I WAS STILL IN THE BUSINESS **MYSELF,** I'D CUT HIM OUT OF THERE IN A SECOND.
WHAT DO YOU THINK, SWEETIE? ARE YOU **UP** TO IT?
USO-TSUKI, CAN WE--?
I'LL **TRY.**
I can sever **voice** from breath, Hasharito, and light from a **lantern.**
So long as he doesn't **wake,** this will be easy.
ESS YOU, WEETIE.
NOW, LADIES, DON'T **FRET.**
THE LITTLE GIRL IS GOING TO **CUT** ME, BUT IT WILL BE ALL RIGHT. LET HER WORK.
Hold me over her **stomach,** Hasharito.
Let me trace his **outline.**
He's big and strong. But **lazy.** He's only tied himself to her by **three** threads.
Head. Heart. Crotch. Then it's **done.**

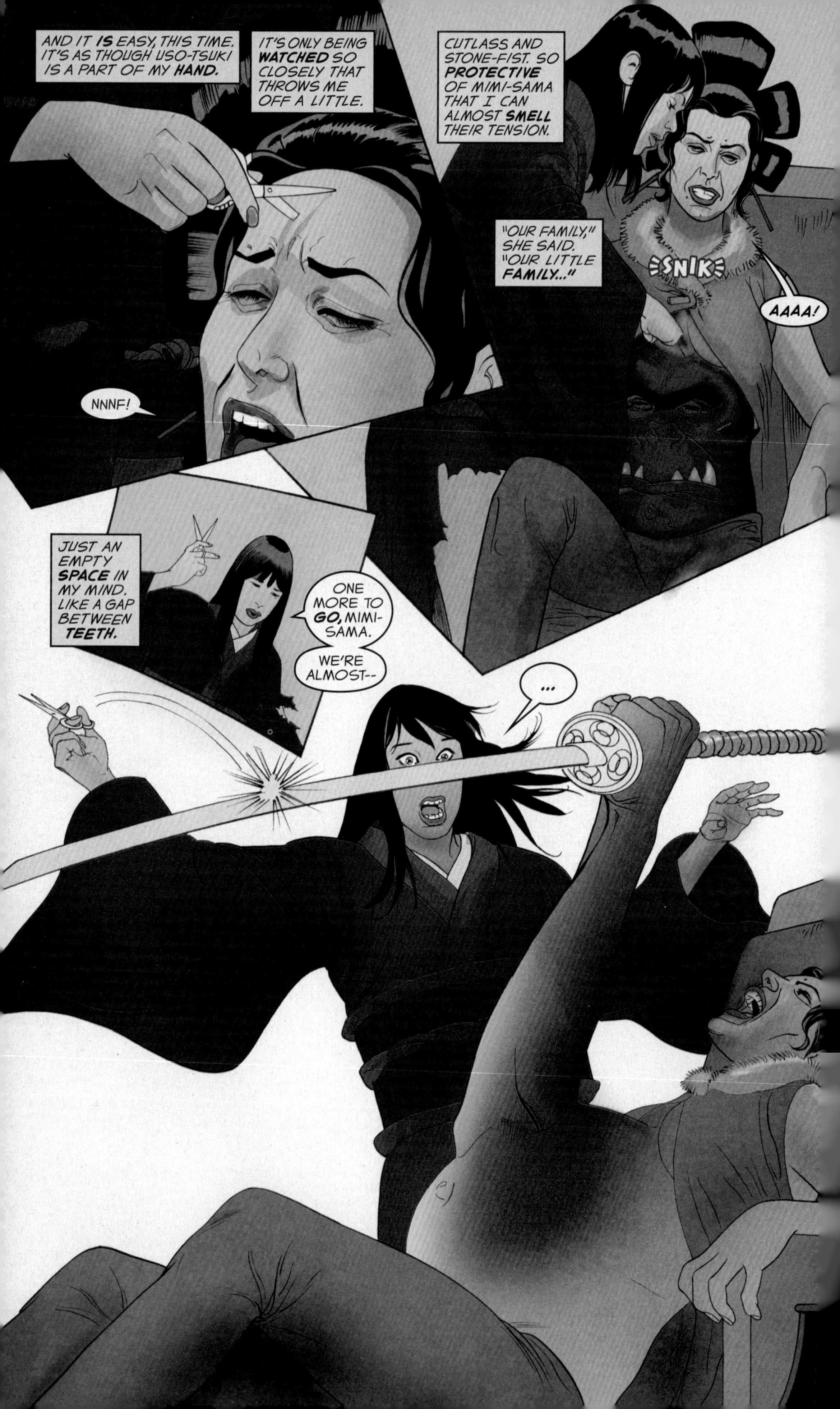
AND IT IS EASY, THIS TIME. IT'S AS THOUGH USO-TSUKI IS A PART OF MY HAND.
IT'S ONLY BEING WATCHED SO CLOSELY THAT THROWS ME OFF A LITTLE.
CUTLASS AND STONE-FIST. SO PROTECTIVE OF MIMI-SAMA THAT I CAN ALMOST SMELL THEIR TENSION.
"OUR FAMILY," SHE SAID. "OUR LITTLE FAMILY..."
SNIK
AAAA!
NNNF!
JUST AN EMPTY SPACE IN MY MIND. LIKE A GAP BETWEEN TEETH.
ONE MORE TO GO, MIMI-SAMA.
WE'RE ALMOST--
...

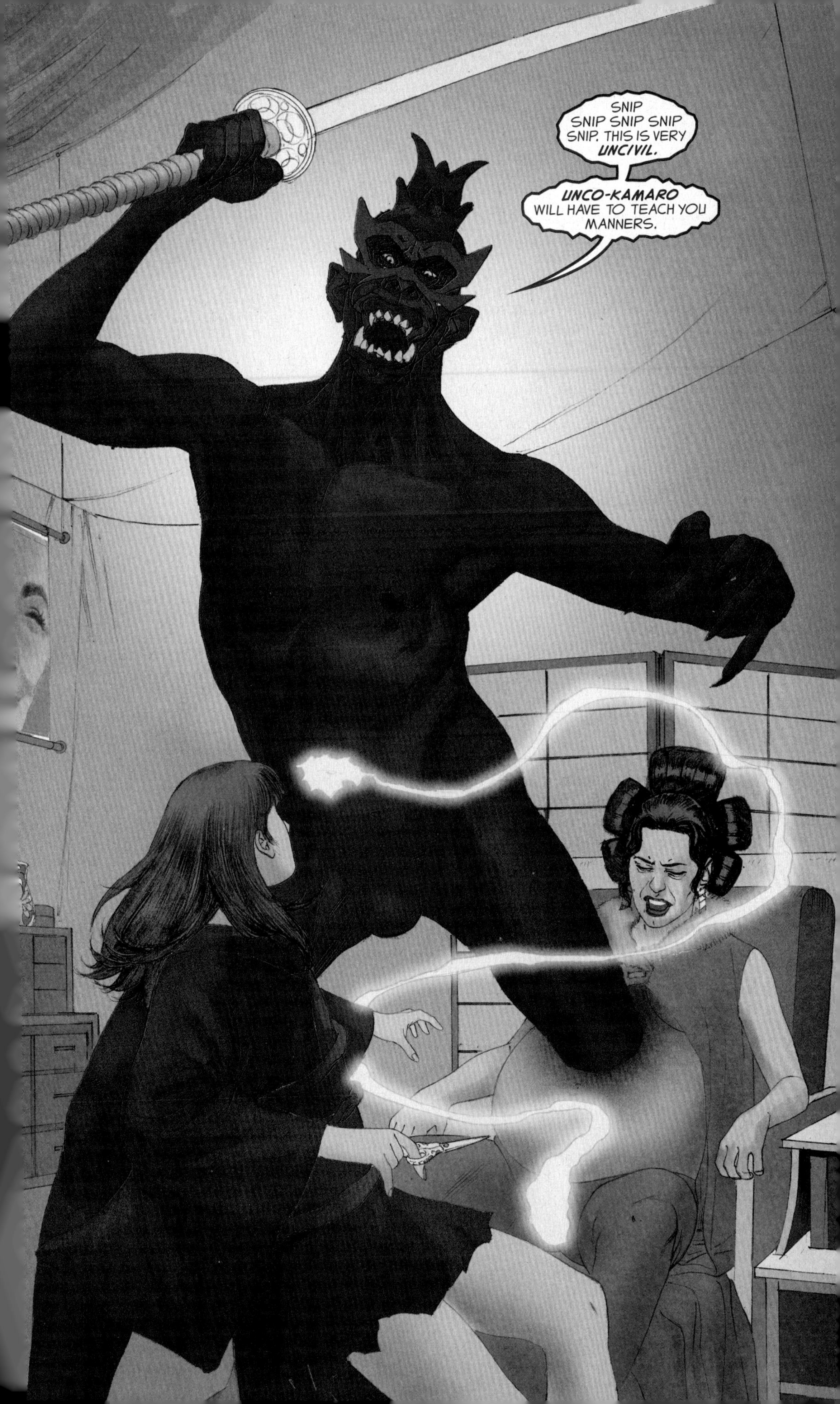
SNIP SNIP SNIP SNIP SNIP. THIS IS VERY UNCIVIL.
UNCO-KAMARO WILL HAVE TO TEACH YOU MANNERS.

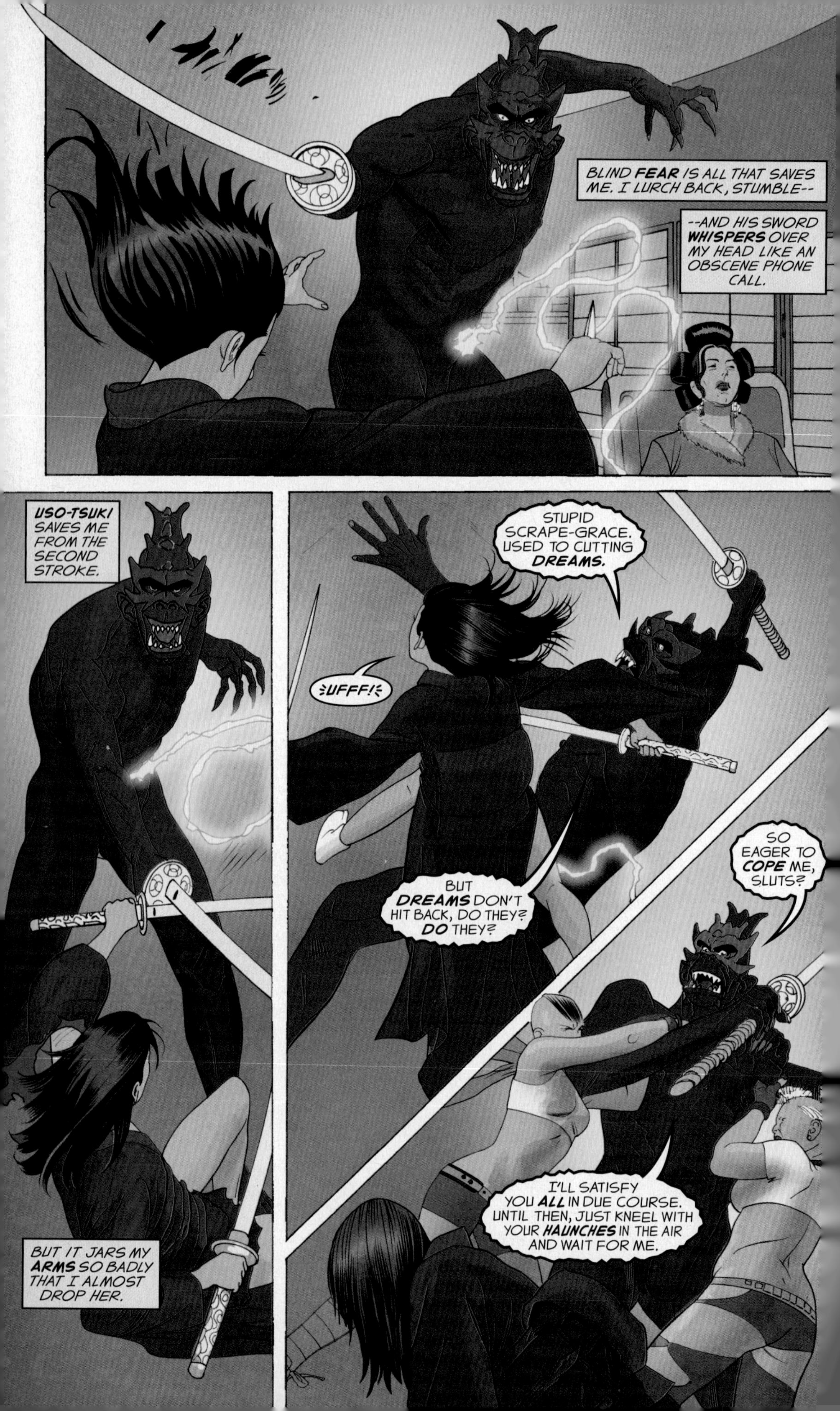
BLIND **FEAR** IS ALL THAT SAVES ME. I LURCH BACK, STUMBLE--
--AND HIS SWORD **WHISPERS** OVER MY HEAD LIKE AN OBSCENE PHONE CALL.
USO-TSUKI SAVES ME FROM THE SECOND STROKE.
BUT IT JARS MY **ARMS** SO BADLY THAT I ALMOST DROP HER.
STUPID SCRAPE-GRACE. USED TO CUTTING **DREAMS.**
UFFF!
BUT **DREAMS** DON'T HIT BACK, DO THEY? **DO** THEY?
SO EAGER TO **COPE** ME, SLUTS?
I'LL SATISFY YOU **ALL** IN DUE COURSE. UNTIL THEN, JUST KNEEL WITH YOUR **HAUNCHES** IN THE AIR AND WAIT FOR ME.

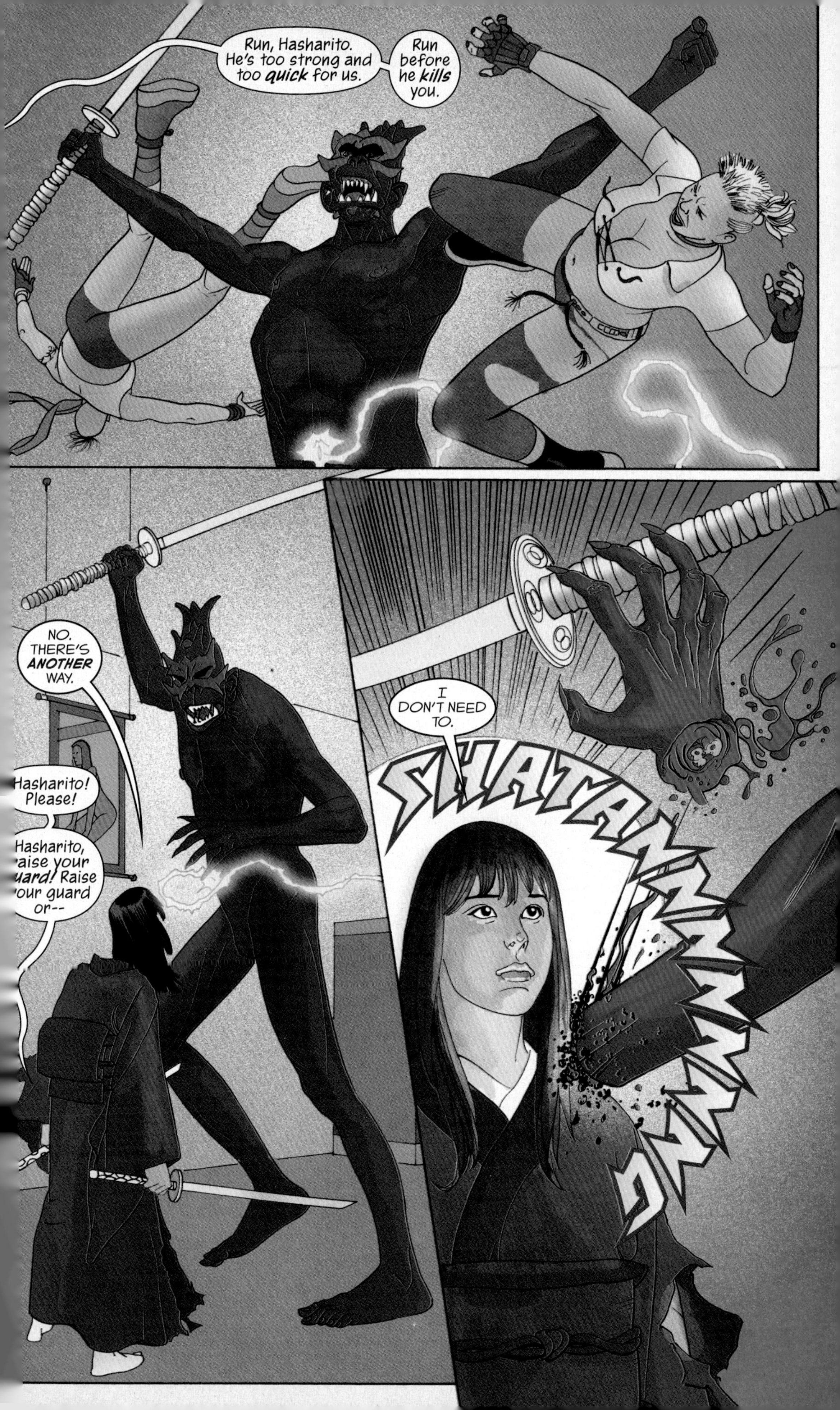

Run, Hasharito. He's too strong and too *quick* for us.
Run before he *kills* you.
NO. THERE'S *ANOTHER* WAY.
Hasharito! Please!
Hasharito, raise your guard! Raise your guard or--
I DON'T NEED TO.
SHATANNNNNG

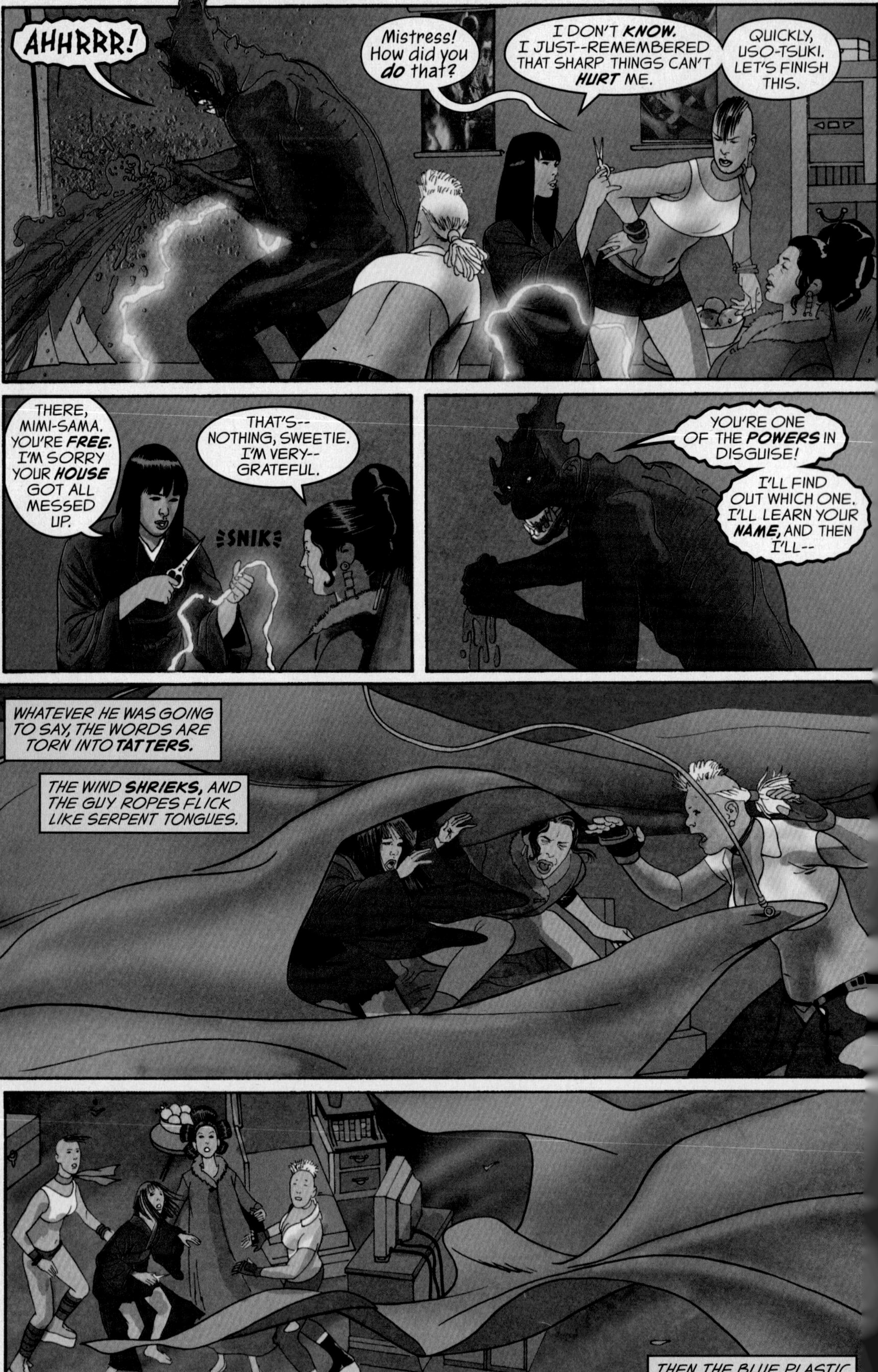

AHHRRR!
Mistress! How did you do that?
I DON'T KNOW. I JUST--REMEMBERED THAT SHARP THINGS CAN'T HURT ME.
QUICKLY, USO-TSUKI. LET'S FINISH THIS.
THERE, MIMI-SAMA. YOU'RE FREE. I'M SORRY YOUR HOUSE GOT ALL MESSED UP.
SNIK
THAT'S-- NOTHING, SWEETIE. I'M VERY-- GRATEFUL.
YOU'RE ONE OF THE POWERS IN DISGUISE!
I'LL FIND OUT WHICH ONE. I'LL LEARN YOUR NAME, AND THEN I'LL--
WHATEVER HE WAS GOING TO SAY, THE WORDS ARE TORN INTO TATTERS.
THE WIND SHRIEKS, AND THE GUY ROPES FLICK LIKE SERPENT TONGUES.
THEN THE BLUE PLASTIC SHEETS TAKE FLIGHT, LIKE TERRIFIED BIRDS--

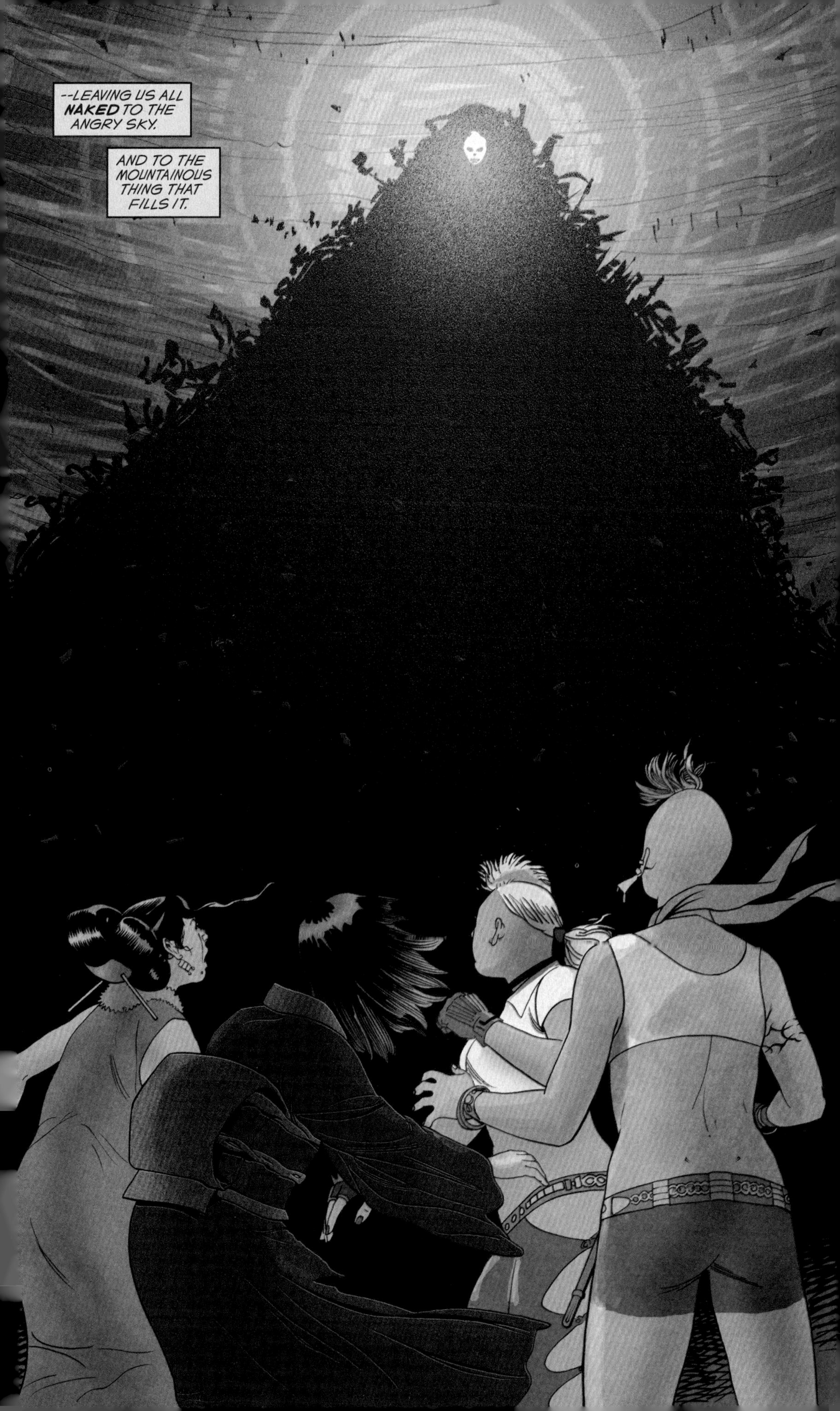
--LEAVING US ALL NAKED TO THE ANGRY SKY.
AND TO THE MOUNTAINOUS THING THAT FILLS IT.

chapter four

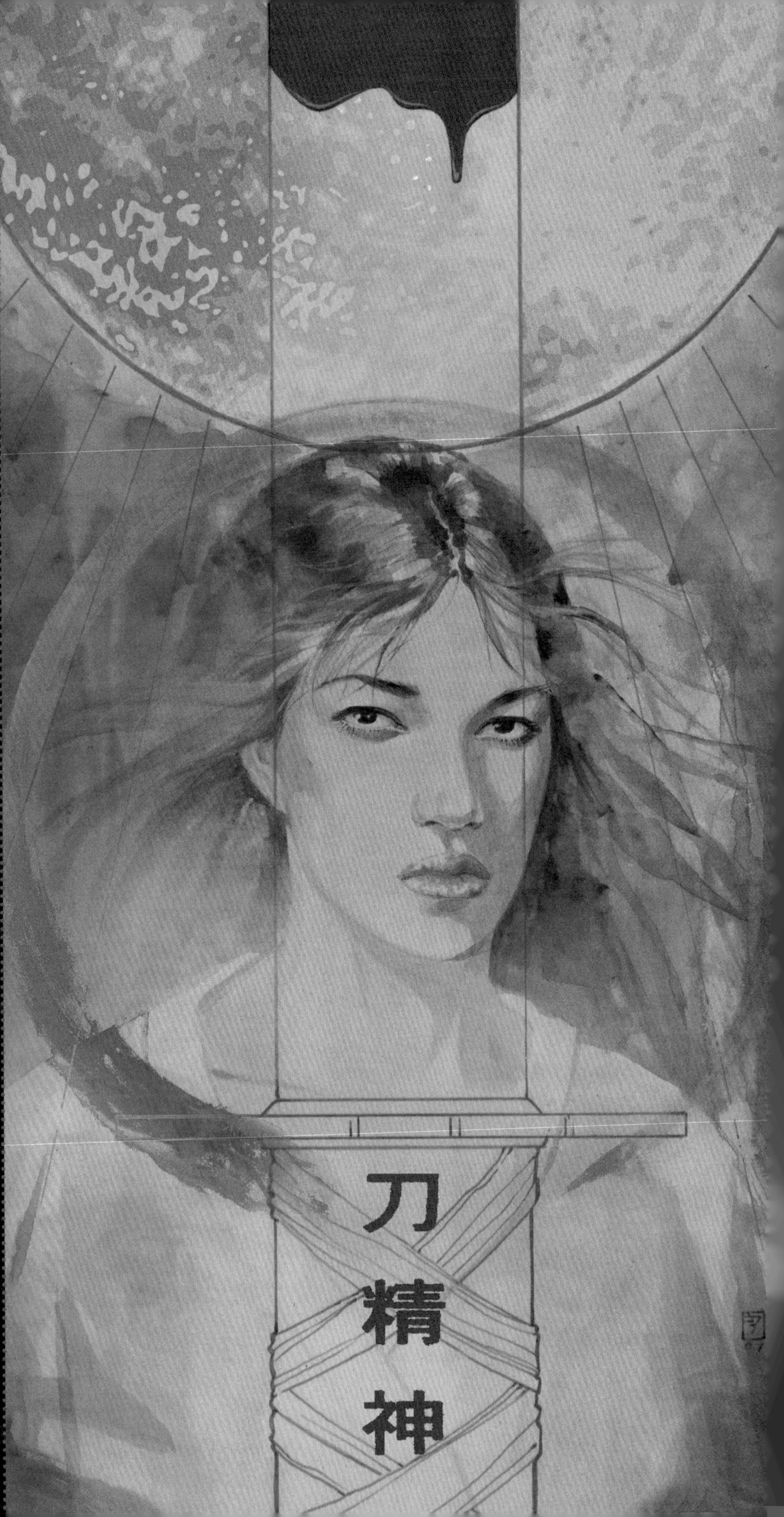
刀精神

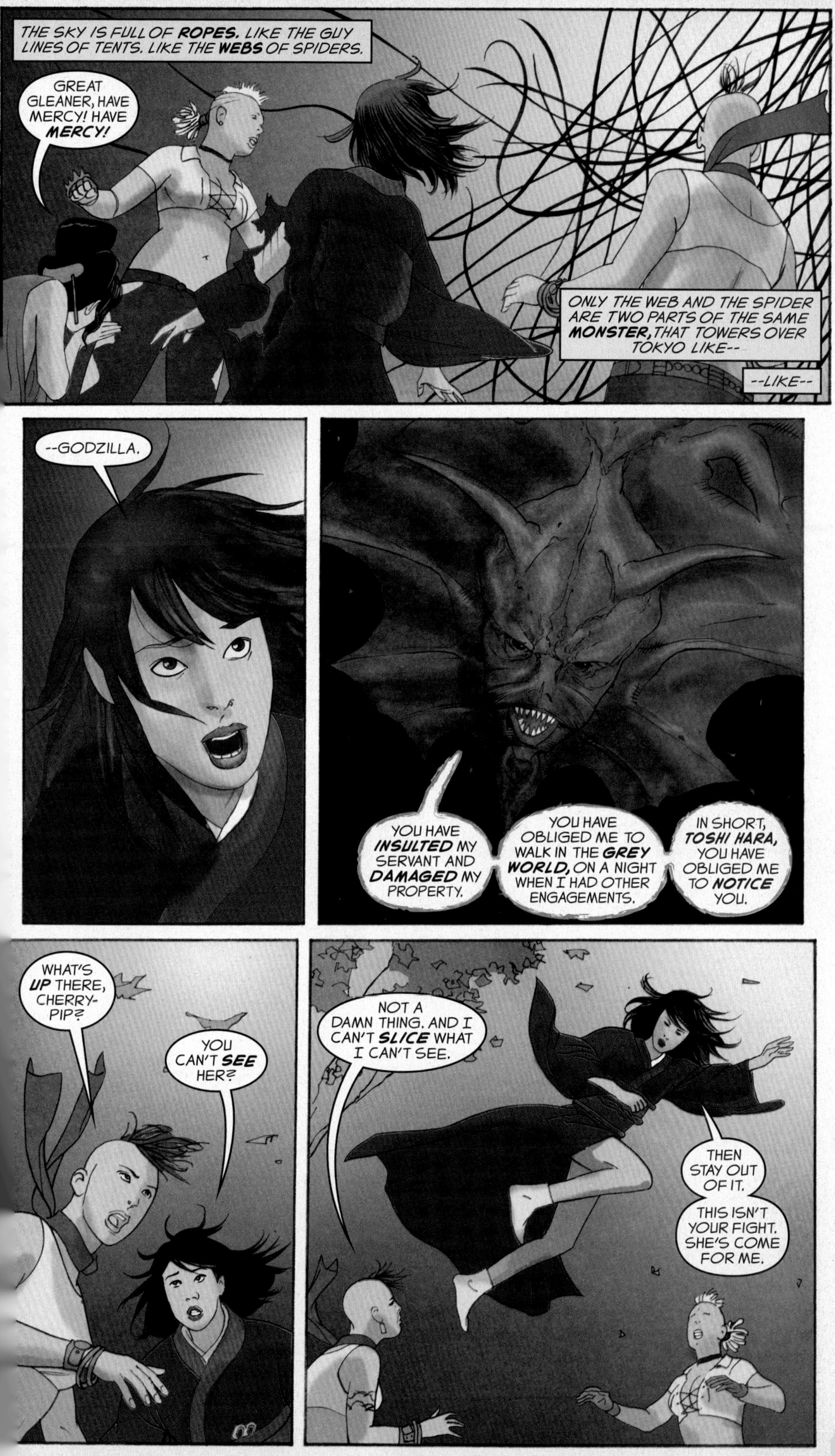
THE SKY IS FULL OF ROPES. LIKE THE GUY LINES OF TENTS. LIKE THE WEBS OF SPIDERS.
GREAT GLEANER, HAVE MERCY! HAVE MERCY!
ONLY THE WEB AND THE SPIDER ARE TWO PARTS OF THE SAME MONSTER, THAT TOWERS OVER TOKYO LIKE--
--LIKE--
--GODZILLA.
YOU HAVE INSULTED MY SERVANT AND DAMAGED MY PROPERTY.
YOU HAVE OBLIGED ME TO WALK IN THE GREY WORLD, ON A NIGHT WHEN I HAD OTHER ENGAGEMENTS.
IN SHORT, TOSHI HARA, YOU HAVE OBLIGED ME TO NOTICE YOU.
WHAT'S UP THERE, CHERRY-PIP?
YOU CAN'T SEE HER?
NOT A DAMN THING. AND I CAN'T SLICE WHAT I CAN'T SEE.
THEN STAY OUT OF IT.
THIS ISN'T YOUR FIGHT. SHE'S COME FOR ME.

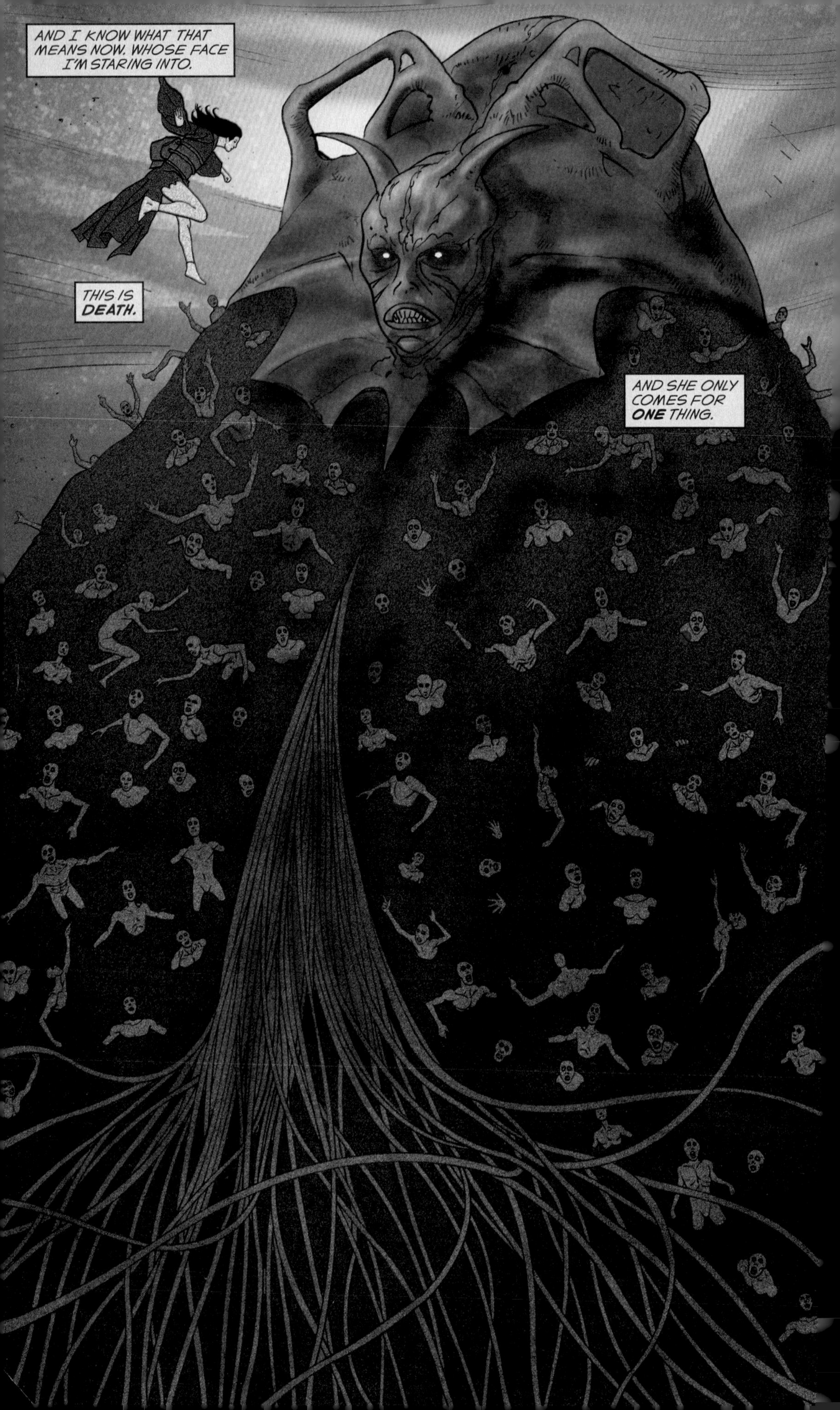
AND I KNOW WHAT THAT MEANS NOW. WHOSE FACE I'M STARING INTO.
THIS IS **DEATH.**
AND SHE ONLY COMES FOR **ONE** THING.

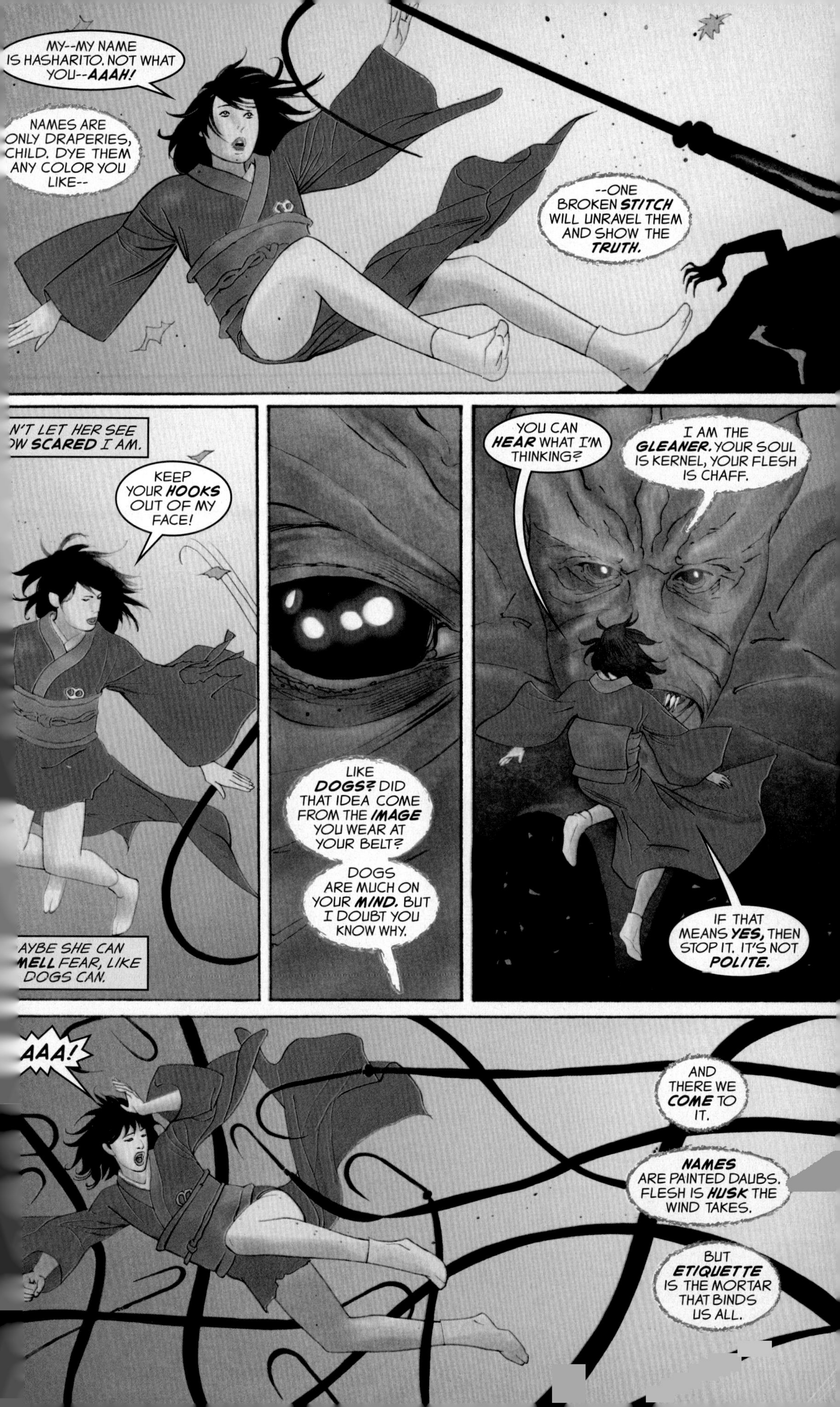
MY--MY NAME IS HASHARITO. NOT WHAT YOU--AAAH!
NAMES ARE ONLY DRAPERIES, CHILD. DYE THEM ANY COLOR YOU LIKE--
--ONE BROKEN STITCH WILL UNRAVEL THEM AND SHOW THE TRUTH.
N'T LET HER SEE OW SCARED I AM.
KEEP YOUR HOOKS OUT OF MY FACE!
AYBE SHE CAN MELL FEAR, LIKE DOGS CAN.
LIKE DOGS? DID THAT IDEA COME FROM THE IMAGE YOU WEAR AT YOUR BELT?
DOGS ARE MUCH ON YOUR MIND. BUT I DOUBT YOU KNOW WHY.
YOU CAN HEAR WHAT I'M THINKING?
I AM THE GLEANER. YOUR SOUL IS KERNEL, YOUR FLESH IS CHAFF.
IF THAT MEANS YES, THEN STOP IT. IT'S NOT POLITE.
AAA!
AND THERE WE COME TO IT.
NAMES ARE PAINTED DAUBS. FLESH IS HUSK THE WIND TAKES.
BUT ETIQUETTE IS THE MORTAR THAT BINDS US ALL.

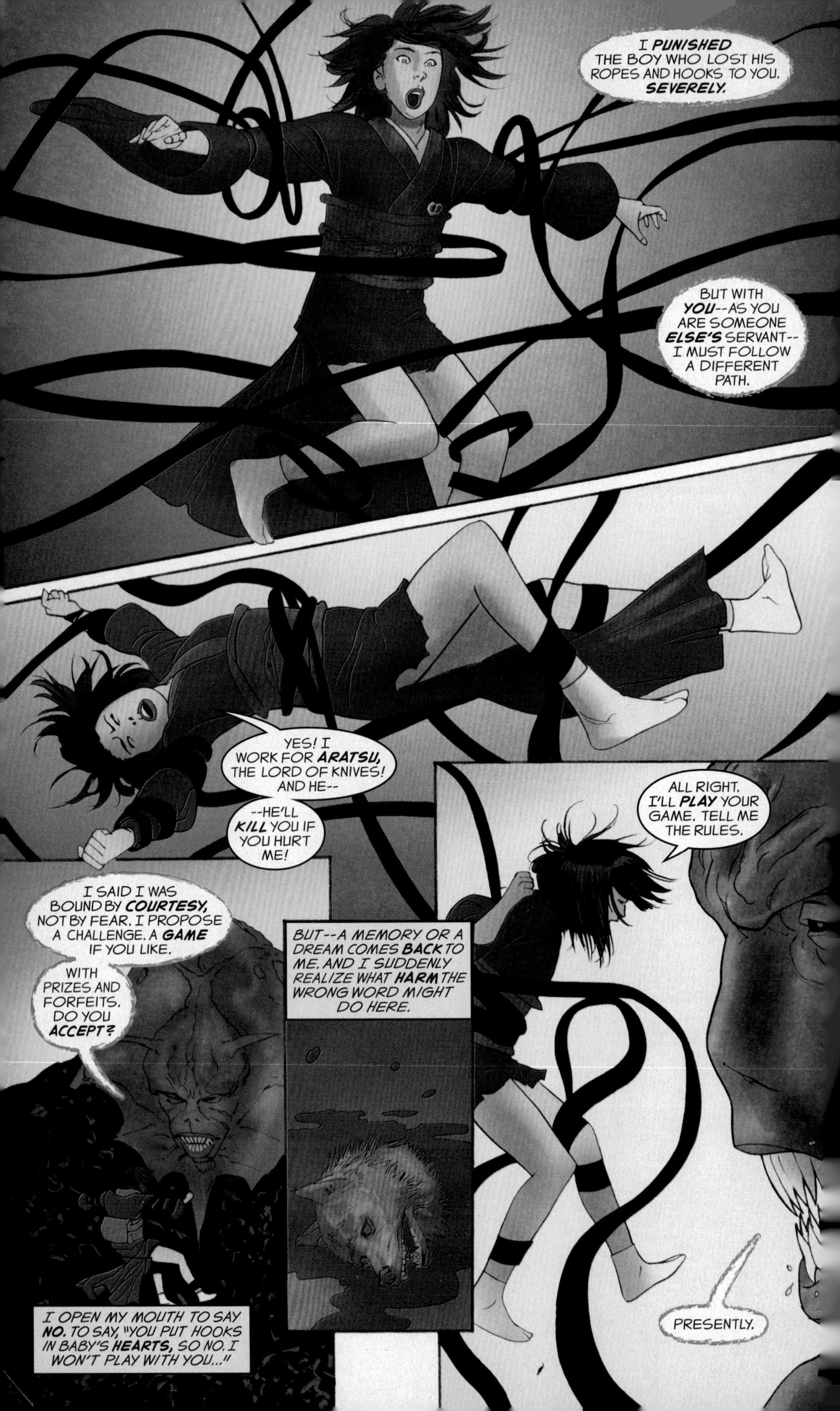
I PUNISHED THE BOY WHO LOST HIS ROPES AND HOOKS TO YOU. SEVERELY.
BUT WITH YOU--AS YOU ARE SOMEONE ELSE'S SERVANT--I MUST FOLLOW A DIFFERENT PATH.
YES! I WORK FOR ARATSU, THE LORD OF KNIVES! AND HE--
--HE'LL KILL YOU IF YOU HURT ME!
I SAID I WAS BOUND BY COURTESY, NOT BY FEAR. I PROPOSE A CHALLENGE. A GAME IF YOU LIKE.
WITH PRIZES AND FORFEITS. DO YOU ACCEPT?
I OPEN MY MOUTH TO SAY NO. TO SAY, "YOU PUT HOOKS IN BABY'S HEARTS, SO NO. I WON'T PLAY WITH YOU..."
BUT--A MEMORY OR A DREAM COMES BACK TO ME. AND I SUDDENLY REALIZE WHAT HARM THE WRONG WORD MIGHT DO HERE.
ALL RIGHT. I'LL PLAY YOUR GAME. TELL ME THE RULES.
PRESENTLY.

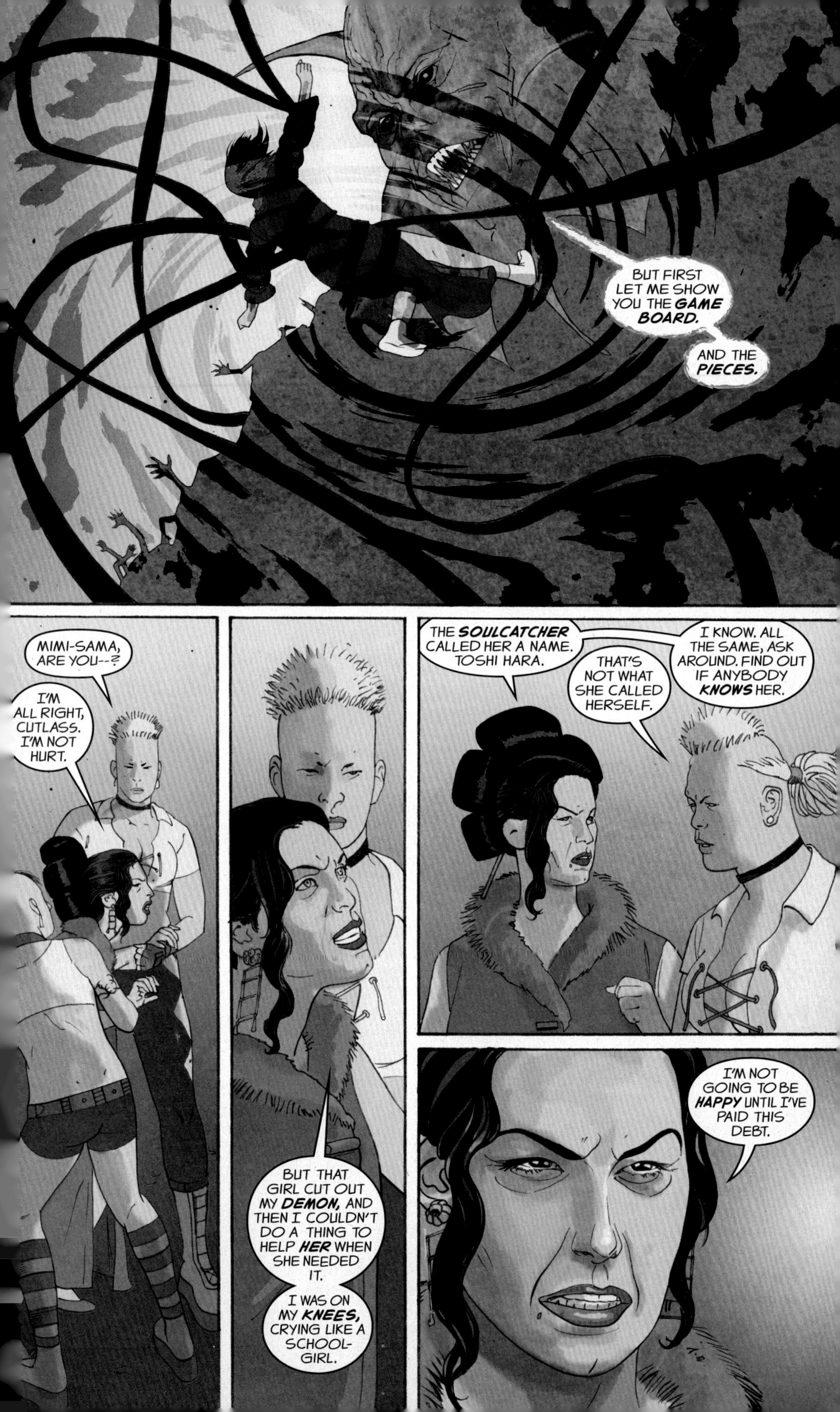
BUT FIRST LET ME SHOW YOU THE GAME BOARD.
AND THE PIECES.
MIMI-SAMA, ARE YOU--?
I'M ALL RIGHT, CUTLASS. I'M NOT HURT.
BUT THAT GIRL CUT OUT MY DEMON, AND THEN I COULDN'T DO A THING TO HELP HER WHEN SHE NEEDED IT.
I WAS ON MY KNEES, CRYING LIKE A SCHOOL-GIRL.
THE SOULCATCHER CALLED HER A NAME. TOSHI HARA.
THAT'S NOT WHAT SHE CALLED HERSELF.
I KNOW. ALL THE SAME, ASK AROUND. FIND OUT IF ANYBODY KNOWS HER.
I'M NOT GOING TO BE HAPPY UNTIL I'VE PAID THIS DEBT.

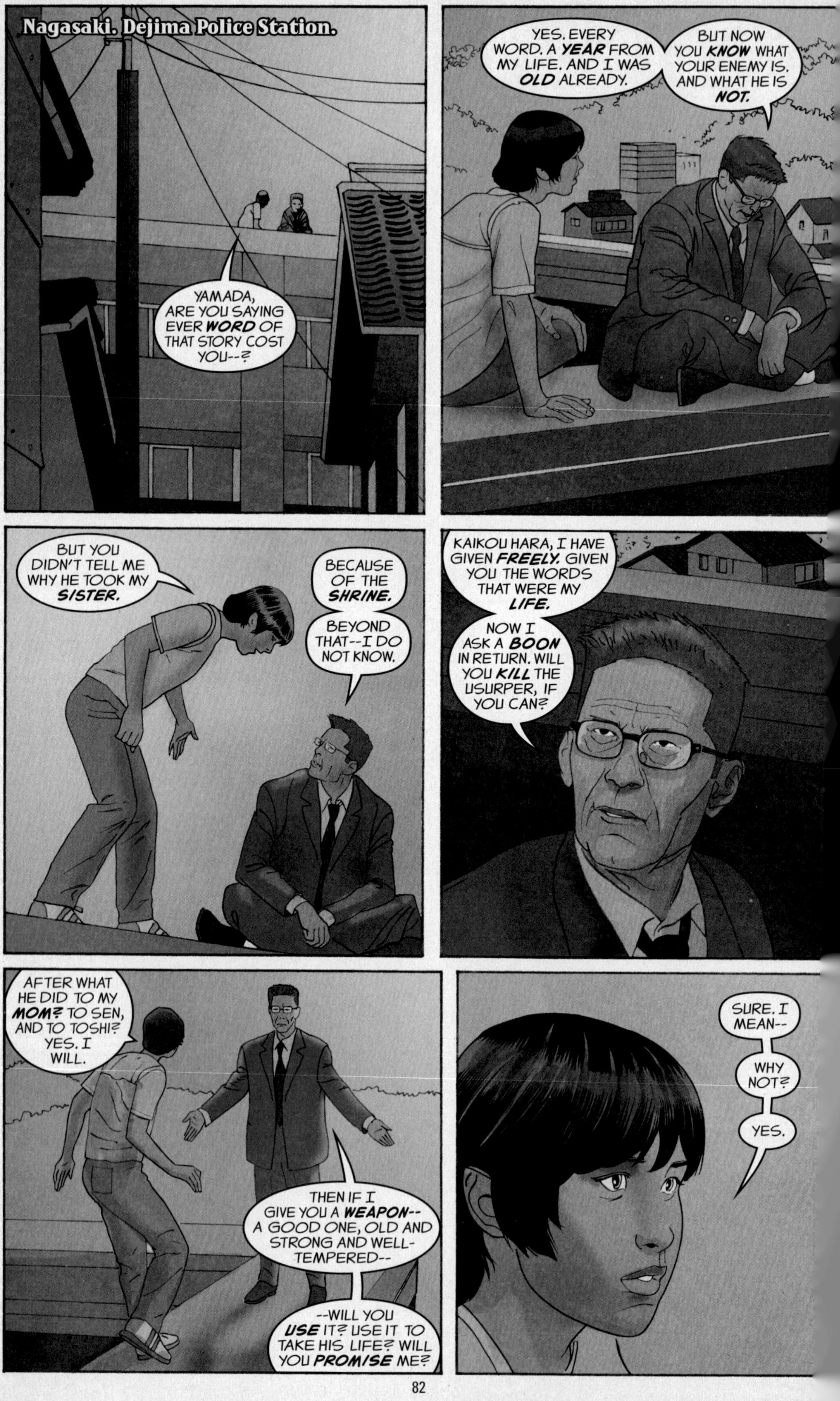
Nagasaki. Dejima Police Station.
YAMADA, ARE YOU SAYING EVER WORD OF THAT STORY COST YOU--?
YES. EVERY WORD. A YEAR FROM MY LIFE. AND I WAS OLD ALREADY.
BUT NOW YOU KNOW WHAT YOUR ENEMY IS. AND WHAT HE IS NOT.
BUT YOU DIDN'T TELL ME WHY HE TOOK MY SISTER.
BECAUSE OF THE SHRINE.
BEYOND THAT--I DO NOT KNOW.
KAIKOU HARA, I HAVE GIVEN FREELY. GIVEN YOU THE WORDS THAT WERE MY LIFE.
NOW I ASK A BOON IN RETURN. WILL YOU KILL THE USURPER, IF YOU CAN?
AFTER WHAT HE DID TO MY MOM? TO SEN, AND TO TOSHI? YES. I WILL.
THEN IF I GIVE YOU A WEAPON-- A GOOD ONE, OLD AND STRONG AND WELL-TEMPERED--
--WILL YOU USE IT? USE IT TO TAKE HIS LIFE? WILL YOU PROMISE ME?
SURE. I MEAN--
WHY NOT?
YES.

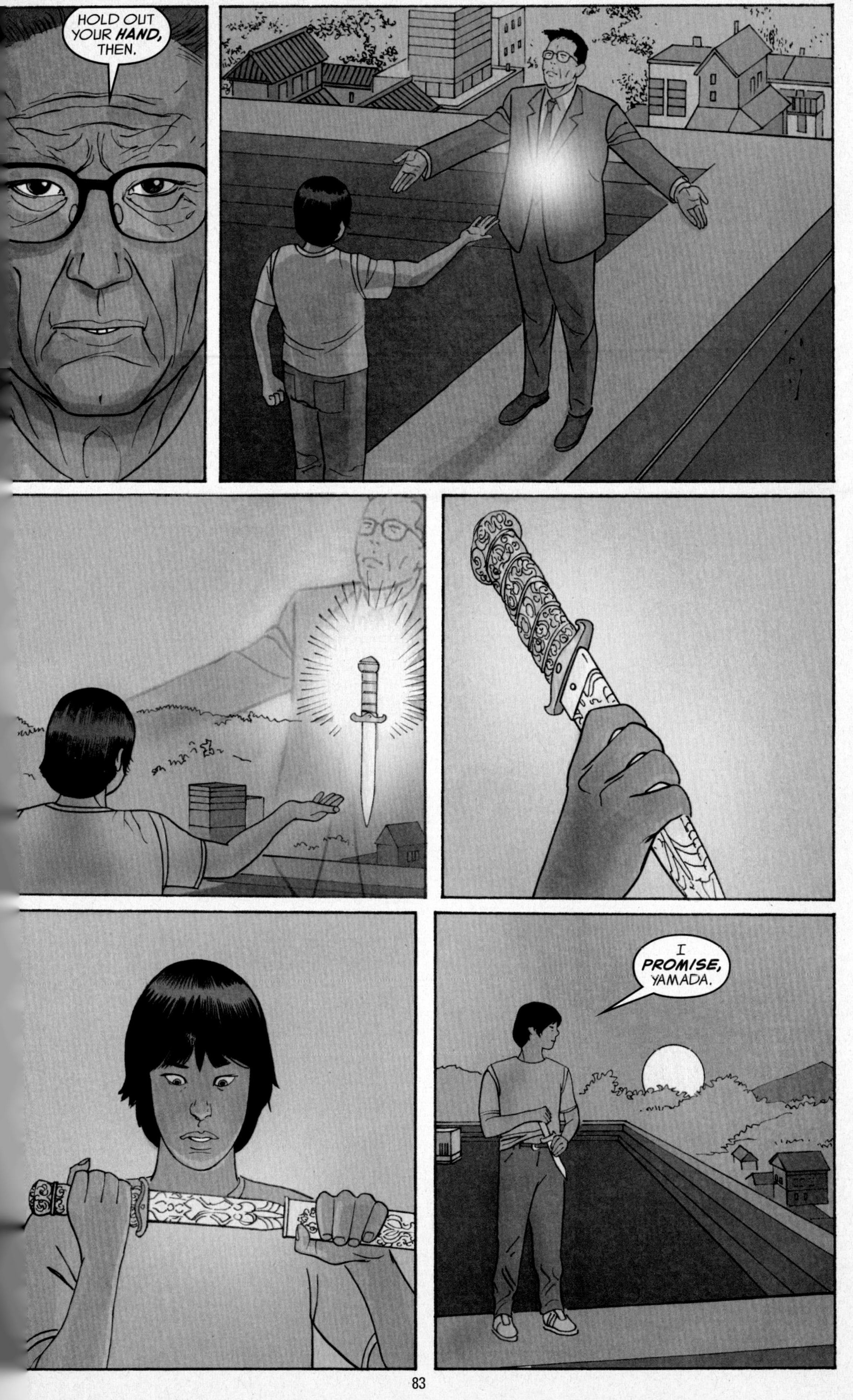
HOLD OUT YOUR **HAND,** THEN.
I **PROMISE,** YAMADA.

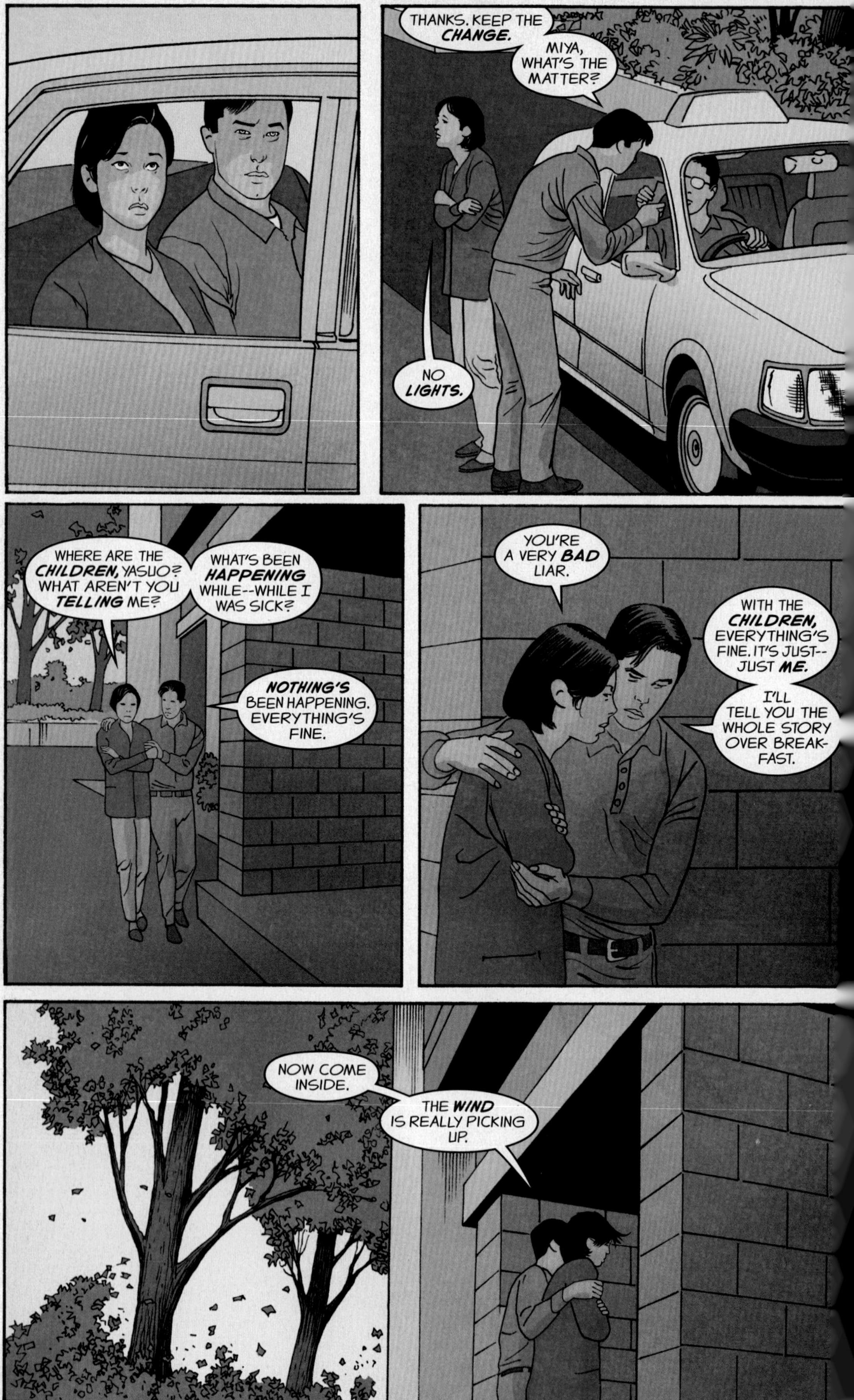
THANKS. KEEP THE CHANGE.
MIYA, WHAT'S THE MATTER?
NO LIGHTS.
WHERE ARE THE CHILDREN, YASUO? WHAT AREN'T YOU TELLING ME?
WHAT'S BEEN HAPPENING WHILE--WHILE I WAS SICK?
NOTHING'S BEEN HAPPENING. EVERYTHING'S FINE.
YOU'RE A VERY BAD LIAR.
WITH THE CHILDREN, EVERYTHING'S FINE. IT'S JUST--JUST ME.
I'LL TELL YOU THE WHOLE STORY OVER BREAK-FAST.
NOW COME INSIDE.
THE WIND IS REALLY PICKING UP.

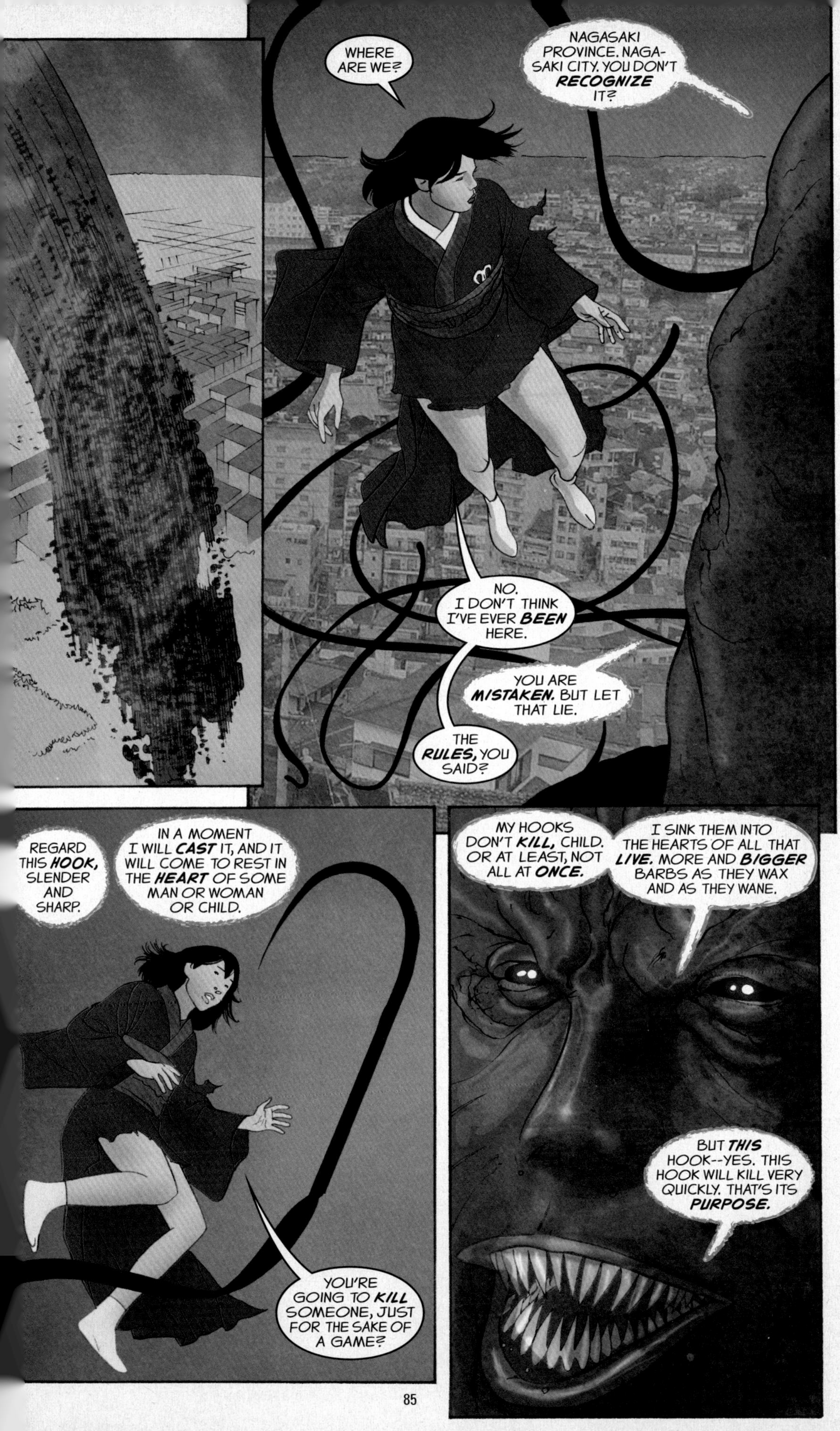
WHERE ARE WE?
NAGASAKI PROVINCE. NAGA-SAKI CITY. YOU DON'T RECOGNIZE IT?
NO. I DON'T THINK I'VE EVER BEEN HERE.
YOU ARE MISTAKEN. BUT LET THAT LIE.
THE RULES, YOU SAID?
REGARD THIS HOOK, SLENDER AND SHARP.
IN A MOMENT I WILL CAST IT, AND IT WILL COME TO REST IN THE HEART OF SOME MAN OR WOMAN OR CHILD.
YOU'RE GOING TO KILL SOMEONE, JUST FOR THE SAKE OF A GAME?
MY HOOKS DON'T KILL, CHILD. OR AT LEAST, NOT ALL AT ONCE.
I SINK THEM INTO THE HEARTS OF ALL THAT LIVE. MORE AND BIGGER BARBS AS THEY WAX AND AS THEY WANE.
BUT THIS HOOK--YES. THIS HOOK WILL KILL VERY QUICKLY. THAT'S ITS PURPOSE.

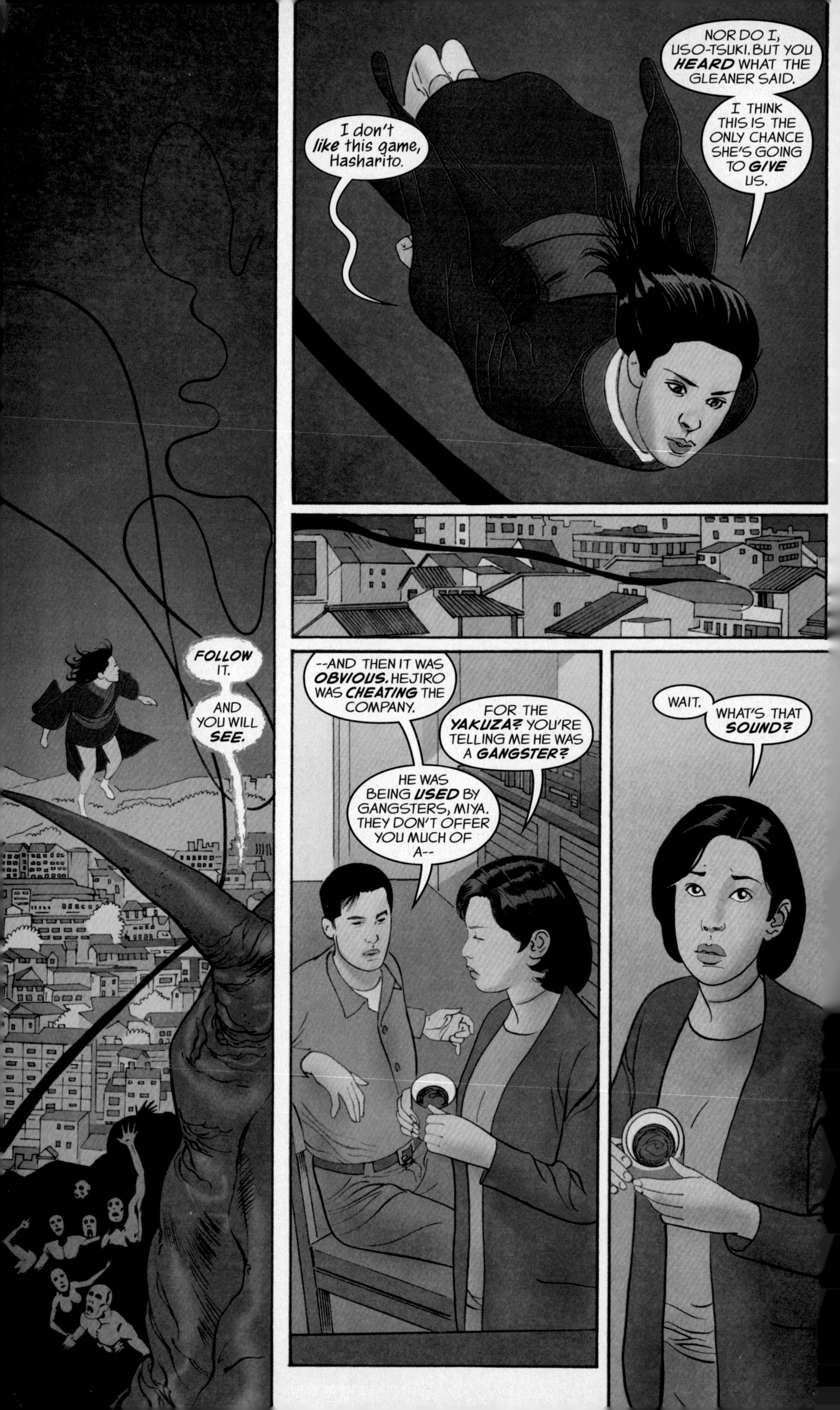
FOLLOW IT.
AND YOU WILL SEE.
I don't like this game, Hasharito.
NOR DO I, USO-TSUKI. BUT YOU HEARD WHAT THE GLEANER SAID.
I THINK THIS IS THE ONLY CHANCE SHE'S GOING TO GIVE US.
--AND THEN IT WAS OBVIOUS. HEJIRO WAS CHEATING THE COMPANY.
FOR THE YAKUZA? YOU'RE TELLING ME HE WAS A GANGSTER?
HE WAS BEING USED BY GANGSTERS, MIYA. THEY DON'T OFFER YOU MUCH OF A--
WAIT.
WHAT'S THAT SOUND?

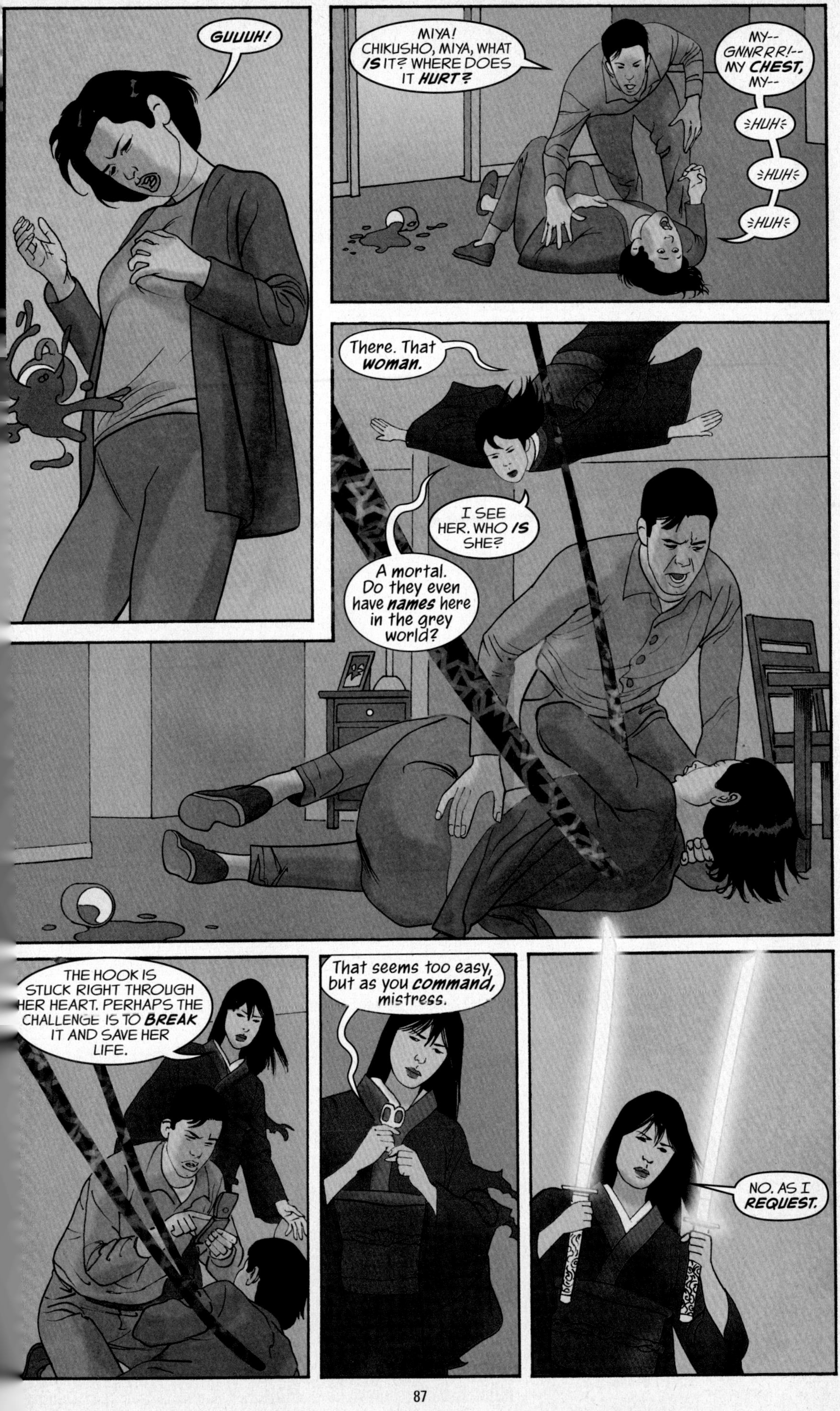
GUUUH!
MIYA! CHIKUSHO, MIYA, WHAT IS IT? WHERE DOES IT HURT?
MY-- GNNRRR!-- MY CHEST, MY--
HUH
HUH
HUH
There. That woman.
I SEE HER. WHO IS SHE?
A mortal. Do they even have names here in the grey world?
THE HOOK IS STUCK RIGHT THROUGH HER HEART. PERHAPS THE CHALLENGE IS TO BREAK IT AND SAVE HER LIFE.
That seems too easy, but as you command, mistress.
NO. AS I REQUEST.

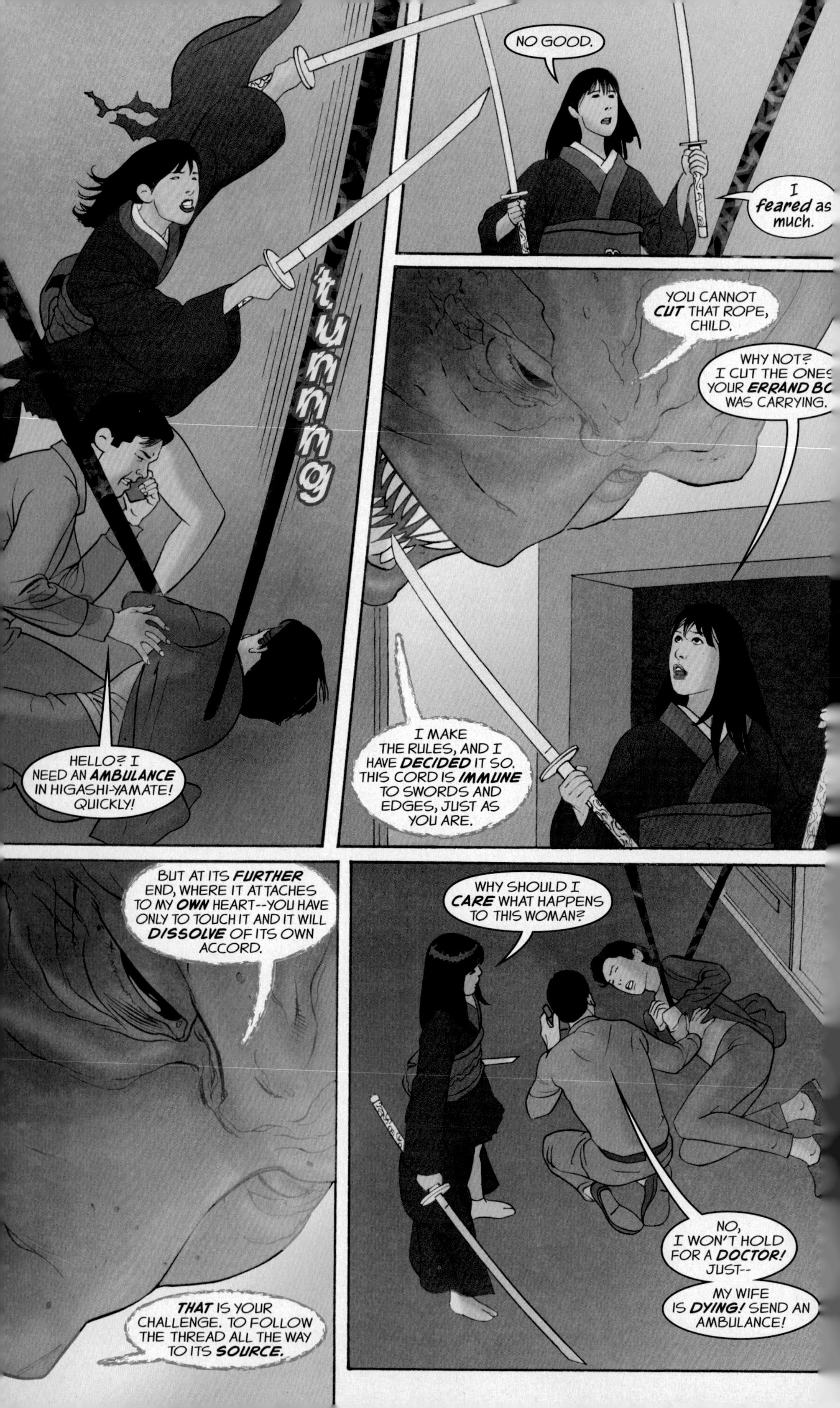

tunnng
NO GOOD.
I feared as much.
HELLO? I NEED AN AMBULANCE IN HIGASHI-YAMATE! QUICKLY!
YOU CANNOT CUT THAT ROPE, CHILD.
WHY NOT? I CUT THE ONES YOUR ERRAND BO WAS CARRYING.
I MAKE THE RULES, AND I HAVE DECIDED IT SO. THIS CORD IS IMMUNE TO SWORDS AND EDGES, JUST AS YOU ARE.
BUT AT ITS FURTHER END, WHERE IT ATTACHES TO MY OWN HEART--YOU HAVE ONLY TO TOUCH IT AND IT WILL DISSOLVE OF ITS OWN ACCORD.
THAT IS YOUR CHALLENGE. TO FOLLOW THE THREAD ALL THE WAY TO ITS SOURCE.
WHY SHOULD I CARE WHAT HAPPENS TO THIS WOMAN?
NO, I WON'T HOLD FOR A DOCTOR! JUST--
MY WIFE IS DYING! SEND AN AMBULANCE!

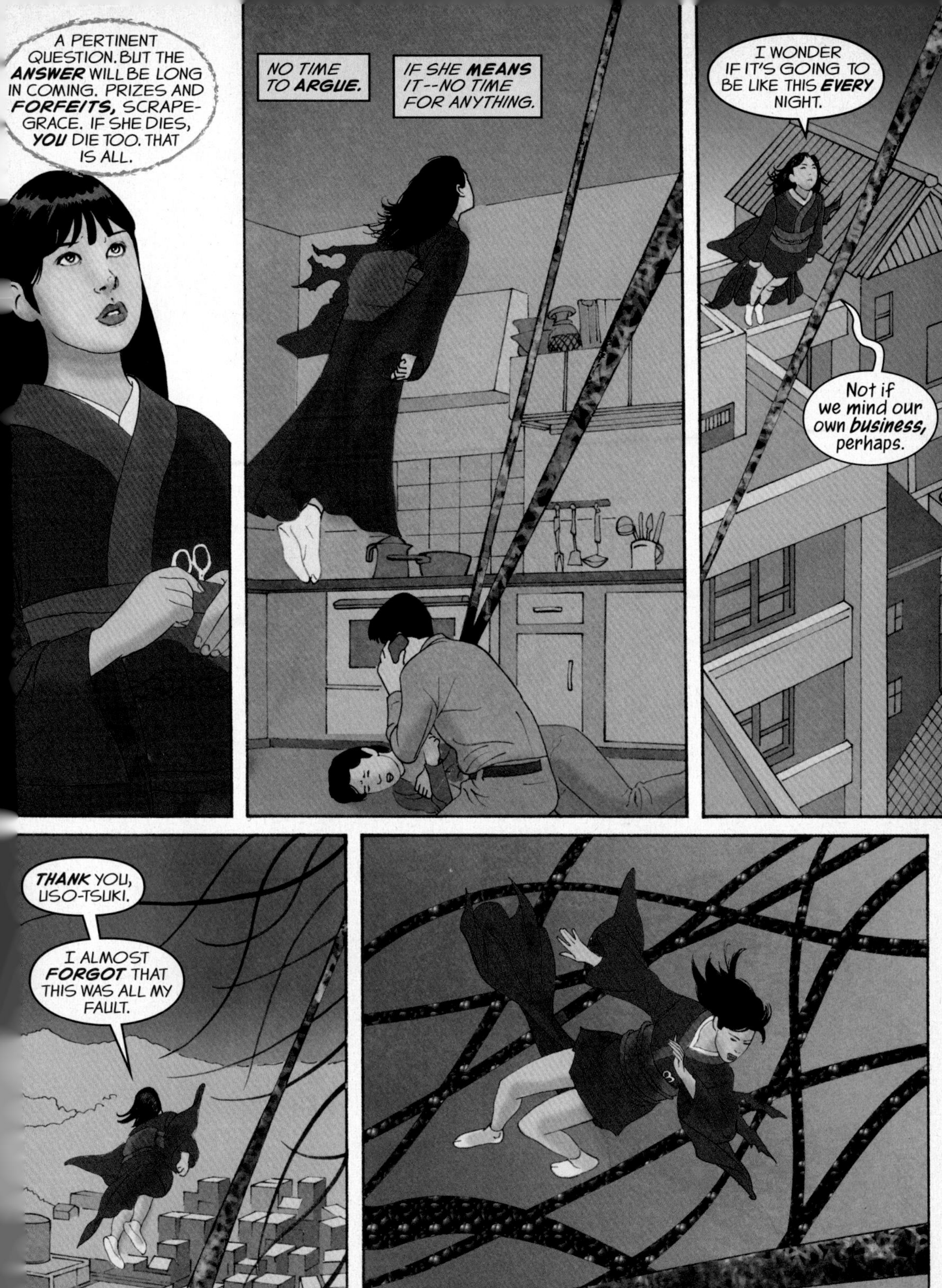
A PERTINENT QUESTION. BUT THE ANSWER WILL BE LONG IN COMING. PRIZES AND FORFEITS, SCRAPE-GRACE. IF SHE DIES, YOU DIE TOO. THAT IS ALL.
NO TIME TO ARGUE.
IF SHE MEANS IT--NO TIME FOR ANYTHING.
I WONDER IF IT'S GOING TO BE LIKE THIS EVERY NIGHT.
Not if we mind our own business, perhaps.
THANK YOU, USO-TSUKI.
I ALMOST FORGOT THAT THIS WAS ALL MY FAULT.
IT SEEMS EASY ENOUGH, ALL THE SAME.
THE OTHER THREADS MOSTLY HAVE DIFFERENT TEXTURES OR THICKNESSES. YOU'VE ONLY GOT TO KEEP YOUR EYES OPEN.

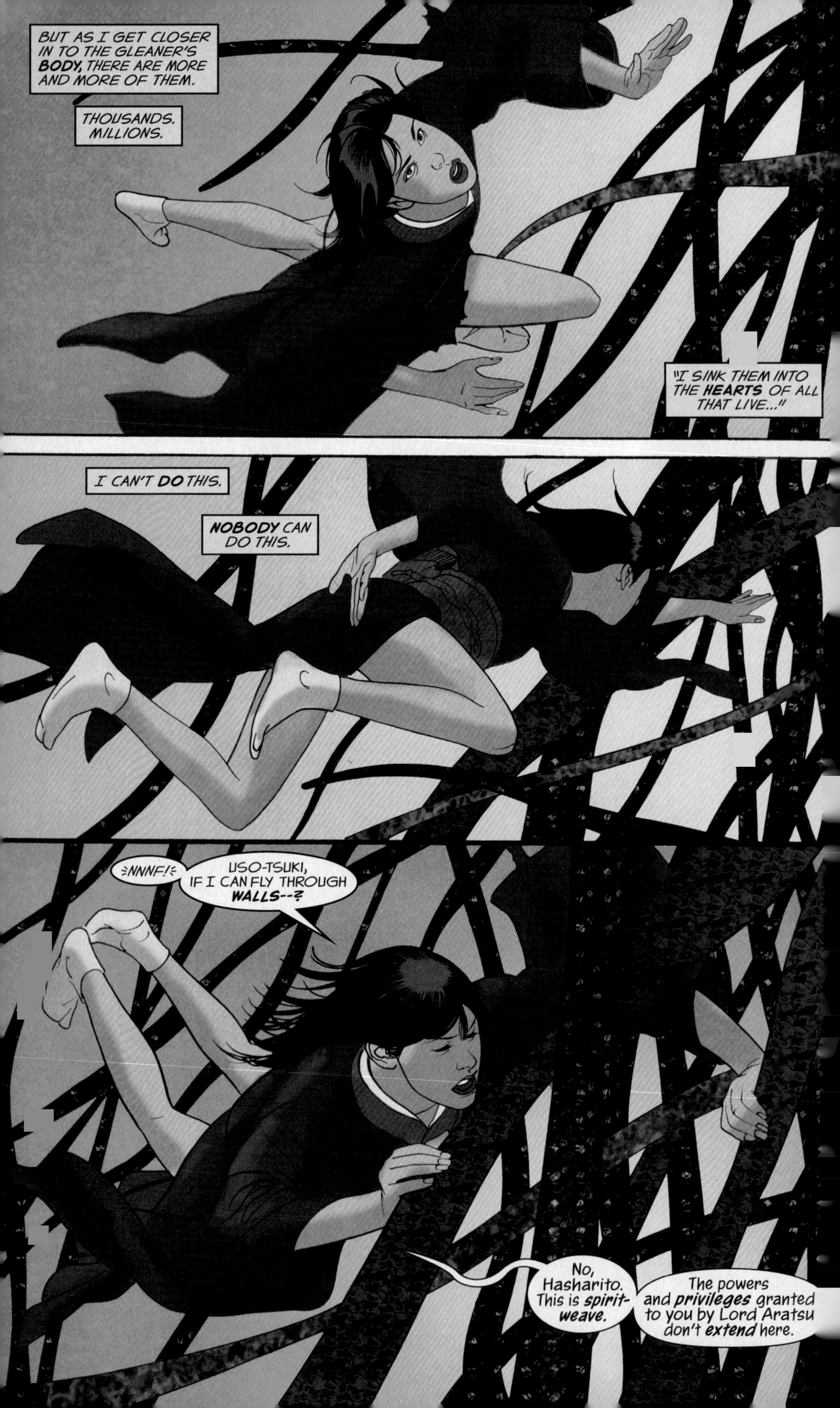
BUT AS I GET CLOSER IN TO THE GLEANER'S **BODY,** THERE ARE MORE AND MORE OF THEM.
THOUSANDS. MILLIONS.
"I SINK THEM INTO THE **HEARTS** OF ALL THAT LIVE..."
I CAN'T **DO** THIS.
NOBODY CAN DO THIS.
NNNF!
USO-TSUKI, IF I CAN FLY THROUGH **WALLS--?**
No, Hasharito. This is *spirit-weave.*
The powers and *privileges* granted to you by Lord Aratsu don't *extend* here.

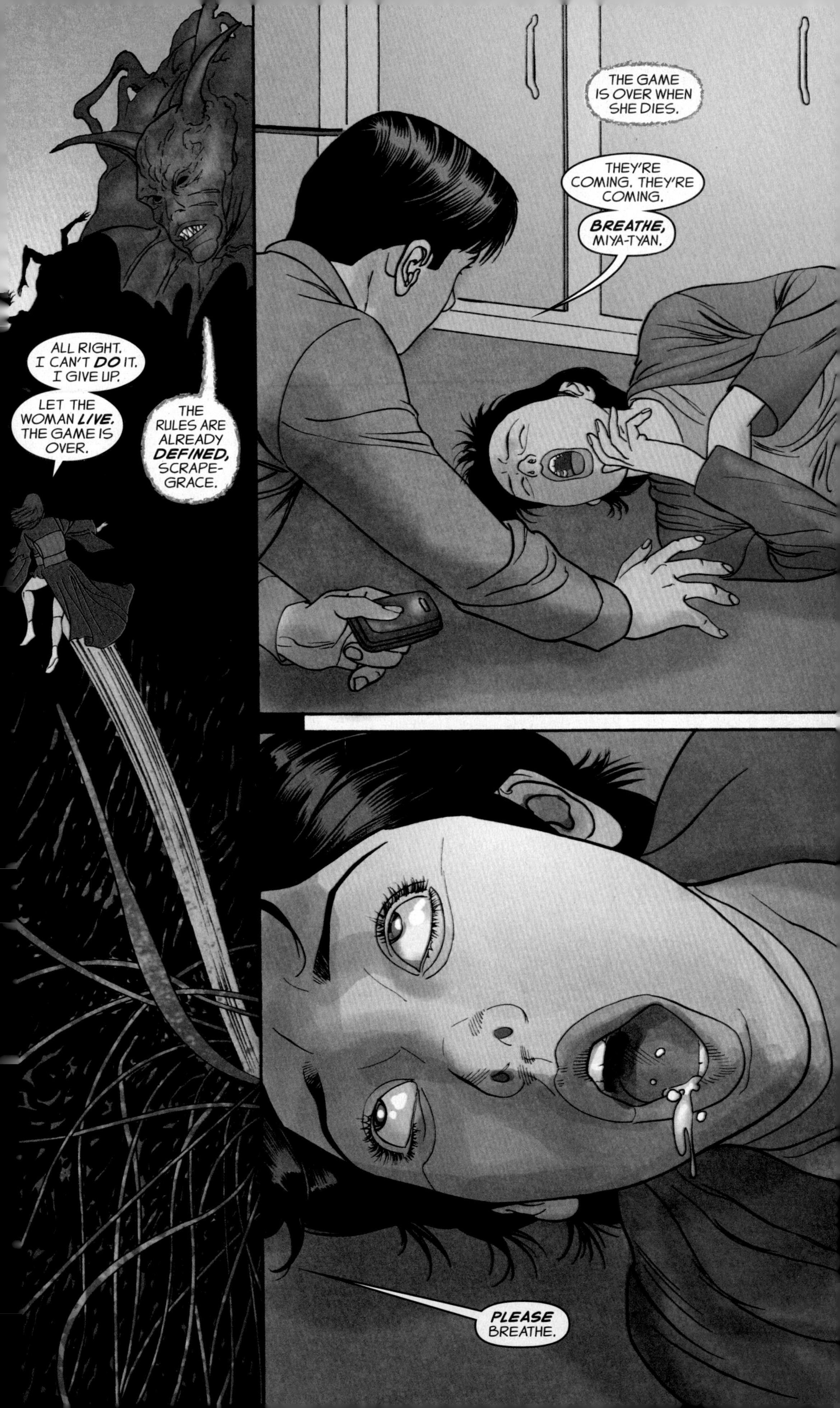
ALL RIGHT. I CAN'T **DO** IT. I GIVE UP.
LET THE WOMAN **LIVE.** THE GAME IS OVER.
THE RULES ARE ALREADY **DEFINED,** SCRAPE-GRACE.
THE GAME IS OVER WHEN SHE DIES.
THEY'RE COMING. THEY'RE COMING.
BREATHE, MIYA-TYAN.
PLEASE BREATHE.

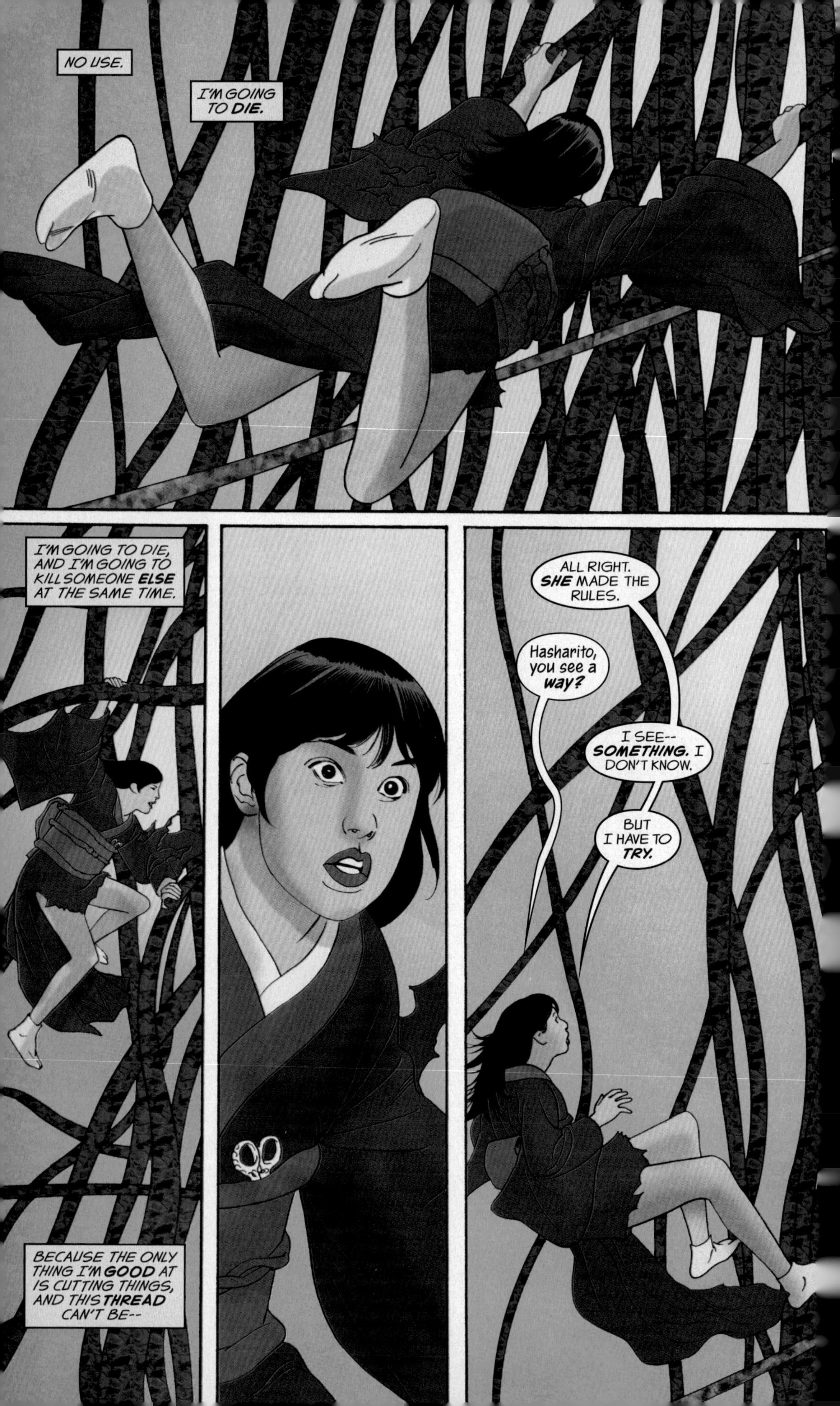
NO USE.
I'M GOING TO DIE.
I'M GOING TO DIE, AND I'M GOING TO KILL SOMEONE ELSE AT THE SAME TIME.
BECAUSE THE ONLY THING I'M GOOD AT IS CUTTING THINGS, AND THIS THREAD CAN'T BE--
ALL RIGHT. SHE MADE THE RULES.
Hasharito, you see a way?
I SEE-- SOMETHING. I DON'T KNOW.
BUT I HAVE TO TRY.

THIS IS **STUPID.** GAMBLING EVERY-THING ON--WHAT?

AN **ACCIDENT.** SOMETHING I DID ONLY ONCE, AND THEN WITHOUT MEANING TO.

BUT IT HAPPENED WHEN I WAS **ANGRY.**

SO I **REMEMBER** IT. AND I TRY TO BE ANGRY **NOW.**

NOTHING.

I THINK ABOUT **KISHIMO-JIN,** WHO I HATE.

AND ABOUT ALL THE **HUMILIATIONS** AND THE SNEAKY, DEADLY LITTLE **TRICKS** SHE PLAYED ON ME.

STILL NOTHING COMES.

WHAT ABOUT THE MOMENT WHEN I WAS **BORN?**

IN ARATSU'S **CHAMBERS.**

MY CHEST **BURNING** WHERE HIS SWORD HAD JUST CUT AWAY MY PAST AND MY **FUTURE.**

OH YES! OH YES, NOW--

NOW IT BUILDS IN E LIKE THE STE OF MY WN BLOOD.

FEEDING ON **ECHOES** OF LONG-DEAD MOMENTS.

DESPERATE TO BE SPOKEN.

CLAWING ITS WAY INTO THE **WORLD**--

93

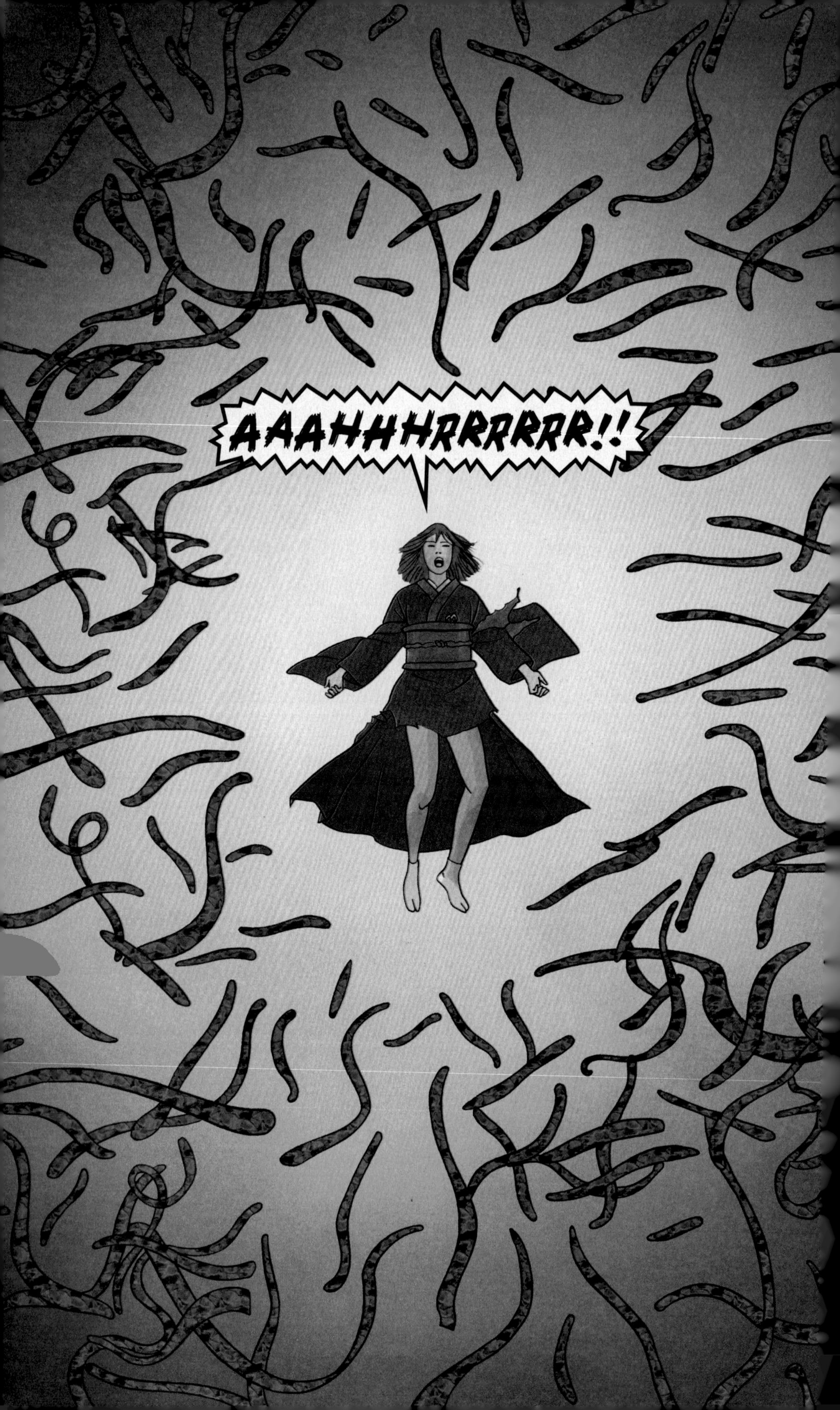
AAAHHHRRRRRR!!

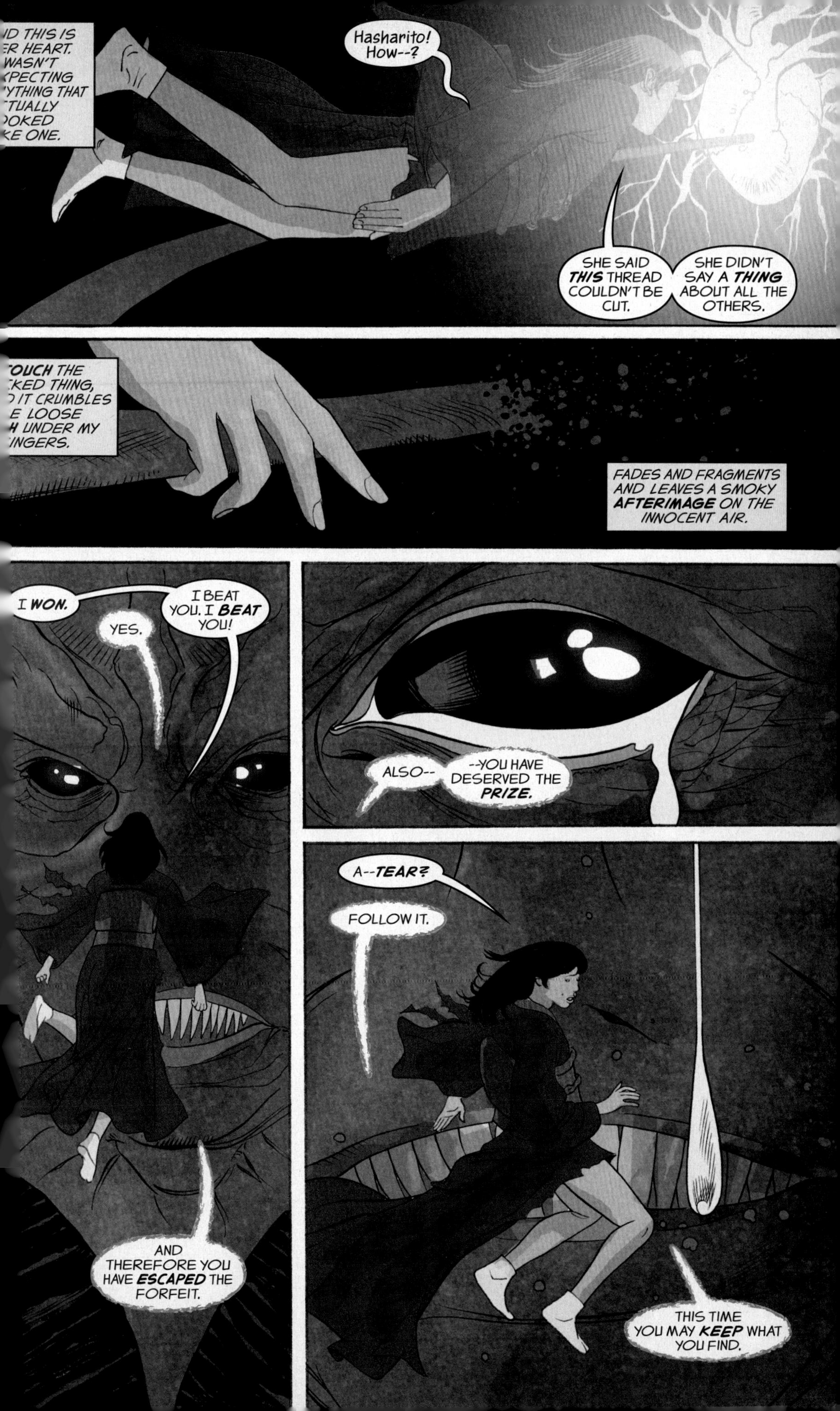

ID THIS IS
ER HEART.
WASN'T
XPECTING
YTHING THAT
TUALLY
OOKED
KE ONE.
Hasharito! How--?
SHE SAID THIS THREAD COULDN'T BE CUT.
SHE DIDN'T SAY A THING ABOUT ALL THE OTHERS.
OUCH THE
KED THING,
D IT CRUMBLES
E LOOSE
H UNDER MY
INGERS.
FADES AND FRAGMENTS AND LEAVES A SMOKY AFTERIMAGE ON THE INNOCENT AIR.
I WON.
I BEAT YOU. I BEAT YOU!
YES.
AND THEREFORE YOU HAVE ESCAPED THE FORFEIT.
ALSO--
--YOU HAVE DESERVED THE PRIZE.
A--TEAR?
FOLLOW IT.
THIS TIME YOU MAY KEEP WHAT YOU FIND.

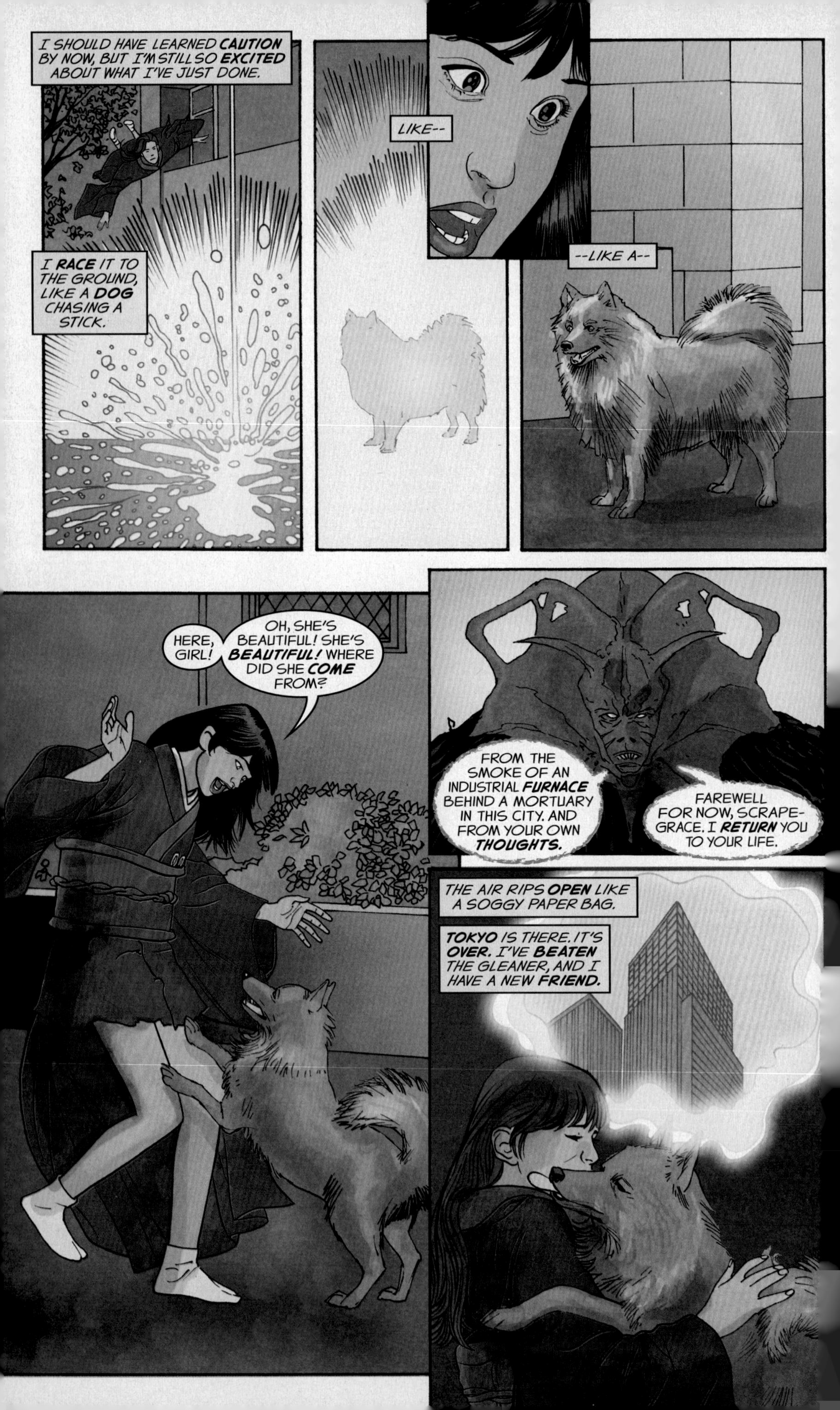

I SHOULD HAVE LEARNED CAUTION BY NOW, BUT I'M STILL SO EXCITED ABOUT WHAT I'VE JUST DONE.
I RACE IT TO THE GROUND, LIKE A DOG CHASING A STICK.
LIKE--
--LIKE A--
HERE, GIRL!
OH, SHE'S BEAUTIFUL! SHE'S BEAUTIFUL! WHERE DID SHE COME FROM?
FROM THE SMOKE OF AN INDUSTRIAL FURNACE BEHIND A MORTUARY IN THIS CITY. AND FROM YOUR OWN THOUGHTS.
FAREWELL FOR NOW, SCRAPE-GRACE. I RETURN YOU TO YOUR LIFE.
THE AIR RIPS OPEN LIKE A SOGGY PAPER BAG.
TOKYO IS THERE. IT'S OVER. I'VE BEATEN THE GLEANER, AND I HAVE A NEW FRIEND.

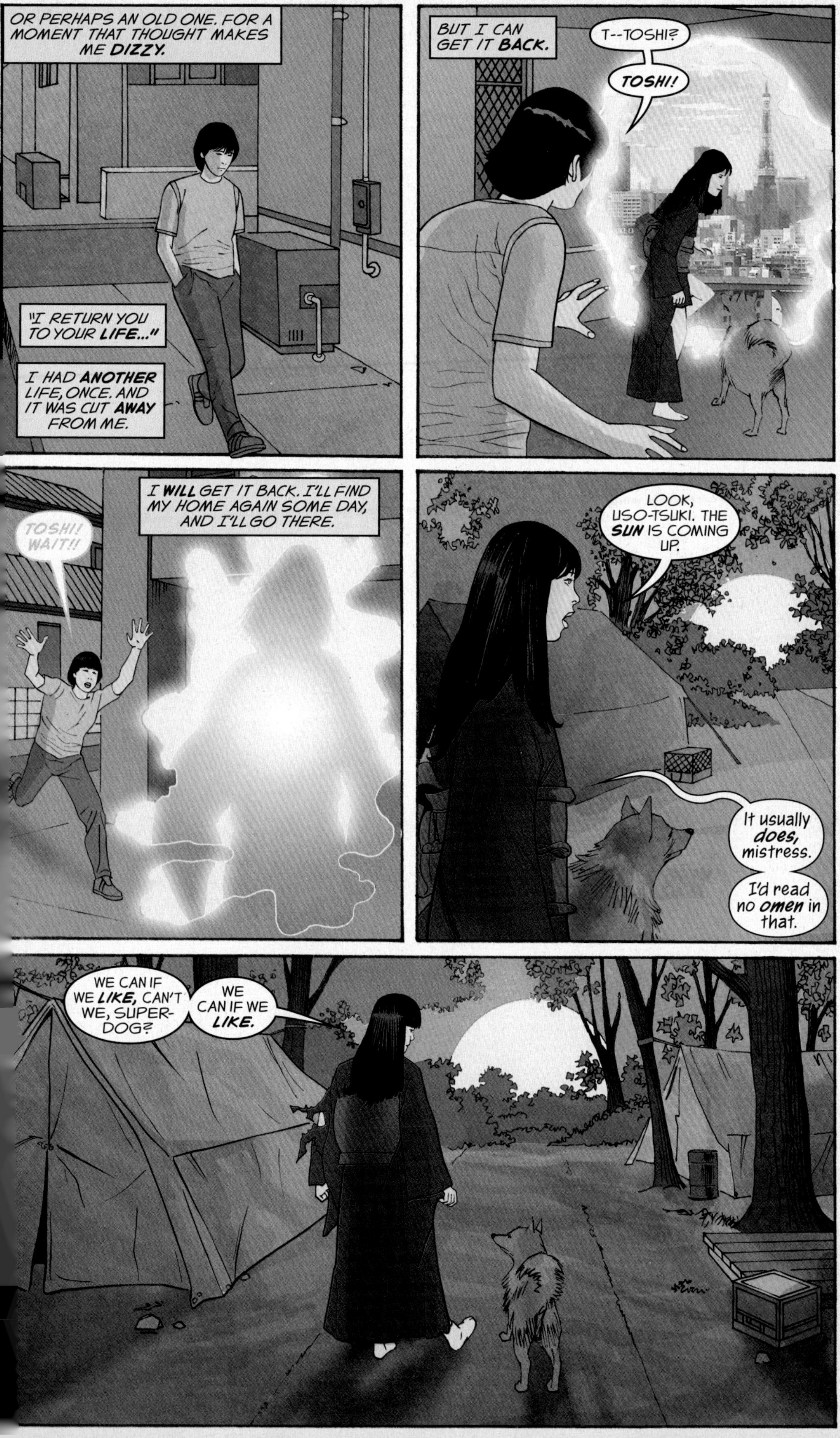

OR PERHAPS AN OLD ONE. FOR A MOMENT THAT THOUGHT MAKES ME DIZZY.
"I RETURN YOU TO YOUR LIFE..."
I HAD ANOTHER LIFE, ONCE. AND IT WAS CUT AWAY FROM ME.
BUT I CAN GET IT BACK.
T--TOSHI?
TOSHI!
I WILL GET IT BACK. I'LL FIND MY HOME AGAIN SOME DAY, AND I'LL GO THERE.
TOSHI! WAIT!!
LOOK, USO-TSUKI. THE SUN IS COMING UP.
It usually does, mistress.
I'd read no omen in that.
WE CAN IF WE LIKE, CAN'T WE, SUPER-DOG?
WE CAN IF WE LIKE.

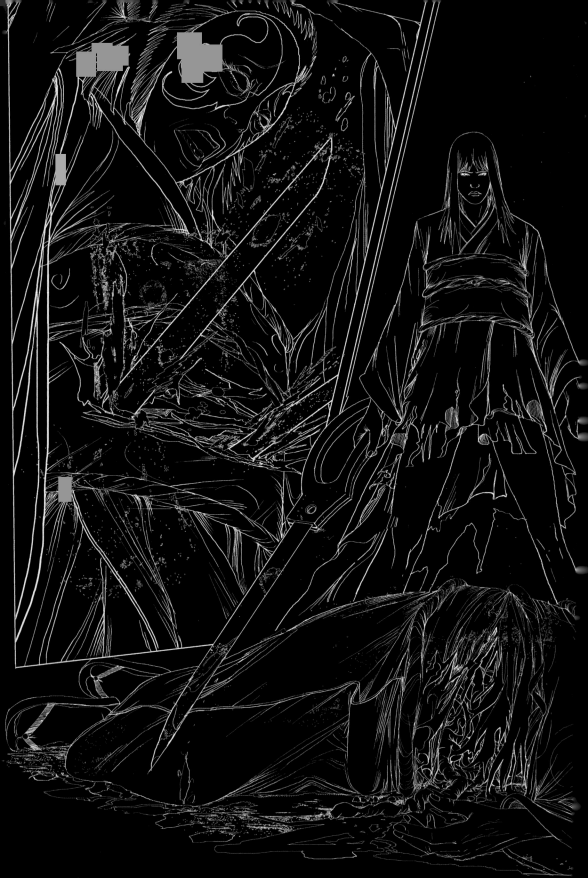

Bedtime Stories

Written by Mike Carey   Art by Eric Nguyen

chapter one

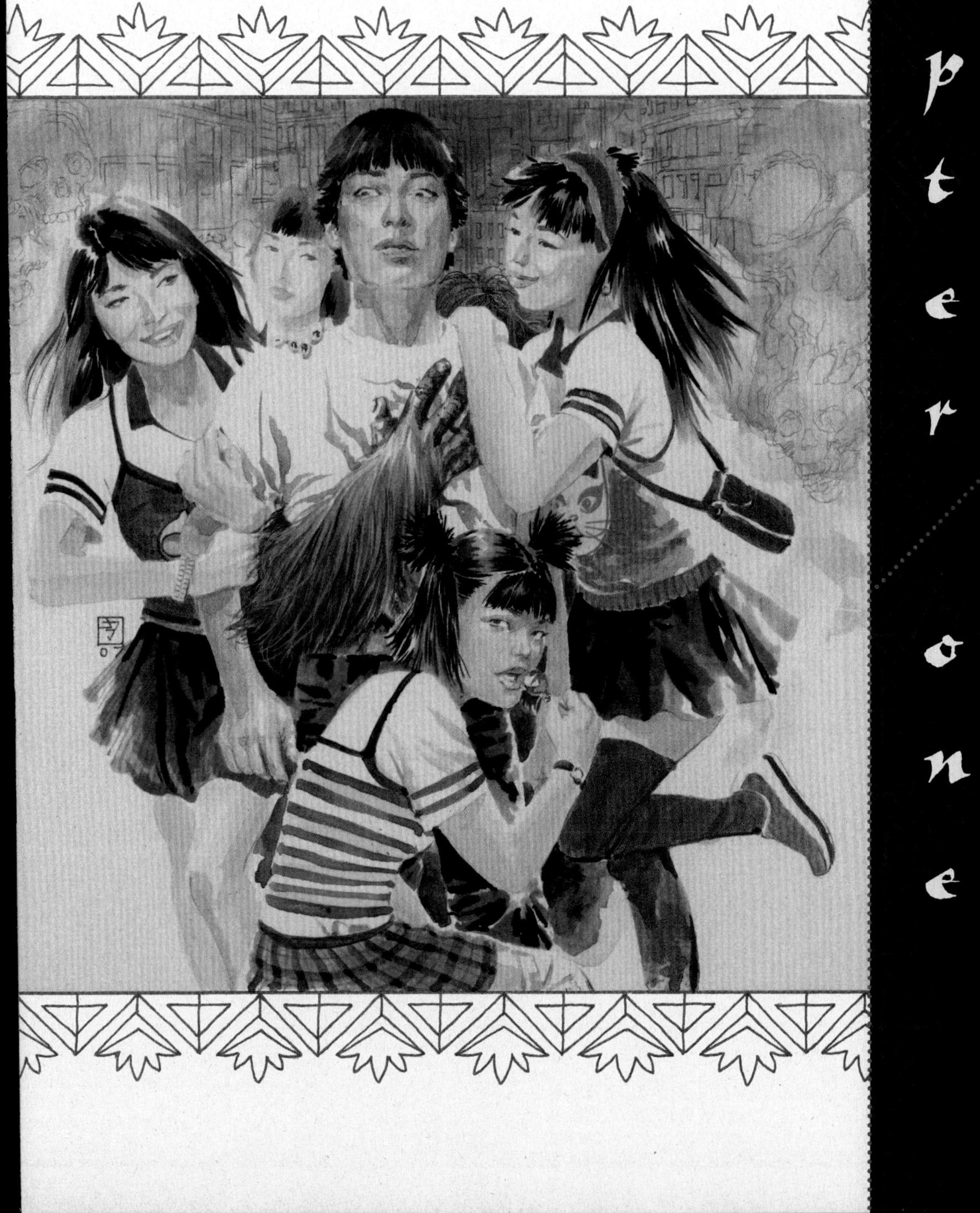

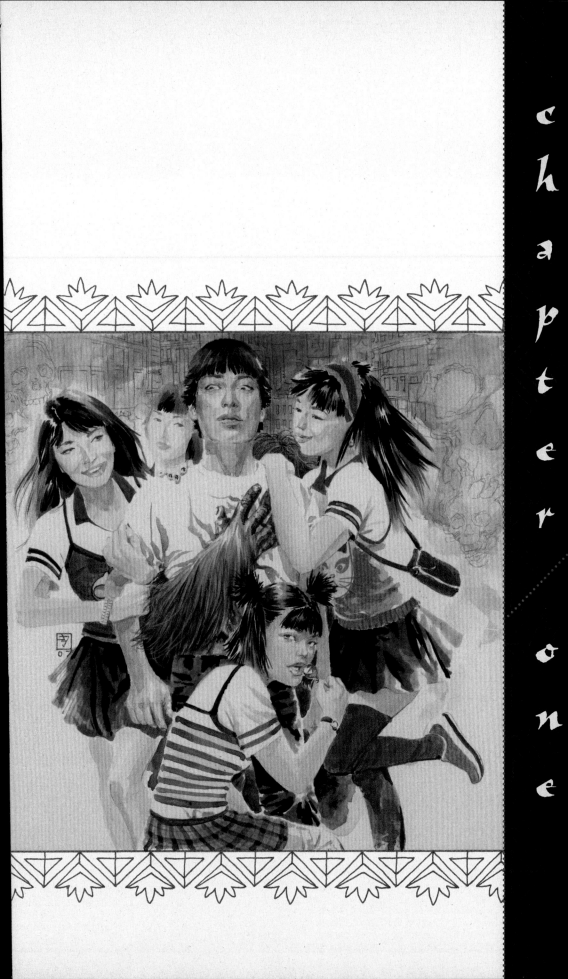

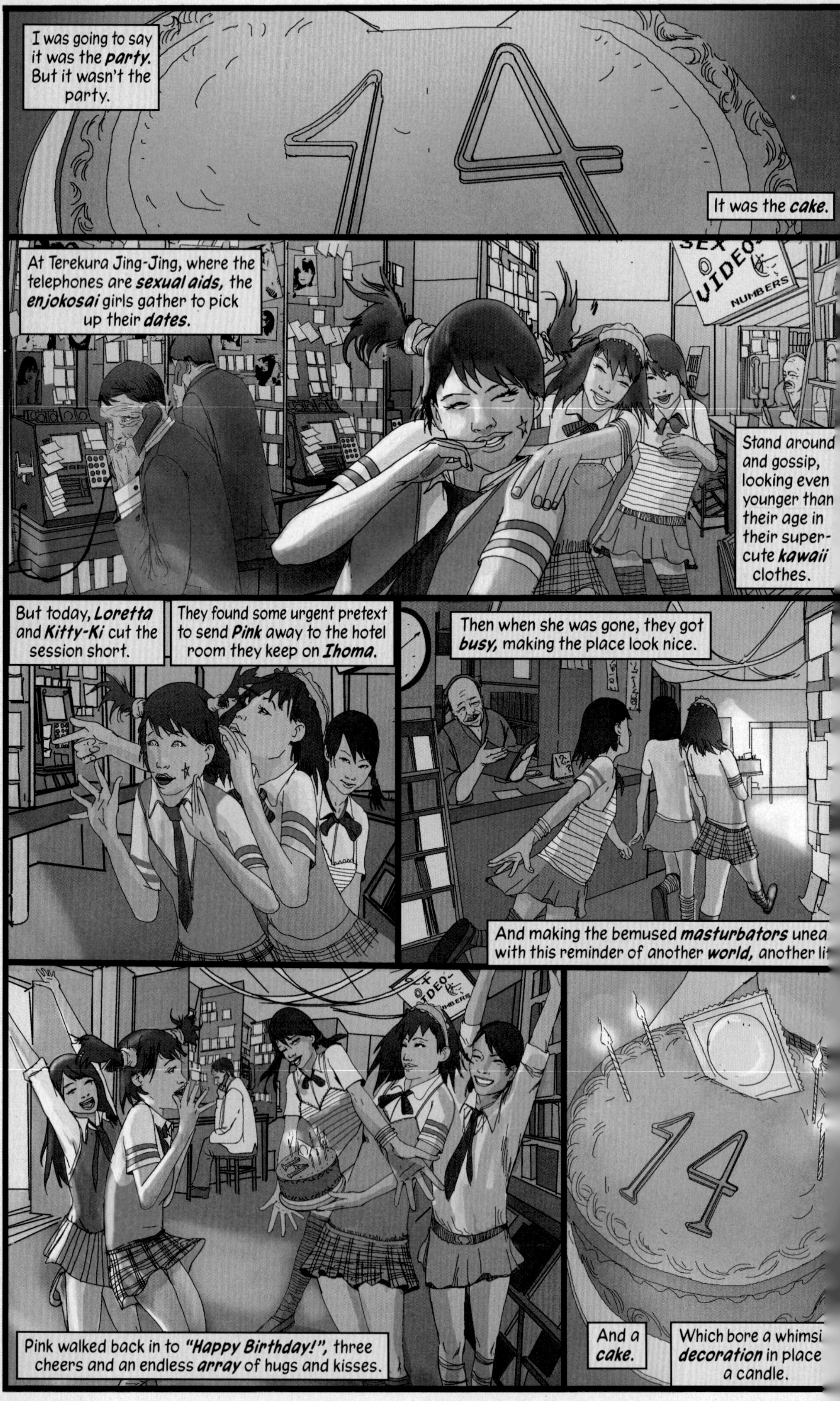
I was going to say it was the *party.* But it wasn't the party.
It was the *cake.*
At Terekura Jing-Jing, where the telephones are *sexual aids,* the *enjokosai* girls gather to pick up their *dates.*
SEX VIDEOS NUMBERS
Stand around and gossip, looking even younger than their age in their super-cute *kawaii* clothes.
But today, *Loretta* and *Kitty-Ki* cut the session short.
They found some urgent pretext to send *Pink* away to the hotel room they keep on *Ihoma.*
Then when she was gone, they got *busy,* making the place look nice.
And making the bemused *masturbators* unea
with this reminder of another *world,* another li
Pink walked back in to *"Happy Birthday!",* three cheers and an endless *array* of hugs and kisses.
And a *cake.*
Which bore a whimsi
decoration in place
a candle.

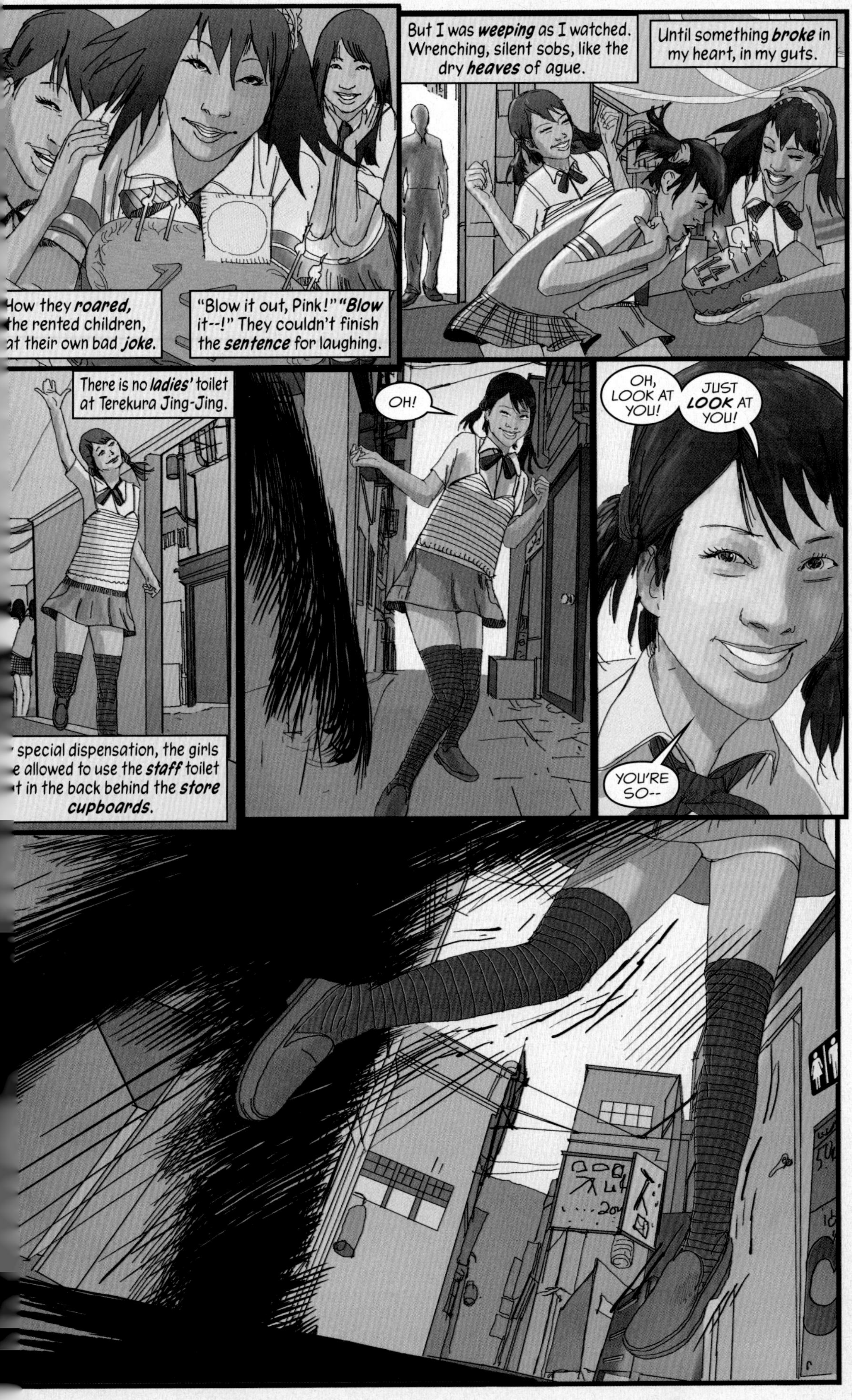
How they roared, the rented children, at their own bad joke.
"Blow it out, Pink!" "Blow it--!" They couldn't finish the sentence for laughing.
But I was weeping as I watched. Wrenching, silent sobs, like the dry heaves of ague.
Until something broke in my heart, in my guts.
There is no ladies' toilet at Terekura Jing-Jing.
y special dispensation, the girls e allowed to use the staff toilet t in the back behind the store cupboards.
OH!
OH, LOOK AT YOU!
JUST LOOK AT YOU!
YOU'RE SO--

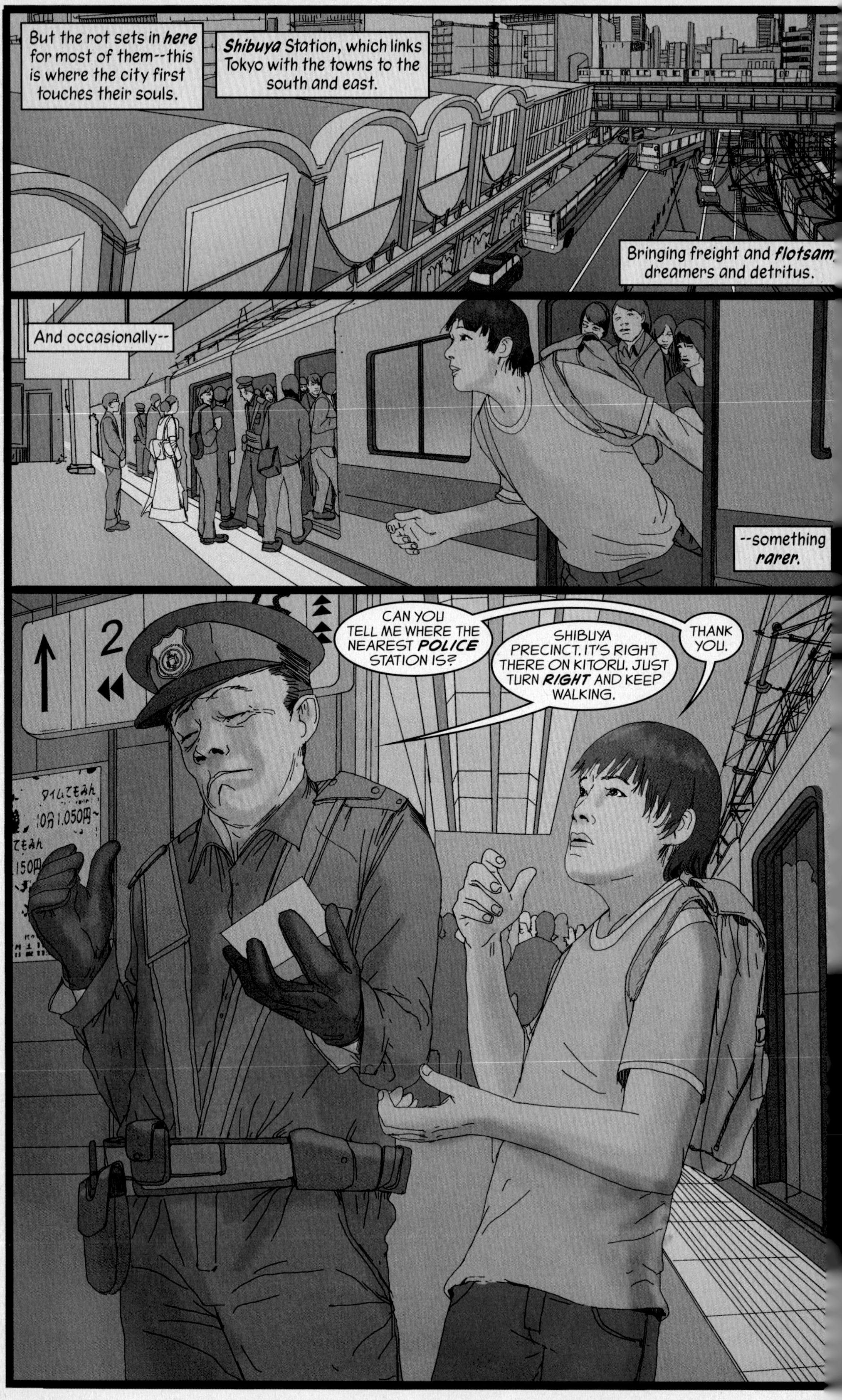

But the rot sets in *here* for most of them--this is where the city first touches their souls.
Shibuya Station, which links Tokyo with the towns to the south and east.
Bringing freight and *flotsam*, dreamers and detritus.
And occasionally--
--something *rarer.*
2
タイムてもみん
10分1,050円~
CAN YOU TELL ME WHERE THE NEAREST *POLICE* STATION IS?
SHIBUYA PRECINCT. IT'S RIGHT THERE ON KITORU. JUST TURN *RIGHT* AND KEEP WALKING.
THANK YOU.

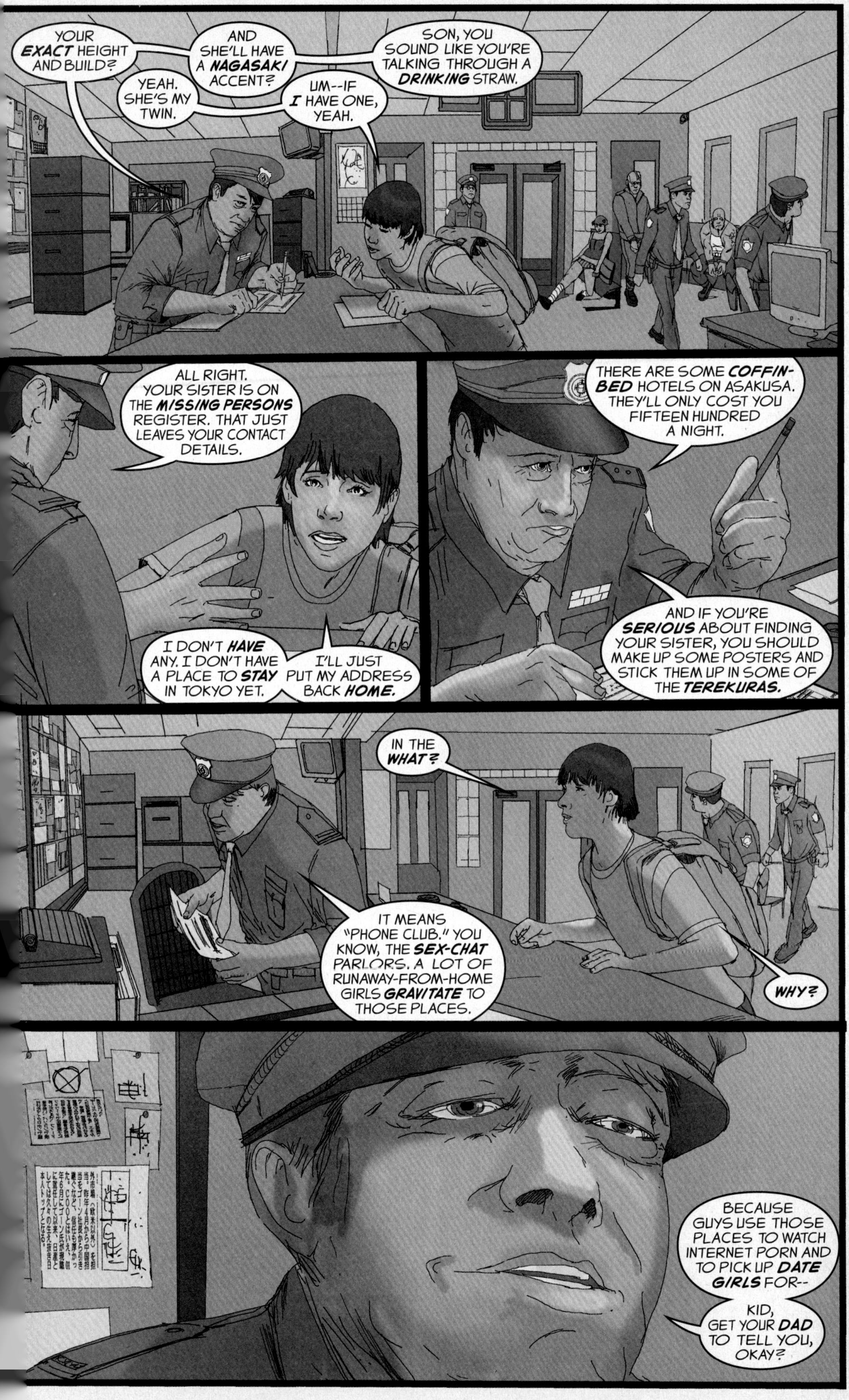
YOUR EXACT HEIGHT AND BUILD?
YEAH. SHE'S MY TWIN.
AND SHE'LL HAVE A NAGASAKI ACCENT?
UM--IF I HAVE ONE, YEAH.
SON, YOU SOUND LIKE YOU'RE TALKING THROUGH A DRINKING STRAW.
ALL RIGHT. YOUR SISTER IS ON THE MISSING PERSONS REGISTER. THAT JUST LEAVES YOUR CONTACT DETAILS.
I DON'T HAVE ANY. I DON'T HAVE A PLACE TO STAY IN TOKYO YET.
I'LL JUST PUT MY ADDRESS BACK HOME.
THERE ARE SOME COFFIN-BED HOTELS ON ASAKUSA. THEY'LL ONLY COST YOU FIFTEEN HUNDRED A NIGHT.
AND IF YOU'RE SERIOUS ABOUT FINDING YOUR SISTER, YOU SHOULD MAKE UP SOME POSTERS AND STICK THEM UP IN SOME OF THE TEREKURAS.
IN THE WHAT?
IT MEANS "PHONE CLUB." YOU KNOW, THE SEX-CHAT PARLORS. A LOT OF RUNAWAY-FROM-HOME GIRLS GRAVITATE TO THOSE PLACES.
WHY?
BECAUSE GUYS USE THOSE PLACES TO WATCH INTERNET PORN AND TO PICK UP DATE GIRLS FOR--
KID, GET YOUR DAD TO TELL YOU, OKAY?

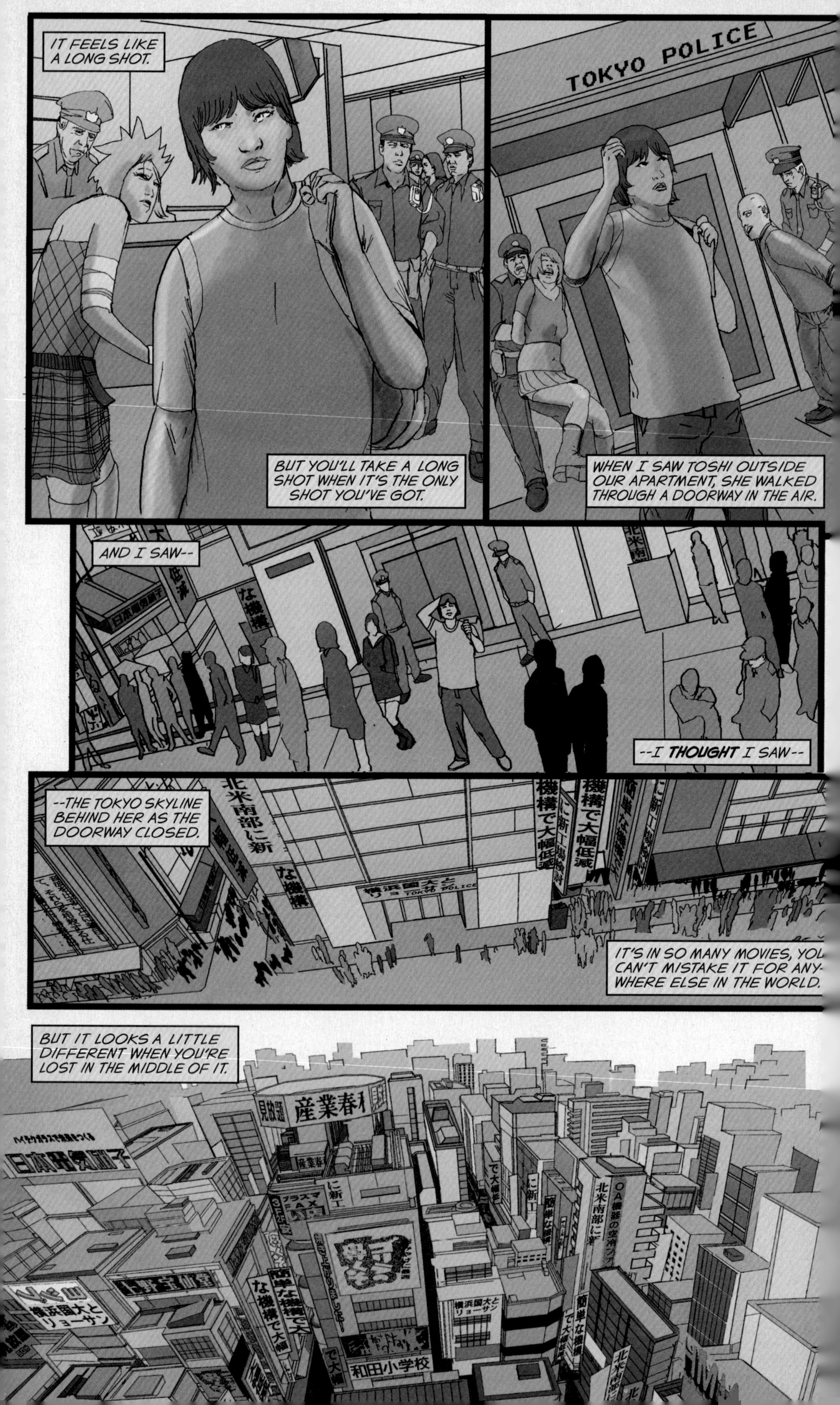
IT FEELS LIKE A LONG SHOT.
BUT YOU'LL TAKE A LONG SHOT WHEN IT'S THE ONLY SHOT YOU'VE GOT.
TOKYO POLICE
WHEN I SAW TOSHI OUTSIDE OUR APARTMENT, SHE WALKED THROUGH A DOORWAY IN THE AIR.
AND I SAW--
--I THOUGHT I SAW--
--THE TOKYO SKYLINE BEHIND HER AS THE DOORWAY CLOSED.
IT'S IN SO MANY MOVIES, YOU CAN'T MISTAKE IT FOR ANY-WHERE ELSE IN THE WORLD.
BUT IT LOOKS A LITTLE DIFFERENT WHEN YOU'RE LOST IN THE MIDDLE OF IT.

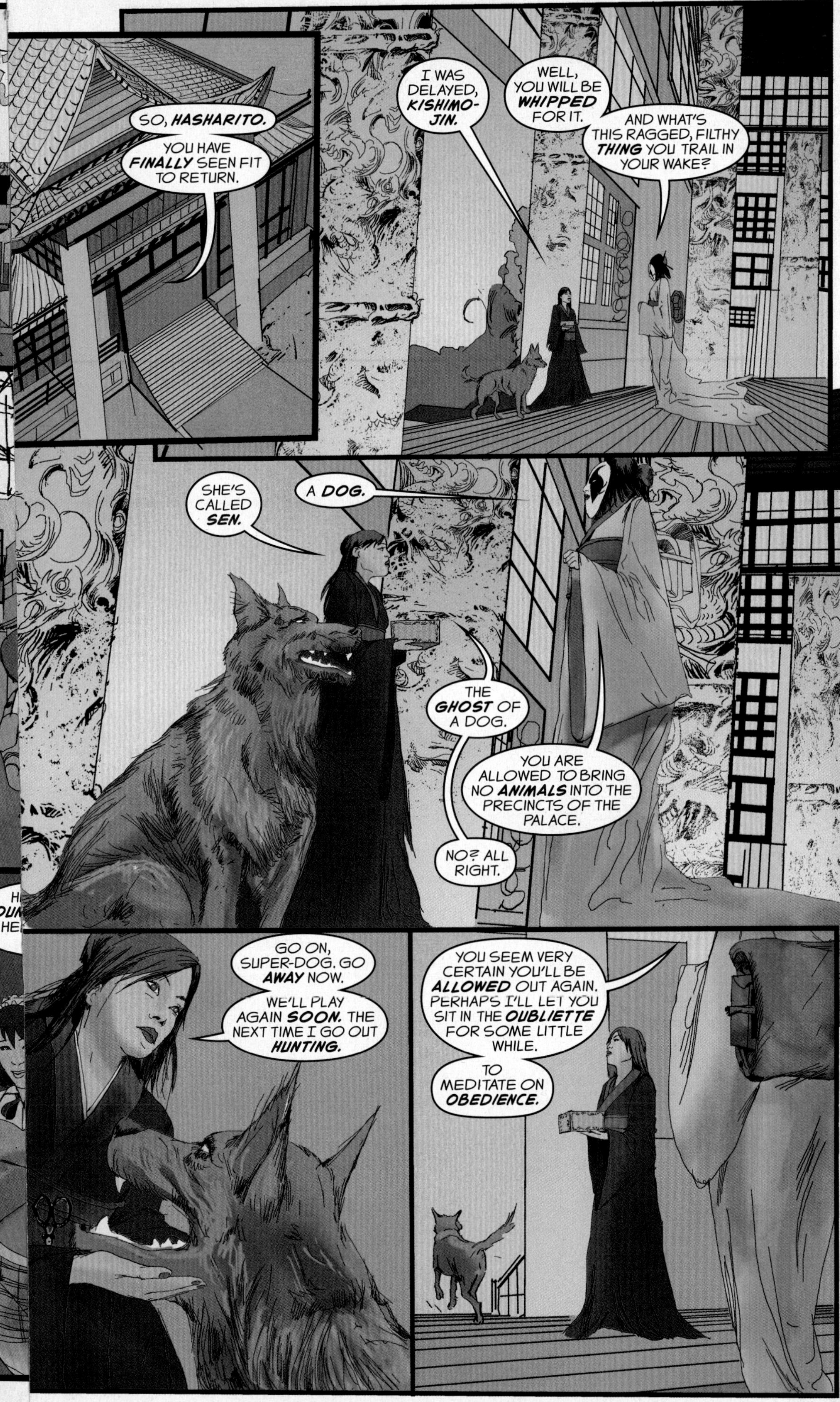

SO, HASHARITO.
YOU HAVE FINALLY SEEN FIT TO RETURN.
I WAS DELAYED, KISHIMO-JIN.
WELL, YOU WILL BE WHIPPED FOR IT.
AND WHAT'S THIS RAGGED, FILTHY THING YOU TRAIL IN YOUR WAKE?
A DOG.
SHE'S CALLED SEN.
THE GHOST OF A DOG.
YOU ARE ALLOWED TO BRING NO ANIMALS INTO THE PRECINCTS OF THE PALACE.
NO? ALL RIGHT.
GO ON, SUPER-DOG. GO AWAY NOW.
WE'LL PLAY AGAIN SOON. THE NEXT TIME I GO OUT HUNTING.
YOU SEEM VERY CERTAIN YOU'LL BE ALLOWED OUT AGAIN. PERHAPS I'LL LET YOU SIT IN THE OUBLIETTE FOR SOME LITTLE WHILE.
TO MEDITATE ON OBEDIENCE.

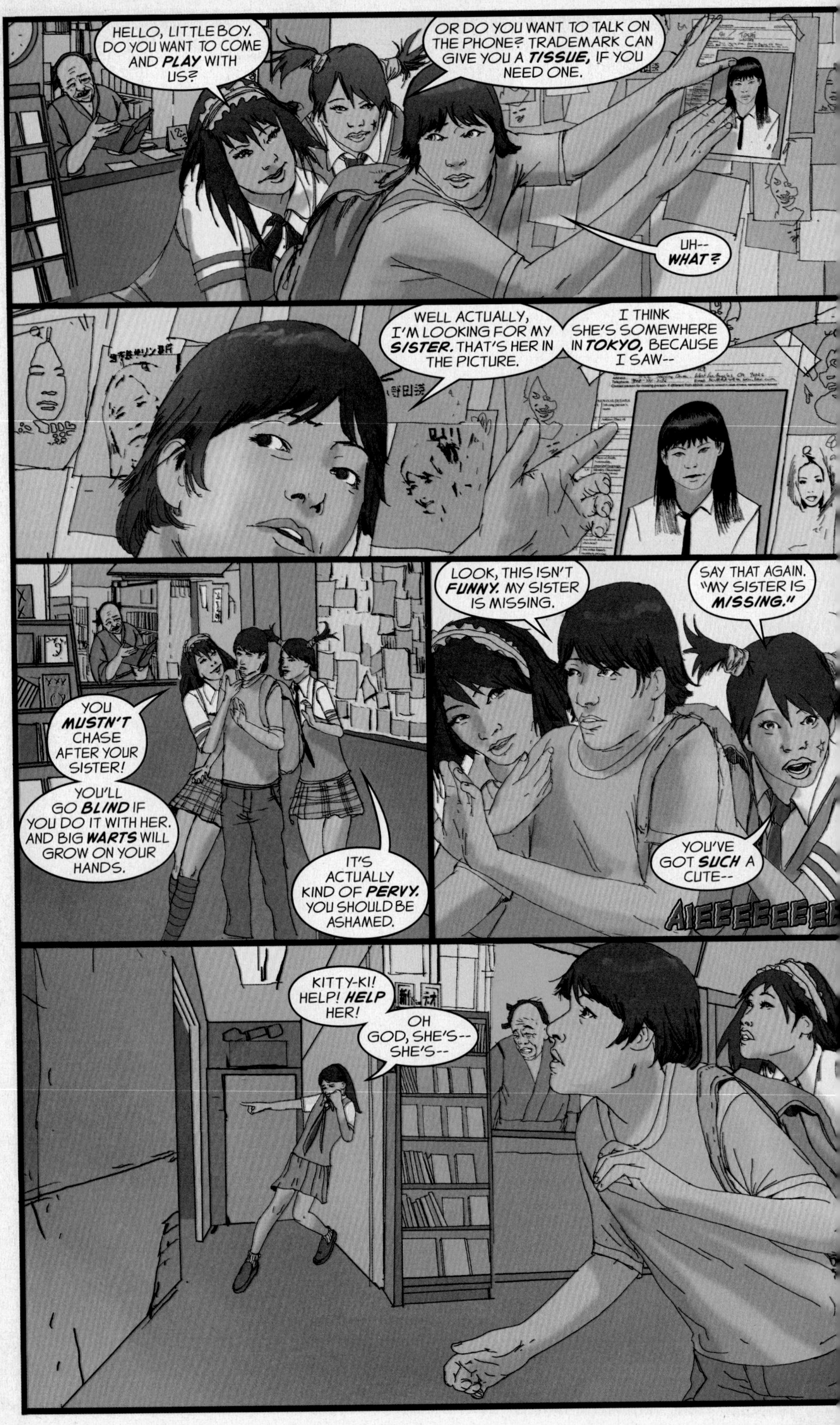
HELLO, LITTLE BOY. DO YOU WANT TO COME AND PLAY WITH US?
OR DO YOU WANT TO TALK ON THE PHONE? TRADEMARK CAN GIVE YOU A TISSUE, IF YOU NEED ONE.
UH-- WHAT?
WELL ACTUALLY, I'M LOOKING FOR MY SISTER. THAT'S HER IN THE PICTURE.
I THINK SHE'S SOMEWHERE IN TOKYO, BECAUSE I SAW--
YOU MUSTN'T CHASE AFTER YOUR SISTER!
YOU'LL GO BLIND IF YOU DO IT WITH HER. AND BIG WARTS WILL GROW ON YOUR HANDS.
IT'S ACTUALLY KIND OF PERVY. YOU SHOULD BE ASHAMED.
LOOK, THIS ISN'T FUNNY. MY SISTER IS MISSING.
SAY THAT AGAIN. "MY SISTER IS MISSING."
YOU'VE GOT SUCH A CUTE--
AIEEEEEEE
KITTY-KI! HELP! HELP HER!
OH GOD, SHE'S-- SHE'S--

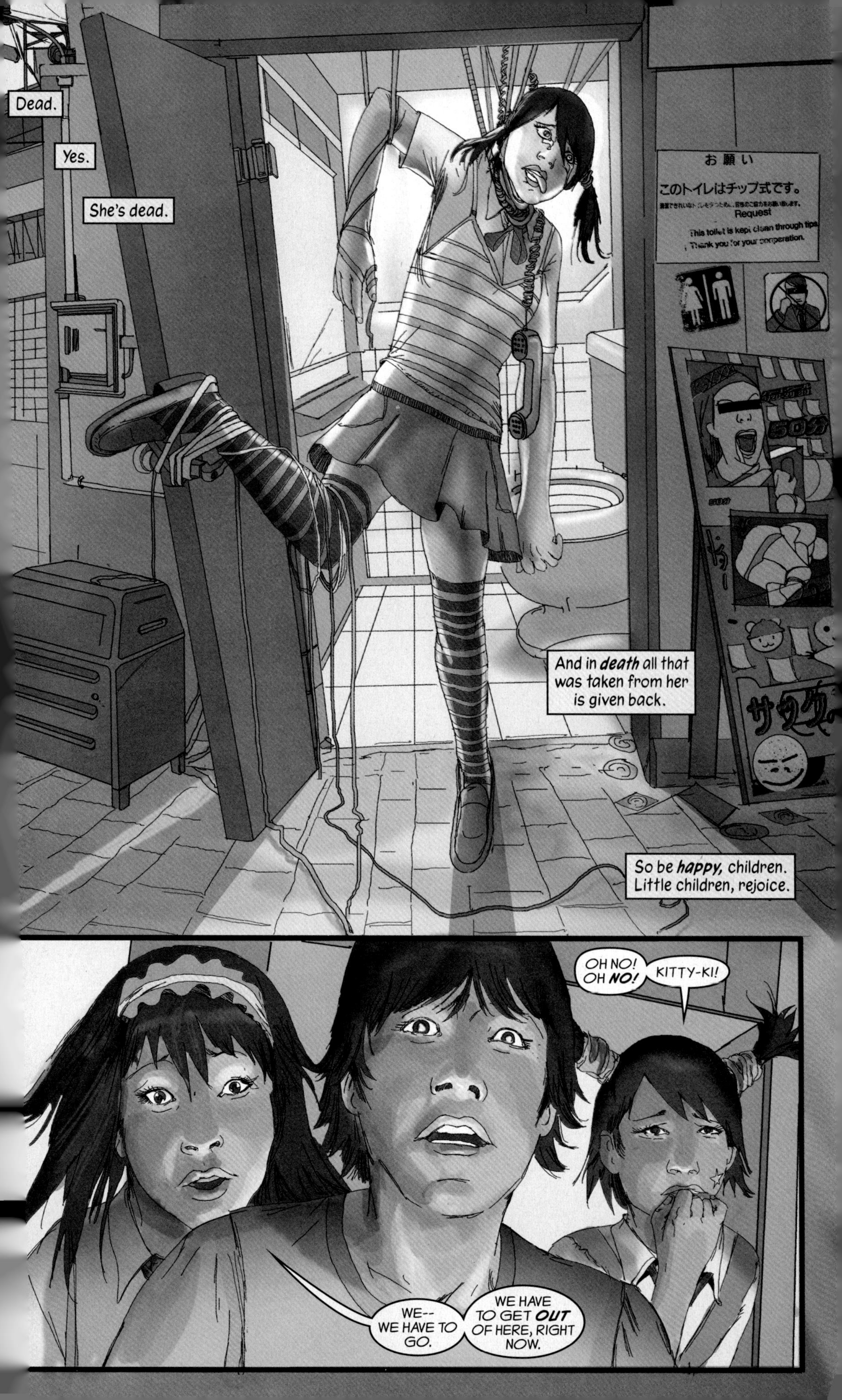
Dead.
Yes.
She's dead.
お願い
このトイレはチップ式です。
Request
This toilet is kept clean through tips.
Thank you for your cooperation.
And in *death* all that was taken from her is given back.
So be *happy,* children. Little children, rejoice.
OH NO! OH *NO!*
KITTY-KI!
WE-- WE HAVE TO GO.
WE HAVE TO GET *OUT* OF HERE, RIGHT NOW.

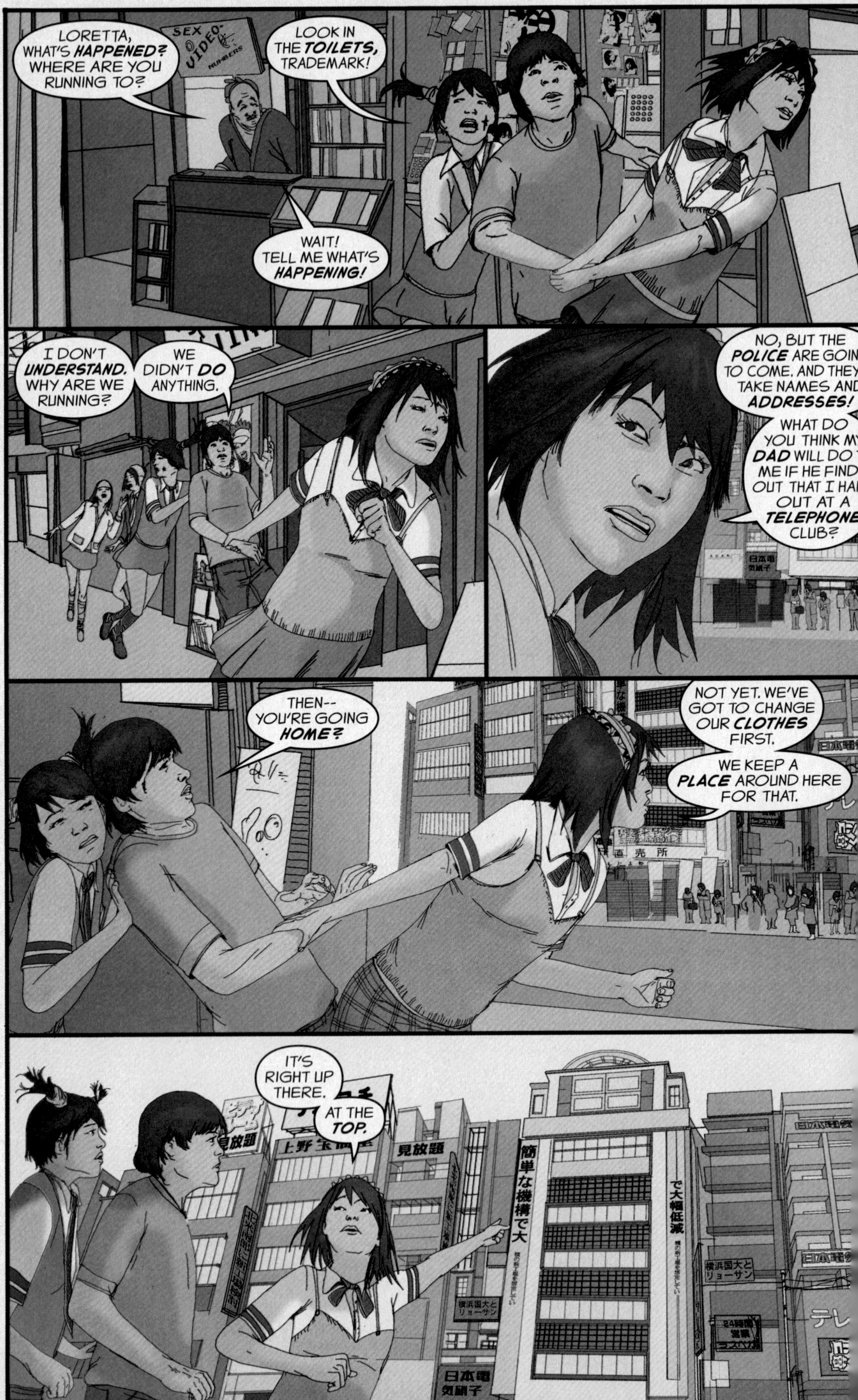
LORETTA, WHAT'S HAPPENED? WHERE ARE YOU RUNNING TO?
SEX VIDEO NUMBERS
LOOK IN THE TOILETS, TRADEMARK!
WAIT! TELL ME WHAT'S HAPPENING!
I DON'T UNDERSTAND. WHY ARE WE RUNNING?
WE DIDN'T DO ANYTHING.
NO, BUT THE POLICE ARE GOING TO COME. AND THEY' TAKE NAMES AND ADDRESSES!
WHAT DO YOU THINK MY DAD WILL DO TO ME IF HE FIND OUT THAT I HAN OUT AT A TELEPHONE CLUB?
THEN-- YOU'RE GOING HOME?
NOT YET. WE'VE GOT TO CHANGE OUR CLOTHES FIRST.
WE KEEP A PLACE AROUND HERE FOR THAT.
直売所
IT'S RIGHT UP THERE.
AT THE TOP.
見放題
見放題
簡単な機構で大
で大幅低減
横浜国大と リョーサン
横浜国大と リョーサン
日本電 気硝子

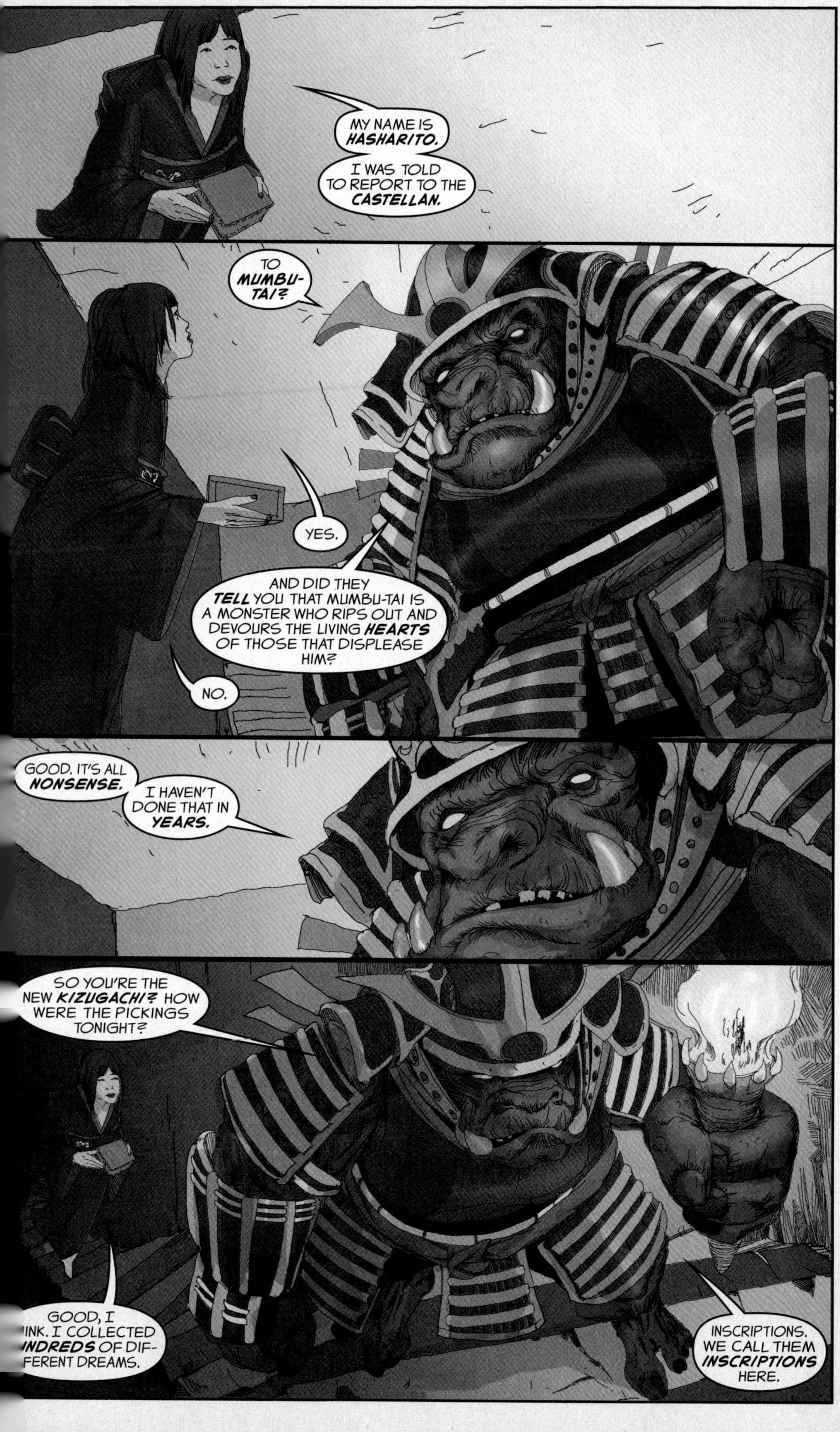
MY NAME IS **HASHARITO.**
I WAS TOLD TO REPORT TO THE **CASTELLAN.**
TO **MUMBU-TAI?**
YES.
AND DID THEY **TELL** YOU THAT MUMBU-TAI IS A MONSTER WHO RIPS OUT AND DEVOURS THE LIVING **HEARTS** OF THOSE THAT DISPLEASE HIM?
NO.
GOOD. IT'S ALL **NONSENSE.**
I HAVEN'T DONE THAT IN **YEARS.**
SO YOU'RE THE NEW **KIZUGACHI?** HOW WERE THE PICKINGS TONIGHT?
GOOD, I
INK. I COLLECTED
NDREDS OF DIF-
FERENT DREAMS.
INSCRIPTIONS. WE CALL THEM **INSCRIPTIONS** HERE.

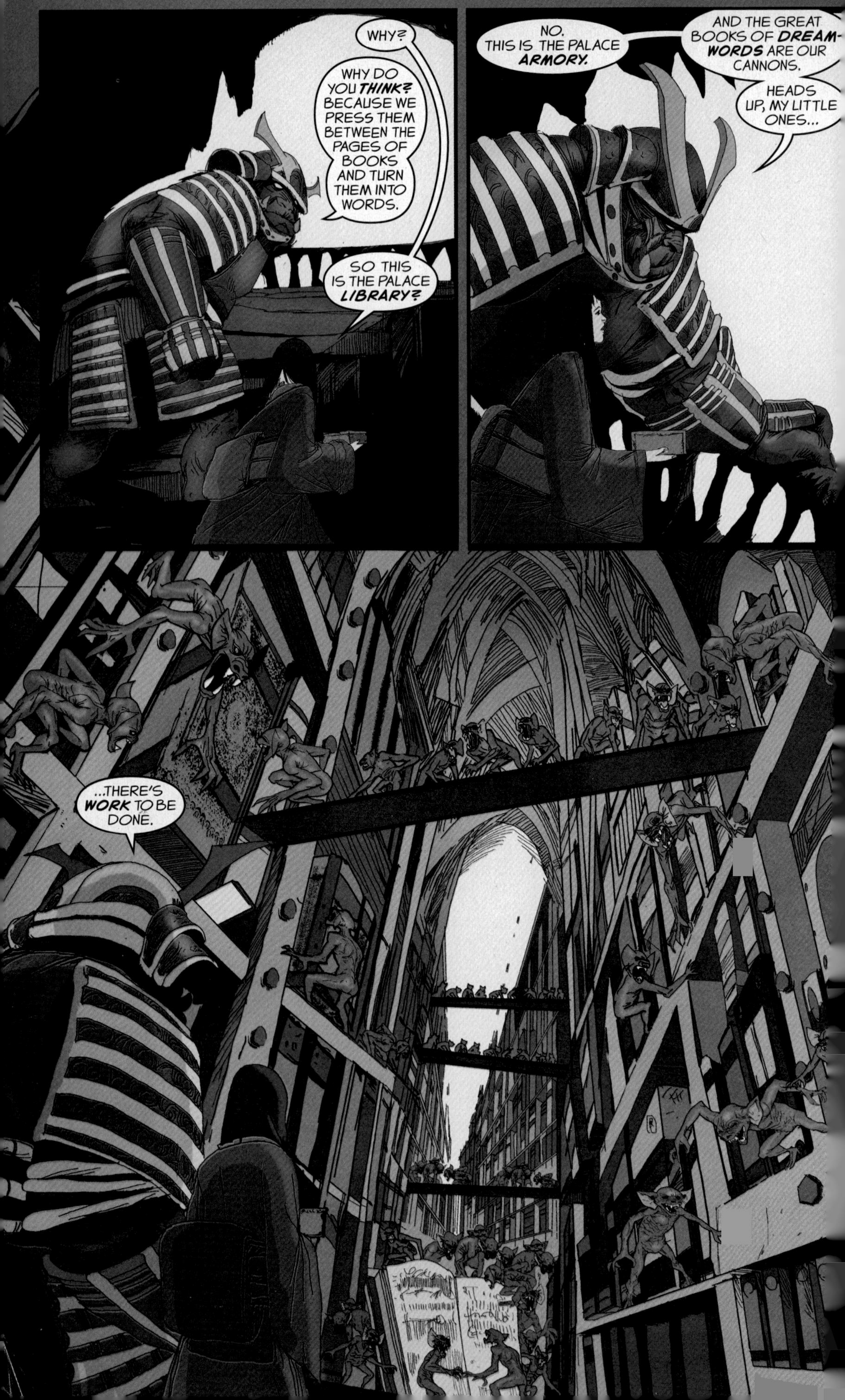
WHY?
WHY DO YOU THINK? BECAUSE WE PRESS THEM BETWEEN THE PAGES OF BOOKS AND TURN THEM INTO WORDS.
SO THIS IS THE PALACE LIBRARY?
NO. THIS IS THE PALACE ARMORY.
AND THE GREAT BOOKS OF DREAM-WORDS ARE OUR CANNONS.
HEADS UP, MY LITTLE ONES...
...THERE'S WORK TO BE DONE.

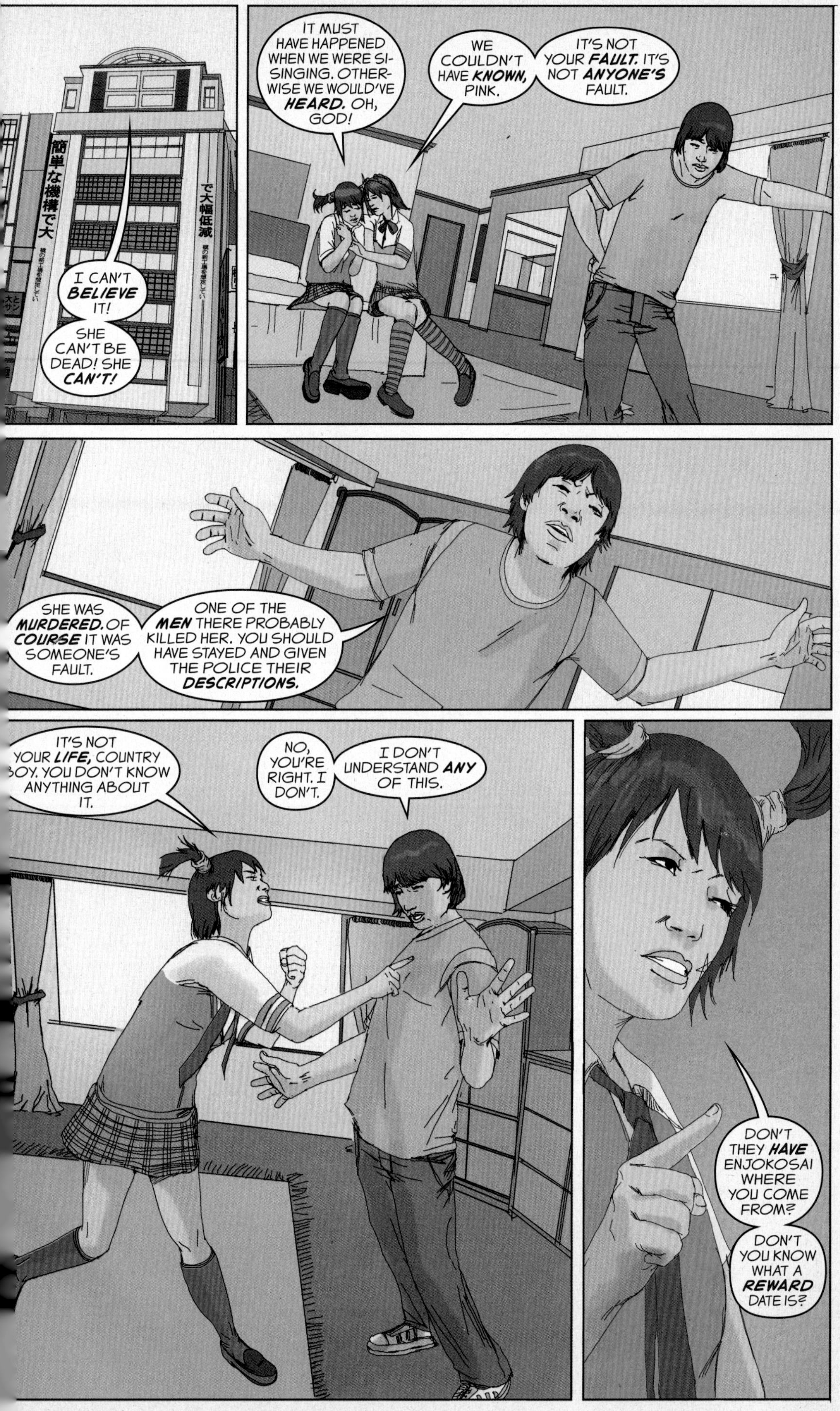

簡単な機構で大
で大幅低減
I CAN'T BELIEVE IT!
SHE CAN'T BE DEAD! SHE CAN'T!
IT MUST HAVE HAPPENED WHEN WE WERE SI-SINGING. OTHER-WISE WE WOULD'VE HEARD. OH, GOD!
WE COULDN'T HAVE KNOWN, PINK.
IT'S NOT YOUR FAULT. IT'S NOT ANYONE'S FAULT.
SHE WAS MURDERED. OF COURSE IT WAS SOMEONE'S FAULT.
ONE OF THE MEN THERE PROBABLY KILLED HER. YOU SHOULD HAVE STAYED AND GIVEN THE POLICE THEIR DESCRIPTIONS.
IT'S NOT YOUR LIFE, COUNTRY BOY. YOU DON'T KNOW ANYTHING ABOUT IT.
NO, YOU'RE RIGHT. I DON'T.
I DON'T UNDERSTAND ANY OF THIS.
DON'T THEY HAVE ENJOKOSAI WHERE YOU COME FROM?
DON'T YOU KNOW WHAT A REWARD DATE IS?

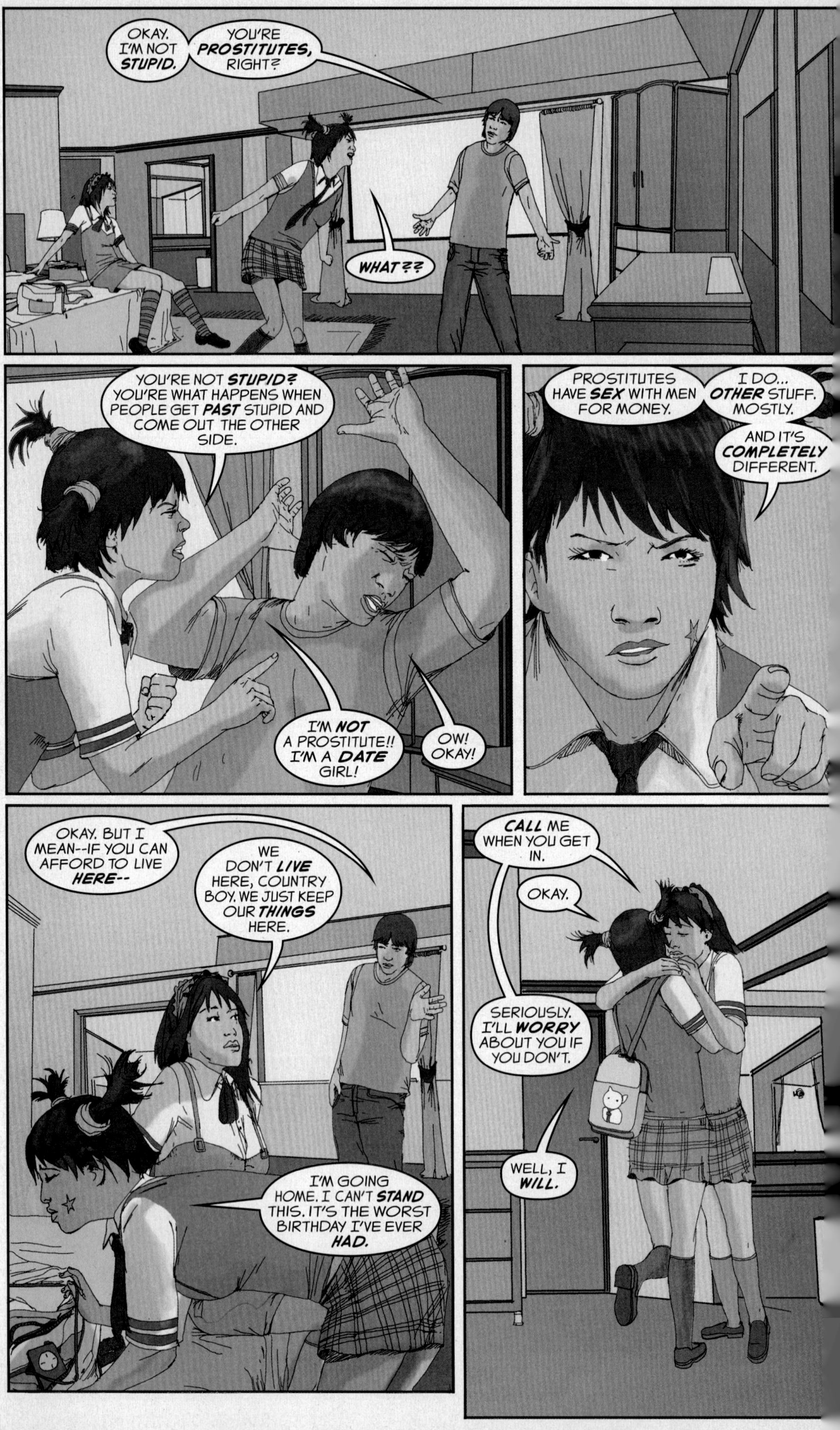
OKAY. I'M NOT STUPID.
YOU'RE PROSTITUTES, RIGHT?
WHAT??
YOU'RE NOT STUPID? YOU'RE WHAT HAPPENS WHEN PEOPLE GET PAST STUPID AND COME OUT THE OTHER SIDE.
I'M NOT A PROSTITUTE!! I'M A DATE GIRL!
OW! OKAY!
PROSTITUTES HAVE SEX WITH MEN FOR MONEY.
I DO... OTHER STUFF. MOSTLY.
AND IT'S COMPLETELY DIFFERENT.
OKAY. BUT I MEAN--IF YOU CAN AFFORD TO LIVE HERE--
WE DON'T LIVE HERE, COUNTRY BOY. WE JUST KEEP OUR THINGS HERE.
I'M GOING HOME. I CAN'T STAND THIS. IT'S THE WORST BIRTHDAY I'VE EVER HAD.
CALL ME WHEN YOU GET IN.
OKAY.
SERIOUSLY. I'LL WORRY ABOUT YOU IF YOU DON'T.
WELL, I WILL.

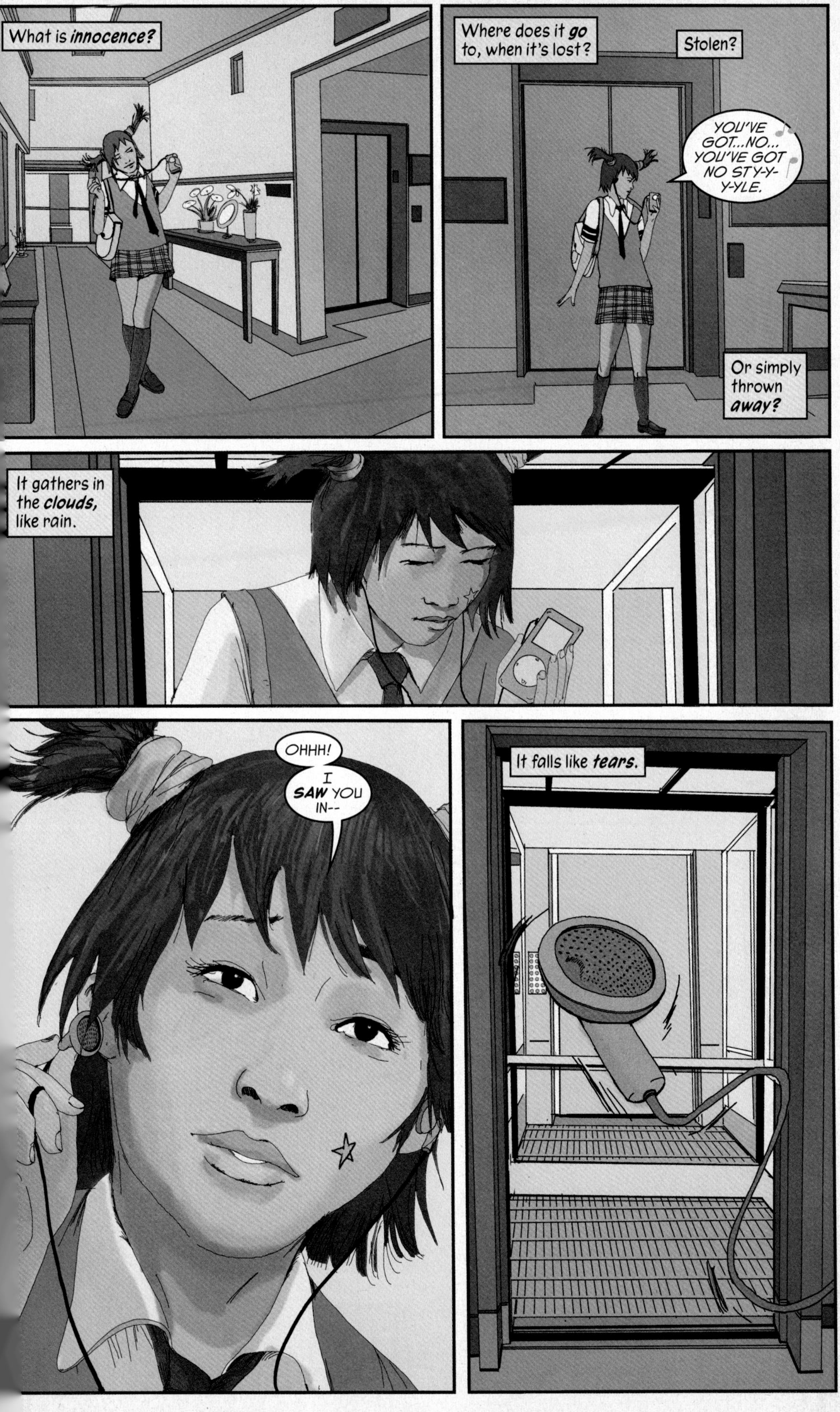
What is innocence?
Where does it go to, when it's lost?
Stolen?
YOU'VE GOT...NO... YOU'VE GOT NO STY-Y-Y-YLE.
Or simply thrown away?
It gathers in the clouds, like rain.
OHHH!
I SAW YOU IN--
It falls like tears.

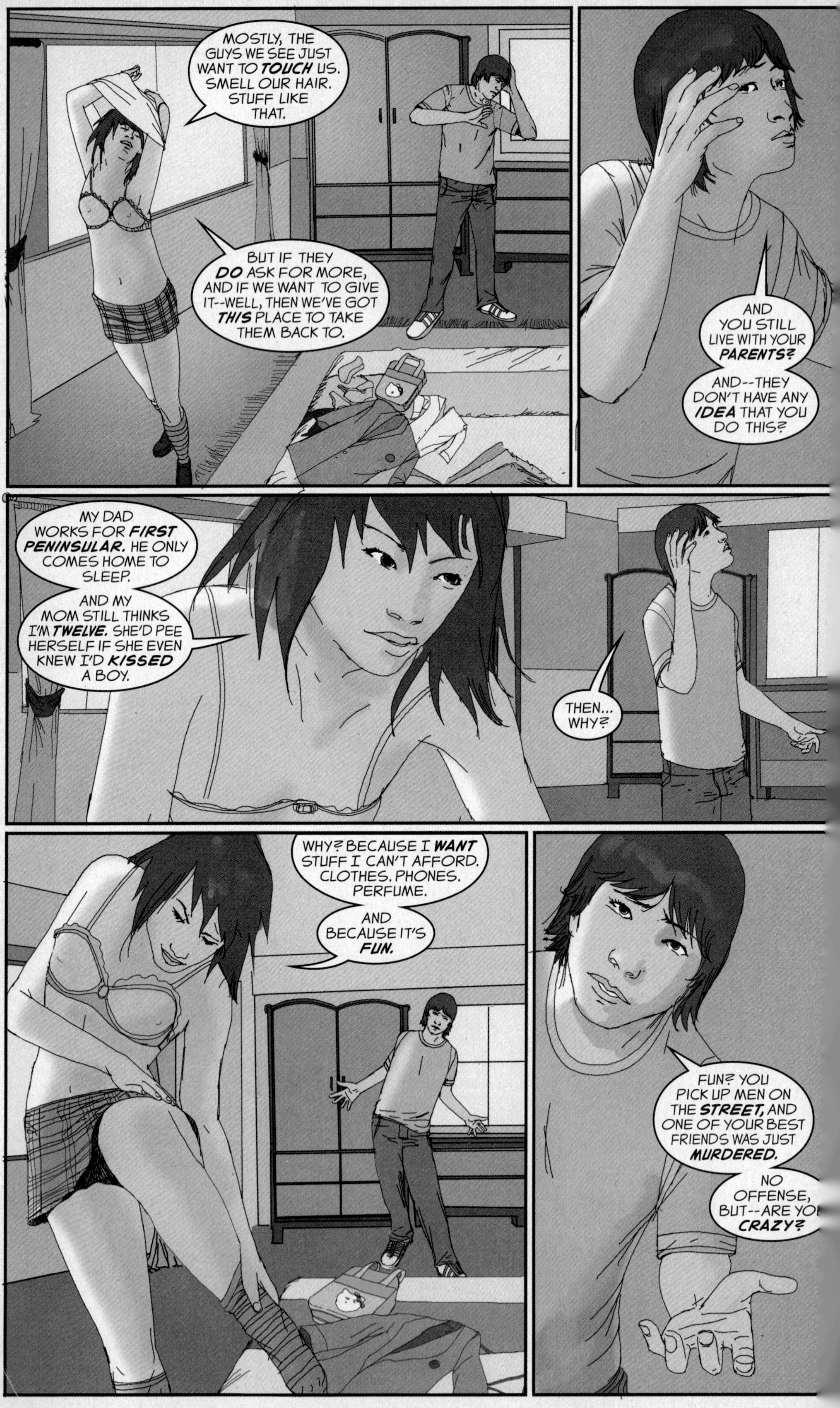

MOSTLY, THE GUYS WE SEE JUST WANT TO TOUCH US. SMELL OUR HAIR. STUFF LIKE THAT.
BUT IF THEY DO ASK FOR MORE, AND IF WE WANT TO GIVE IT--WELL, THEN WE'VE GOT THIS PLACE TO TAKE THEM BACK TO.
AND YOU STILL LIVE WITH YOUR PARENTS?
AND--THEY DON'T HAVE ANY IDEA THAT YOU DO THIS?
MY DAD WORKS FOR FIRST PENINSULAR. HE ONLY COMES HOME TO SLEEP.
AND MY MOM STILL THINKS I'M TWELVE. SHE'D PEE HERSELF IF SHE EVEN KNEW I'D KISSED A BOY.
THEN... WHY?
WHY? BECAUSE I WANT STUFF I CAN'T AFFORD. CLOTHES. PHONES. PERFUME.
AND BECAUSE IT'S FUN.
FUN? YOU PICK UP MEN ON THE STREET, AND ONE OF YOUR BEST FRIENDS WAS JUST MURDERED.
NO OFFENSE, BUT--ARE YO CRAZY?

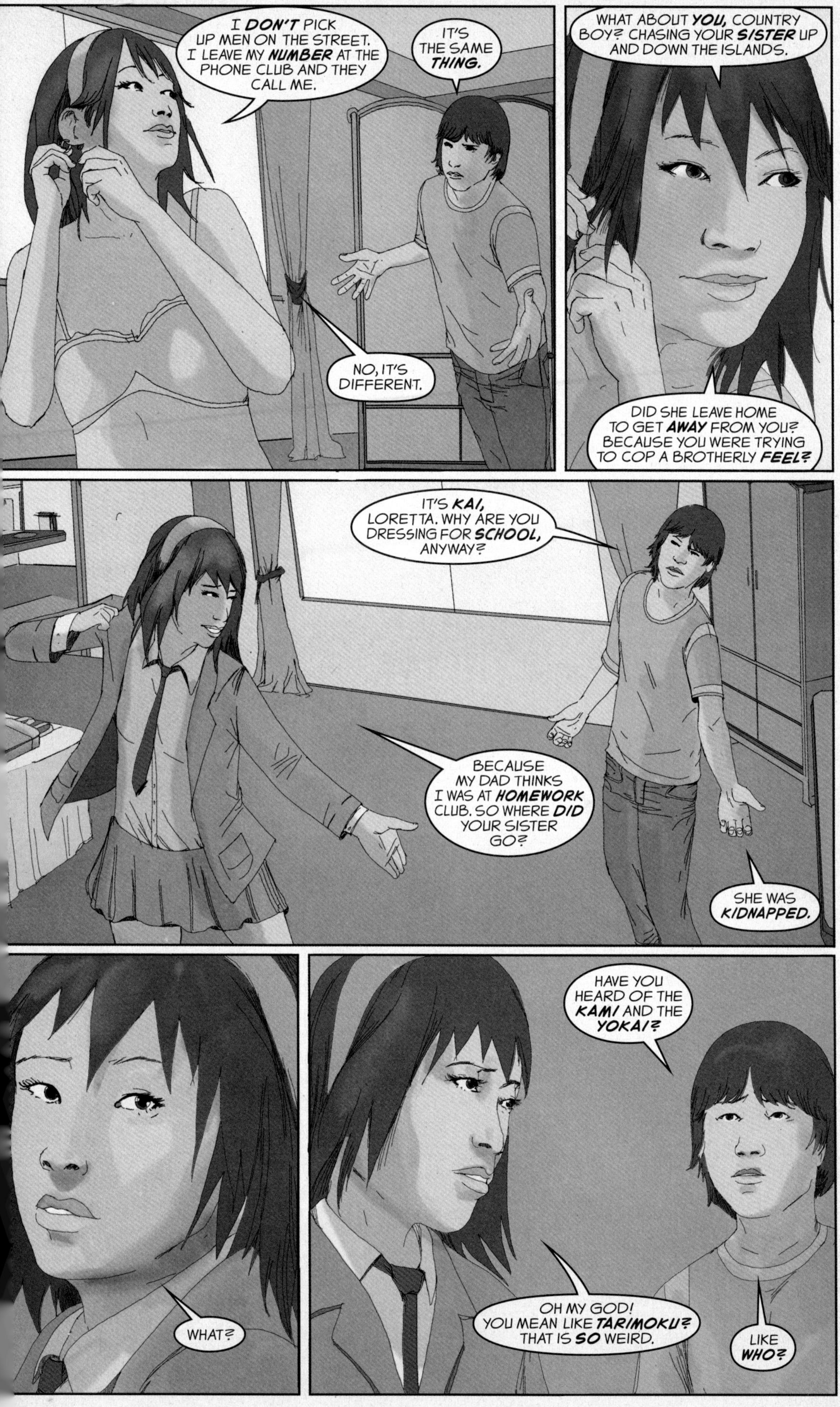
I DON'T PICK UP MEN ON THE STREET. I LEAVE MY NUMBER AT THE PHONE CLUB AND THEY CALL ME.
IT'S THE SAME THING.
NO, IT'S DIFFERENT.
WHAT ABOUT YOU, COUNTRY BOY? CHASING YOUR SISTER UP AND DOWN THE ISLANDS.
DID SHE LEAVE HOME TO GET AWAY FROM YOU? BECAUSE YOU WERE TRYING TO COP A BROTHERLY FEEL?
IT'S KAI, LORETTA. WHY ARE YOU DRESSING FOR SCHOOL, ANYWAY?
BECAUSE MY DAD THINKS I WAS AT HOMEWORK CLUB. SO WHERE DID YOUR SISTER GO?
SHE WAS KIDNAPPED.
WHAT?
HAVE YOU HEARD OF THE KAMI AND THE YOKAI?
OH MY GOD! YOU MEAN LIKE TARIMOKU? THAT IS SO WEIRD.
LIKE WHO?

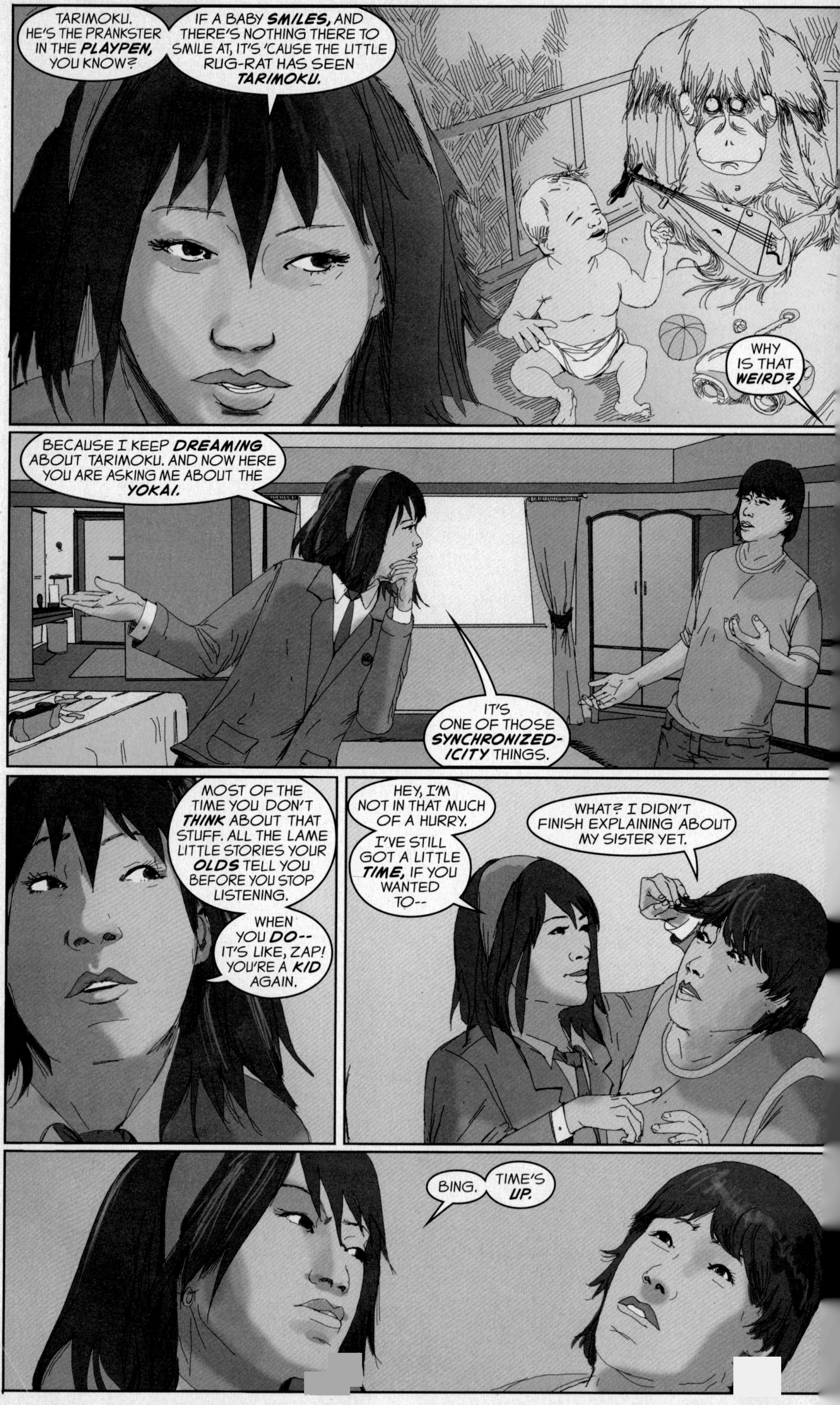
TARIMOKU. HE'S THE PRANKSTER IN THE PLAYPEN, YOU KNOW?
IF A BABY SMILES, AND THERE'S NOTHING THERE TO SMILE AT, IT'S 'CAUSE THE LITTLE RUG-RAT HAS SEEN TARIMOKU.
WHY IS THAT WEIRD?
BECAUSE I KEEP DREAMING ABOUT TARIMOKU. AND NOW HERE YOU ARE ASKING ME ABOUT THE YOKAI.
IT'S ONE OF THOSE SYNCHRONIZED-ICITY THINGS.
MOST OF THE TIME YOU DON'T THINK ABOUT THAT STUFF. ALL THE LAME LITTLE STORIES YOUR OLDS TELL YOU BEFORE YOU STOP LISTENING.
WHEN YOU DO-- IT'S LIKE, ZAP! YOU'RE A KID AGAIN.
HEY, I'M NOT IN THAT MUCH OF A HURRY.
I'VE STILL GOT A LITTLE TIME, IF YOU WANTED TO--
WHAT? I DIDN'T FINISH EXPLAINING ABOUT MY SISTER YET.
BING.
TIME'S UP.

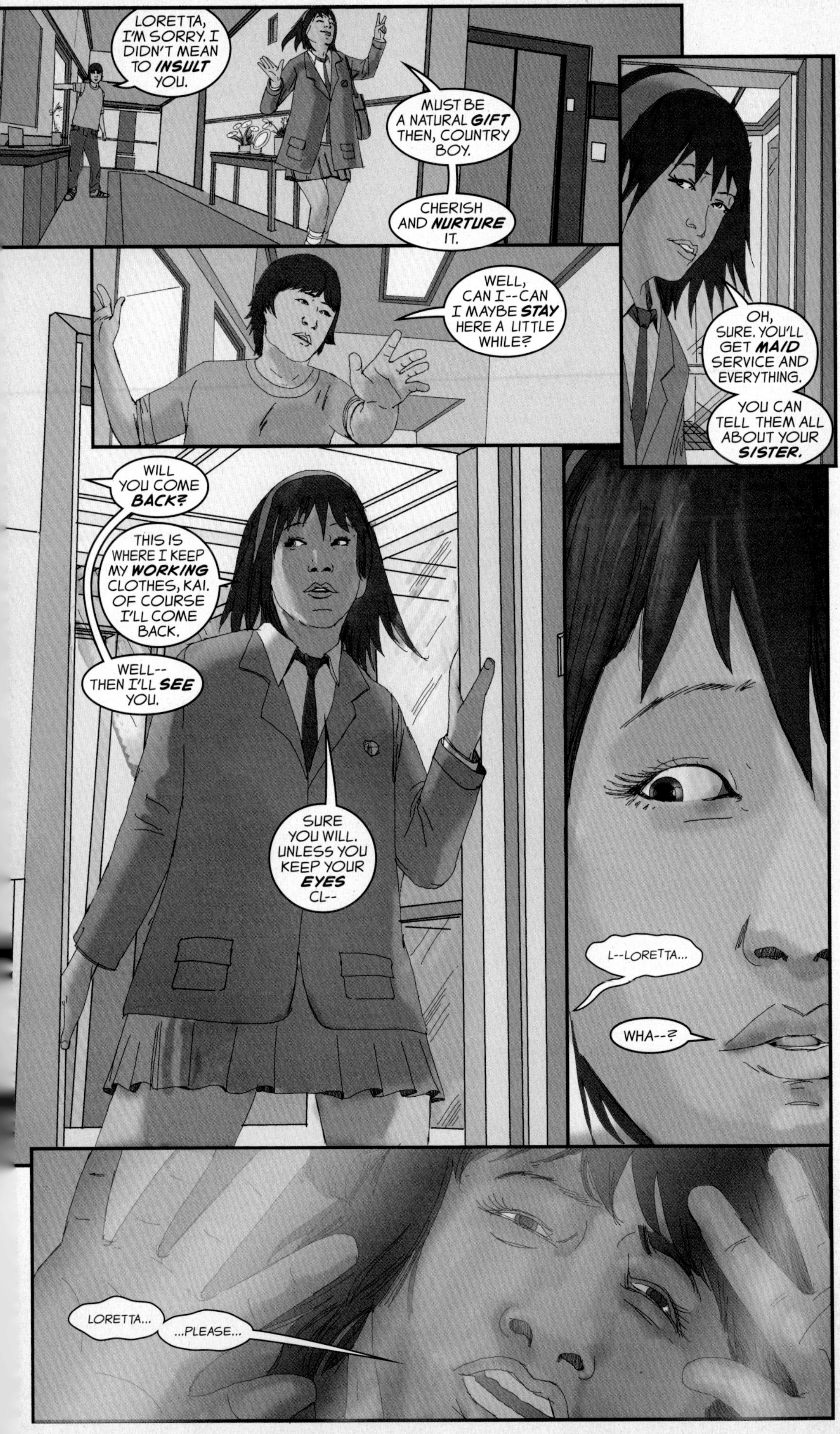
LORETTA, I'M SORRY. I DIDN'T MEAN TO INSULT YOU.
MUST BE A NATURAL GIFT THEN, COUNTRY BOY.
CHERISH AND NURTURE IT.
WELL, CAN I--CAN I MAYBE STAY HERE A LITTLE WHILE?
OH, SURE. YOU'LL GET MAID SERVICE AND EVERYTHING.
YOU CAN TELL THEM ALL ABOUT YOUR SISTER.
WILL YOU COME BACK?
THIS IS WHERE I KEEP MY WORKING CLOTHES, KAI. OF COURSE I'LL COME BACK.
WELL-- THEN I'LL SEE YOU.
SURE YOU WILL. UNLESS YOU KEEP YOUR EYES CL--
L--LORETTA...
WHA--?
LORETTA...
...PLEASE...

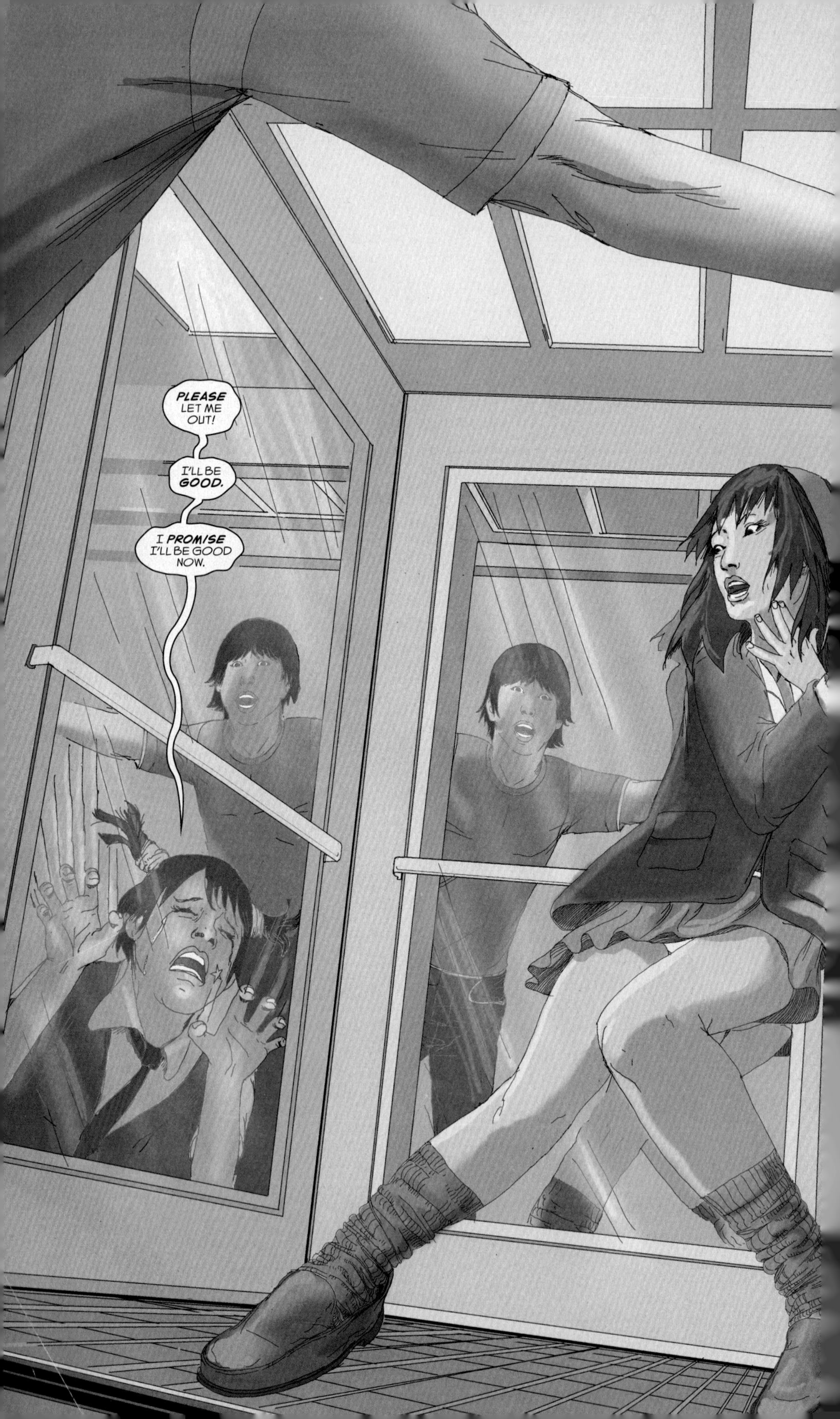
PLEASE LET ME OUT!
I'LL BE GOOD.
I PROMISE I'LL BE GOOD NOW.

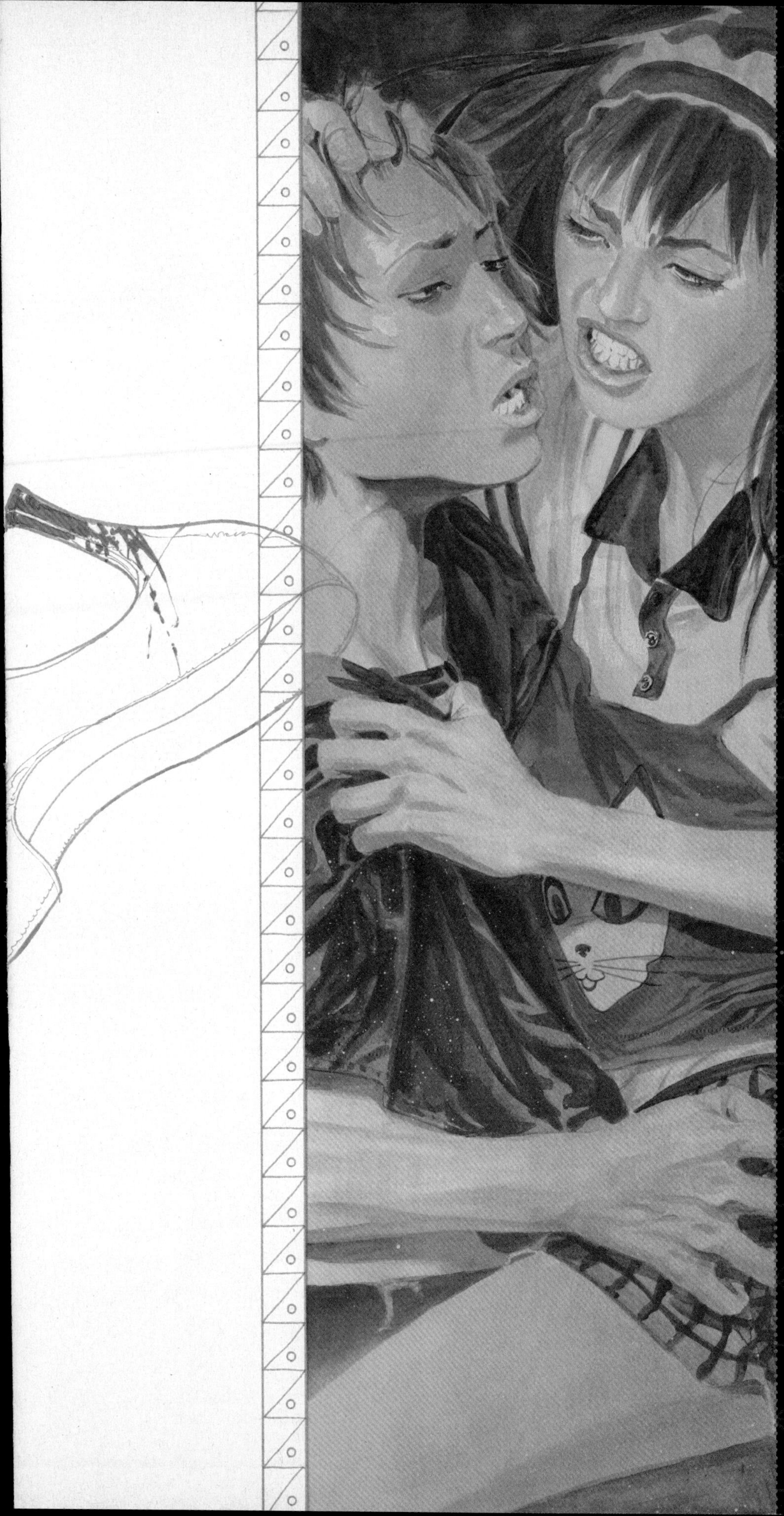

chapter two

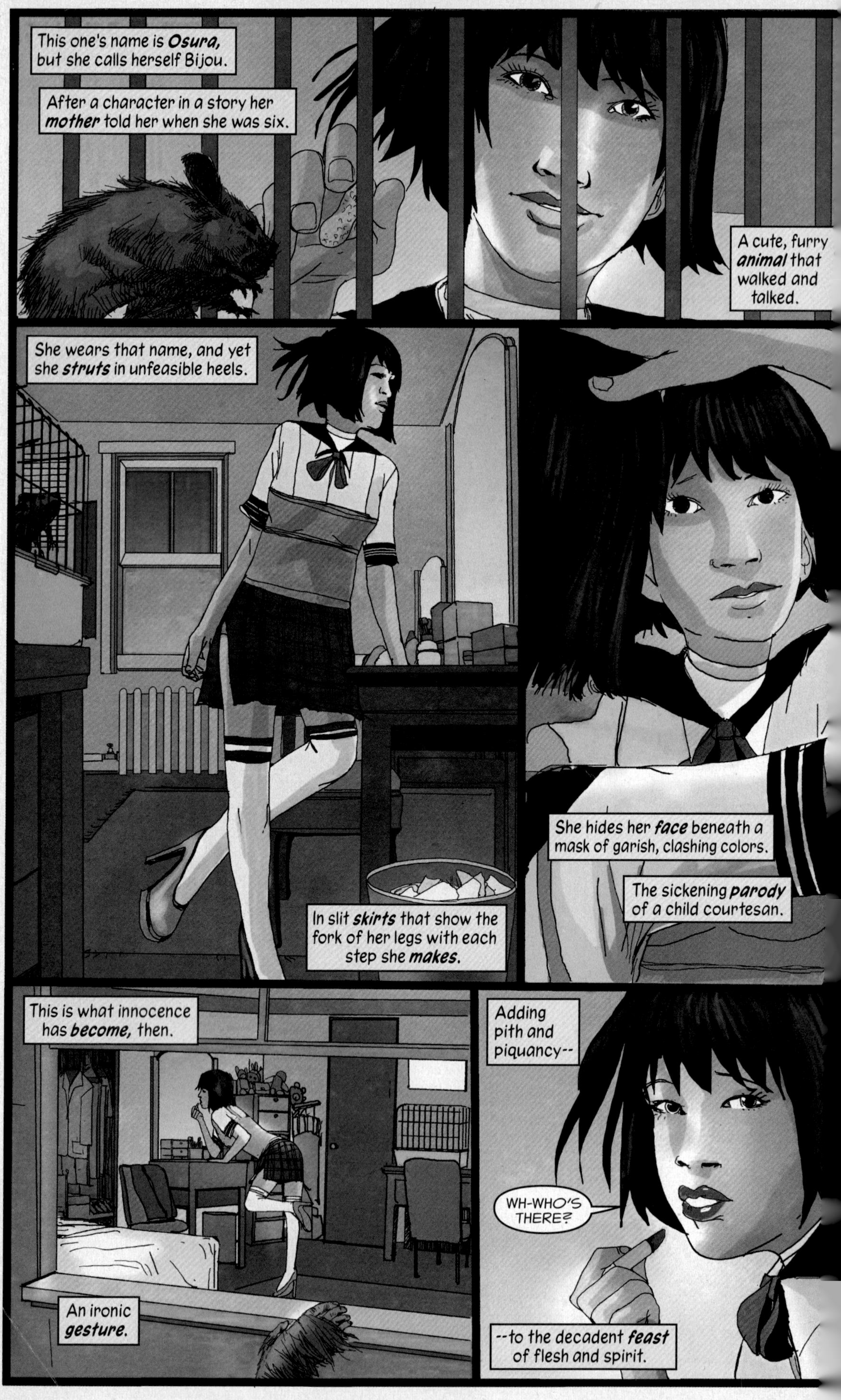
This one's name is **Osura,** but she calls herself Bijou.
After a character in a story her **mother** told her when she was six.
A cute, furry **animal** that walked and talked.
She wears that name, and yet she **struts** in unfeasible heels.
In slit **skirts** that show the fork of her legs with each step she **makes.**
She hides her **face** beneath a mask of garish, clashing colors.
The sickening **parody** of a child courtesan.
This is what innocence has **become,** then.
An ironic **gesture.**
Adding pith and piquancy--
WH-WHO'S THERE?
--to the decadent **feast** of flesh and spirit.

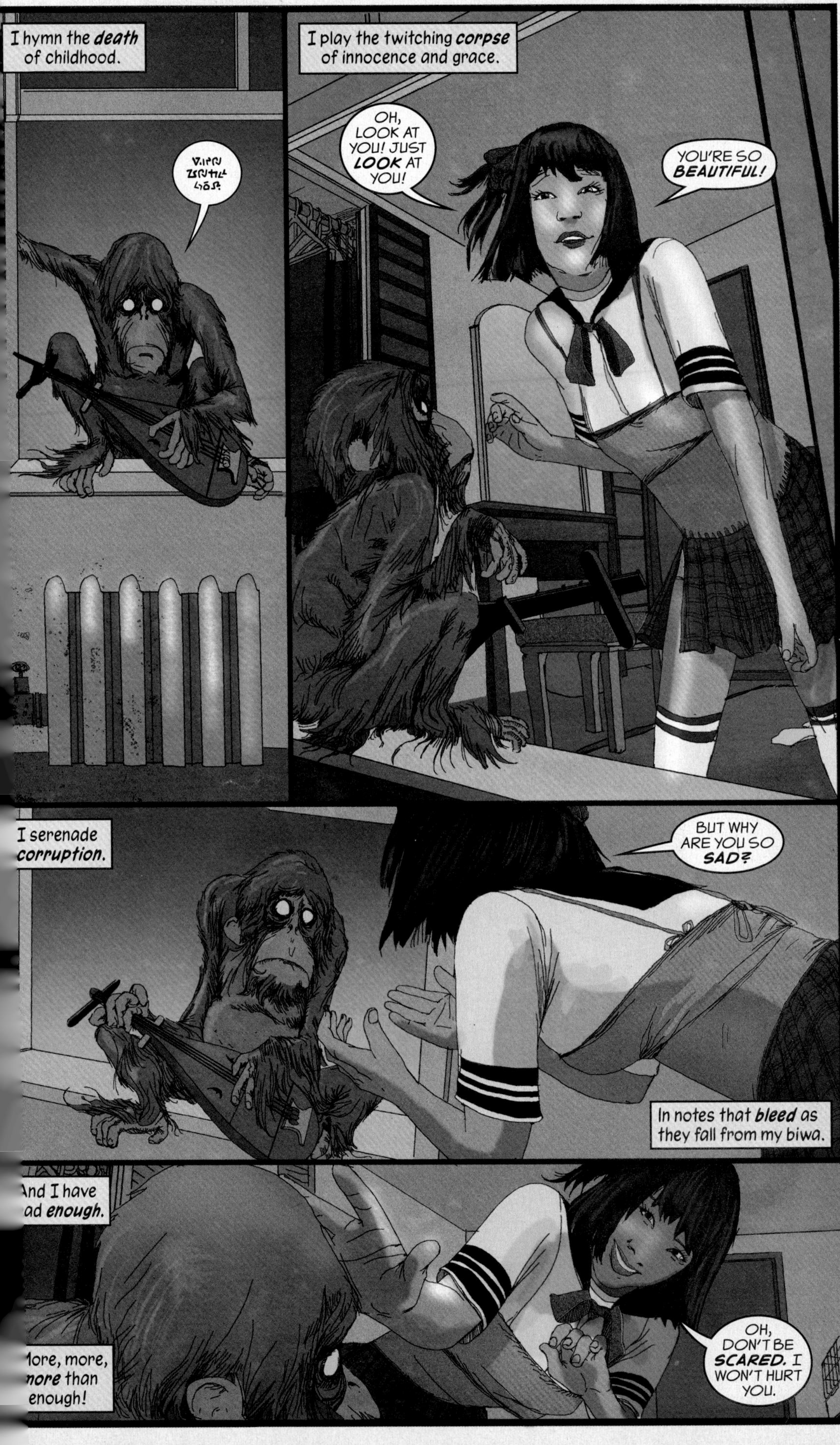
I hymn the *death* of childhood.
I play the twitching *corpse* of innocence and grace.
OH, LOOK AT YOU! JUST **LOOK** AT YOU!
YOU'RE SO **BEAUTIFUL!**
I serenade *corruption*.
BUT WHY ARE YOU SO **SAD?**
In notes that *bleed* as they fall from my biwa.
And I have ad *enough*.
ore, more, *more* than enough!
OH, DON'T BE **SCARED.** I WON'T HURT YOU.

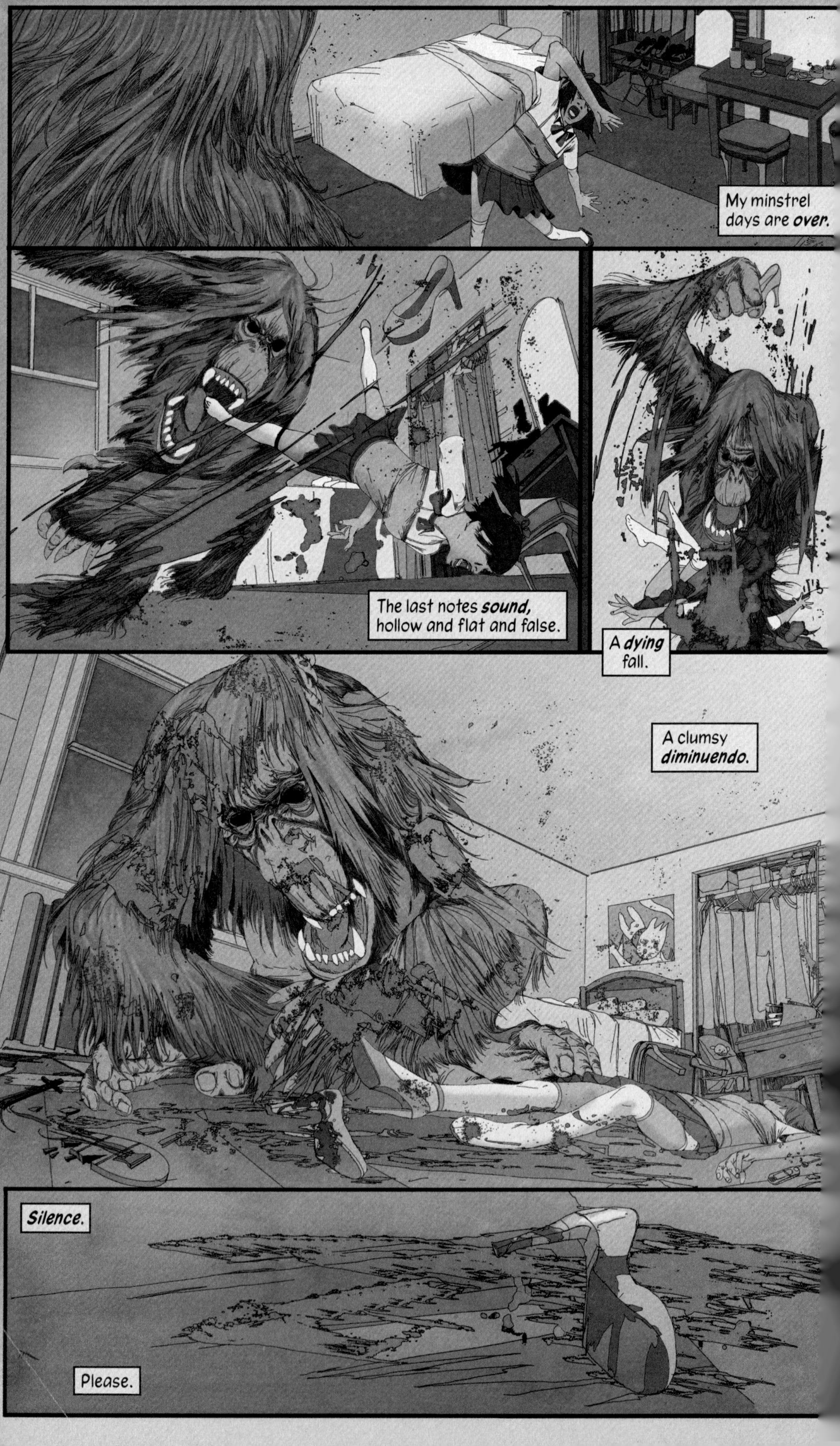
My minstrel days are *over*.
The last notes *sound*, hollow and flat and false.
A *dying* fall.
A clumsy *diminuendo*.
Silence.
Please.

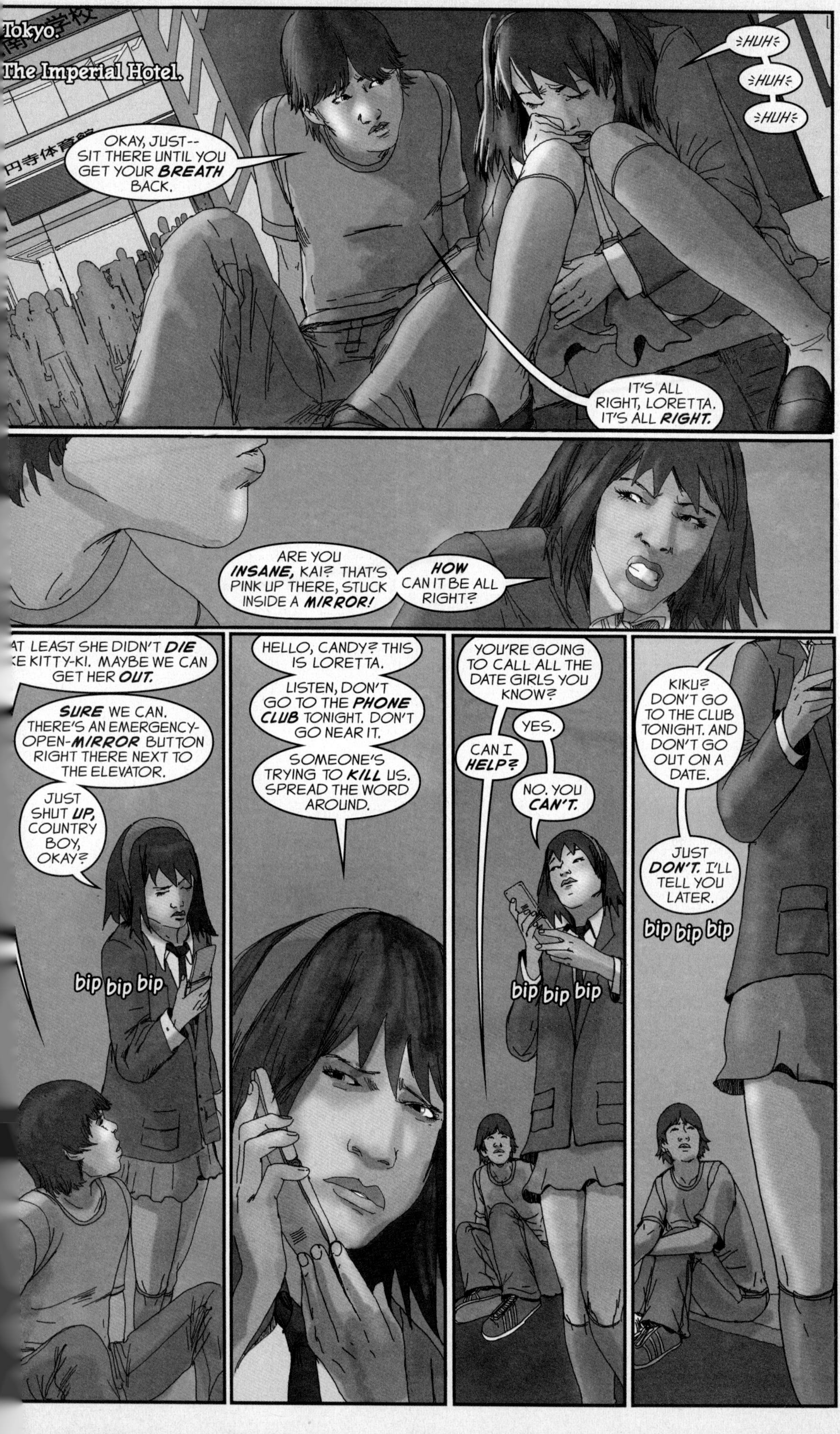
Tokyo.
The Imperial Hotel.
HUH
HUH
HUH
OKAY, JUST-- SIT THERE UNTIL YOU GET YOUR BREATH BACK.
IT'S ALL RIGHT, LORETTA. IT'S ALL RIGHT.
ARE YOU INSANE, KAI? THAT'S PINK UP THERE, STUCK INSIDE A MIRROR!
HOW CAN IT BE ALL RIGHT?
AT LEAST SHE DIDN'T DIE LIKE KITTY-KI. MAYBE WE CAN GET HER OUT.
SURE WE CAN. THERE'S AN EMERGENCY-OPEN-MIRROR BUTTON RIGHT THERE NEXT TO THE ELEVATOR.
JUST SHUT UP, COUNTRY BOY, OKAY?
bip bip bip
HELLO, CANDY? THIS IS LORETTA.
LISTEN, DON'T GO TO THE PHONE CLUB TONIGHT. DON'T GO NEAR IT.
SOMEONE'S TRYING TO KILL US. SPREAD THE WORD AROUND.
YOU'RE GOING TO CALL ALL THE DATE GIRLS YOU KNOW?
YES.
CAN I HELP?
NO. YOU CAN'T.
bip bip bip
KIKU? DON'T GO TO THE CLUB TONIGHT. AND DON'T GO OUT ON A DATE.
JUST DON'T. I'LL TELL YOU LATER.
bip bip bip

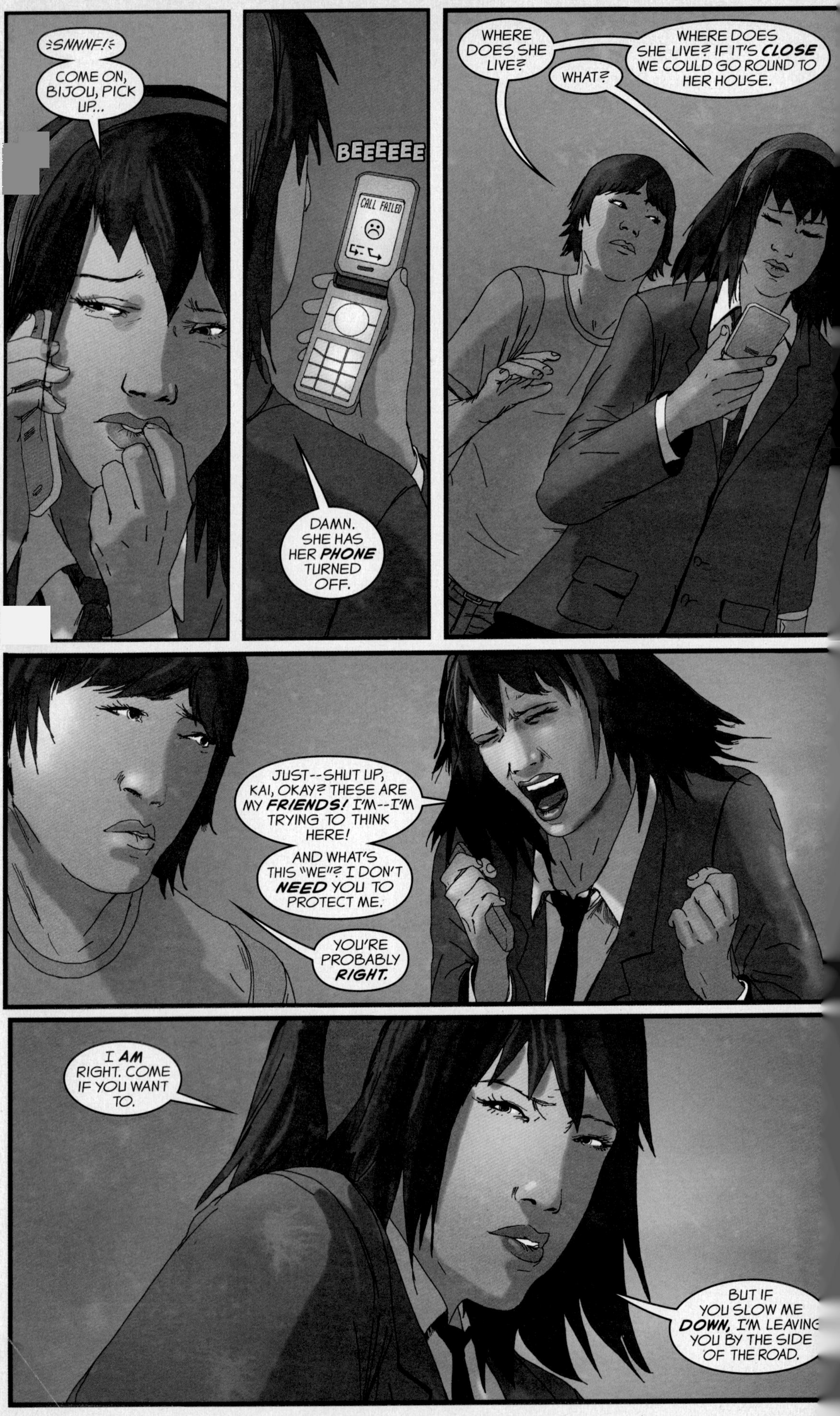

SNNNF!
COME ON, BIJOU, PICK UP...
BEEEEEE
CALL FAILED
DAMN. SHE HAS HER PHONE TURNED OFF.
WHERE DOES SHE LIVE?
WHAT?
WHERE DOES SHE LIVE? IF IT'S CLOSE WE COULD GO ROUND TO HER HOUSE.
JUST--SHUT UP, KAI, OKAY? THESE ARE MY FRIENDS! I'M--I'M TRYING TO THINK HERE!
AND WHAT'S THIS "WE"? I DON'T NEED YOU TO PROTECT ME.
YOU'RE PROBABLY RIGHT.
I AM RIGHT. COME IF YOU WANT TO.
BUT IF YOU SLOW ME DOWN, I'M LEAVING YOU BY THE SIDE OF THE ROAD.

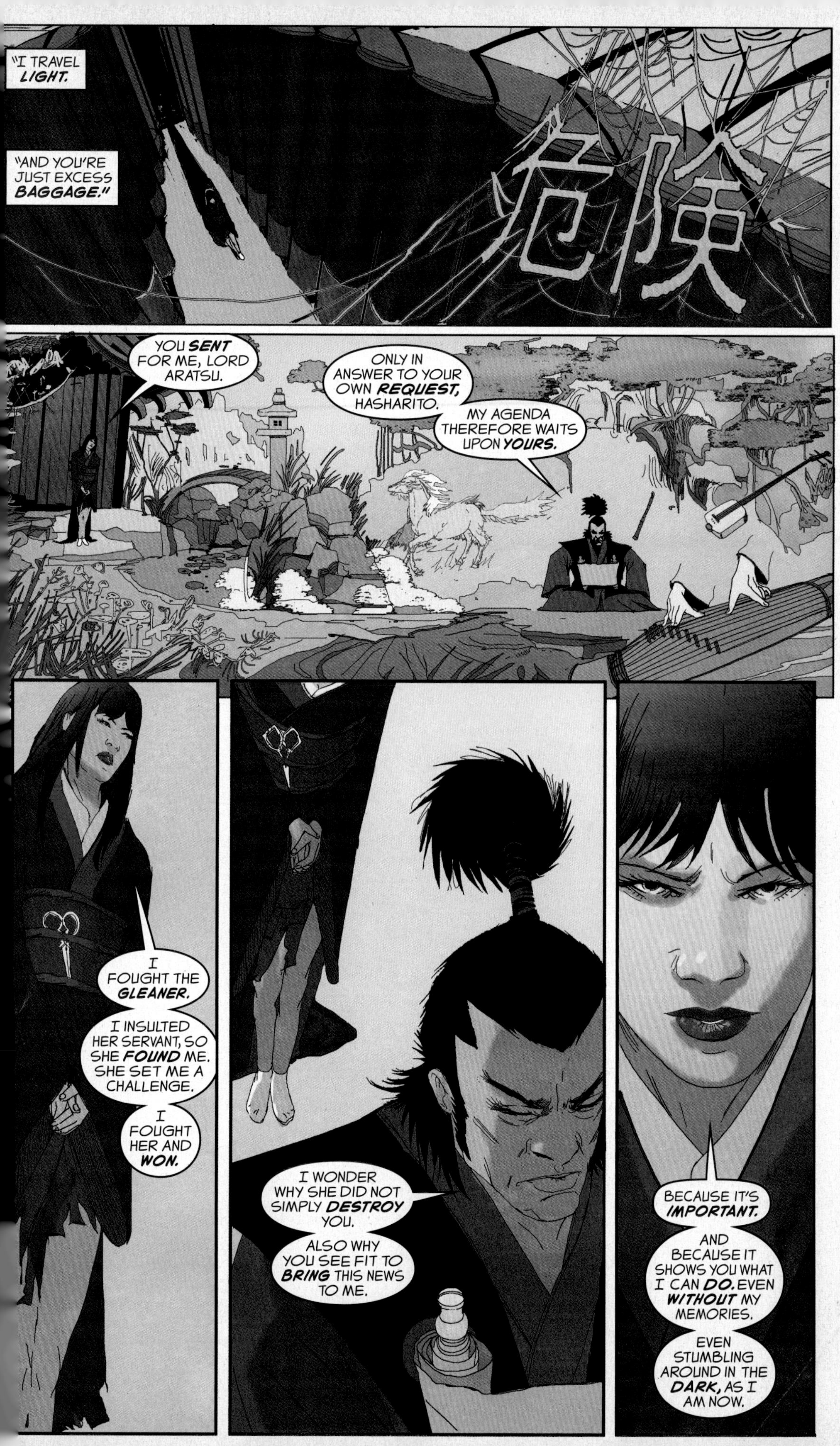

"I TRAVEL LIGHT.
"AND YOU'RE JUST EXCESS BAGGAGE."
危険
YOU SENT FOR ME, LORD ARATSU.
ONLY IN ANSWER TO YOUR OWN REQUEST, HASHARITO.
MY AGENDA THEREFORE WAITS UPON YOURS.
I FOUGHT THE GLEANER.
I INSULTED HER SERVANT, SO SHE FOUND ME. SHE SET ME A CHALLENGE.
I FOUGHT HER AND WON.
I WONDER WHY SHE DID NOT SIMPLY DESTROY YOU.
ALSO WHY YOU SEE FIT TO BRING THIS NEWS TO ME.
BECAUSE IT'S IMPORTANT.
AND BECAUSE IT SHOWS YOU WHAT I CAN DO. EVEN WITHOUT MY MEMORIES.
EVEN STUMBLING AROUND IN THE DARK, AS I AM NOW.

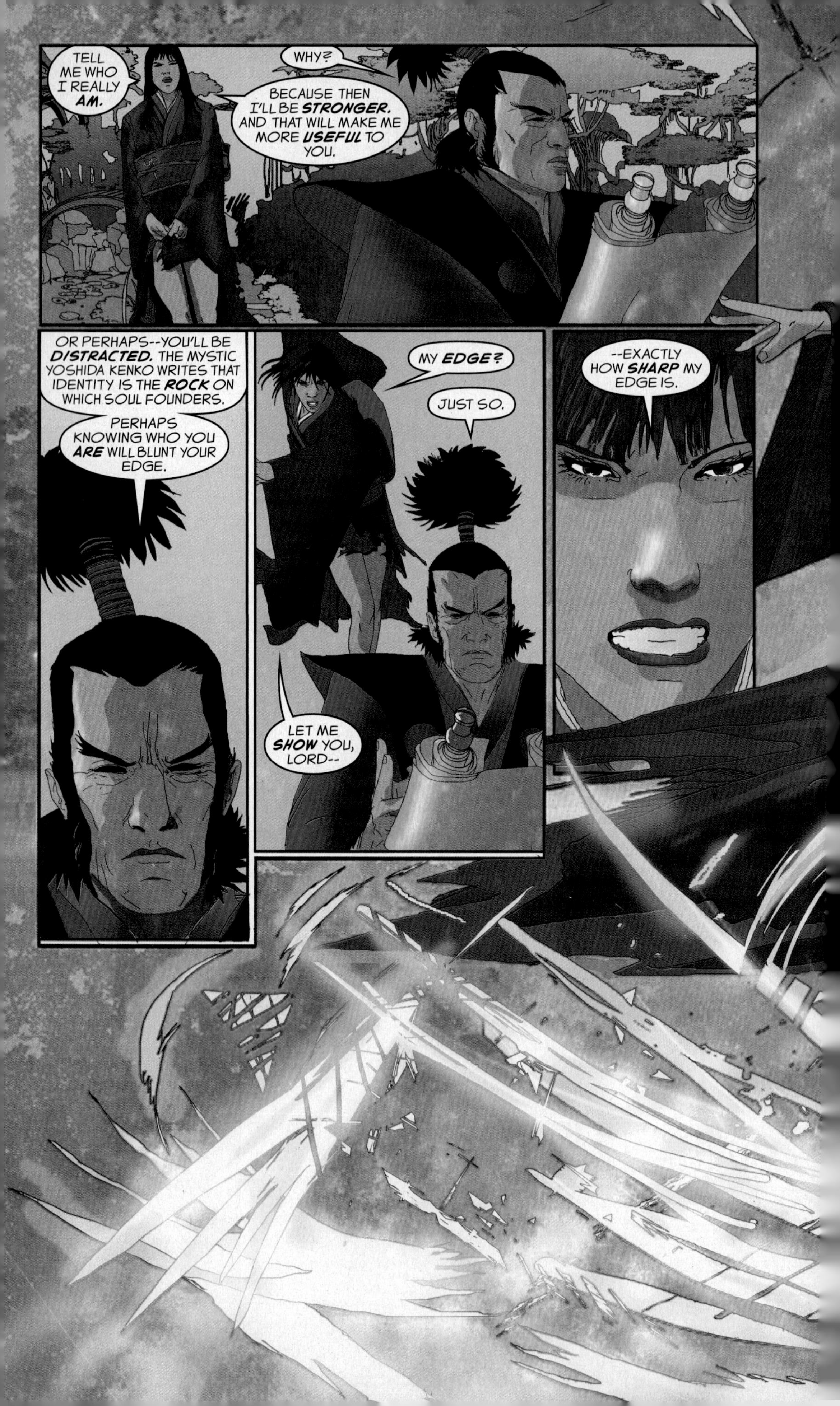

TELL ME WHO I REALLY **AM.**
WHY?
BECAUSE THEN I'LL BE **STRONGER.** AND THAT WILL MAKE ME MORE **USEFUL** TO YOU.
OR PERHAPS--YOU'LL BE **DISTRACTED.** THE MYSTIC YOSHIDA KENKO WRITES THAT IDENTITY IS THE **ROCK** ON WHICH SOUL FOUNDERS.
PERHAPS KNOWING WHO YOU **ARE** WILL BLUNT YOUR EDGE.
MY **EDGE?**
JUST SO.
LET ME **SHOW** YOU, LORD--
--EXACTLY HOW **SHARP** MY EDGE IS.

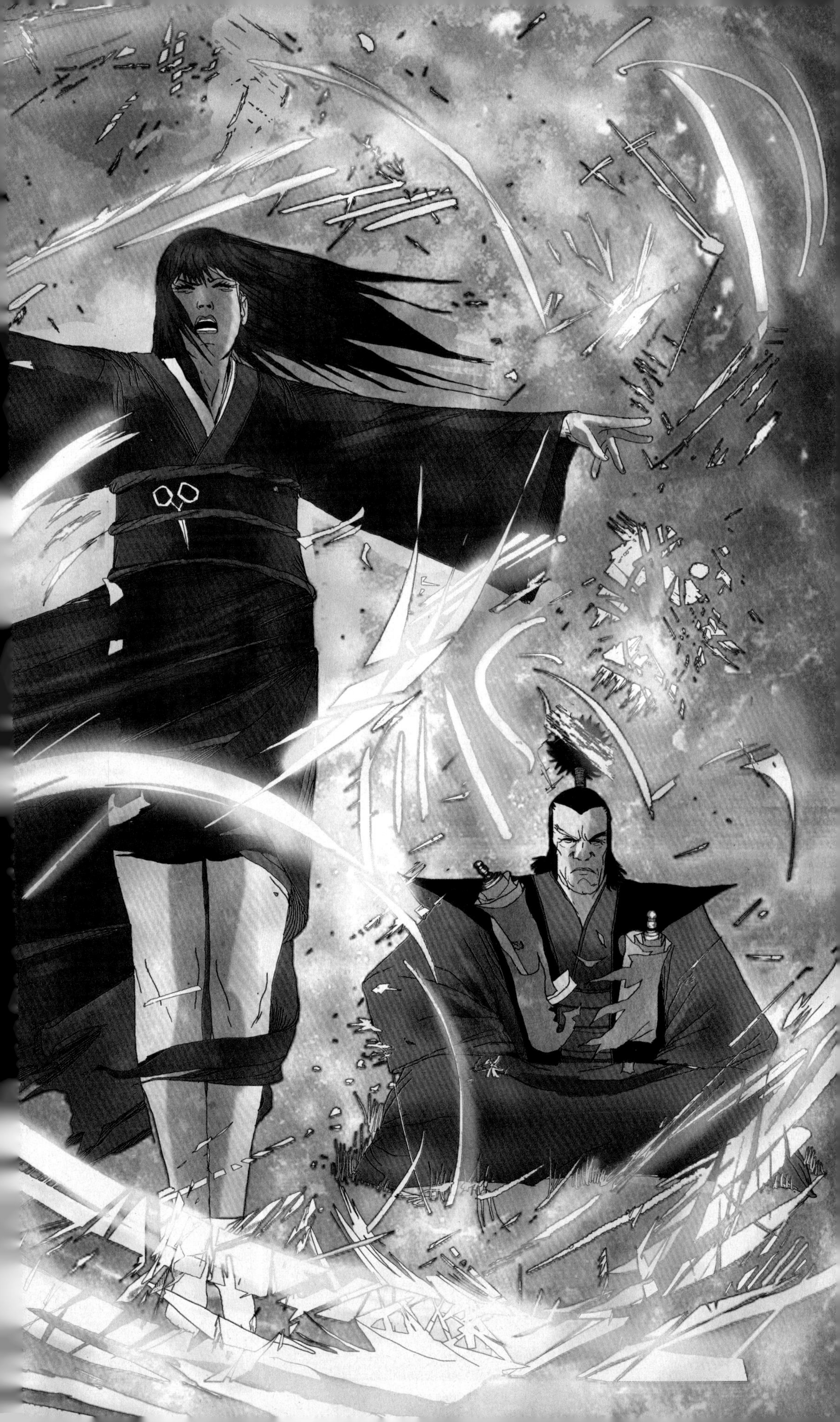

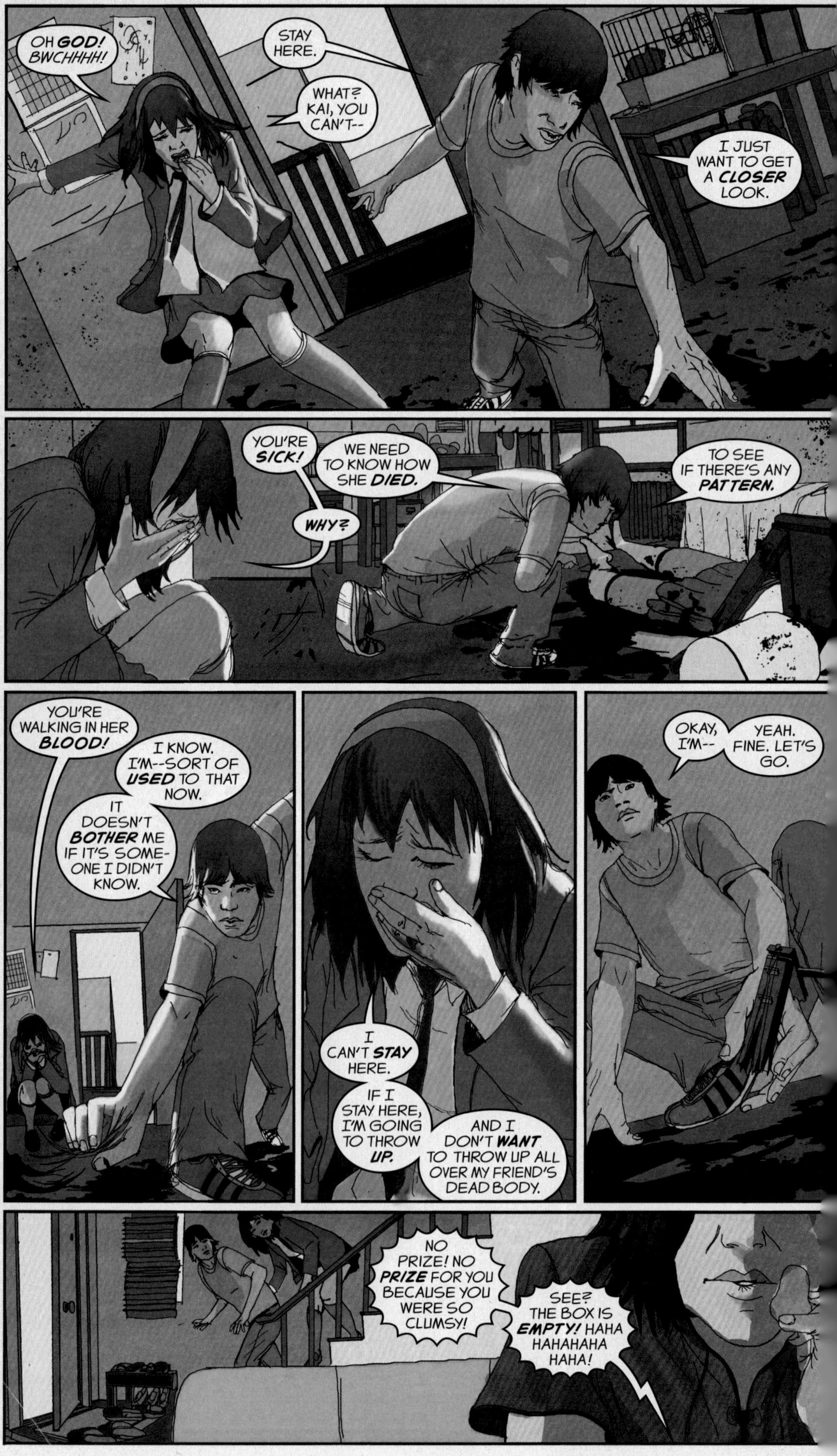
OH **GOD!** BWCHHHH!
STAY HERE.
WHAT? KAI, YOU CAN'T--
I JUST WANT TO GET A **CLOSER** LOOK.
YOU'RE **SICK!**
WE NEED TO KNOW HOW SHE **DIED.**
WHY?
TO SEE IF THERE'S ANY **PATTERN.**
YOU'RE WALKING IN HER **BLOOD!**
I KNOW. I'M--SORT OF **USED** TO THAT NOW.
IT DOESN'T **BOTHER** ME IF IT'S SOME-ONE I DIDN'T KNOW.
I CAN'T **STAY** HERE.
IF I STAY HERE, I'M GOING TO THROW **UP.**
AND I DON'T **WANT** TO THROW UP ALL OVER MY FRIEND'S DEAD BODY.
OKAY, I'M--
YEAH. FINE. LET'S GO.
NO PRIZE! NO **PRIZE** FOR YOU BECAUSE YOU WERE SO CLUMSY!
SEE? THE BOX IS **EMPTY!** HAHA HAHAHAHA HAHA!

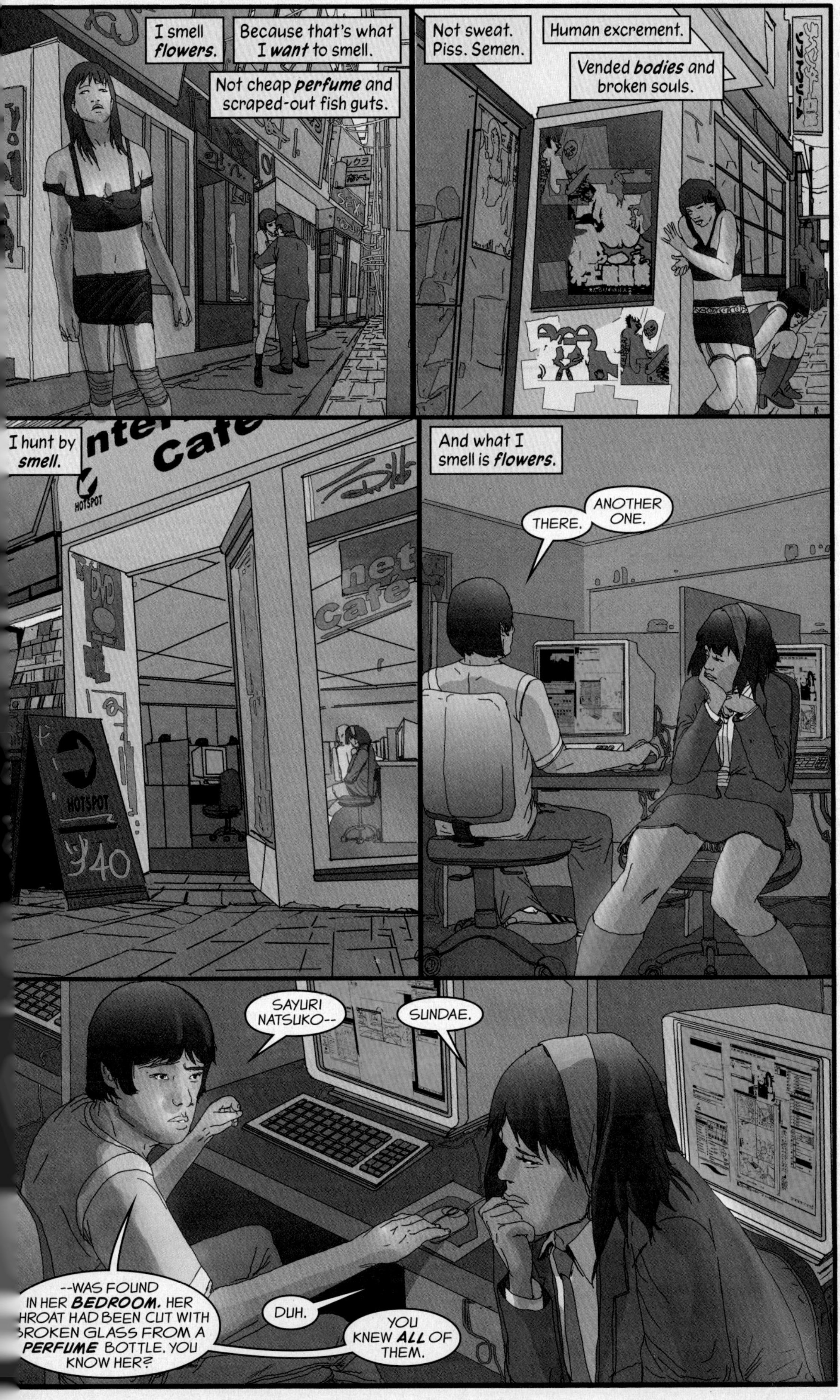
I smell flowers.
Because that's what I want to smell.
Not cheap perfume and scraped-out fish guts.
Not sweat. Piss. Semen.
Human excrement.
Vended bodies and broken souls.
I hunt by smell.
And what I smell is flowers.
THERE.
ANOTHER ONE.
SAYURI NATSUKO--
SUNDAE.
--WAS FOUND IN HER BEDROOM. HER THROAT HAD BEEN CUT WITH BROKEN GLASS FROM A PERFUME BOTTLE. YOU KNOW HER?
DUH.
YOU KNEW ALL OF THEM.

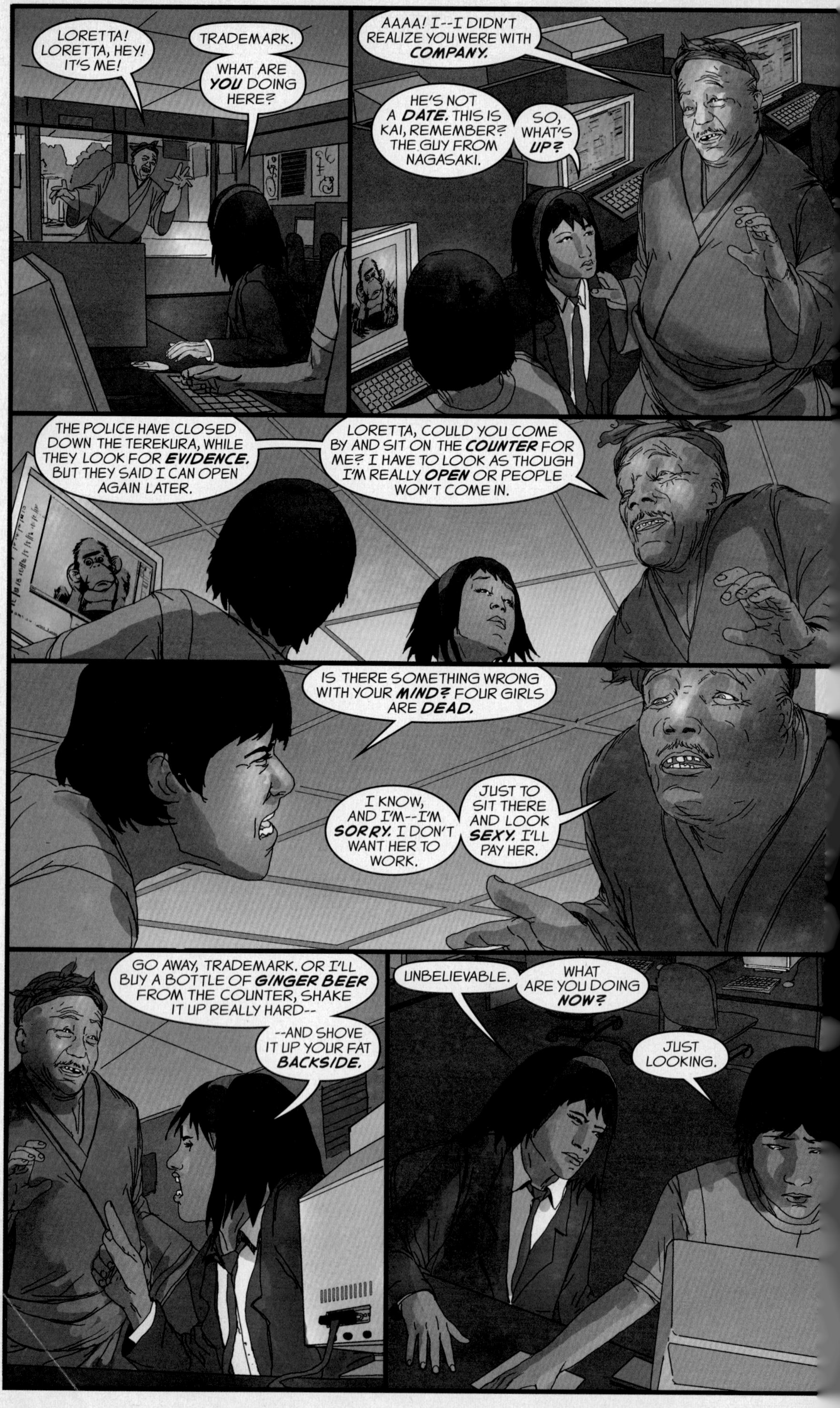
LORETTA! LORETTA, HEY! IT'S ME!
TRADEMARK.
WHAT ARE YOU DOING HERE?
AAAA! I--I DIDN'T REALIZE YOU WERE WITH COMPANY.
HE'S NOT A DATE. THIS IS KAI, REMEMBER? THE GUY FROM NAGASAKI.
SO, WHAT'S UP?
THE POLICE HAVE CLOSED DOWN THE TEREKURA, WHILE THEY LOOK FOR EVIDENCE. BUT THEY SAID I CAN OPEN AGAIN LATER.
LORETTA, COULD YOU COME BY AND SIT ON THE COUNTER FOR ME? I HAVE TO LOOK AS THOUGH I'M REALLY OPEN OR PEOPLE WON'T COME IN.
IS THERE SOMETHING WRONG WITH YOUR MIND? FOUR GIRLS ARE DEAD.
I KNOW, AND I'M--I'M SORRY. I DON'T WANT HER TO WORK.
JUST TO SIT THERE AND LOOK SEXY. I'LL PAY HER.
GO AWAY, TRADEMARK. OR I'LL BUY A BOTTLE OF GINGER BEER FROM THE COUNTER, SHAKE IT UP REALLY HARD--
--AND SHOVE IT UP YOUR FAT BACKSIDE.
UNBELIEVABLE.
WHAT ARE YOU DOING NOW?
JUST LOOKING.

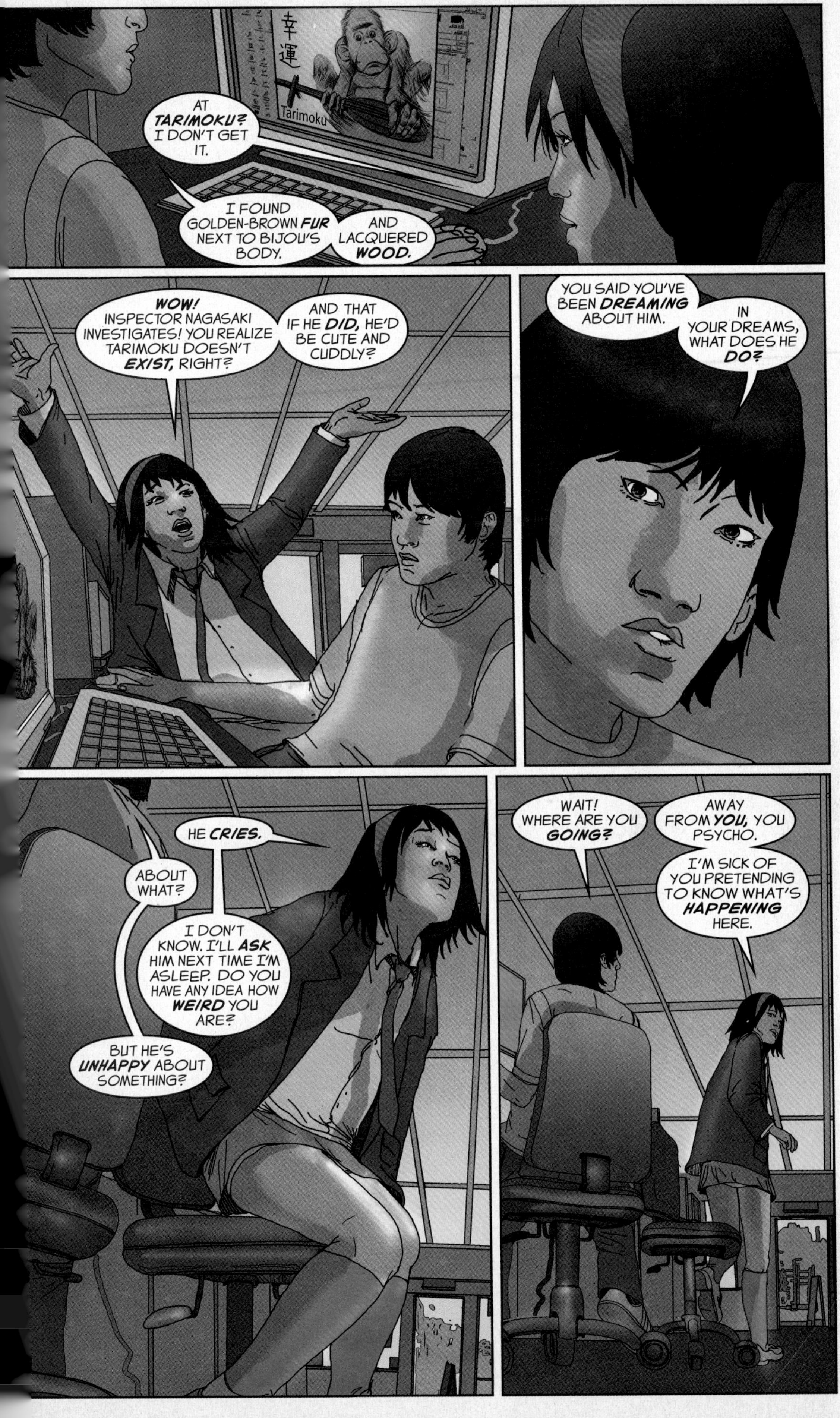

Tarimoku
幸運
AT TARIMOKU? I DON'T GET IT.
I FOUND GOLDEN-BROWN FUR NEXT TO BIJOU'S BODY.
AND LACQUERED WOOD.
WOW! INSPECTOR NAGASAKI INVESTIGATES! YOU REALIZE TARIMOKU DOESN'T EXIST, RIGHT?
AND THAT IF HE DID, HE'D BE CUTE AND CUDDLY?
YOU SAID YOU'VE BEEN DREAMING ABOUT HIM.
IN YOUR DREAMS, WHAT DOES HE DO?
HE CRIES.
ABOUT WHAT?
I DON'T KNOW. I'LL ASK HIM NEXT TIME I'M ASLEEP. DO YOU HAVE ANY IDEA HOW WEIRD YOU ARE?
BUT HE'S UNHAPPY ABOUT SOMETHING?
WAIT! WHERE ARE YOU GOING?
AWAY FROM YOU, YOU PSYCHO.
I'M SICK OF YOU PRETENDING TO KNOW WHAT'S HAPPENING HERE.

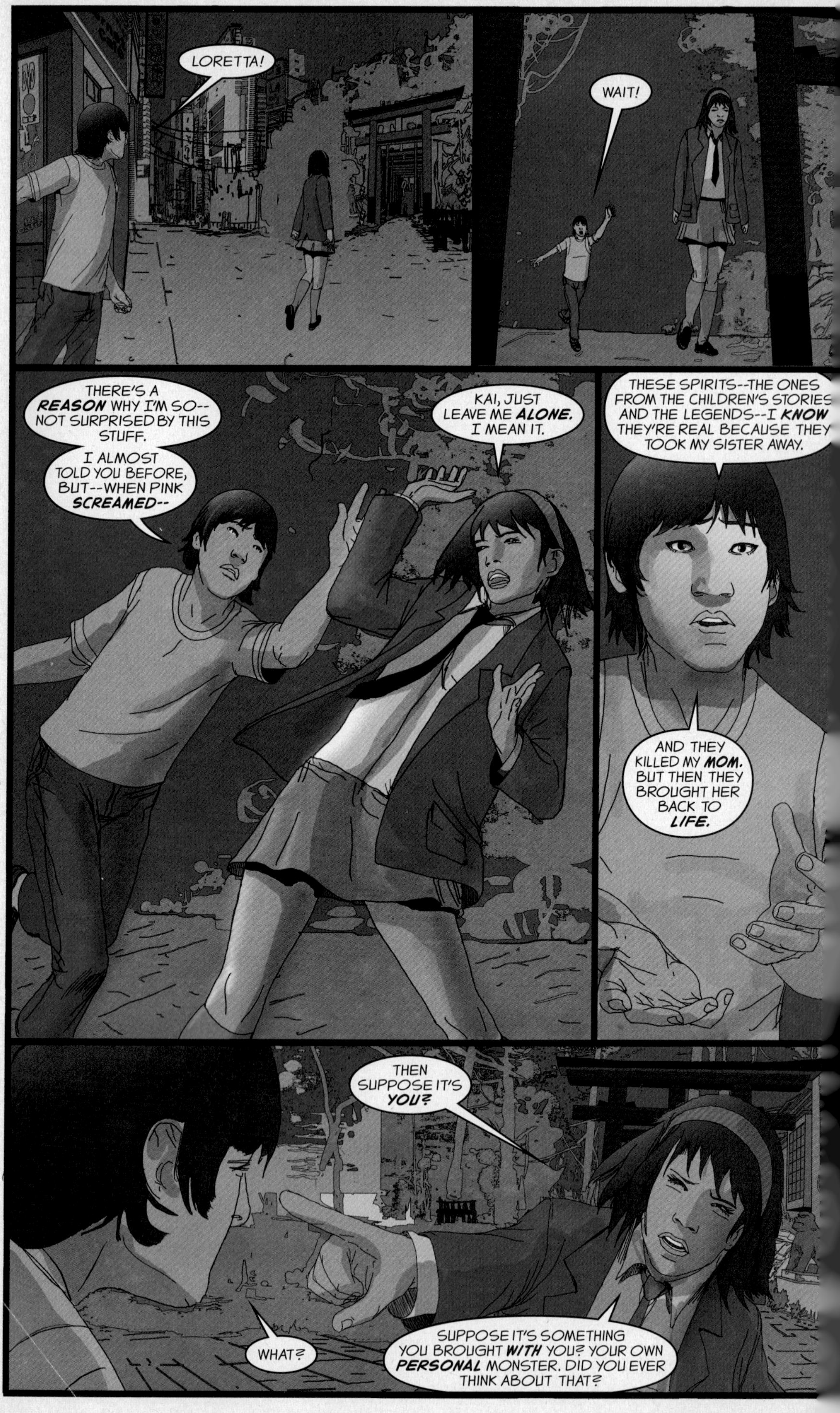
LORETTA!
WAIT!
THERE'S A REASON WHY I'M SO--NOT SURPRISED BY THIS STUFF.
I ALMOST TOLD YOU BEFORE, BUT--WHEN PINK SCREAMED--
KAI, JUST LEAVE ME ALONE. I MEAN IT.
THESE SPIRITS--THE ONES FROM THE CHILDREN'S STORIES AND THE LEGENDS--I KNOW THEY'RE REAL BECAUSE THEY TOOK MY SISTER AWAY.
AND THEY KILLED MY MOM. BUT THEN THEY BROUGHT HER BACK TO LIFE.
THEN SUPPOSE IT'S YOU?
WHAT?
SUPPOSE IT'S SOMETHING YOU BROUGHT WITH YOU? YOUR OWN PERSONAL MONSTER. DID YOU EVER THINK ABOUT THAT?

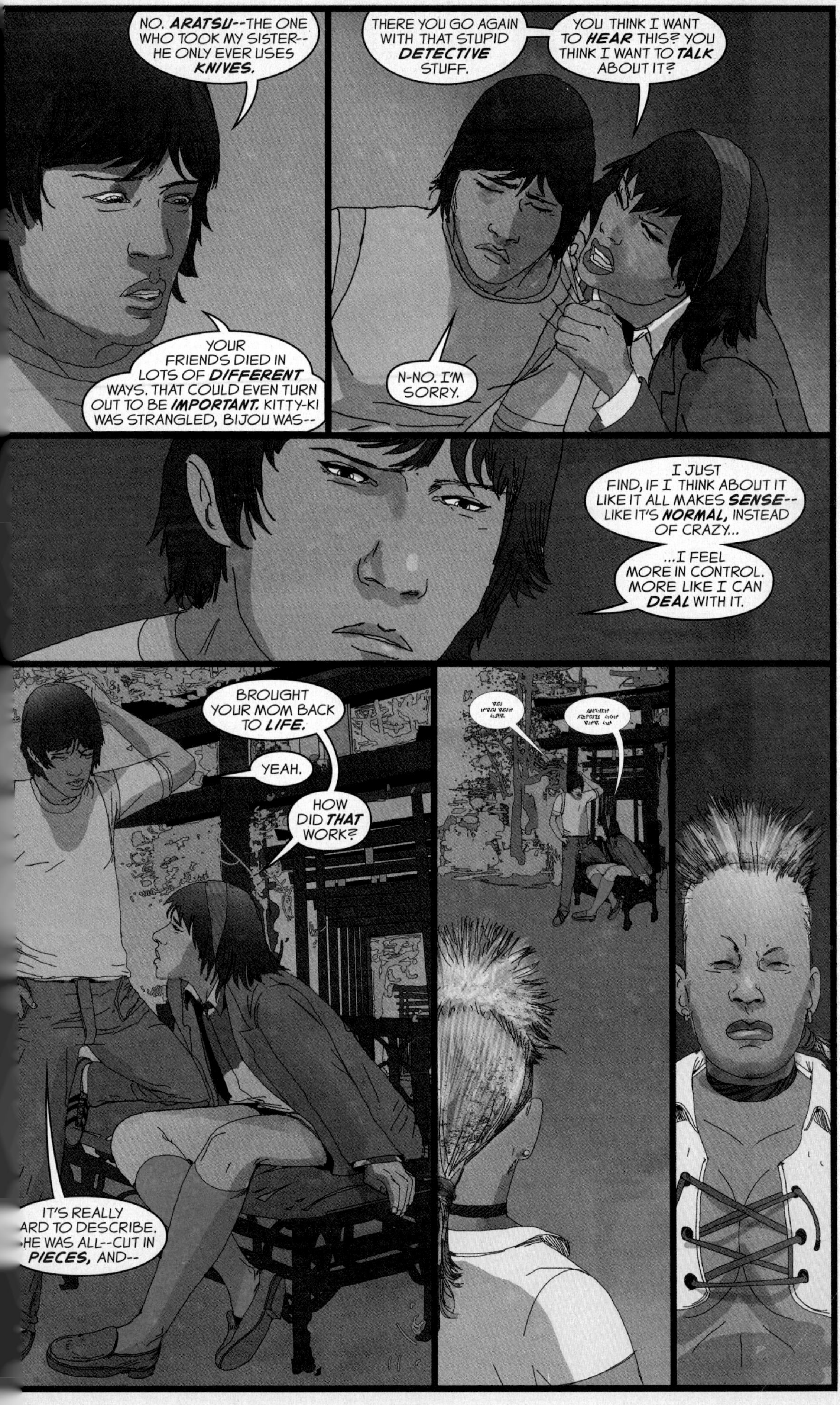
NO. ARATSU--THE ONE WHO TOOK MY SISTER-- HE ONLY EVER USES KNIVES.
YOUR FRIENDS DIED IN LOTS OF DIFFERENT WAYS. THAT COULD EVEN TURN OUT TO BE IMPORTANT. KITTY-KI WAS STRANGLED, BIJOU WAS--
THERE YOU GO AGAIN WITH THAT STUPID DETECTIVE STUFF.
YOU THINK I WANT TO HEAR THIS? YOU THINK I WANT TO TALK ABOUT IT?
N-NO. I'M SORRY.
I JUST FIND, IF I THINK ABOUT IT LIKE IT ALL MAKES SENSE-- LIKE IT'S NORMAL, INSTEAD OF CRAZY...
...I FEEL MORE IN CONTROL. MORE LIKE I CAN DEAL WITH IT.
BROUGHT YOUR MOM BACK TO LIFE.
YEAH.
HOW DID THAT WORK?
IT'S REALLY
ARD TO DESCRIBE.
HE WAS ALL--CUT IN
PIECES, AND--

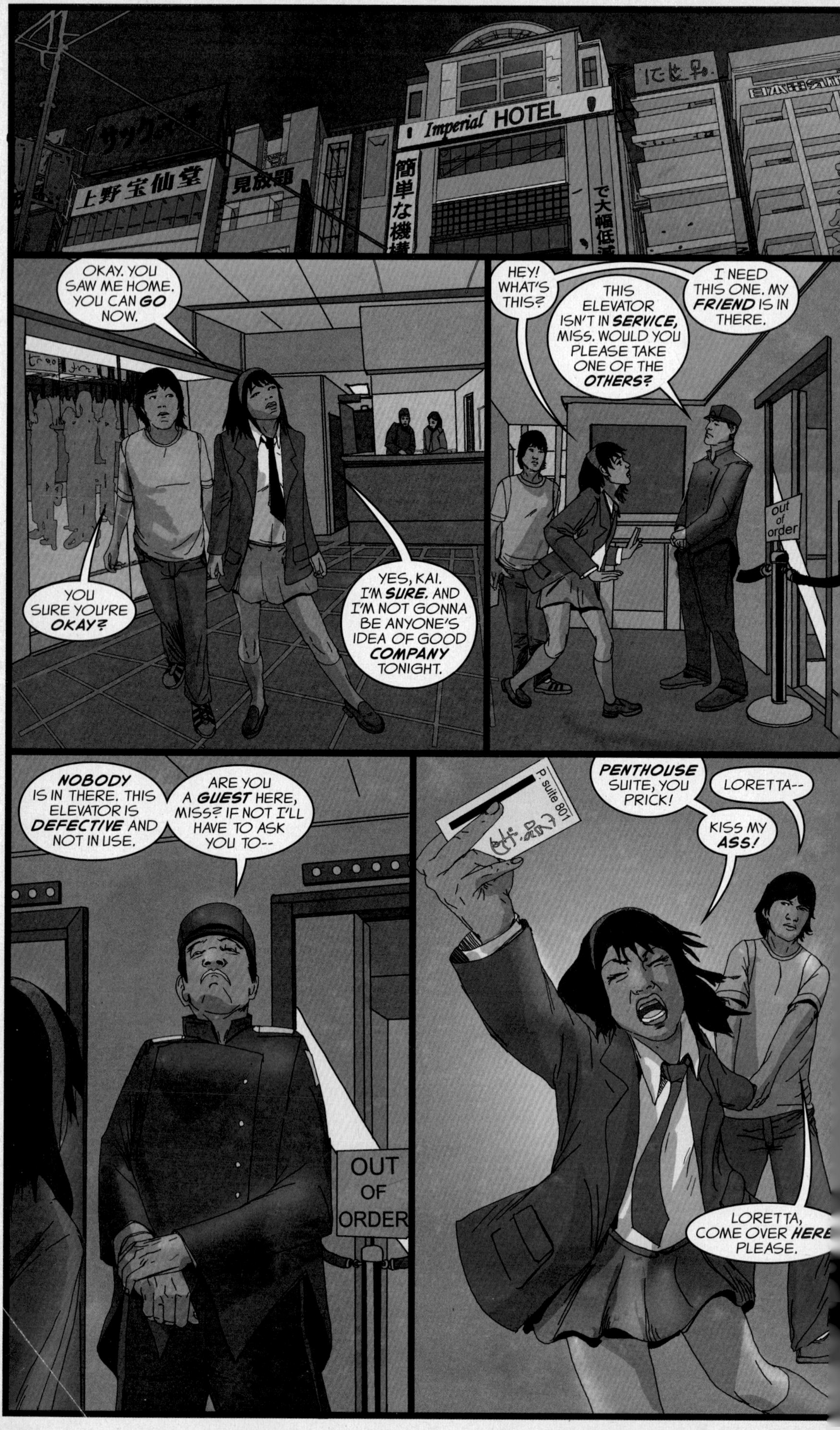

Imperial HOTEL
上野宝仙堂
見放題
OKAY. YOU SAW ME HOME. YOU CAN **GO** NOW.
YOU SURE YOU'RE **OKAY?**
YES, KAI. I'M **SURE.** AND I'M NOT GONNA BE ANYONE'S IDEA OF GOOD **COMPANY** TONIGHT.
HEY! WHAT'S THIS?
I NEED THIS ONE. MY **FRIEND** IS IN THERE.
THIS ELEVATOR ISN'T IN **SERVICE,** MISS. WOULD YOU PLEASE TAKE ONE OF THE **OTHERS?**
out of order
NOBODY IS IN THERE. THIS ELEVATOR IS **DEFECTIVE** AND NOT IN USE.
ARE YOU A **GUEST** HERE, MISS? IF NOT I'LL HAVE TO ASK YOU TO--
OUT OF ORDER
P. suite 801
PENTHOUSE SUITE, YOU PRICK!
LORETTA--
KISS MY **ASS!**
LORETTA, COME OVER **HERE** PLEASE.

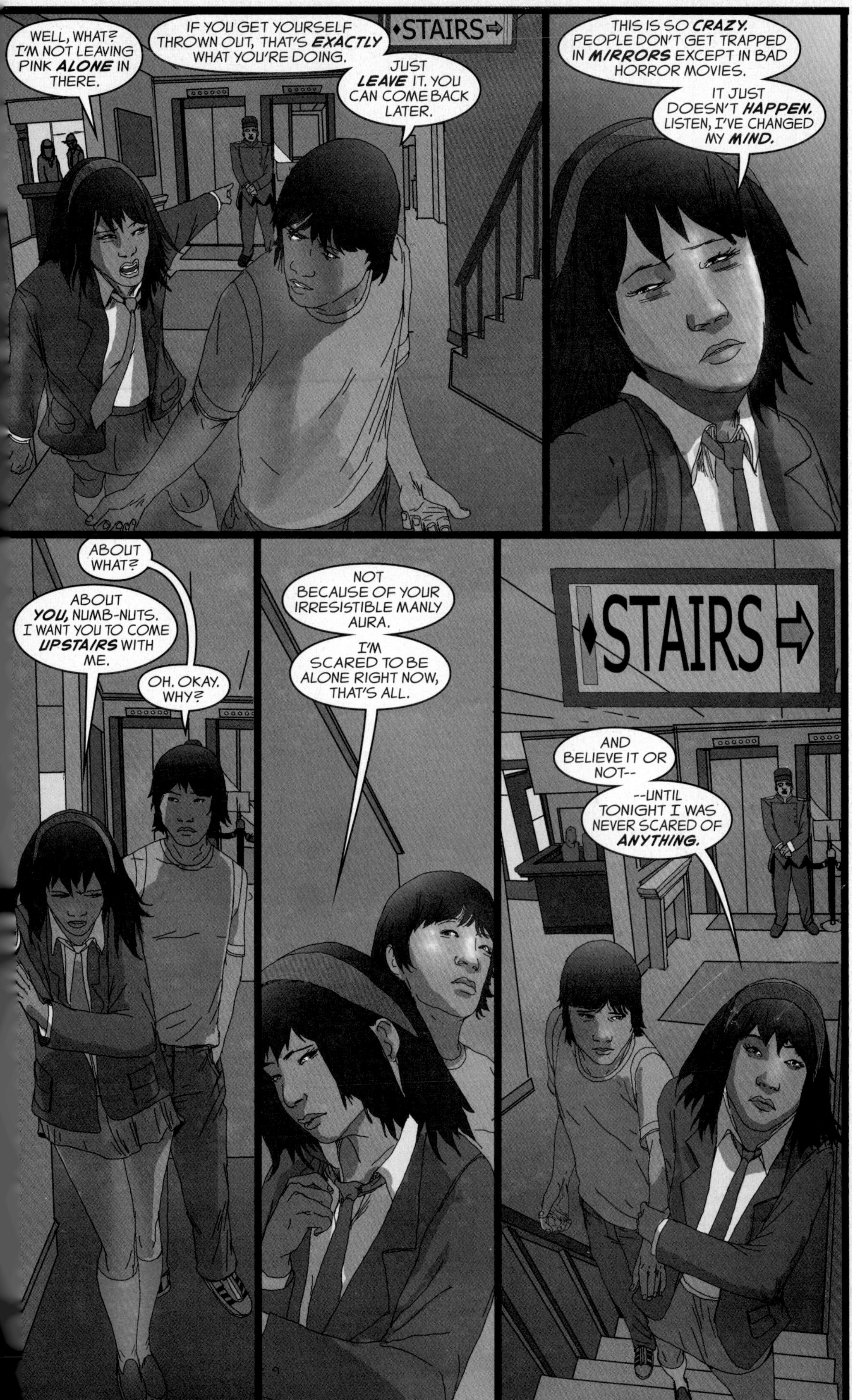
STAIRS
WELL, WHAT? I'M NOT LEAVING PINK ALONE IN THERE.
IF YOU GET YOURSELF THROWN OUT, THAT'S EXACTLY WHAT YOU'RE DOING.
JUST LEAVE IT. YOU CAN COME BACK LATER.
THIS IS SO CRAZY. PEOPLE DON'T GET TRAPPED IN MIRRORS EXCEPT IN BAD HORROR MOVIES.
IT JUST DOESN'T HAPPEN. LISTEN, I'VE CHANGED MY MIND.
ABOUT WHAT?
ABOUT YOU, NUMB-NUTS. I WANT YOU TO COME UPSTAIRS WITH ME.
OH. OKAY. WHY?
NOT BECAUSE OF YOUR IRRESISTIBLE MANLY AURA.
I'M SCARED TO BE ALONE RIGHT NOW, THAT'S ALL.
STAIRS
AND BELIEVE IT OR NOT--
--UNTIL TONIGHT I WAS NEVER SCARED OF ANYTHING.

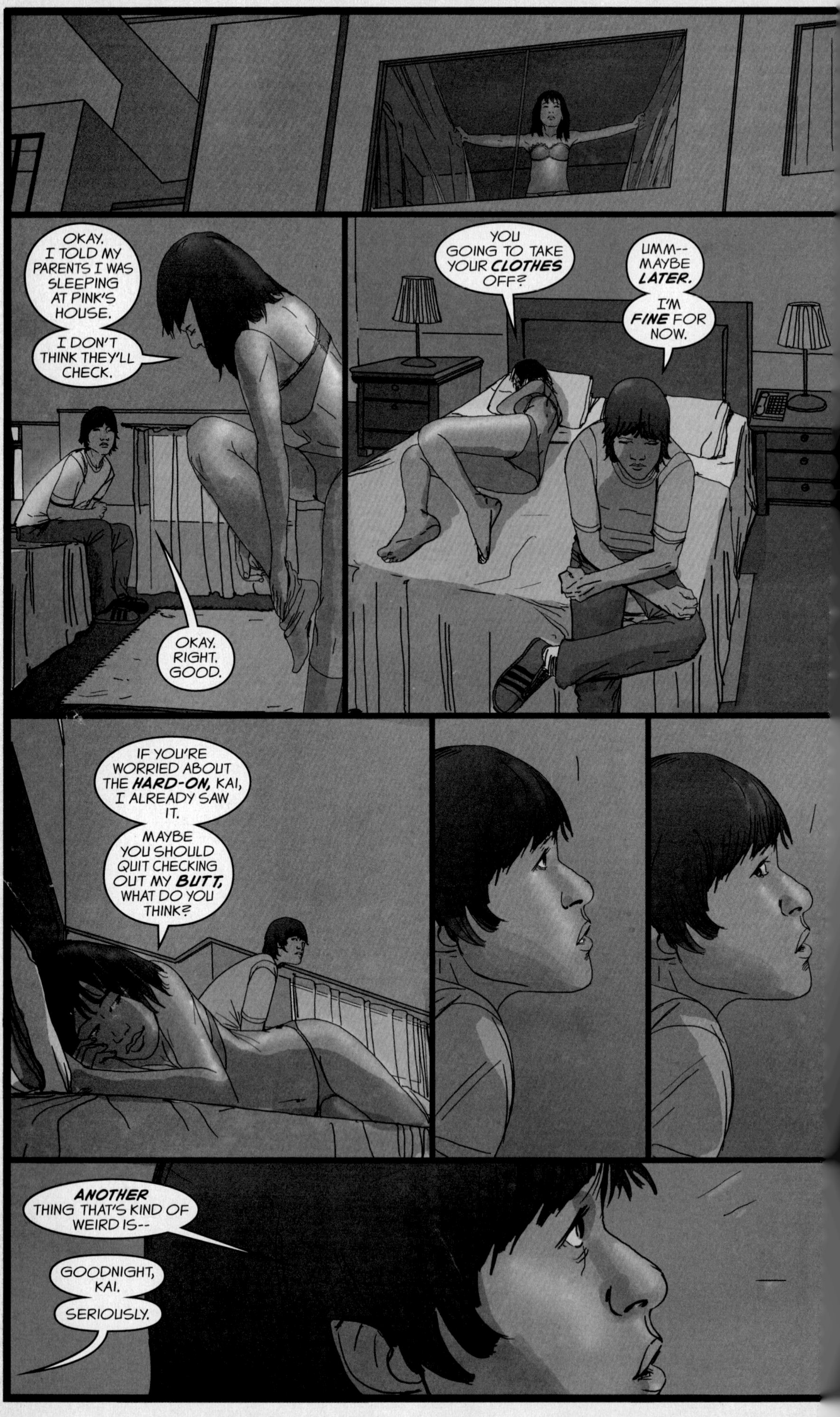
OKAY. I TOLD MY PARENTS I WAS SLEEPING AT PINK'S HOUSE.
I DON'T THINK THEY'LL CHECK.
OKAY. RIGHT. GOOD.
YOU GOING TO TAKE YOUR CLOTHES OFF?
UMM-- MAYBE LATER.
I'M FINE FOR NOW.
IF YOU'RE WORRIED ABOUT THE HARD-ON, KAI, I ALREADY SAW IT.
MAYBE YOU SHOULD QUIT CHECKING OUT MY BUTT, WHAT DO YOU THINK?
ANOTHER THING THAT'S KIND OF WEIRD IS--
GOODNIGHT, KAI.
SERIOUSLY.

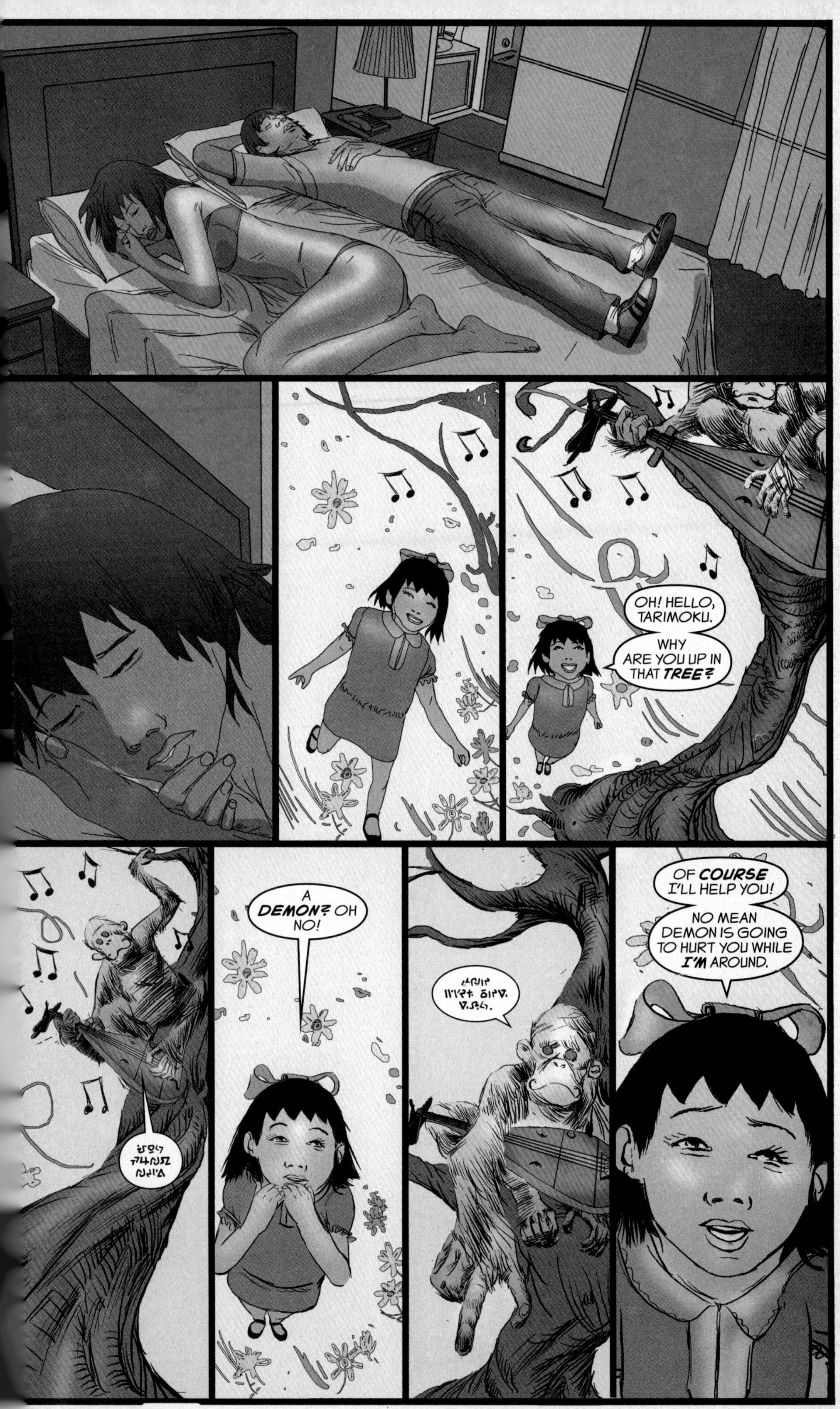
OH! HELLO, TARIMOKU.
WHY ARE YOU UP IN THAT **TREE?**
A **DEMON?** OH NO!
OF **COURSE** I'LL HELP YOU!
NO MEAN DEMON IS GOING TO HURT YOU WHILE ***I'M*** AROUND.

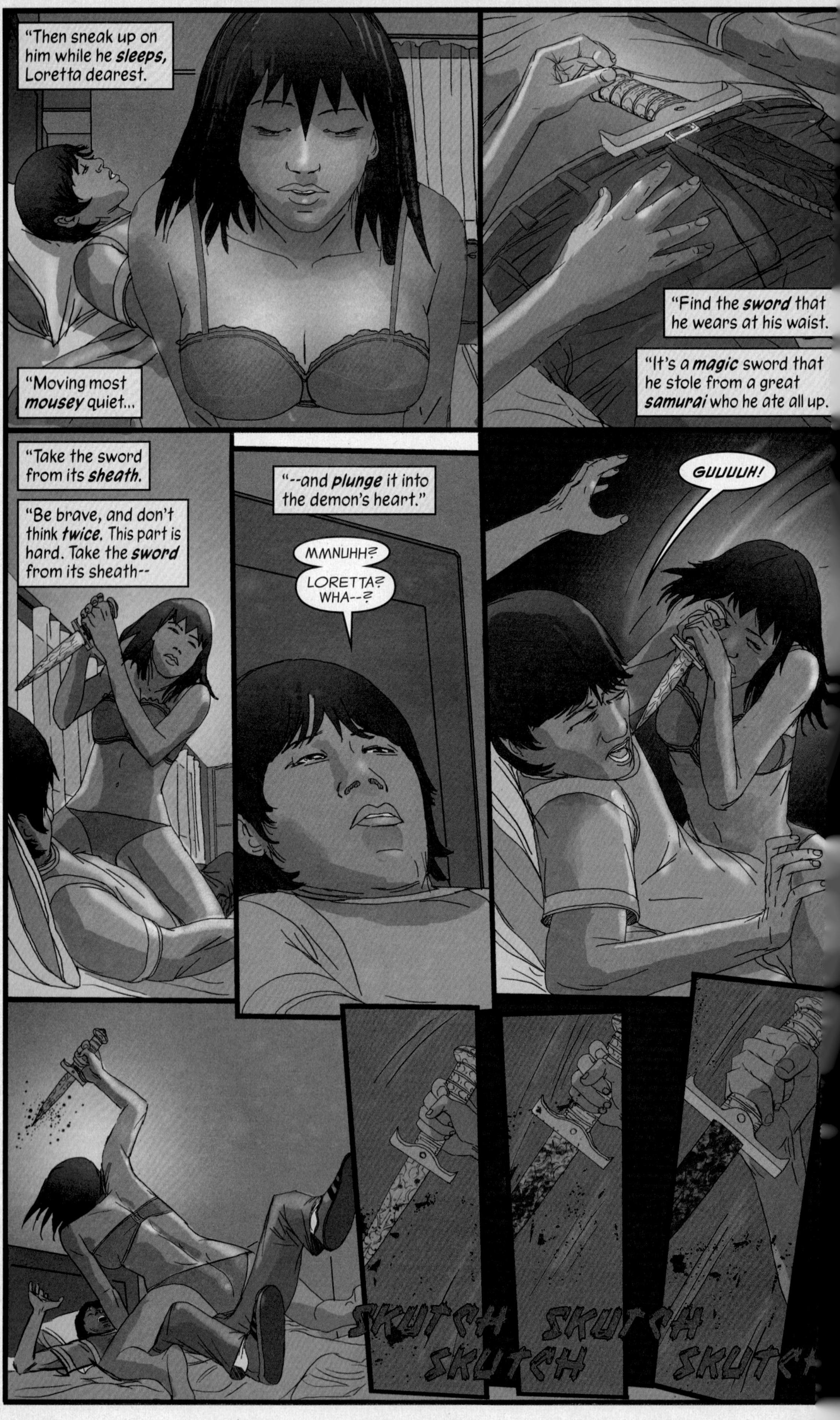
"Then sneak up on him while he *sleeps,* Loretta dearest.
"Moving most *mousey* quiet...
"Find the *sword* that he wears at his waist.
"It's a *magic* sword that he stole from a great *samurai* who he ate all up.
"Take the sword from its *sheath.*
"Be brave, and don't think *twice.* This part is hard. Take the *sword* from its sheath--
"--and *plunge* it into the demon's heart."
MMNUHH?
LORETTA? WHA--?
GUUUUH!
SKUTCH
SKUTCH
SKUTCH

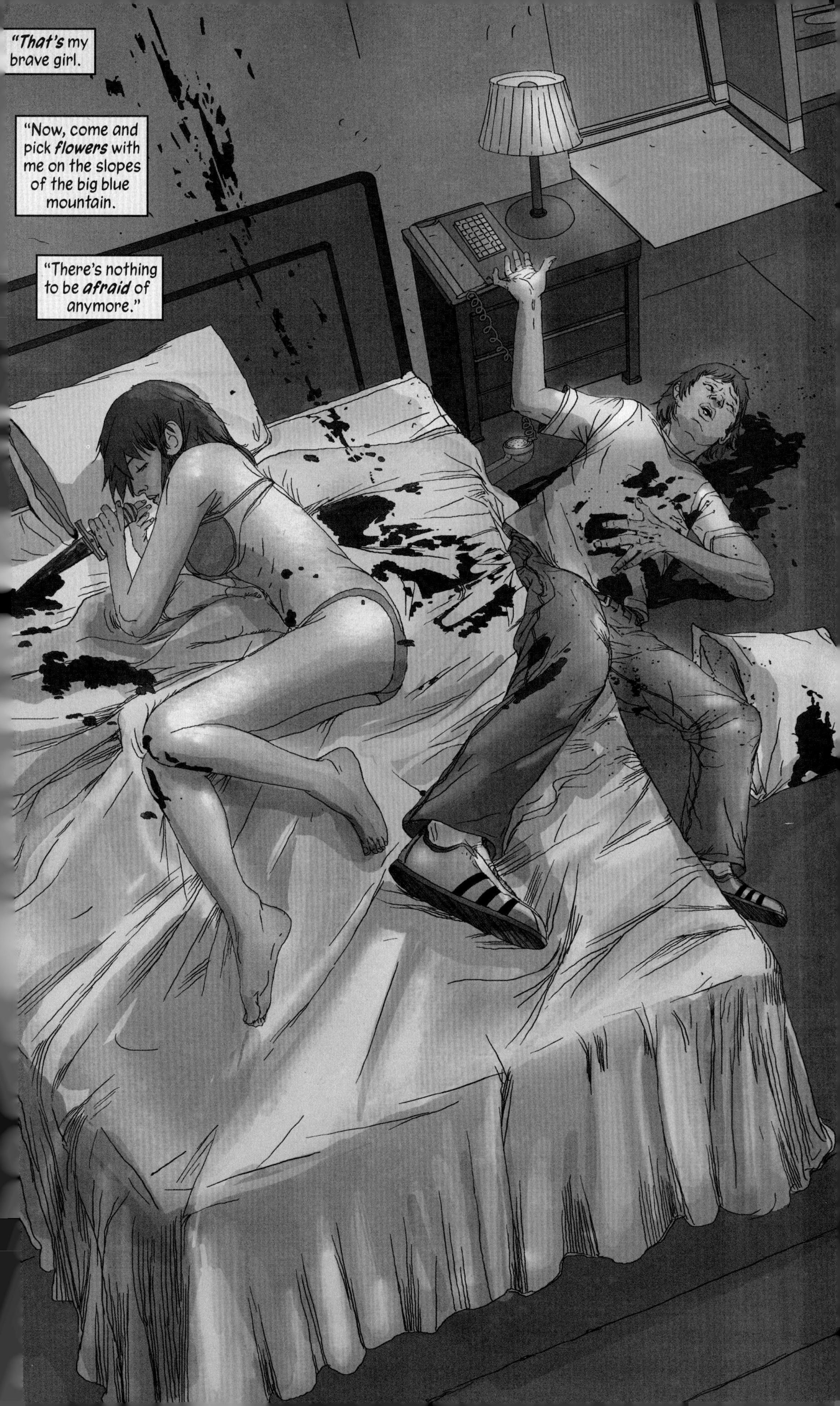
"That's my brave girl.
"Now, come and pick flowers with me on the slopes of the big blue mountain.
"There's nothing to be afraid of anymore."

chapter three

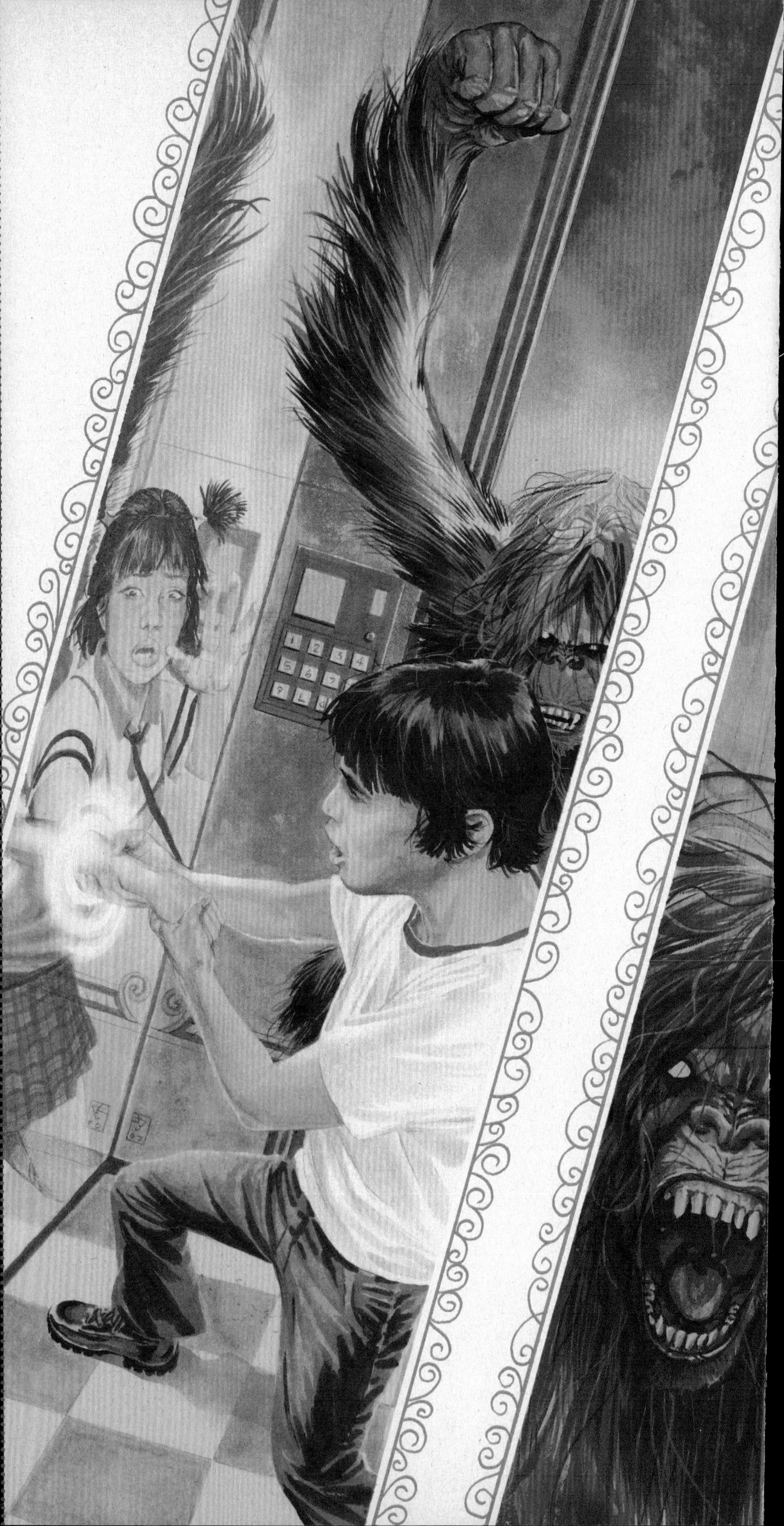

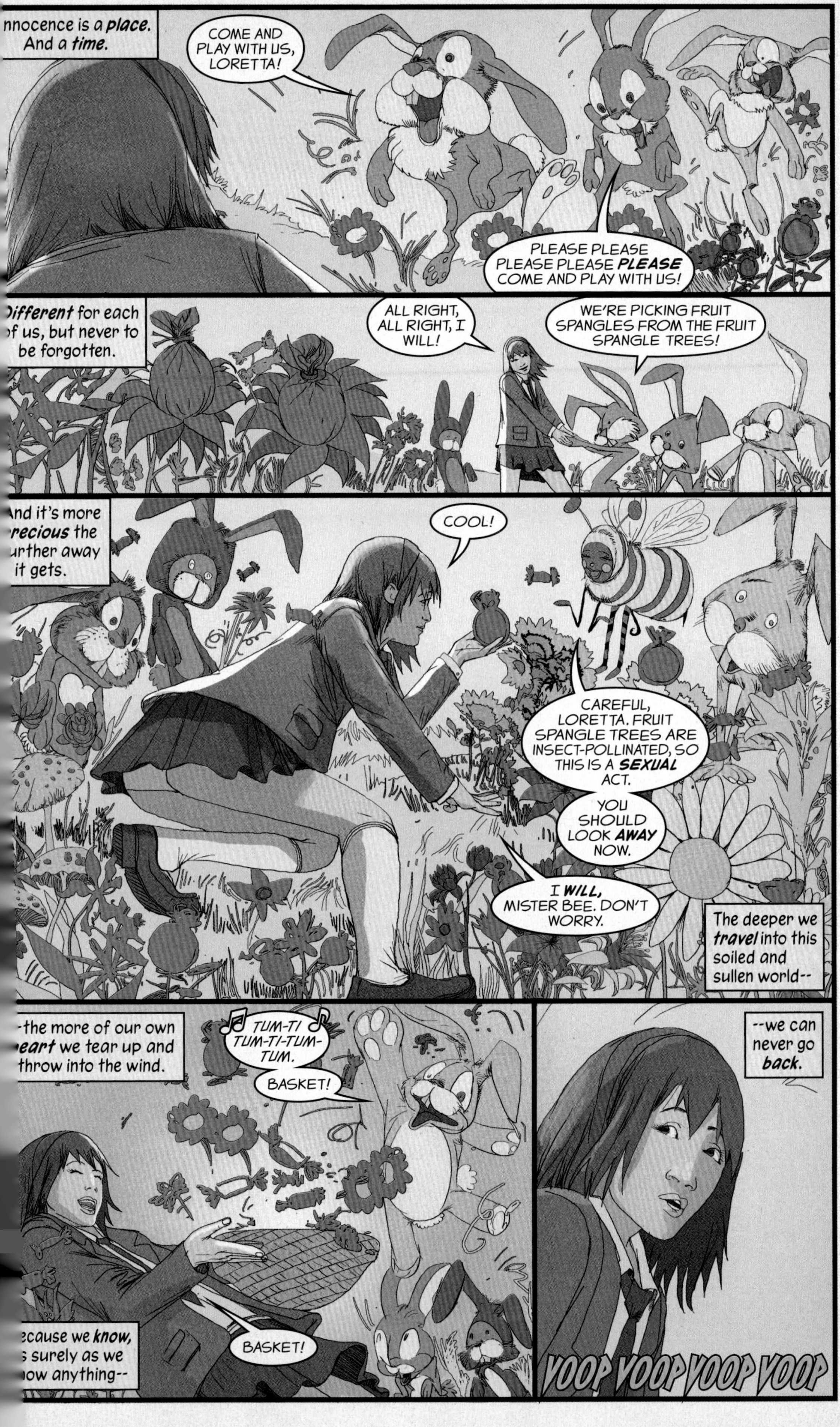
nnocence is a place. And a time.
COME AND PLAY WITH US, LORETTA!
PLEASE PLEASE PLEASE PLEASE PLEASE COME AND PLAY WITH US!
ifferent for each f us, but never to be forgotten.
ALL RIGHT, ALL RIGHT, I WILL!
WE'RE PICKING FRUIT SPANGLES FROM THE FRUIT SPANGLE TREES!
nd it's more recious the urther away it gets.
COOL!
CAREFUL, LORETTA. FRUIT SPANGLE TREES ARE INSECT-POLLINATED, SO THIS IS A SEXUAL ACT.
YOU SHOULD LOOK AWAY NOW.
I WILL, MISTER BEE. DON'T WORRY.
The deeper we travel into this soiled and sullen world--
-the more of our own eart we tear up and throw into the wind.
TUM-TI TUM-TI-TUM-TUM.
BASKET!
BASKET!
ecause we know, s surely as we now anything--
--we can never go back.
VOOP VOOP VOOP VOOP

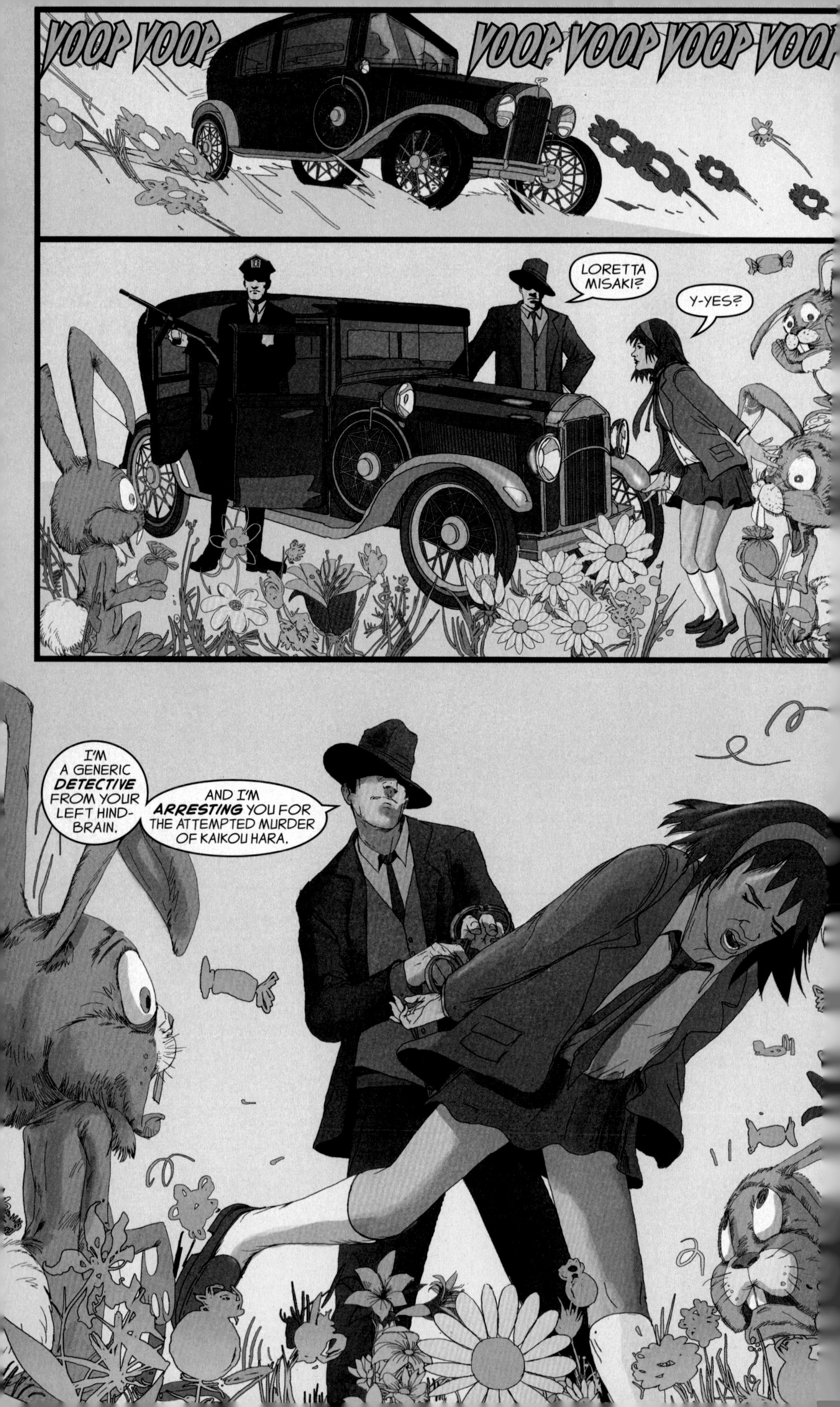
VOOP VOOP
VOOP VOOP VOOP VOOP VOO
LORETTA MISAKI?
Y-YES?
I'M A GENERIC **DETECTIVE** FROM YOUR LEFT HIND-BRAIN.
AND I'M **ARRESTING** YOU FOR THE ATTEMPTED MURDER OF KAIKOU HARA.

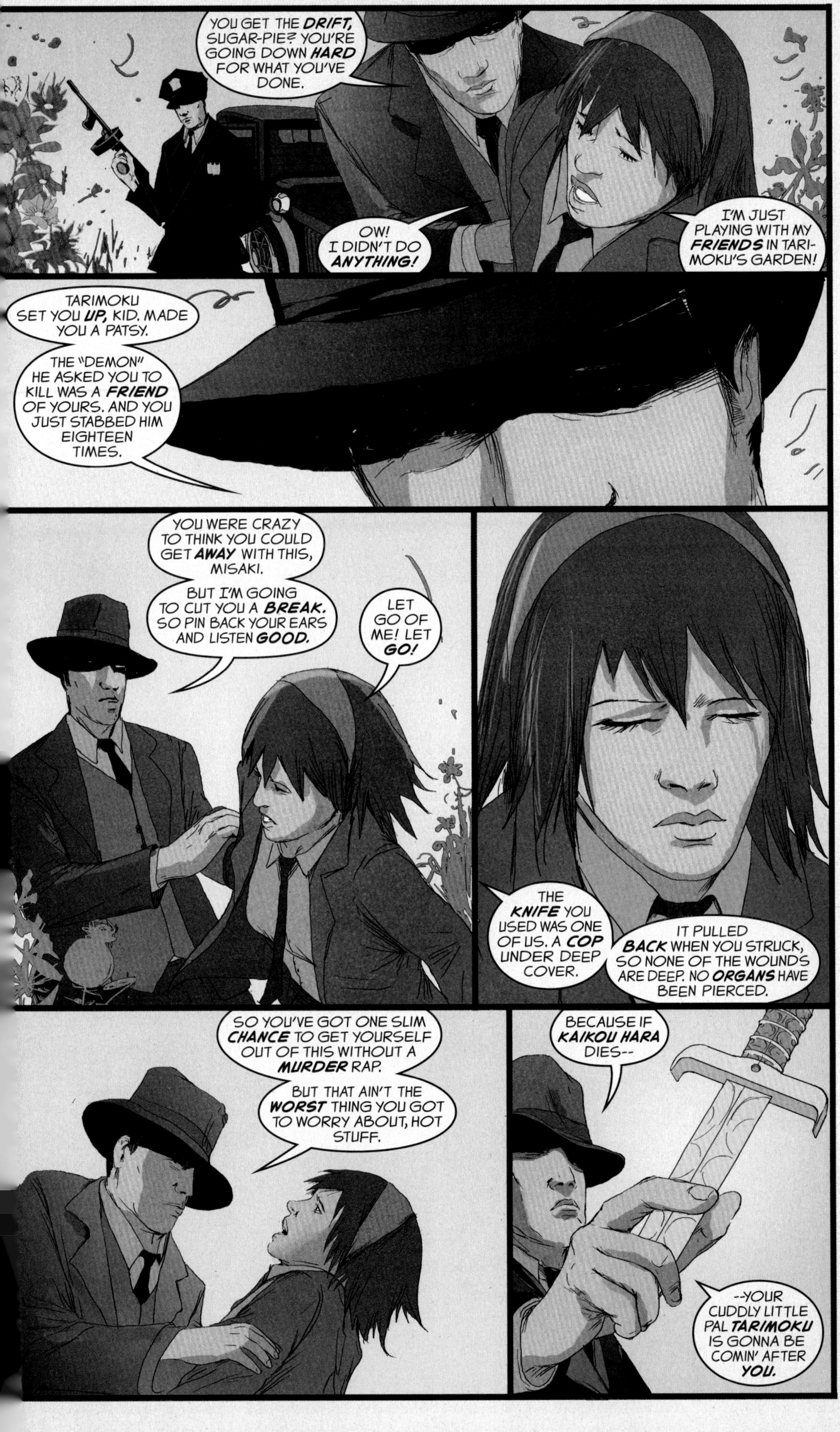
YOU GET THE DRIFT, SUGAR-PIE? YOU'RE GOING DOWN HARD FOR WHAT YOU'VE DONE.
OW! I DIDN'T DO ANYTHING!
I'M JUST PLAYING WITH MY FRIENDS IN TARI-MOKU'S GARDEN!
TARIMOKU SET YOU UP, KID. MADE YOU A PATSY.
THE "DEMON" HE ASKED YOU TO KILL WAS A FRIEND OF YOURS. AND YOU JUST STABBED HIM EIGHTEEN TIMES.
YOU WERE CRAZY TO THINK YOU COULD GET AWAY WITH THIS, MISAKI.
BUT I'M GOING TO CUT YOU A BREAK. SO PIN BACK YOUR EARS AND LISTEN GOOD.
LET GO OF ME! LET GO!
THE KNIFE YOU USED WAS ONE OF US. A COP UNDER DEEP COVER.
IT PULLED BACK WHEN YOU STRUCK, SO NONE OF THE WOUNDS ARE DEEP. NO ORGANS HAVE BEEN PIERCED.
SO YOU'VE GOT ONE SLIM CHANCE TO GET YOURSELF OUT OF THIS WITHOUT A MURDER RAP.
BUT THAT AIN'T THE WORST THING YOU GOT TO WORRY ABOUT, HOT STUFF.
BECAUSE IF KAIKOU HARA DIES--
--YOUR CUDDLY LITTLE PAL TARIMOKU IS GONNA BE COMIN' AFTER YOU.

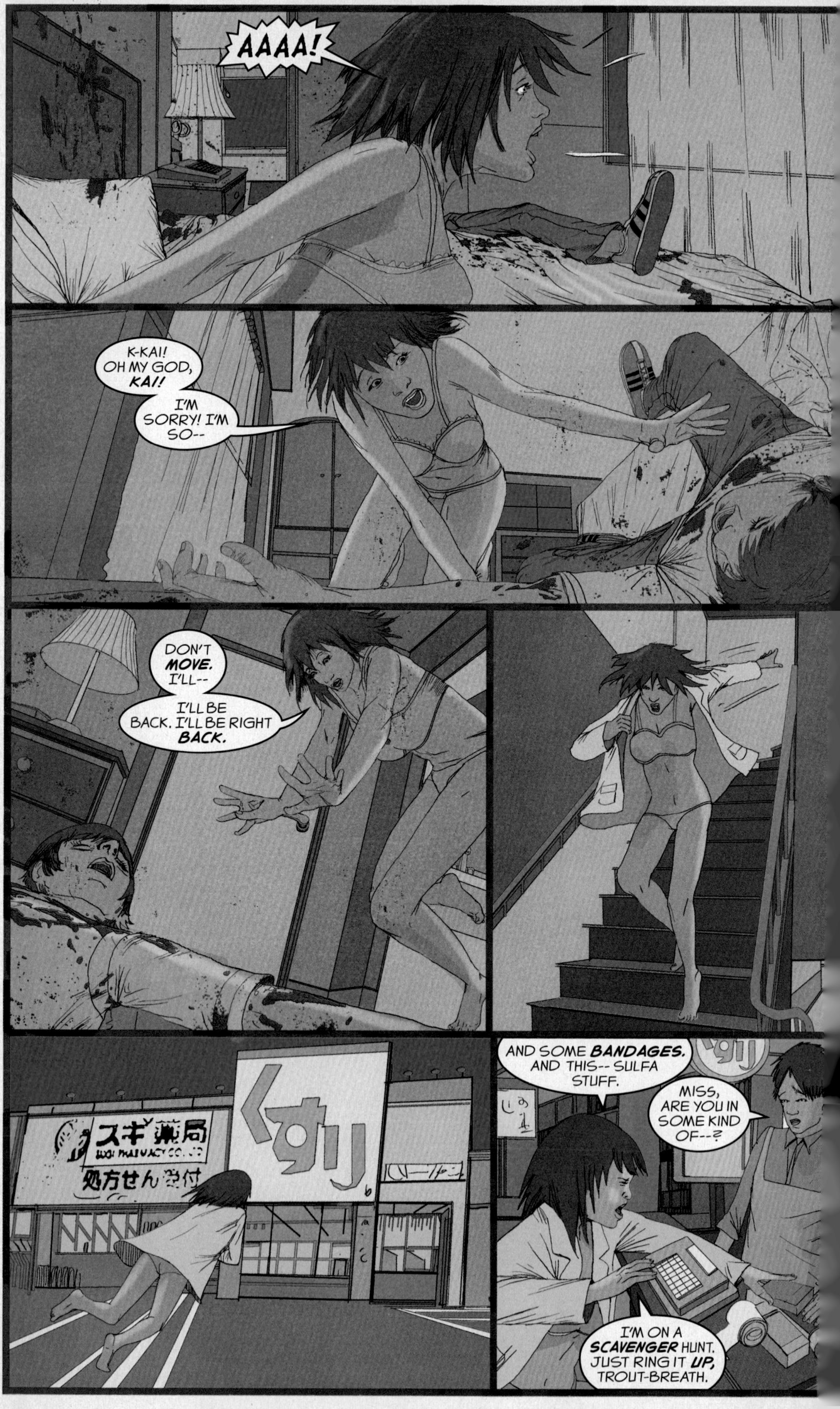
AAAA!
K-KAI! OH MY GOD, KAI!
I'M SORRY! I'M SO--
DON'T MOVE. I'LL--
I'LL BE BACK. I'LL BE RIGHT BACK.
スギ薬局
処方せん受付
くすり
AND SOME BANDAGES. AND THIS-- SULFA STUFF.
MISS, ARE YOU IN SOME KIND OF--?
I'M ON A SCAVENGER HUNT. JUST RING IT UP, TROUT-BREATH.

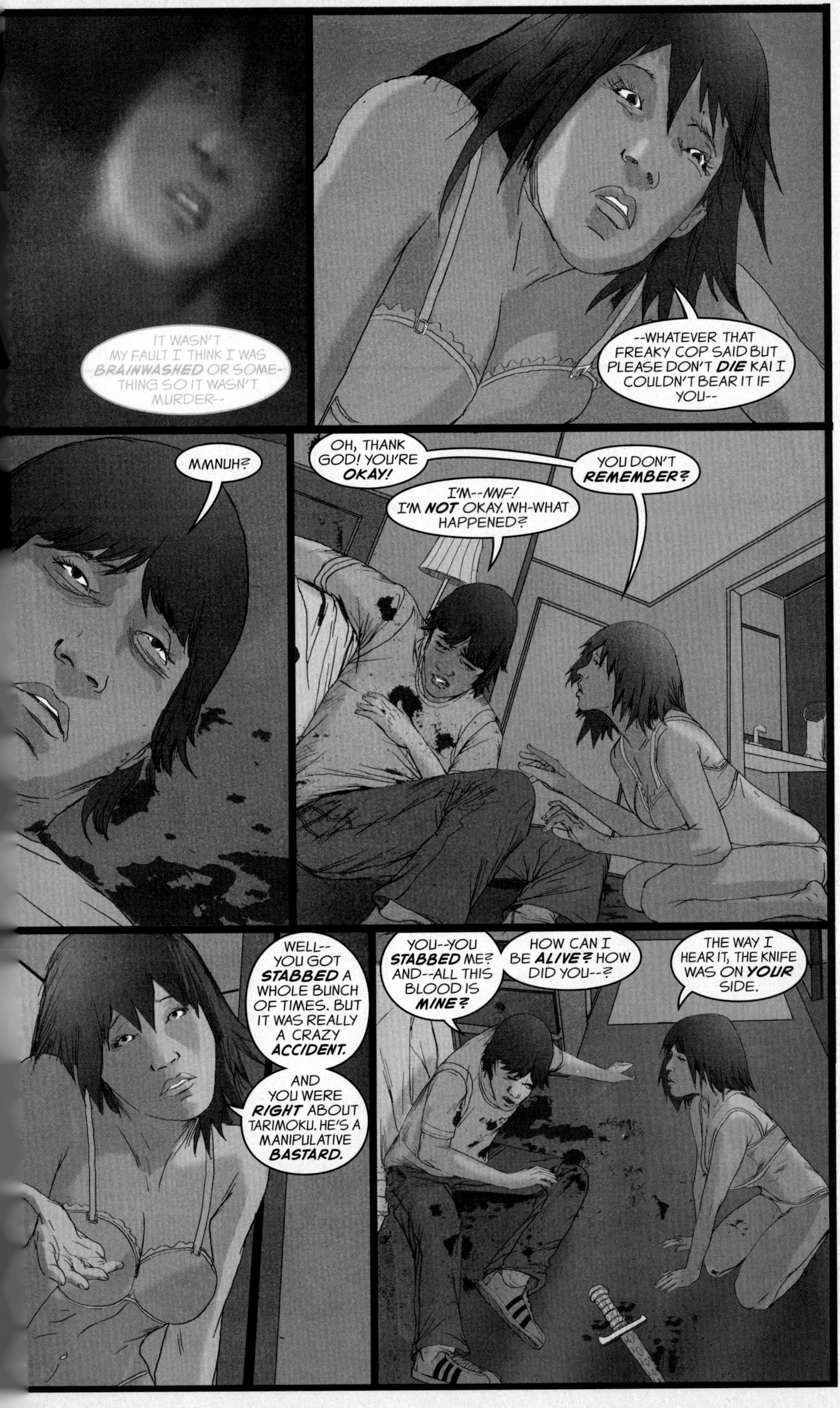

IT WASN'T MY FAULT I THINK I WAS BRAINWASHED OR SOMETHING SO IT WASN'T MURDER--
--WHATEVER THAT FREAKY COP SAID BUT PLEASE DON'T DIE KAI I COULDN'T BEAR IT IF YOU--
MMNUH?
OH, THANK GOD! YOU'RE OKAY!
YOU DON'T REMEMBER?
I'M--NNF! I'M NOT OKAY. WH-WHAT HAPPENED?
WELL--YOU GOT STABBED A WHOLE BUNCH OF TIMES. BUT IT WAS REALLY A CRAZY ACCIDENT.
AND YOU WERE RIGHT ABOUT TARIMOKU. HE'S A MANIPULATIVE BASTARD.
YOU--YOU STABBED ME? AND--ALL THIS BLOOD IS MINE?
HOW CAN I BE ALIVE? HOW DID YOU--?
THE WAY I HEAR IT, THE KNIFE WAS ON YOUR SIDE.

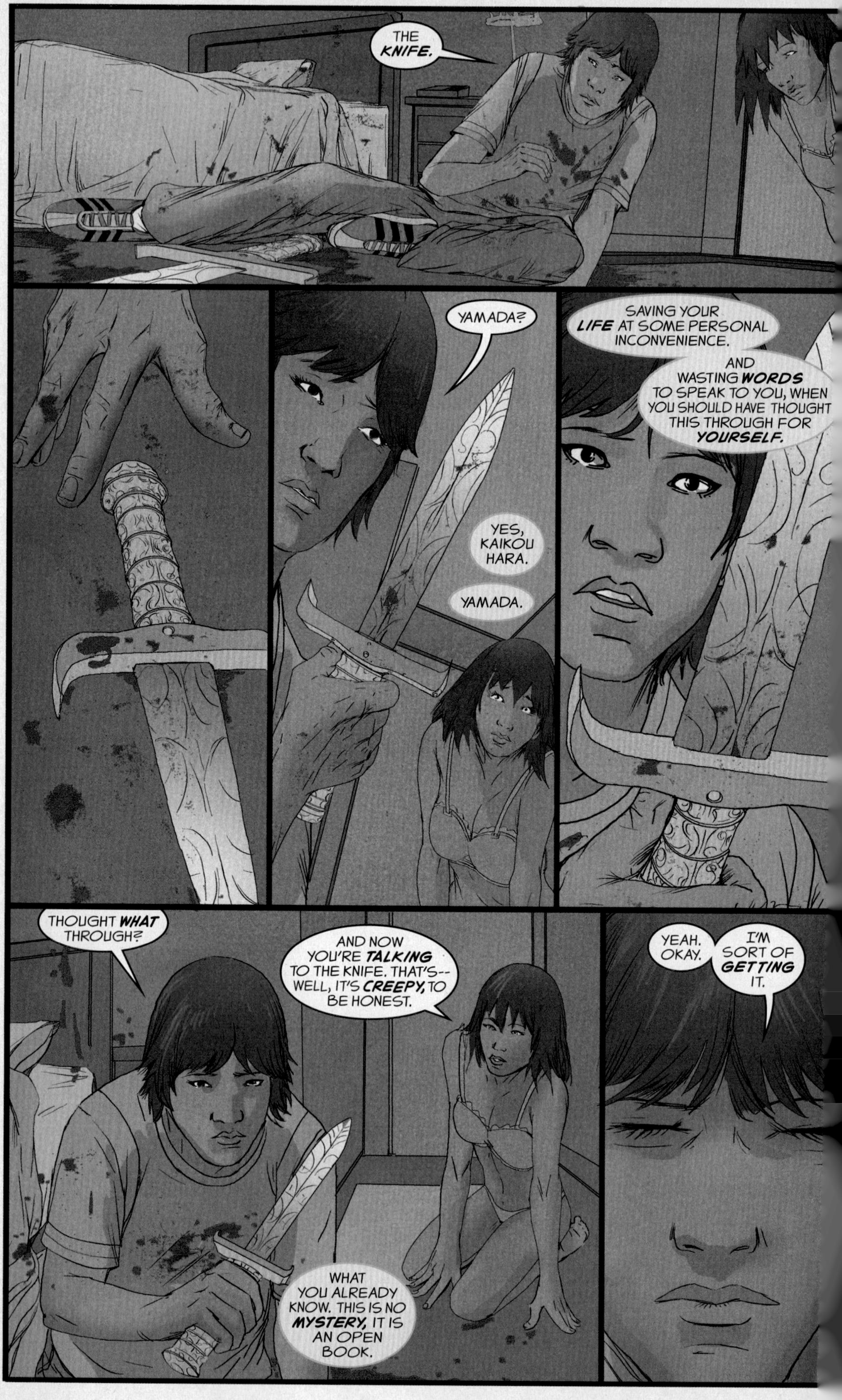

THE KNIFE.
YAMADA?
YES, KAIKOU HARA.
YAMADA.
SAVING YOUR LIFE AT SOME PERSONAL INCONVENIENCE.
AND WASTING WORDS TO SPEAK TO YOU, WHEN YOU SHOULD HAVE THOUGHT THIS THROUGH FOR YOURSELF.
THOUGHT WHAT THROUGH?
AND NOW YOU'RE TALKING TO THE KNIFE. THAT'S-- WELL, IT'S CREEPY, TO BE HONEST.
WHAT YOU ALREADY KNOW. THIS IS NO MYSTERY, IT IS AN OPEN BOOK.
YEAH. OKAY.
I'M SORT OF GETTING IT.

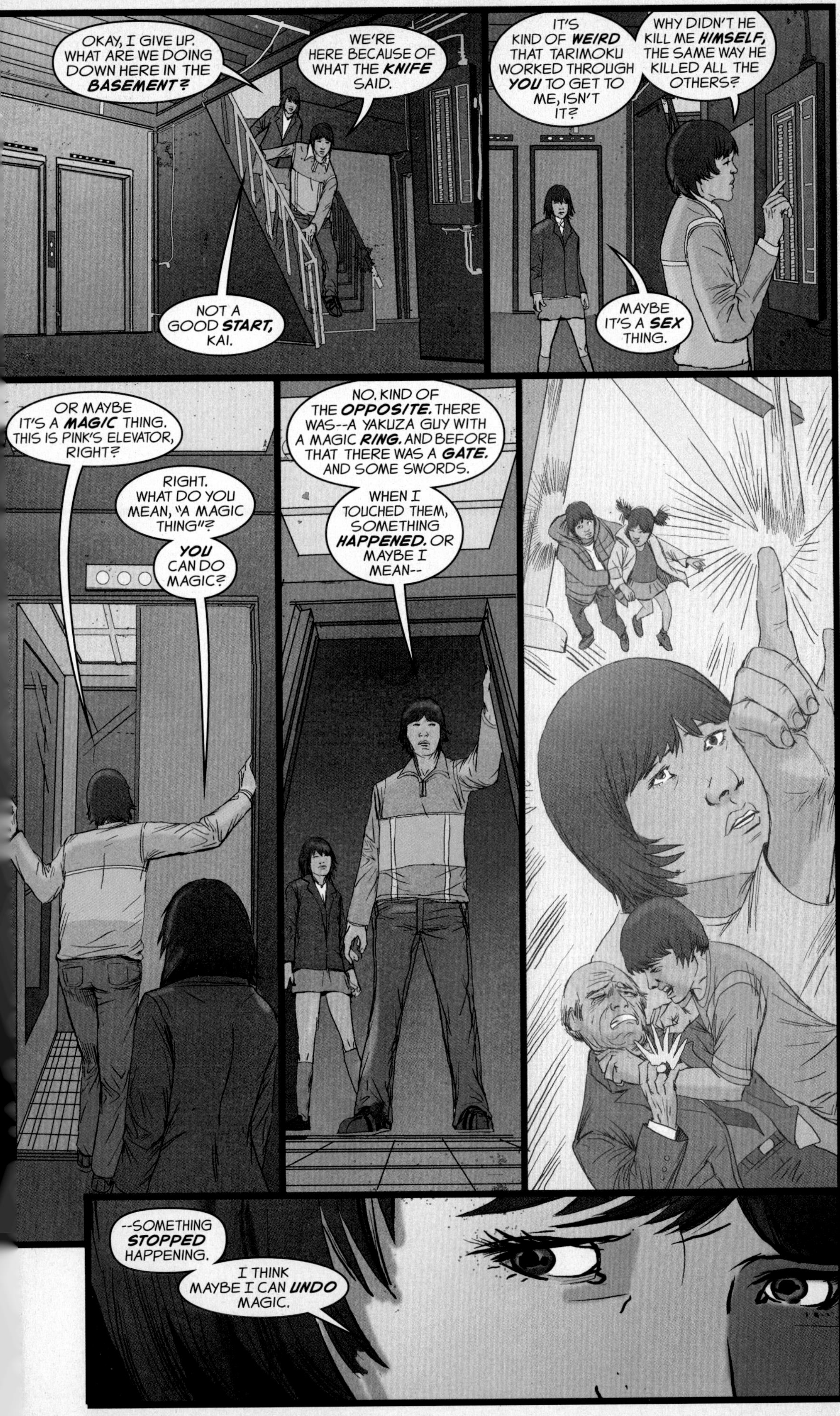
OKAY, I GIVE UP. WHAT ARE WE DOING DOWN HERE IN THE BASEMENT?
WE'RE HERE BECAUSE OF WHAT THE KNIFE SAID.
NOT A GOOD START, KAI.
IT'S KIND OF WEIRD THAT TARIMOKU WORKED THROUGH YOU TO GET TO ME, ISN'T IT?
WHY DIDN'T HE KILL ME HIMSELF, THE SAME WAY HE KILLED ALL THE OTHERS?
MAYBE IT'S A SEX THING.
OR MAYBE IT'S A MAGIC THING. THIS IS PINK'S ELEVATOR, RIGHT?
RIGHT. WHAT DO YOU MEAN, "A MAGIC THING"?
YOU CAN DO MAGIC?
NO. KIND OF THE OPPOSITE. THERE WAS--A YAKUZA GUY WITH A MAGIC RING. AND BEFORE THAT THERE WAS A GATE. AND SOME SWORDS.
WHEN I TOUCHED THEM, SOMETHING HAPPENED. OR MAYBE I MEAN--
--SOMETHING STOPPED HAPPENING.
I THINK MAYBE I CAN UNDO MAGIC.

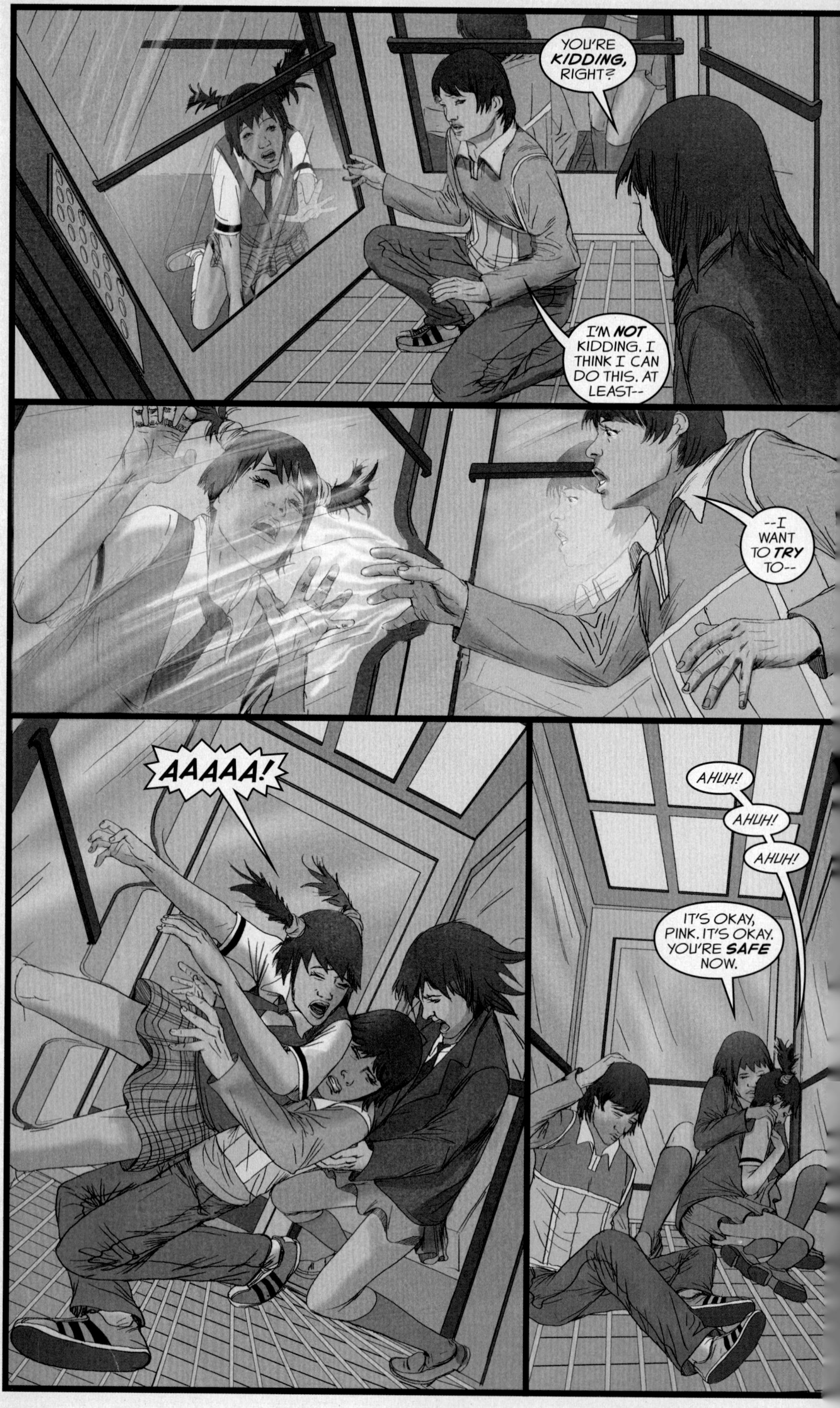

YOU'RE KIDDING, RIGHT?
I'M NOT KIDDING. I THINK I CAN DO THIS. AT LEAST--
--I WANT TO TRY TO--
AAAAA!
AHUH!
AHUH!
AHUH!
IT'S OKAY, PINK. IT'S OKAY. YOU'RE SAFE NOW.

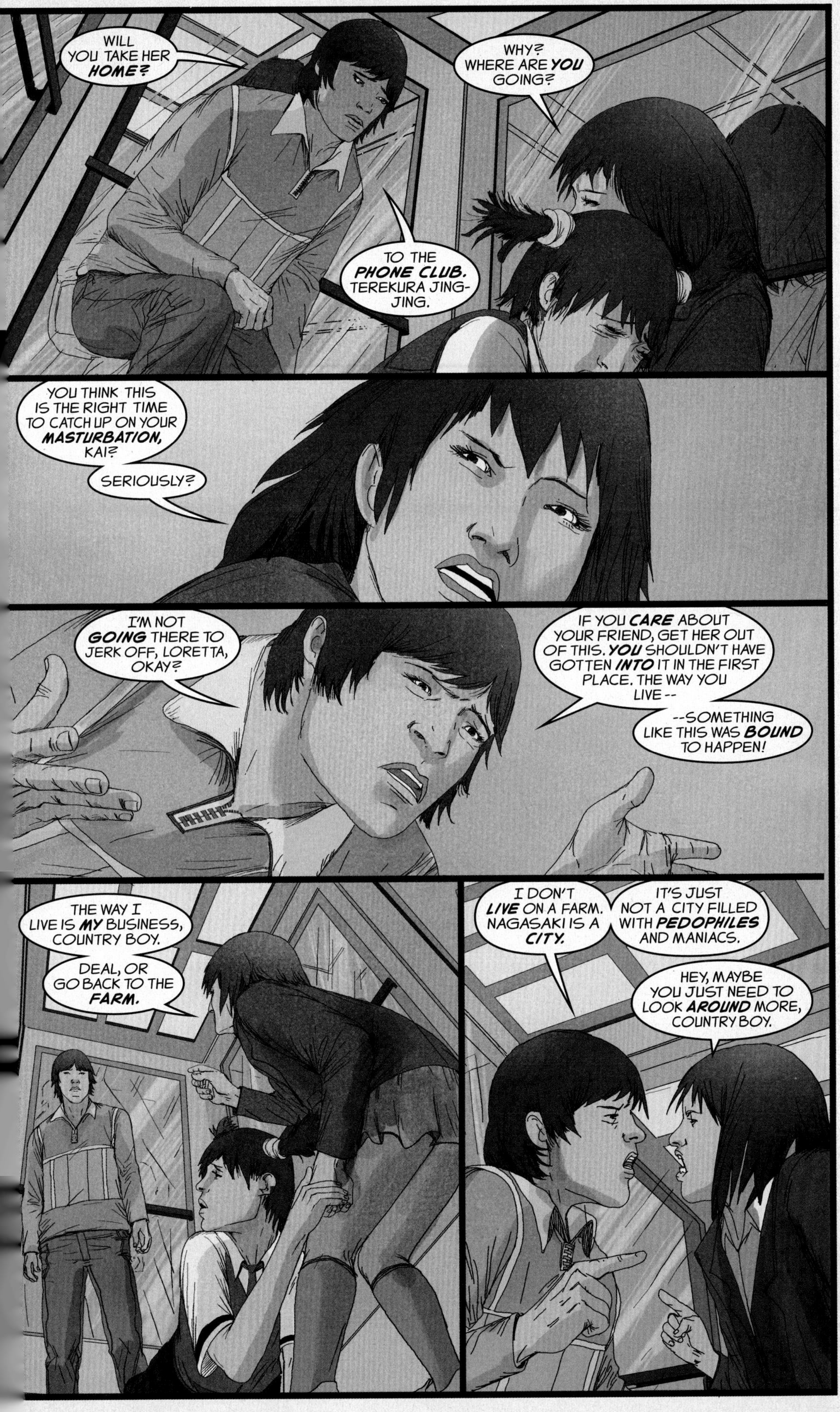

WILL YOU TAKE HER HOME?
WHY? WHERE ARE YOU GOING?
TO THE PHONE CLUB. TEREKURA JING-JING.
YOU THINK THIS IS THE RIGHT TIME TO CATCH UP ON YOUR MASTURBATION, KAI?
SERIOUSLY?
I'M NOT GOING THERE TO JERK OFF, LORETTA, OKAY?
IF YOU CARE ABOUT YOUR FRIEND, GET HER OUT OF THIS. YOU SHOULDN'T HAVE GOTTEN INTO IT IN THE FIRST PLACE. THE WAY YOU LIVE --
--SOMETHING LIKE THIS WAS BOUND TO HAPPEN!
THE WAY I LIVE IS MY BUSINESS, COUNTRY BOY.
DEAL, OR GO BACK TO THE FARM.
I DON'T LIVE ON A FARM. NAGASAKI IS A CITY.
IT'S JUST NOT A CITY FILLED WITH PEDOPHILES AND MANIACS.
HEY, MAYBE YOU JUST NEED TO LOOK AROUND MORE, COUNTRY BOY.

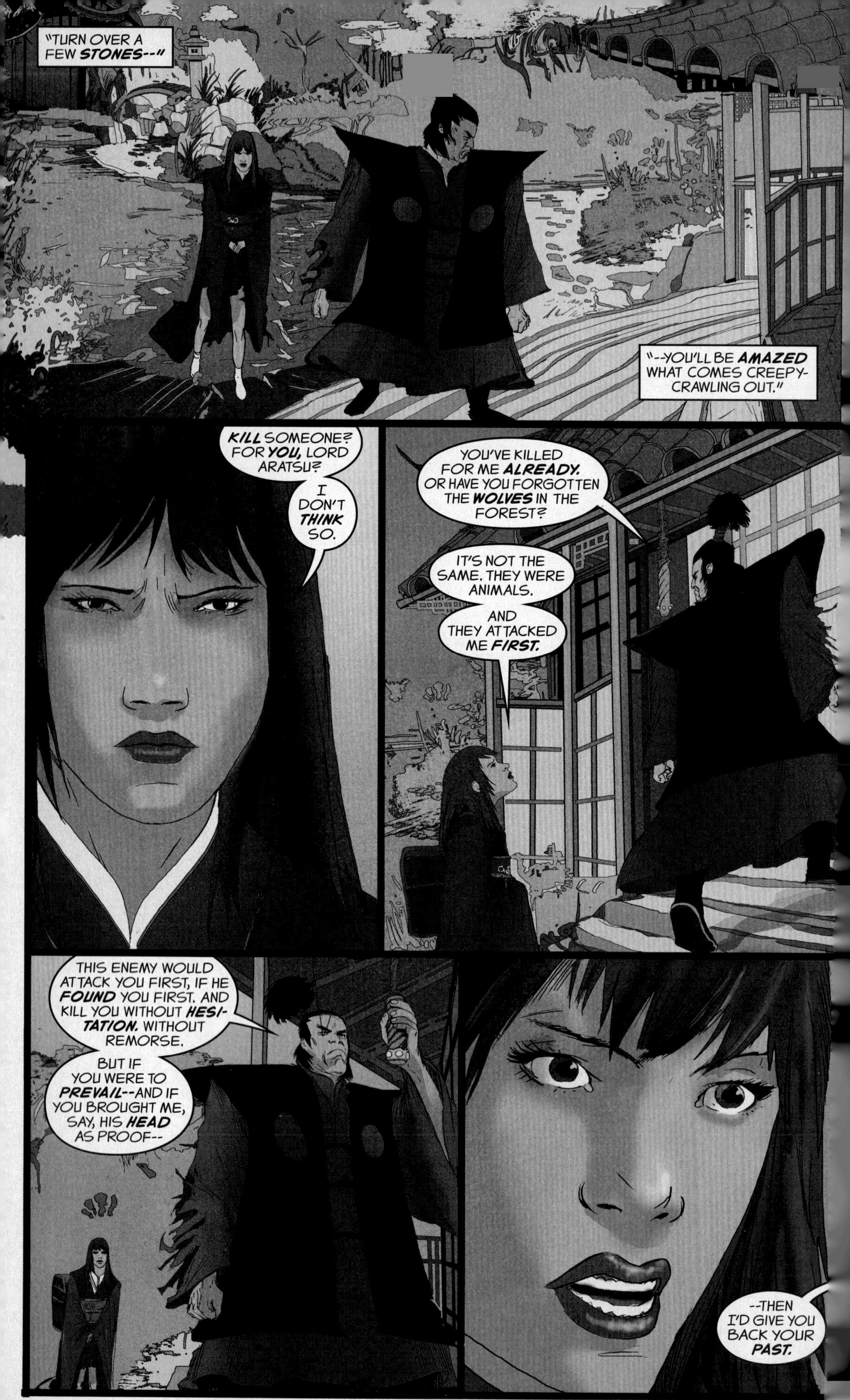
"TURN OVER A FEW STONES--"
"--YOU'LL BE AMAZED WHAT COMES CREEPY-CRAWLING OUT."
KILL SOMEONE? FOR YOU, LORD ARATSU?
I DON'T THINK SO.
YOU'VE KILLED FOR ME ALREADY. OR HAVE YOU FORGOTTEN THE WOLVES IN THE FOREST?
IT'S NOT THE SAME. THEY WERE ANIMALS.
AND THEY ATTACKED ME FIRST.
THIS ENEMY WOULD ATTACK YOU FIRST, IF HE FOUND YOU FIRST. AND KILL YOU WITHOUT HESI-TATION. WITHOUT REMORSE.
BUT IF YOU WERE TO PREVAIL--AND IF YOU BROUGHT ME, SAY, HIS HEAD AS PROOF--
--THEN I'D GIVE YOU BACK YOUR PAST.

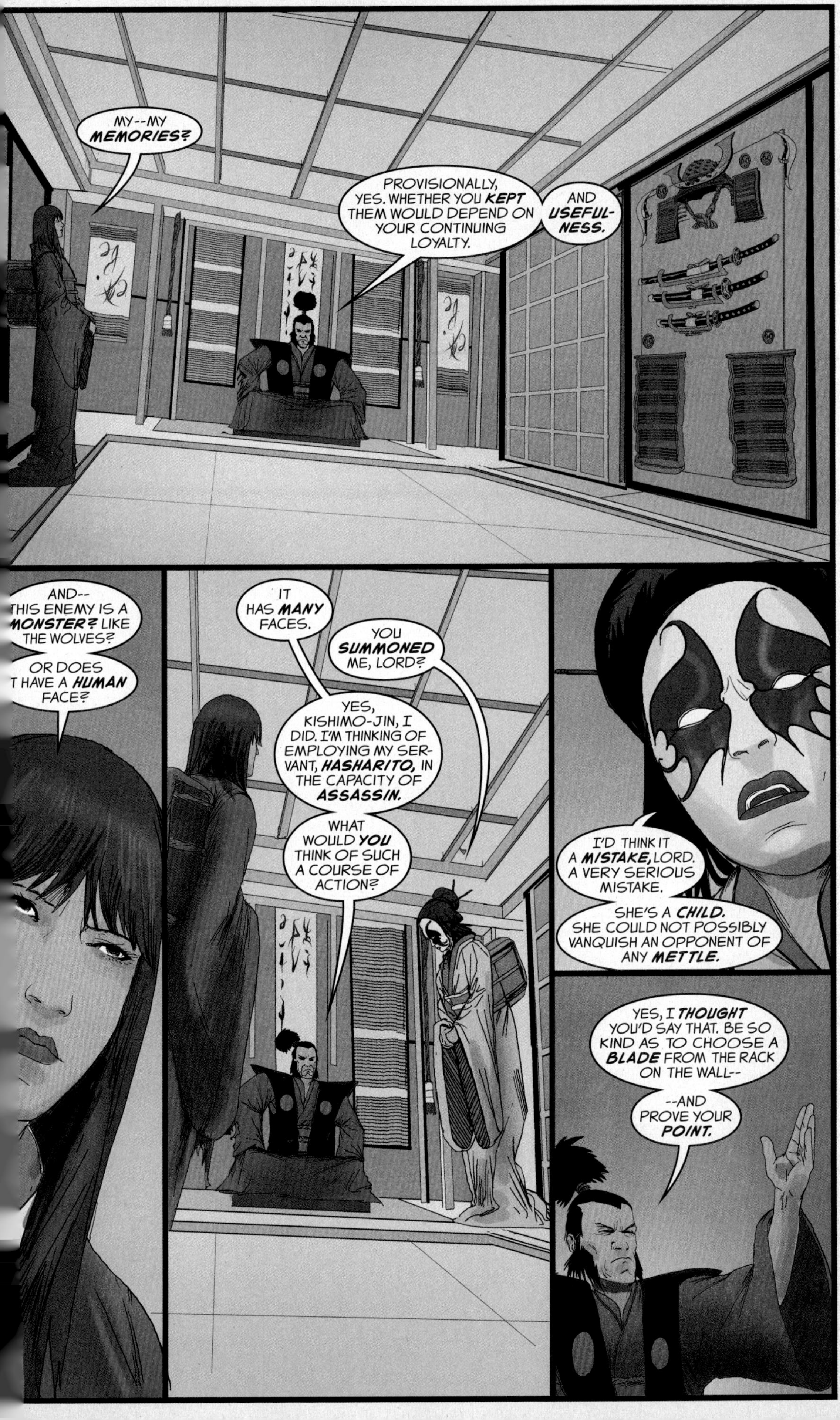
MY--MY MEMORIES?
PROVISIONALLY, YES. WHETHER YOU KEPT THEM WOULD DEPEND ON YOUR CONTINUING LOYALTY.
AND USEFUL-NESS.
AND-- THIS ENEMY IS A MONSTER? LIKE THE WOLVES?
OR DOES IT HAVE A HUMAN FACE?
IT HAS MANY FACES.
YOU SUMMONED ME, LORD?
YES, KISHIMO-JIN, I DID. I'M THINKING OF EMPLOYING MY SER-VANT, HASHARITO, IN THE CAPACITY OF ASSASSIN.
WHAT WOULD YOU THINK OF SUCH A COURSE OF ACTION?
I'D THINK IT A MISTAKE, LORD. A VERY SERIOUS MISTAKE.
SHE'S A CHILD. SHE COULD NOT POSSIBLY VANQUISH AN OPPONENT OF ANY METTLE.
YES, I THOUGHT YOU'D SAY THAT. BE SO KIND AS TO CHOOSE A BLADE FROM THE RACK ON THE WALL--
--AND PROVE YOUR POINT.

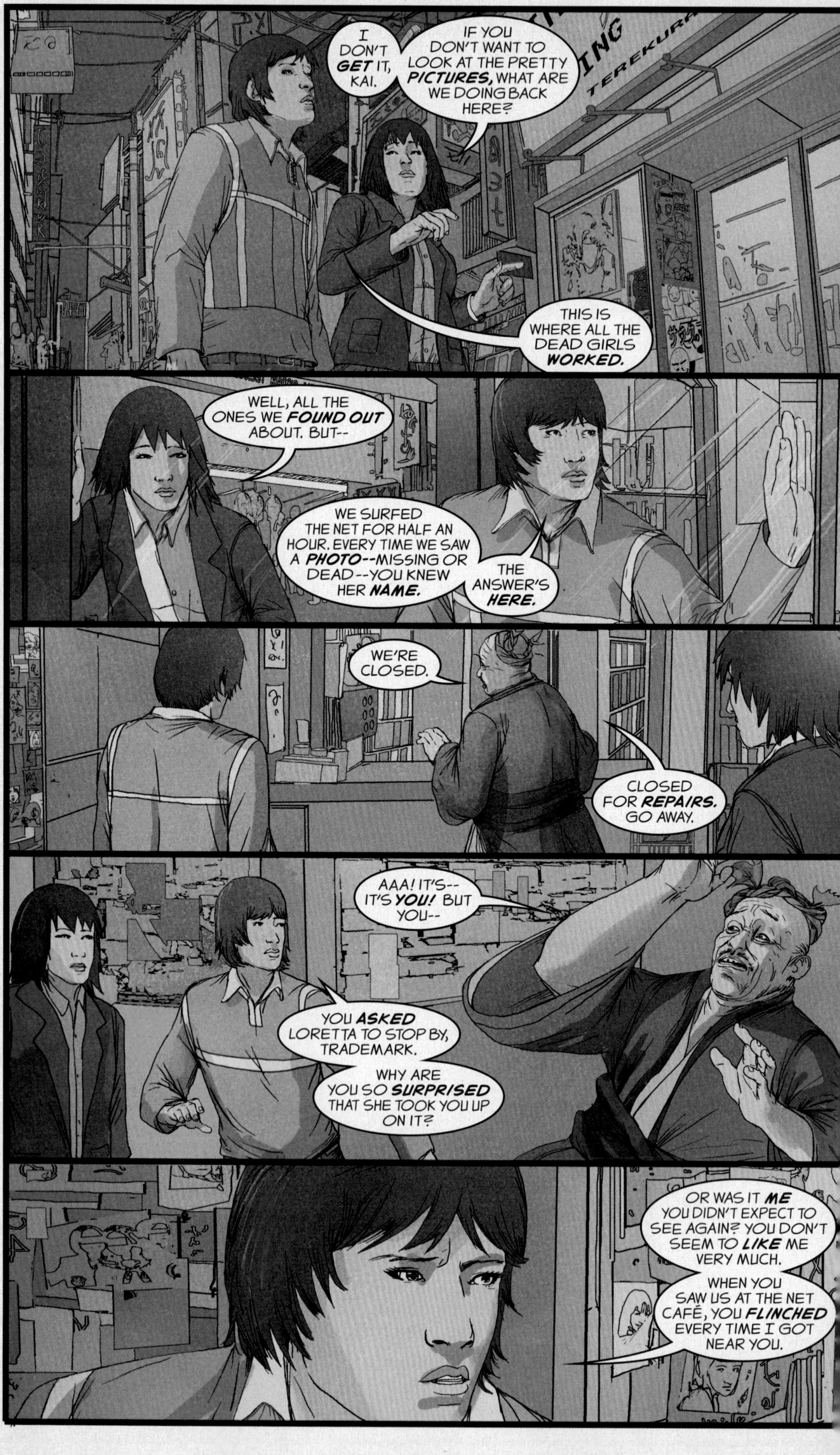

TEREKURA
I DON'T GET IT, KAI.
IF YOU DON'T WANT TO LOOK AT THE PRETTY PICTURES, WHAT ARE WE DOING BACK HERE?
THIS IS WHERE ALL THE DEAD GIRLS WORKED.
WELL, ALL THE ONES WE FOUND OUT ABOUT. BUT--
WE SURFED THE NET FOR HALF AN HOUR. EVERY TIME WE SAW A PHOTO--MISSING OR DEAD--YOU KNEW HER NAME.
THE ANSWER'S HERE.
WE'RE CLOSED.
CLOSED FOR REPAIRS. GO AWAY.
AAA! IT'S-- IT'S YOU! BUT YOU--
YOU ASKED LORETTA TO STOP BY, TRADEMARK.
WHY ARE YOU SO SURPRISED THAT SHE TOOK YOU UP ON IT?
OR WAS IT ME YOU DIDN'T EXPECT TO SEE AGAIN? YOU DON'T SEEM TO LIKE ME VERY MUCH.
WHEN YOU SAW US AT THE NET CAFÉ, YOU FLINCHED EVERY TIME I GOT NEAR YOU.

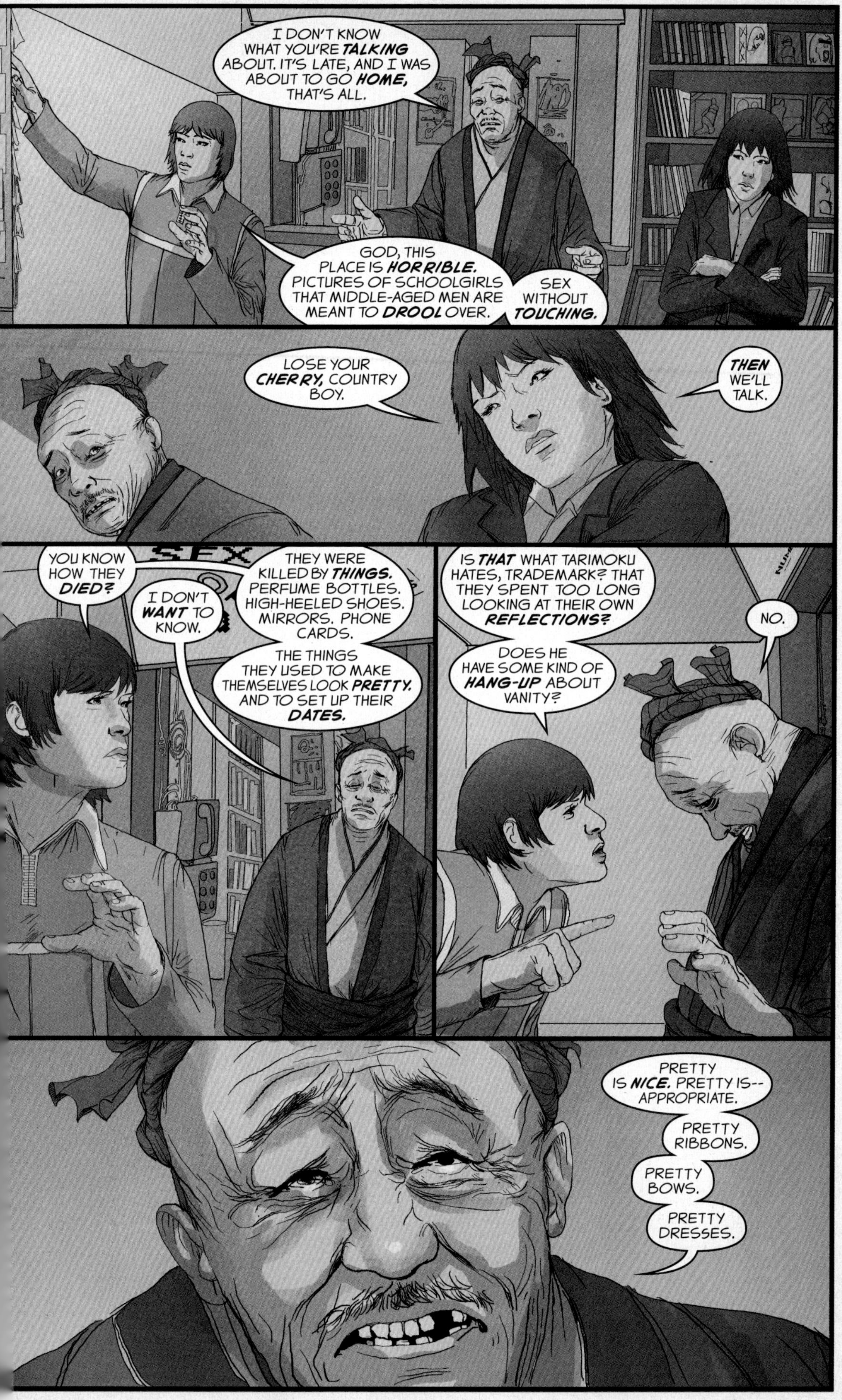
I DON'T KNOW WHAT YOU'RE TALKING ABOUT. IT'S LATE, AND I WAS ABOUT TO GO HOME, THAT'S ALL.
GOD, THIS PLACE IS HORRIBLE. PICTURES OF SCHOOLGIRLS THAT MIDDLE-AGED MEN ARE MEANT TO DROOL OVER.
SEX WITHOUT TOUCHING.
LOSE YOUR CHERRY, COUNTRY BOY.
THEN WE'LL TALK.
YOU KNOW HOW THEY DIED?
THEY WERE KILLED BY THINGS. PERFUME BOTTLES. HIGH-HEELED SHOES. MIRRORS. PHONE CARDS.
I DON'T WANT TO KNOW.
THE THINGS THEY USED TO MAKE THEMSELVES LOOK PRETTY. AND TO SET UP THEIR DATES.
SFX
IS THAT WHAT TARIMOKU HATES, TRADEMARK? THAT THEY SPENT TOO LONG LOOKING AT THEIR OWN REFLECTIONS?
DOES HE HAVE SOME KIND OF HANG-UP ABOUT VANITY?
NO.
PRETTY IS NICE. PRETTY IS-- APPROPRIATE.
PRETTY RIBBONS.
PRETTY BOWS.
PRETTY DRESSES.

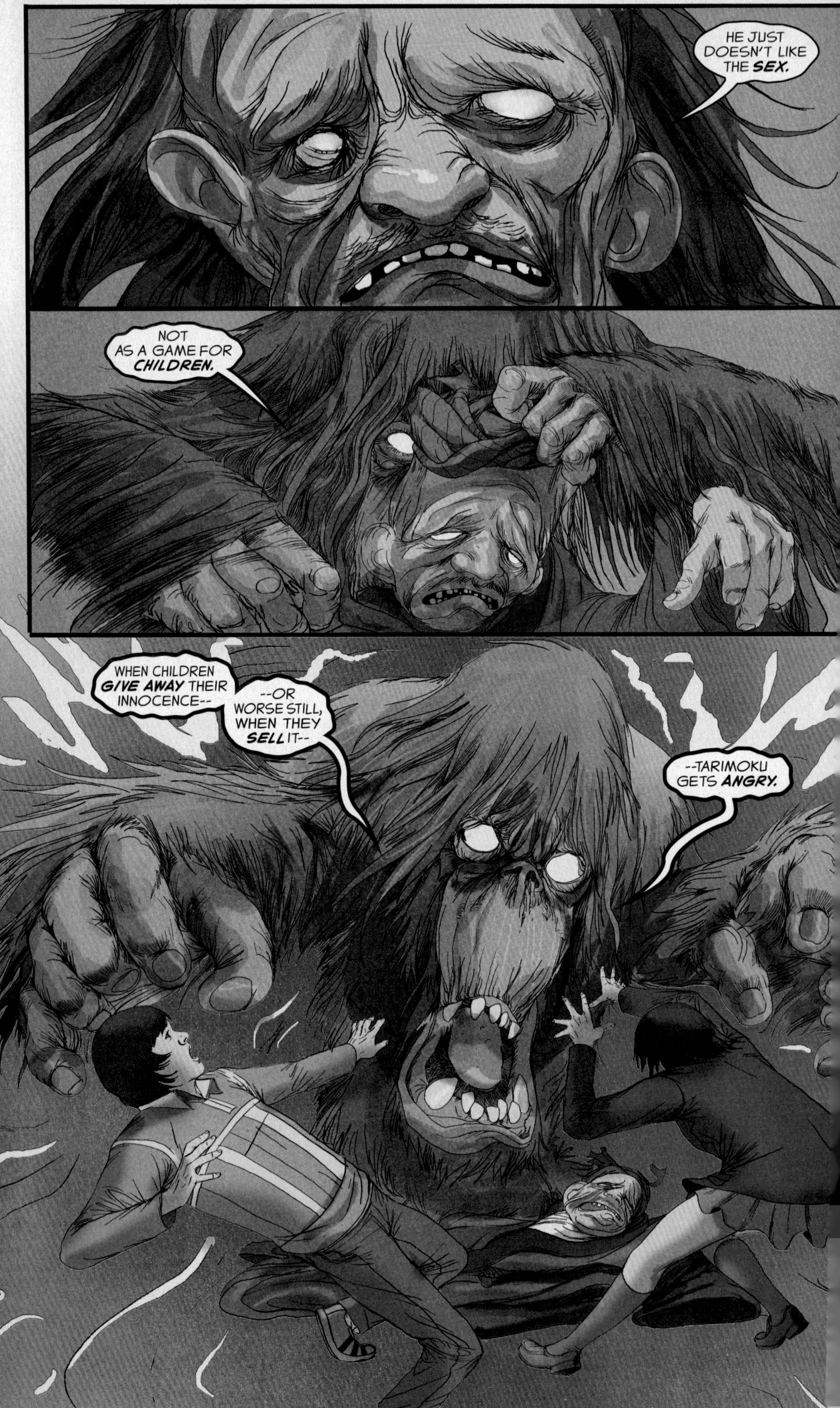
HE JUST DOESN'T LIKE THE SEX.
NOT AS A GAME FOR CHILDREN.
WHEN CHILDREN GIVE AWAY THEIR INNOCENCE--
--OR WORSE STILL, WHEN THEY SELL IT--
--TARIMOKU GETS ANGRY.

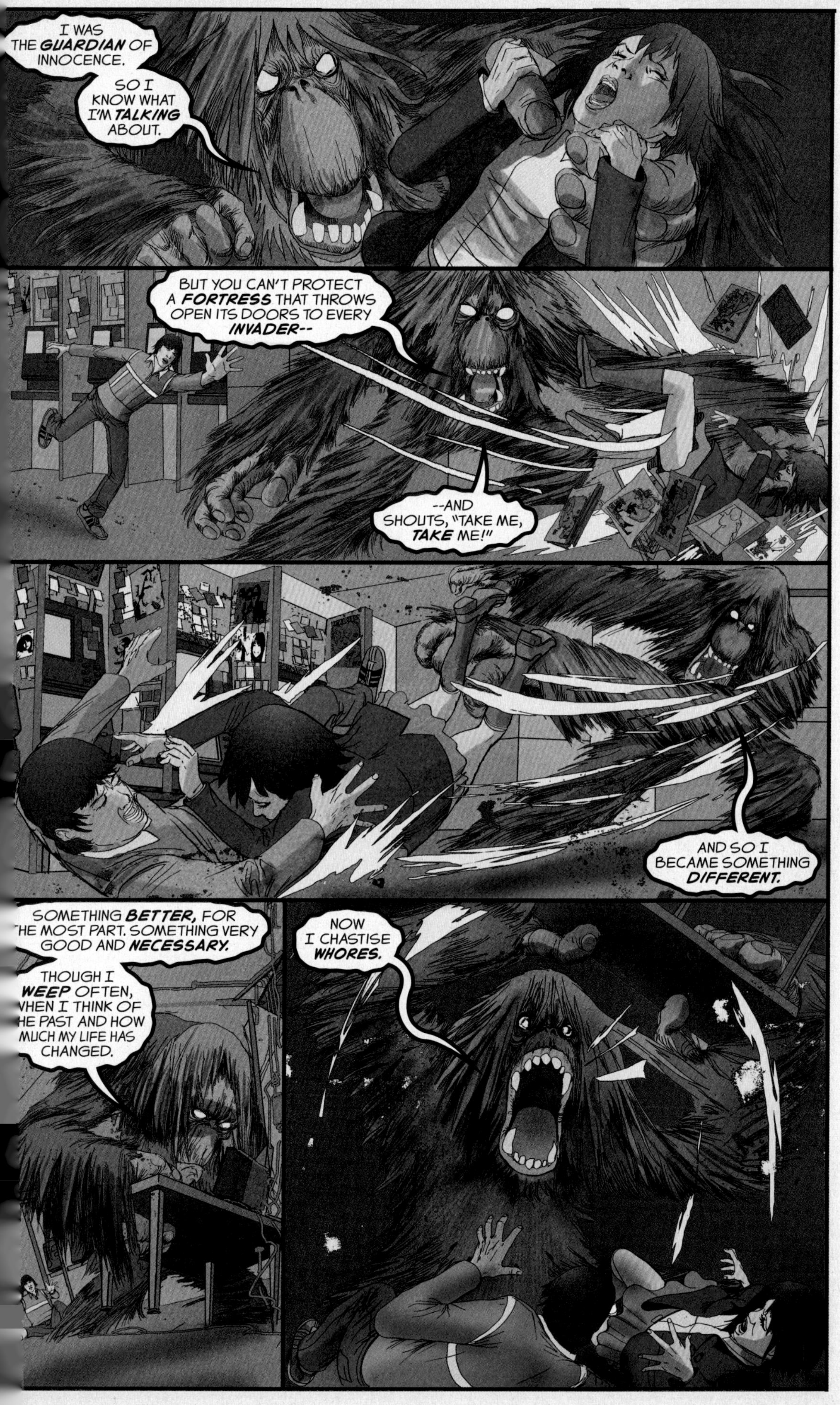

I WAS THE GUARDIAN OF INNOCENCE.
SO I KNOW WHAT I'M TALKING ABOUT.
BUT YOU CAN'T PROTECT A FORTRESS THAT THROWS OPEN ITS DOORS TO EVERY INVADER--
--AND SHOUTS, "TAKE ME, TAKE ME!"
AND SO I BECAME SOMETHING DIFFERENT.
SOMETHING BETTER, FOR THE MOST PART. SOMETHING VERY GOOD AND NECESSARY.
THOUGH I WEEP OFTEN, WHEN I THINK OF THE PAST AND HOW MUCH MY LIFE HAS CHANGED.
NOW I CHASTISE WHORES.

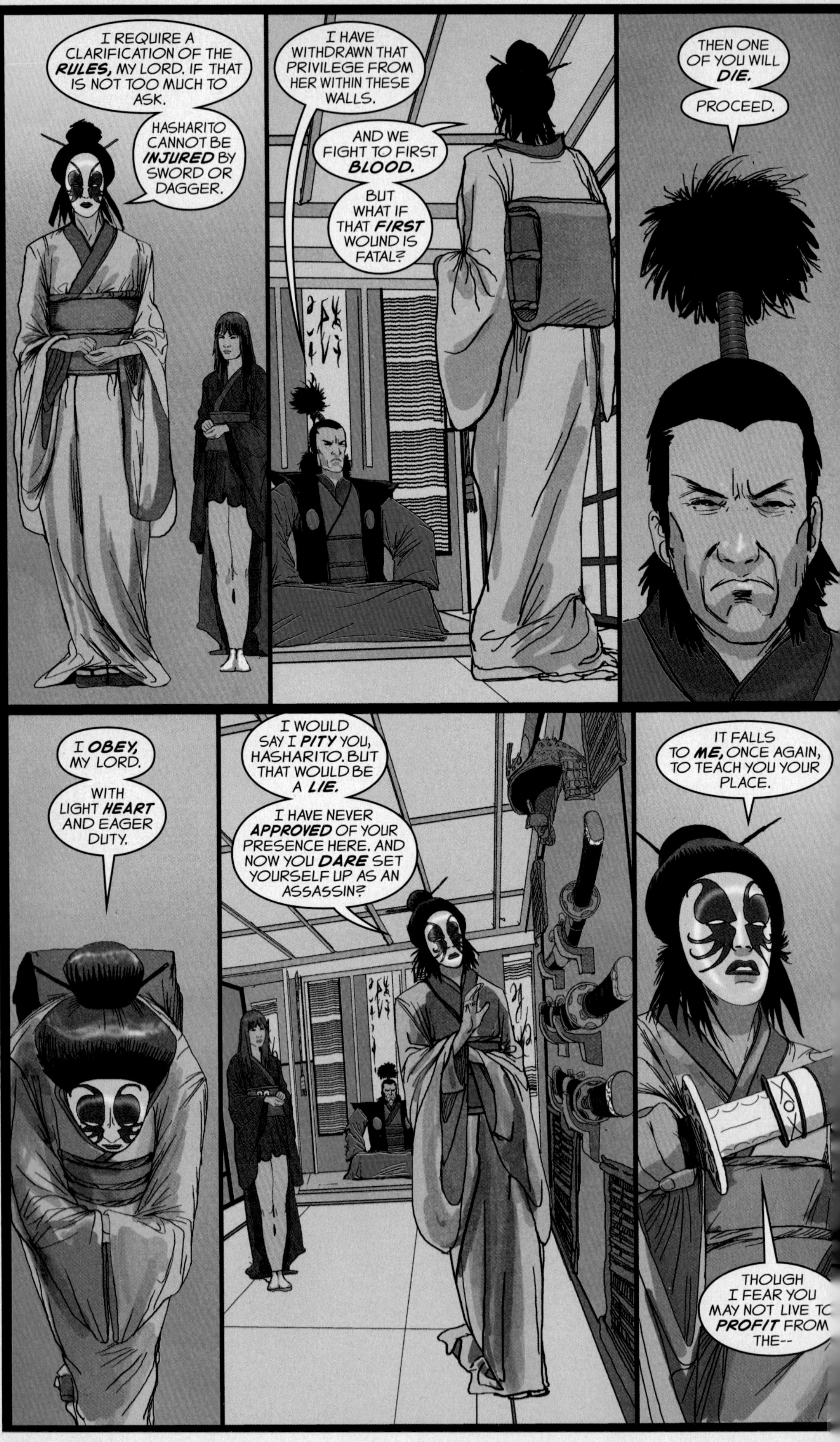
I REQUIRE A CLARIFICATION OF THE RULES, MY LORD. IF THAT IS NOT TOO MUCH TO ASK.
HASHARITO CANNOT BE INJURED BY SWORD OR DAGGER.
I HAVE WITHDRAWN THAT PRIVILEGE FROM HER WITHIN THESE WALLS.
AND WE FIGHT TO FIRST BLOOD.
BUT WHAT IF THAT FIRST WOUND IS FATAL?
THEN ONE OF YOU WILL DIE.
PROCEED.
I OBEY, MY LORD.
WITH LIGHT HEART AND EAGER DUTY.
I WOULD SAY I PITY YOU, HASHARITO. BUT THAT WOULD BE A LIE.
I HAVE NEVER APPROVED OF YOUR PRESENCE HERE. AND NOW YOU DARE SET YOURSELF UP AS AN ASSASSIN?
IT FALLS TO ME, ONCE AGAIN, TO TEACH YOU YOUR PLACE.
THOUGH I FEAR YOU MAY NOT LIVE TO PROFIT FROM THE--

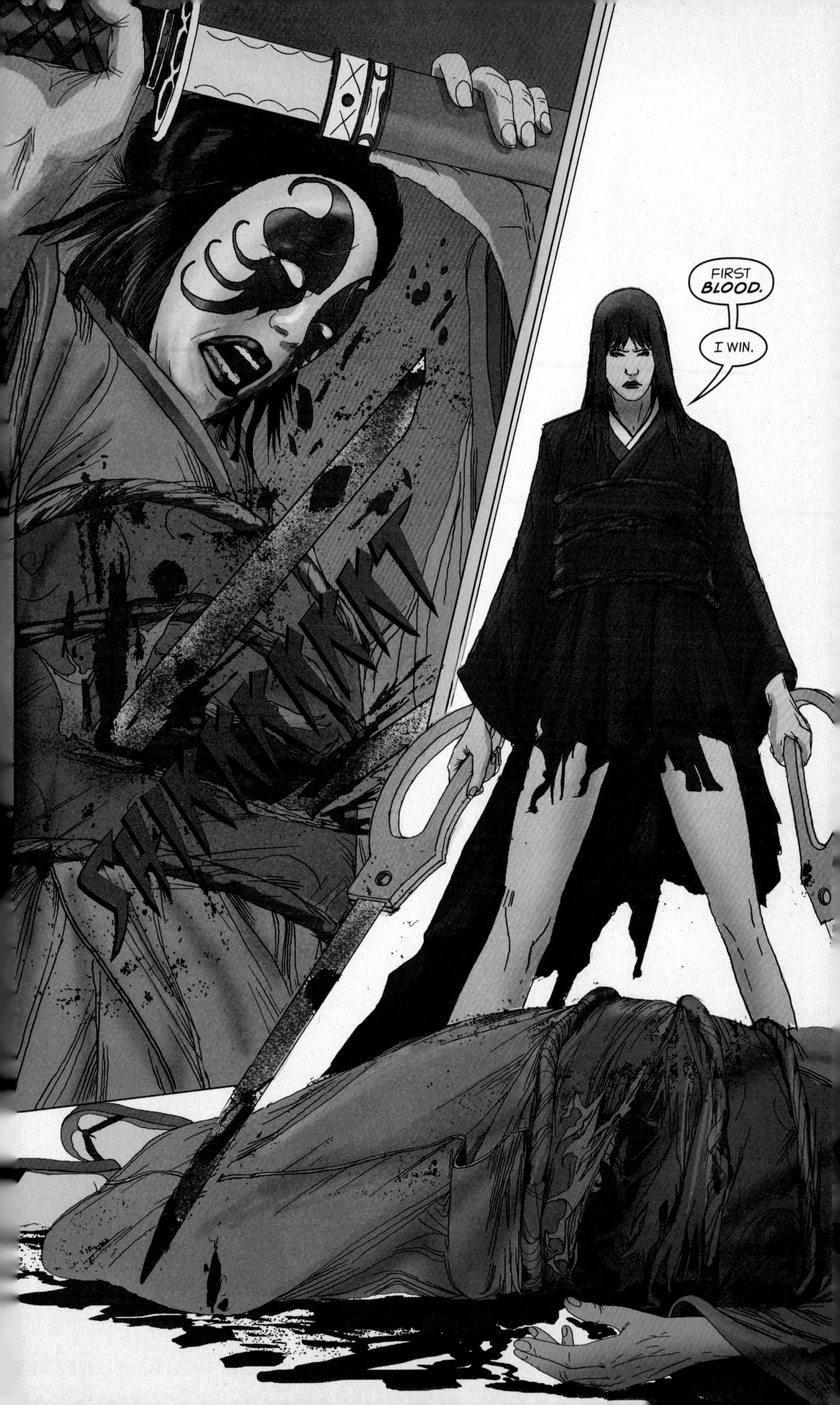
FIRST BLOOD.
I WIN.

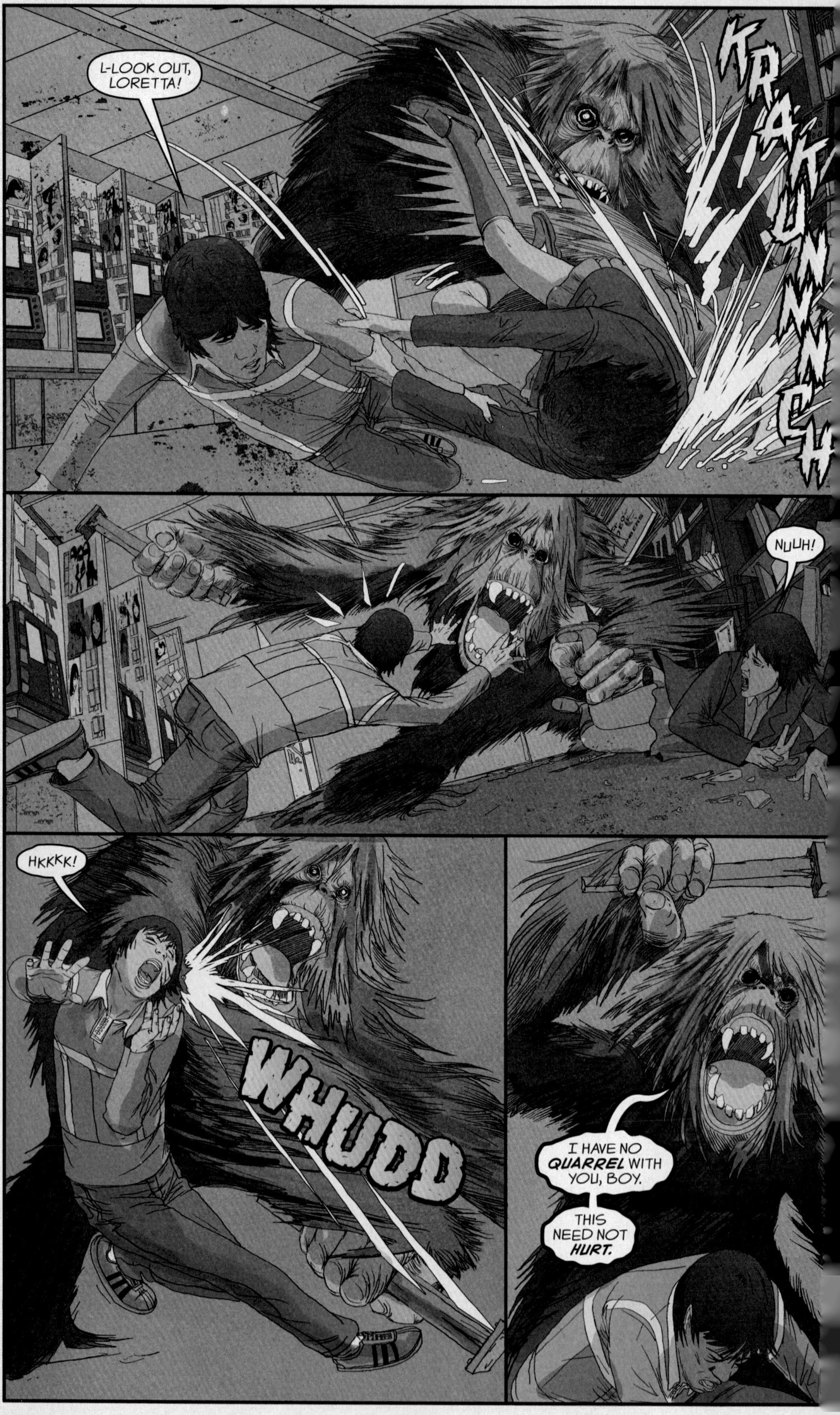

L-LOOK OUT, LORETTA!
KRAKUNNCH
NUUH!
HKKKK!
WHUDD
I HAVE NO QUARREL WITH YOU, BOY.
THIS NEED NOT HURT.

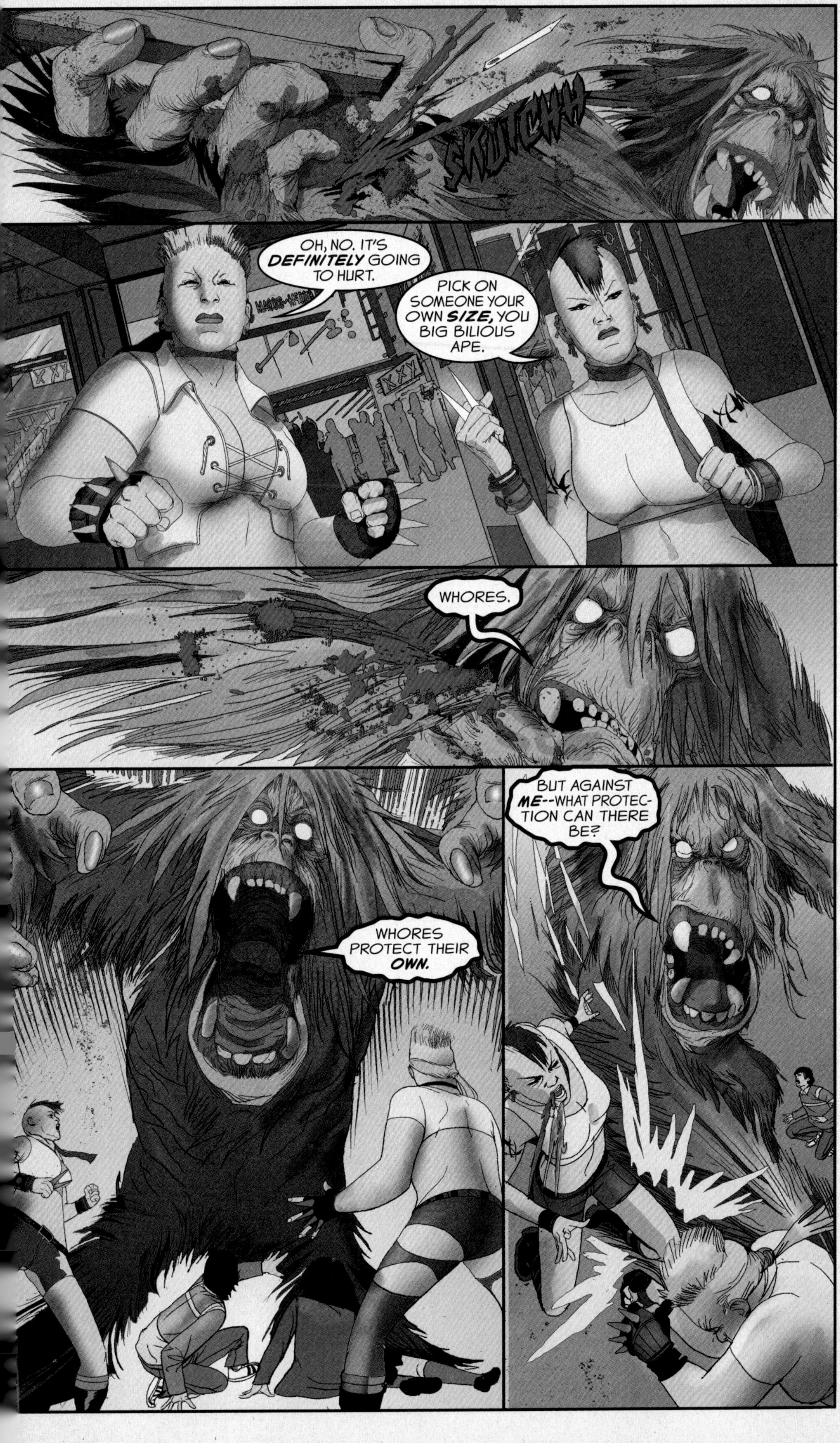
SKLITCHH
OH, NO. IT'S DEFINITELY GOING TO HURT.
PICK ON SOMEONE YOUR OWN SIZE, YOU BIG BILIOUS APE.
WHORES.
WHORES PROTECT THEIR OWN.
BUT AGAINST ME--WHAT PROTECTION CAN THERE BE?

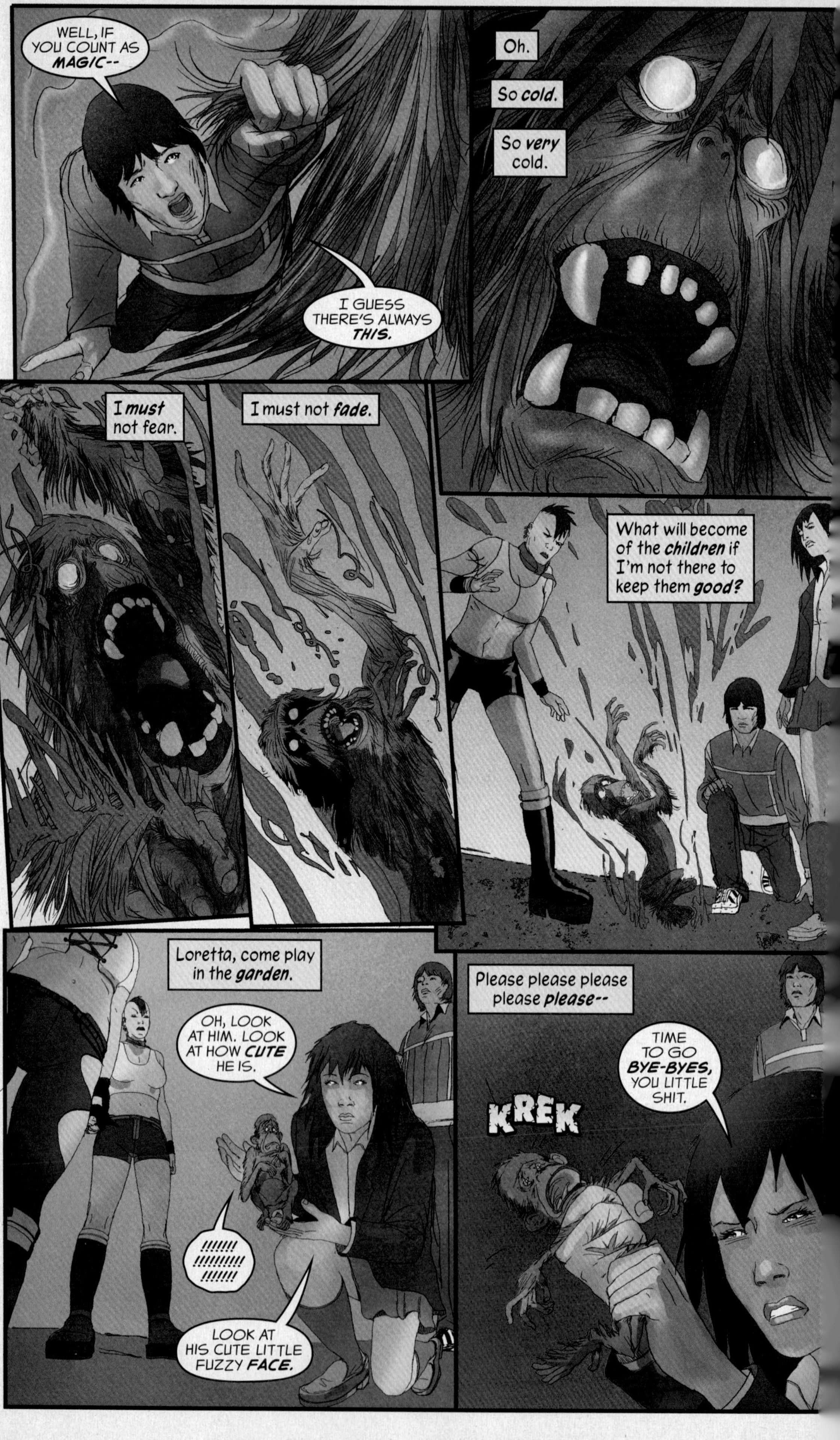
WELL, IF YOU COUNT AS MAGIC--
I GUESS THERE'S ALWAYS THIS.
Oh.
So cold.
So very cold.
I must not fear.
I must not fade.
What will become of the children if I'm not there to keep them good?
Loretta, come play in the garden.
OH, LOOK AT HIM. LOOK AT HOW CUTE HE IS.
!!!!!!! !!!!!!!!!! !!!!!!!
LOOK AT HIS CUTE LITTLE FUZZY FACE.
Please please please please please--
TIME TO GO BYE-BYES, YOU LITTLE SHIT.
KREK

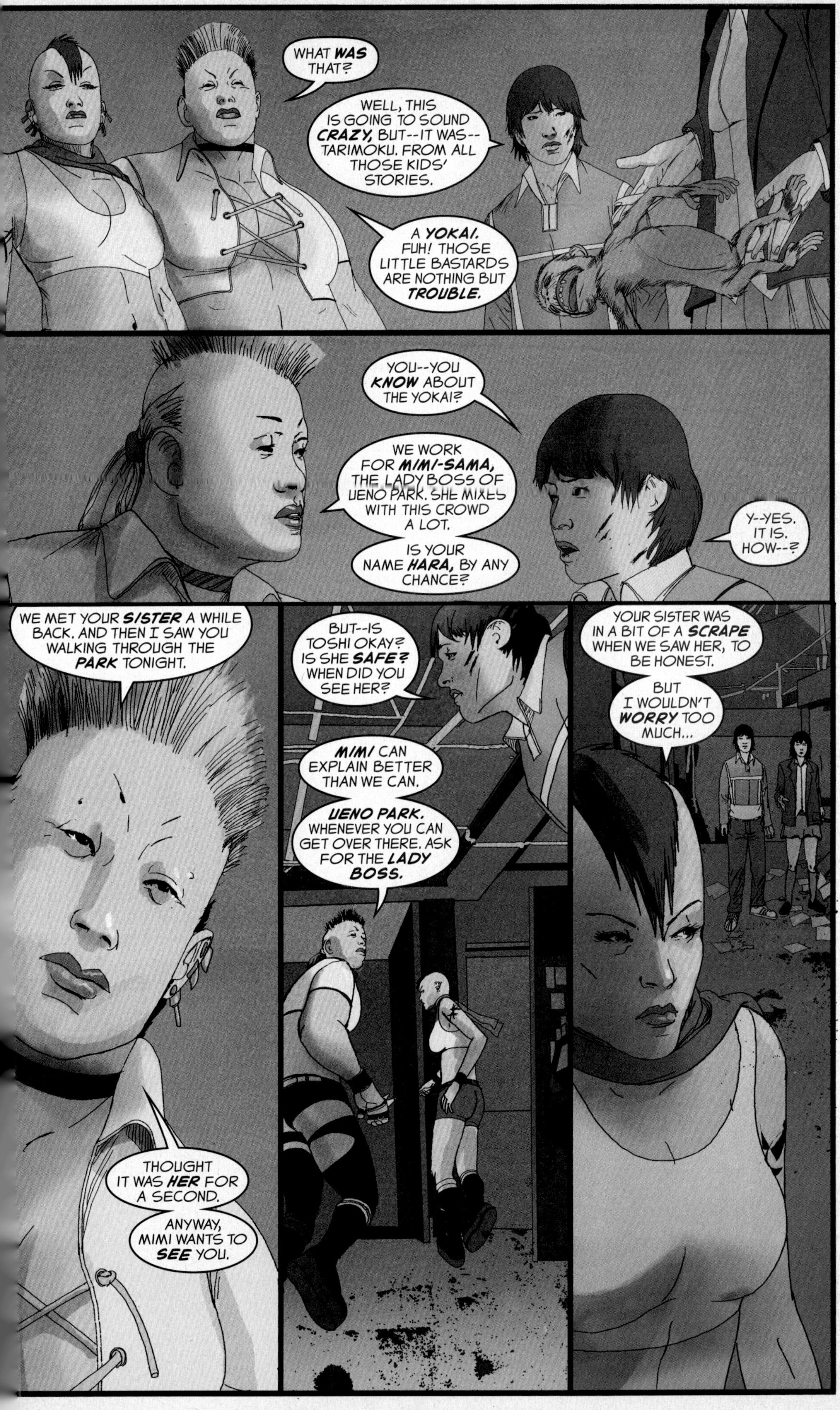
WHAT **WAS** THAT?
WELL, THIS IS GOING TO SOUND **CRAZY,** BUT--IT WAS--TARIMOKU. FROM ALL THOSE KIDS' STORIES.
A **YOKAI.** FUH! THOSE LITTLE BASTARDS ARE NOTHING BUT **TROUBLE.**
YOU--YOU **KNOW** ABOUT THE YOKAI?
WE WORK FOR **MIMI-SAMA,** THE LADY BOSS OF UENO PARK. SHE MIXES WITH THIS CROWD A LOT.
IS YOUR NAME **HARA,** BY ANY CHANCE?
Y--YES. IT IS. HOW--?
WE MET YOUR **SISTER** A WHILE BACK. AND THEN I SAW YOU WALKING THROUGH THE **PARK** TONIGHT.
THOUGHT IT WAS **HER** FOR A SECOND.
ANYWAY, MIMI WANTS TO **SEE** YOU.
BUT--IS TOSHI OKAY? IS SHE **SAFE?** WHEN DID YOU SEE HER?
MIMI CAN EXPLAIN BETTER THAN WE CAN.
UENO PARK. WHENEVER YOU CAN GET OVER THERE. ASK FOR THE **LADY BOSS.**
YOUR SISTER WAS IN A BIT OF A **SCRAPE** WHEN WE SAW HER, TO BE HONEST.
BUT I WOULDN'T **WORRY** TOO MUCH...

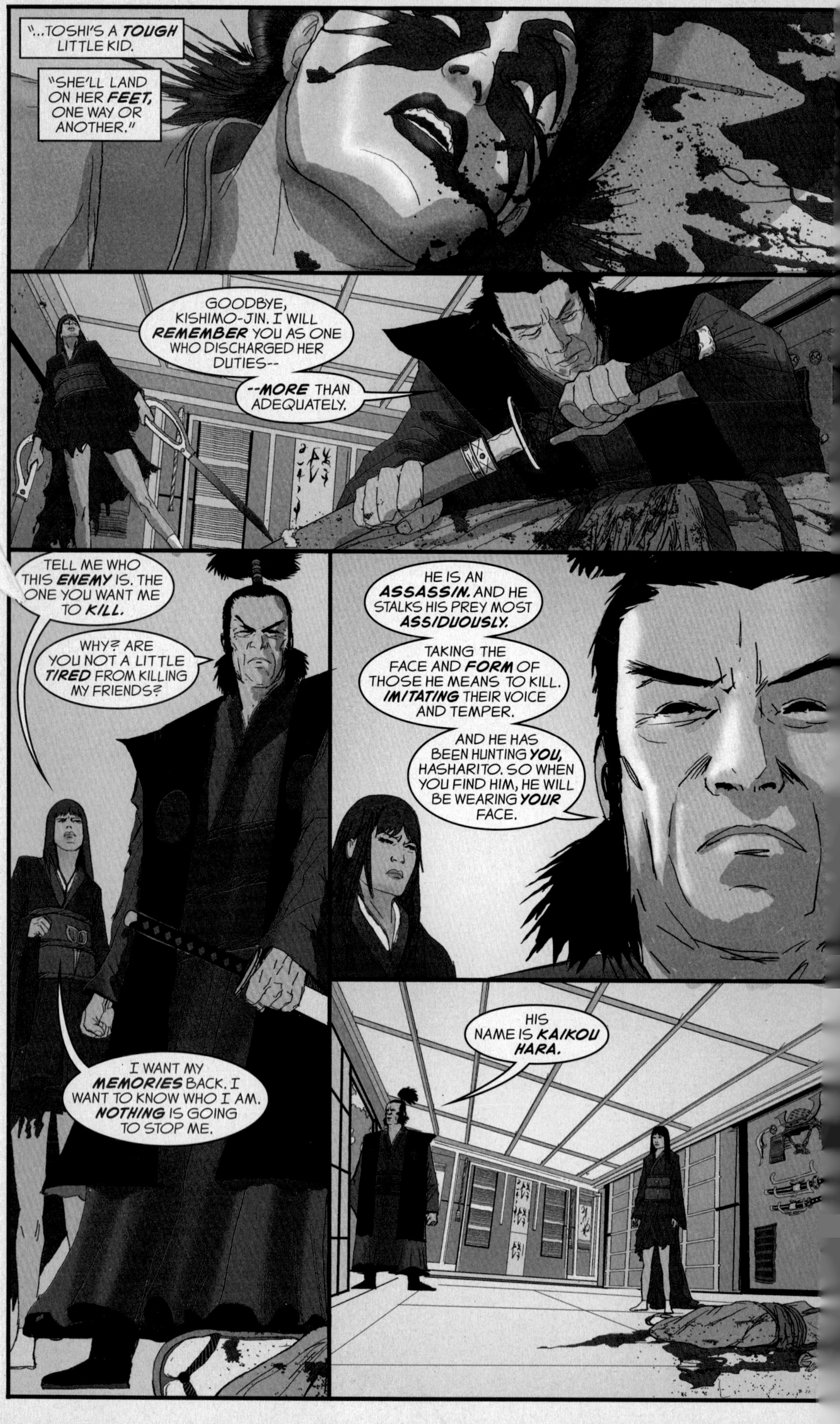
"...TOSHI'S A **TOUGH** LITTLE KID.
"SHE'LL LAND ON HER **FEET,** ONE WAY OR ANOTHER."
GOODBYE, KISHIMO-JIN. I WILL **REMEMBER** YOU AS ONE WHO DISCHARGED HER DUTIES--
--**MORE** THAN ADEQUATELY.
TELL ME WHO THIS **ENEMY** IS. THE ONE YOU WANT ME TO **KILL.**
WHY? ARE YOU NOT A LITTLE **TIRED** FROM KILLING MY FRIENDS?
HE IS AN **ASSASSIN.** AND HE STALKS HIS PREY MOST **ASSIDUOUSLY.**
TAKING THE FACE AND **FORM** OF THOSE HE MEANS TO KILL. **IMITATING** THEIR VOICE AND TEMPER.
AND HE HAS BEEN HUNTING **YOU,** HASHARITO. SO WHEN YOU FIND HIM, HE WILL BE WEARING **YOUR** FACE.
I WANT MY **MEMORIES** BACK. I WANT TO KNOW WHO I AM. **NOTHING** IS GOING TO STOP ME.
HIS NAME IS **KAIKOU HARA.**

Innocence for Sale or Rent

The second story arc in this collection deals with a phenomenon which is both very difficult for Westerners to understand and hugely controversial within Japan itself: the phenomenon of *enjokosai*, which is usually translated as "reward dating" or "compensated dating." I thought it might be useful to add a few comments here about this practice and its place in Japanese culture, for the benefit of readers who may find their minds gently boggling as they read through this chapter and encounter the characters of Loretta, Kitty-Ki and Pink.

Obviously, teenage prostitution is a worldwide problem. It's not restricted to Japan, and it's not something we can ever afford to think of as "someone else's problem." But the situation in Japan has some features that aren't reproduced elsewhere, and the cultural context is different. Japanese popular culture openly eroticizes underage girls, with a large and mostly legal industry catering to a sexual fetish which in the West is more aggressively legislated against. Manga images of children in sexual poses and acts are available to buy in ordinary news outlets, and high school girls who want to engage in prostitution find a sophisticated support network already in place to help them do so.

The most important element in this support network is the *terekura*: the telephone club. In Europe and America, sex chat lines mostly advertise through magazines and websites, and the men who use them make their calls from home. In Japan, the men are more likely to go to phone clubs. Here, they can engage in sex chats with women, and, if they want to, they can masturbate while they're talking. But they can also access lists of phone numbers left at the club by girls looking for an actual meeting — and a significant proportion of these girls will be of middle school and high school age.

The resulting "reward date" may not involve actual sex. Each girl — in theory at least — can choose how far she wants to go and how much she wants to charge for it. The girls are aware that the commodity they're really offering, their unique selling point, is innocence. They typically dress in *kawaii* styles, emphasizing their youth and cuteness. The men they meet may either pay them in cash or buy them expensive gifts. The date may be a one-off or may be the start of a protracted relationship.

In some ways, this can all look a lot less malign than teenage prostitution in the West. The girls seem to have more control over the transaction. They're not owned or victimized by a pimp, and they're not sleeping rough on the streets or living in disease-ridden squats. They get to keep whatever they make (many seem motivated by a desire to buy designer clothes and accessories) and they can stop at any time — in theory, anyway. Jennifer Liddy, writing in the online magazine *Freezebox*, remarks that when she discusses *enjokosai* with her Japanese friends and colleagues, they're very unwilling to see the girls as victims, or to attach any stigma to the men who pay for their (insert euphemistic quote marks) company.

It's difficult to get an estimate for how widespread this whole phenomenon is, but according to a Tokyo Metropolitan Authority survey of 1996, 4% of all high school girls in Tokyo admitted to having acted as paid escorts. A more recent survey across the whole of Japan, by the Congress of Parents' and Teachers' Associations, found that 25% of their teenaged sample were "regularly" involved with telephone clubs in one way or another — either just chatting or using them to set up reward dates.

I'm not making these points in order to raise any kind of moral panic or to encourage anyone to shake their heads in holier-than-thou horror at how depraved Japanese men are. Let's be blunt: I don't know about the United States, but London appears to be becoming the forced prostitution capital of the goddamned world, with up to a quarter of all girls kidnapped or coerced into sex work in Europe probably going through the UK at some point in their nightmare journey. Speaking as a Brit, I am in no position to cast the first stone here.

All I'm doing is trying to give you a sense of where Loretta and her friends are coming from. They're a product of their culture, and they're a part of something that's real and significant and ongoing — neither fantastic nor exaggerated for effect. And if they make you feel uneasy, good. They really should.

PS: In the UK, there's a charity called Eaves Housing which works to get young girls out of prostitution. In the U.S., there's a group called ECPAT with a similar but broader mission, and in Japan itself there's *Kanita Fujin No Mura*, the "Women's Village" organization. If you want to donate, they're only a Google search away.

MIKE CAREY 2007

WALKING OUT OF HELL (AND OUT OF THE PAGES OF THE SANDMAN), AN AMBITIOUS LUCIFER MORNINGSTAR CREATES A NEW COSMOS MODELLED AFTER HIS OWN IMAGE IN THESE COLLECTIONS FROM WRITER MIKE CAREY AND VERTIGO:

LUCIFER

VOLUME 1:
DEVIL IN THE GATEWAY

ALSO AVAILABLE:

VOL. 2: CHILDREN AND MONSTERS
VOL. 3: A DALLIANCE WITH THE DAMNED
VOL. 4: THE DIVINE COMEDY
VOL. 5: INFERNO
VOL. 6: MANSIONS OF THE SILENCE
VOL. 7: EXODUS
VOL. 8: THE WOLF BENEATH THE TREE
VOL. 9: CRUX

VERTIGO

"Mike Carey's Lucifer is even more manipulative, charming and dangerous than I could have hoped."
— Neil Gaiman, from his Foreword

Lucifer
Devil in the Gateway

Mike Carey
Scott Hampton
Chris Weston
James Hodgkins
Warren Pleece
Dean Ormston

"THE BEST FANTASY COMIC AROUND."
— *COMICS INTERNATIONAL*

"AN ORIGINAL TAKE ON THE FORCES OF GOOD, EVIL AND BEYOND EVIL."
— *PUBLISHERS WEEKLY*

ALL TITLES ARE SUGGESTED FOR MATURE READERS.

SEARCH THE GRAPHIC NOVELS SECTION OF

www.VERTIGOCOMICS.com

FOR ART AND INFORMATION ON ALL OF OUR BOOKS!